语言学范畴研究丛书
Person

人称范畴

Anna Siewierska
Lancaster University

北京大学出版社
PEKING UNIVERSITY PRESS

CAMBRIDGE

著作权合同登记　图字:01-2008-1557 号

Person first edition 0-521-77669-4 by Anna Siewierska first published by Cambridge University Press 2004
All rights reserved.
This reprint edition for the People's Republic of China is published by arrangement with the Press Syndicate of the University of Cambridge, Cambridge, United Kingdom.
ⓒ Cambridge University Press & 北京大学出版社,2008

This book is in copyright. No reproduction of any part may take place without the written permission of Cambridge University Press or 北京大学出版社.
This edition is for sale in the mainland of China only, excluding Hong Kong SAR, Macao SAR and Taiwan, and may not be bought for export therefrom.

此版本仅限中华人民共和国境内销售,不包括香港、澳门特别行政区及中国台湾。不得出口。

图书在版编目(CIP)数据

人称范畴/(英)安娜·谢维尔斯卡著.—影印本.—北京:北京大学出版社,2008.12
　(语言学范畴研究丛书)
　ISBN 978-7-301-14616-3

Ⅰ.人… Ⅱ.安… Ⅲ.人称-研究-英文 Ⅳ.H04

中国版本图书馆 CIP 数据核字(2008)第 183231 号

```
书    名:人称范畴
著作责任者:〔英〕Anna Siewierska 著
责 任 编 辑:旷书文
标 准 书 号:ISBN 978-7-301-14616-3/H · 2158
出 版 发 行:北京大学出版社
地      址:北京市海淀区成府路 205 号  100871
网      址:http://www.pup.cn
电 子 信 箱:zpup@pup.pku.edu.cn
电      话:邮购部 62752015  发行部 62750672  出版部 62754962
           编辑部 62753334
印  刷  者:北京汇林印务有限公司
经  销  者:新华书店
           650 毫米×980 毫米  16 开本  22.75 印张  360 千字
           2008 年 12 月第 1 版  2008 年 12 月第 1 次印刷
定      价:38.00 元
```

未经许可,不得以任何方式复制或抄袭本书之部分或全部内容。
版权所有,侵权必究
举报电话:010-62752024　电子信箱:fd@pup.pku.edu.cn

Contents

List of figures	F8
List of tables	F9
导读	F11
Preface	F33
List of abbreviations	F35

1 Introduction — 1
 1.1 Person as a grammatical category — 1
  1.1.1 Person paradigms — 4
  1.1.2 First and second persons vs third person — 5
 1.2 The universality of person markers — 8
 1.3 The nature of this book — 14

2 The typology of person forms — 16
 2.1 Morpho-phonological form — 16
  2.1.1 Independent forms — 17
  2.1.2 Dependent person markers — 21
 2.2 Syntactic function — 40
  2.2.1 Syntactic function and morpho-phonological form — 40
  2.2.2 The encoding of syntactic function — 47
 2.3 Discourse function — 67

3 The structure of person paradigms — 75
 3.1 Fewer than three persons — 75
 3.2 Variation with respect to number — 79
  3.2.1 More than one person and the inclusive/exclusive distinction — 82
  3.2.2 Duals and larger numbers — 88
  3.2.3 Number and the person hierarchy — 92
  3.2.4 Towards a typology of paradigmatic structure — 96
 3.3 Variation in gender — 103
  3.3.1 Gender and the person hierarchy — 104
  3.3.2 Gender and number — 107
  3.3.3 Gender and the inclusive/exclusive distinction — 110
 3.4 Differences between paradigms — 112
  3.4.1 Independent vs dependent paradigms — 112
  3.4.2 Differences between dependent forms — 118

4 Person agreement — 120
- 4.1 Anaphoric pronoun vs person agreement marker — 121
- 4.2 The targets of person agreement — 127
  - 4.2.1 Predicates — 129
  - 4.2.2 Possessed nouns — 138
  - 4.2.3 Adpositions and other targets — 145
- 4.3 The controllers of person agreement — 148
  - 4.3.1 The person hierarchy — 149
  - 4.3.2 The nominal hierarchy — 151
  - 4.3.3 The animacy hierarchy — 154
  - 4.3.4 The referential hierarchy — 156
  - 4.3.5 The focus hierarchy — 159
- 4.4 The markers of person agreement — 162
  - 4.4.1 Person agreement and morpho-phonological form — 162
  - 4.4.2 The location of person markers — 163

5 The function of person forms — 173
- 5.1 Cognitive discourse analysis and referent accessibility — 174
- 5.2 Referent accessibility and the distribution of person forms in discourse — 178
  - 5.2.1 Entity saliency — 178
  - 5.2.2 Unity — 183
- 5.3 Accessibility and the intra-sentential distribution of person forms — 185
  - 5.3.1 Chomsky's Binding Theory — 185
  - 5.3.2 Referent accessibility and BT — 191
  - 5.3.3 The avoid pronoun constraint — 198
- 5.4 Beyond referent accessibility — 200
  - 5.4.1 Long-distance reflexives, logophoricity and point of view — 201
  - 5.4.2 Person marker vs other referential expression and speaker empathy — 207
- 5.5 Person markers and impersonalization — 210

6 Person forms and social deixis — 214
- 6.1 Alternation in semantic categories — 215
  - 6.1.1 Variation in number — 216
  - 6.1.2 Variation in person — 222
  - 6.1.3 The use of reflexives — 224
- 6.2 Special honorific person markers — 228
- 6.3 Omission of person markers — 235

7 Person forms in a diachronic perspective — 246
- 7.1 The sources of person markers — 247
  - 7.1.1 Lexical sources — 247
  - 7.1.2 Demonstratives — 249
  - 7.1.3 Other person markers — 251
  - 7.1.4 Conjugated verbal forms — 255
  - 7.1.5 Other grammatical markers — 260

7.2	From independent person marker to syntactic agreement marker		261
	7.2.1 Three accounts of the early stages of the grammaticalization of person markers		263
	7.2.2 Syntactic agreement markers		268
7.3	Language externally driven changes in person marking		273
	7.3.1 Borrowing of person markers		274
	7.3.2 Loss of person agreement		277

Appendix 1. List of languages in the sample by macro-area 282

Appendix 2. Genetic classification of languages cited in the text 284

References 296
Author index 312
Language index 316
Subject index 324

Figures

1 Morphological alignment types in monotransitive clauses *page* 51
2 Morphological alignment types in ditransitive clauses 58
3 Singular, vertical and horizontal homophonies in person paradigms 98
4 Relationship between type of agreement markers and type of agreement 126

Tables

2.1	Frequency of lexical and pronominal realization of the S, A and P in six languages	*page* 41
2.2	Dependent pronominals (as a group) and argument prominence	43
2.3	The alignment of independent and overt dependent person forms	53
3.1	The subdivision of the first-person complex	86
3.2	Major singular and vertical homophonies in Cysouw's sample	99
3.3	Major horizontal homophonies in Cysouw's sample	101
4.1	Distribution of anaphoric and grammatical agreement with different targets	128
4.2	Person agreement in monotransitive clauses relative to alignment	134
4.3	The distribution of person A prefixes vs suffixes relative to basic monotransitive order	165
4.4	The distribution of person P prefixes vs suffixes relative to basic monotransitive order	165
4.5	The order of the A and P relative to each other in prefixal vs suffixal location	167
6.1	Second-person pronoun usage by caste and age in Nepali	230
6.1	Korean person markers	232
7.1	Frequency of first- and third-person pronouns in English according to text type, per million words, based on Biber et al.'s (1999) 40-million-word corpus	267

导　读

刘丹青　强星娜
（中国社会科学院 语言研究所）

导读小引

人称（person）在语言学上指表示言谈角色（说者、听者和此外的对象等）的语法范畴，其表达形式既包括以封闭性词类出现的人称代词，也包括虚化、黏着程度不等的各种虚语素。本书是一本就人称范畴的方方面面进行跨语言考察的类型学专著，作为剑桥语言学教材丛书之一种于2004年由英国剑桥大学出版社出版。

本书作者安娜·谢维尔斯卡（Anna Siewierska）是欧洲科学院院士，著名语言类型学家，现任国际语言类型学会会长，英国兰开斯特（Lancaster）大学教授，曾在波兰、澳大利亚、荷兰、丹麦等多个国家的大学任教并从事语言学研究。谢维尔斯卡教授著作丰硕，已出版《被动式的比较语言学分析》、《语序规则》、《功能语法》等专著，参与主编《欧洲语言的语序》、《格、类型学和语法》。从这些著作可以看出，她在类型学领域涉猎广泛，既精于语序等句法问题，也擅长被动范畴等形态学问题。本书是作者的又一部类型学专著。

从跨语言的角度看，人称范畴是个相当复杂的语法现象。从形式方面看，表达人称的语法单位具有很不相同的语法属性，从最独立的代词和名词（**导读者按**：如汉语史上表第一人称的"孤、不穀、寡人、仆、臣"等和表第二人称的"子、君"等名词，再如本书所举的日语、泰语等亚洲语言中的名词性人称词语），到完全黏着的、加在动词上的形态标记，二者之间还有独立程度或者说虚化程度不等的呈连续统的多种单位。有些语言同时存在多种人称形式类别，其间还存在如何配合互动的问题。从表达方面看，不同语言在人称系统的语义构造上也相当多样，不是"你我他"三分那么简单。如作者所指出的，人称范畴在形态学及句法学之外，也跟语义、语用/语篇、语法化、语言亲缘关系和接触关系等诸多方面密切相关。以往语言学理论中关于人称范畴的概述,主要植根于对少数语言的观察,远不能概括人类语言的多样性,也不足以总结出真正具有普遍性的规律。对人称范畴认识的提升,离不开大规模的跨语言考察。在这方面,本书可以说是语种基础最为广泛、探讨最为全面深入的一部专著。它以包含七百多种语言的语种库为材料基础,很多结论都是在对这些语言的穷尽性观察和统计的基础上得出的,这提高了相关结论的可信性。本书无论对人称范畴的语言比较、语言理论还是单一语言研究,都具有很高的参考价值。就国内而言,它对研究中国境内众多语言方言的纷繁复杂的人称现象及其历史演化的研究会有直接帮助。例如,上古汉语复杂的人称代词系统,第一第二人称代词的完整系统和第三人称代词系统的残缺("之"只用于宾格),现代汉语方言间人称代词的系统性差异,藏缅语中人称代词和动词人称形式的相关性,景颇语中句法地位特殊的带有人称作用的句尾词的性质,阿尔泰语言和汉语西北方言中第三人称代词和远指指示词的相关性,诸如此类问题的研究,都能从本书的观察和总结中得到启发。

全书正文包括"导言"在内共七章,围绕人称范畴的表达形式、句法语义语用功能以及相关的社会指称、历史演变等方面逐章展开论述。书前除章节目录外还有全书的示意图目录和表格目录,另有一个简短前言和一个详细的术语缩写对照表;对照表便于读者随时查阅文中多语种例句注释时大量采用的术语缩写。下面我们分章介绍本书正文的主要内容。

一、导　言

"导言"部分展示了一幅人称范畴的跨语言多样性的概括图景,以此说明本书的研究范围及研究意义。

1.1 节讨论作为一个语法范畴的人称。人称的本质是不用普通名词而以专用语法形式表示话语交际中不同的言谈角色。绝大部分语言都只用一组封闭性词语来指称说者、听者和第三方。这类词语习称人称代词(personal pronoun)或简称代词(**导读者按**:西方文献中 pronoun 单用一般就指人称代词,指示词用 demonstrative 而不需要加 pronoun),本书作者换用人称标记(person marker)和人称形式(person form)两个术语,因为不是所有表示人称范畴的语法形式都是代词性的。跨语言看,人称范畴的表现复杂多样。人称的三分法并不是普遍有效,有些语言只有第一第二人称,有些语言甚至只有第一人称采用代词一类语法形式,而第三人称取名词或短语形式。对更多语言的调查,尤其是本书的观察已经显示,Greenberg(1963)基于 30 种语言得出的"所有语言都至少包括三种人称和两种数在内的代词范畴"

(共性42)这一概括不能成立。小于这种三身双数的代词系统并不罕见;比其繁复得多的人称系统也大量存在。作者指出,这是因为除了人称及数以外,人称标记还常兼表定指性、旁指性(obviation,与本指性 proximity 对立,二者是根据所指在说话人心目中的重要性或显著度而做出的区别)、时态、体、式(情态)、两极性(肯定否定)等范畴,以至于人称标记可以多如斐济语那样的135个。此外,人称形式中还可以包含所指的社会地位、亲属关系、语体风格等更外部的要素。有些语言的人称范畴可能因人称形式的语法地位差异而形成不同的子系统,如独立代词系统、人称附缀(clitic,又译附着词)系统、人称词缀系统等。不同子系统的内部结构往往不同,词形变化也表现出差异。作者指出,评论某种语言的人称范畴特点时,如果忽略了不同子系统的存在,那么评述难免不够准确。与多样性相反,人称范畴又强烈表现出第一第二人称与第三人称之间的显著对立,主要体现在词形(**导读者按**:汉语第一第二人称原来都是鼻声母且韵部相同相近,而第三人称词形与前二者一向无关)、范畴切分、格系统差异、句法行为诸多方面。诸项对立根本上皆可归因于指称属性的差异——第一第二人称的本性是直指(现场指),而第三人称的本性是回指。至于有些文献中出现的所谓第四人称,其所指因语言而异,作者认为该术语在普遍意义上并无必要。

1.2节专门讨论人称形式的存在是否为人类语言共性的问题。有学者声称没有人称代词的语言是不可思议的,但作者认为人称形式的普遍性并非不可质疑,关键是如何定义人称形式。例如,代词常与名词相对而存在,但泰、缅、越、日等很多东亚语言表人称的单位往往有很强的名词性和实义性(社会地位义、社会关系义等),与另一些语言意义空灵的人称代词很不相同。对此,作者取一种原型论的态度,将营本(Sugamoto 1989)总结的7条特征作为人称代词的典型特征。这7条特征对理解本书至关重要,照译如下:a. 成员呈封闭性;b. 缺少形态音系的稳定性;c. 缺少特定的语义内容;d. 缺少风格或社会含义的属性;e. 表达语法上的人称;f. 不能带定语;g. 对指称解读有限制。据此,可以由左到右画出一条从强名词性到强代词性的横线。越靠左,上述属性越少,越靠右,上述属性越多越全。作者对照上述特征对取样语言逐一测试,最靠左(名词性最强)的是泰语,其次是日语,最靠右(代词性最强)的是波兰语,其次是英语。

本章以介绍本书的性质和全书结构收尾。

二、人称形式类型学

本章对人称形式的形态音系特征、句法功能和语用功能进行考察。

正如从表人称的名词到人称代词是一个连续统,从独立的人称代词到完全依附性的人称词缀也是一个连续统,中间有若干界限模糊的过渡性单位。对于那些兼表时、体、式等其他范畴的人称形式,很难确定它们处于连续统上的哪个位置。作者认为,不同的分析可能都有一定的道理。人称形式在形态音系上首先表现出独立形式(independent forms)和依附形式(dependent forms)的区别。独立人称形式可单用、可带普通词重音;依附性人称形式则相反,不能带词重音、语音上相对于独立形式有所缩减,不能作为一个词单用,至少句法分布比独立的词狭窄。然而作者也注意到独立形式的界定不乏模糊之处。首先,单用不等于单说(在一定条件下单独成句),例如英语中用作定语的领属代词 my、your、her、their 等从不单说(mine、theirs 等可以单说),但可以单用。可见,作者判定"独立"的标准主要基于形态音系而非句法(**导读者按**:这一看法未必准确,句法可能不是唯一标准或主要标准,但"独立"的判定恐难以完全抛弃句法标准)。此外,作者也讨论了学者们测试独立词的几个句法标准,包括并列标准(唯独立单位可并列)、省略标准(唯独立单位可有条件地省略)、被饰标准(唯独立单位可被其他词语修饰)等,并详细说明了这些标准的作用和局限。另外,一些语言的人称形式不是以人称语素为词根的词语,最常见的是以强调语素或指示语素为词根,以人称语素为词缀的词语。虽然词根不表人称,但这类词整体仍可视为一个人称形式。较成问题的是,某些语言中这类词的句法功能不同于人称代词,而用如"是"、"在"一类动词;也有些语言中黏着的人称词缀总是附加在强调语素上(**导读者按**:《祖堂集》等近代汉语文献中和上海郊区方言中含有"是"的人称代词,来自表强调的系动词"是"和人称语素的组合,即同时与系动词和强调语素有关)。也就是说,这类语言没有单纯以名词功能出现的人称代词。作者认为,这类词既可以视为某种非典型的人称形式,也可以视为带人称形态的谓词。按后一种分析,则这些语言确实是无人称代词的语言;不过这种情况非常少见。反观汉语,从来源上看,近代汉语和汉语方言中的"是我、是他"等以系动词"是"为该组合的核心,整体上看它们确实不是典型的名词性成分,但"我、他"等不是词缀而是真正的人称代词,因此与上述情况不同;而且汉语中同时存在不带"是"的人称代词,所以没有是否存在人称代词的问题;此外,这些词的强调义减弱,词汇化后"是"不再作为独立的谓词,"是我"之类整体成为典型的人称代词。

依附性人称形式在独立代词以外构成由实到虚的连续统,依次如下:

弱化形式>附缀>黏着成分>零形式

我们想补充提醒的是,前三类确实常有由左式逐步虚化弱化为右式的情况,但零形式并不都是前三类弱化消失的产物,而常是一种省略策略或结构缺位,如日语的零形式(zero forms)人称表达。

零形式指在表示人称语义的语法位置以非显性形式表示,主要包括三种情况:a. 绝对零形式,即不用任何人称形式,单纯以空位来表人称。书中以人称表达经常采用零形式的日语为例,指出了用零形式表人称的常见位置和条件。b. 独立代词取零形式,即独立句法位置不出现代词,但动词上有人称标记。c. 人称系统中存在空缺项,所以不得不采用零形式(**导读者按**:上古汉语中第三人称缺少主格代词,常用零形式或名词重复来表第三人称主语),或人称词缀系统中某些人称没有实体语素,只是零形式。

黏着成分(bound forms)和附缀性质不同,但形式上又较难区别。黏着成分在这儿主要指加在词干上的表示人称的词缀,广义上也包括通过词干语音交替,甚至单靠声调交替表达人称的形态。黏着的人称形态一般施加于谓语动词,句法上通常被看做一致关系形态,即用以表达主谓或动宾之类的一致关系。独立论元不出现时,黏着成分也可独立担当论元。附缀的独立性强于黏着成分,它在结构上不依附于词,而与大于词的单位发生句法关系,所以是句法成分而非词内形态成分;但在韵律上附缀已失去独立性,依附于词(被依附的词称为宿主(host)),因此表现又不同于独立的词。附缀和词缀的根本区别是与宿主的关系不同。词缀的宿主是它所依附的那个词根或词干,而附缀是加在整个短语上的,宿主只是该短语中碰巧和附缀相邻的那个词,所以附缀和宿主本身不一定有结构关系。作者参考 Zwicky(1985)详细分析了人称附缀的内部小类。附缀有专用和非专用之别。专用指某成分只能作附缀,而非专用指独立的词在一定条件下弱化成附缀。英语口语中 Bring your friends(带你的朋友来)说成 Bring [ye] friends,Give them back(把它们还回去)说成 Give [em] back,[ye]、[em]是 your 和 them 临时弱化的产物,属于非专用附缀,它们无法用在 your 和 them 能自由出现的其他位置。附缀容易出现的位置有句子的第一个词或第一个成分之后、动词短语的最后一个成分后(不管这个成分是什么)或谓语动词之后,也有语言的人称附缀可以加在动词短语的任一成分之后。附缀在不同位置也有常见与否的区别,如句子第二个位置是附缀的常见位置。根据 Anderson(1993)的分析,人称附缀按其位置分为 6 类:句首、句末、第二位置、中间位置、谓语核心前、谓语核心后。进一步归结为三个参项:辖域参项,即和附缀组合的成分的性质(VP、NP、PP 等);附缀的落脚处(句首、句末、谓语核心上等);附加的方向(前置还是后置于落脚点)。作者指出,这三个参项无法覆盖所有的情况。与动词人称附缀或词缀有关的另一个参项是,它们指向哪个成分或跟哪个成分一致。附缀和词缀的另一些差别表现为,词缀常因词干的形态音位条件差异而有不同的变体,常带来词干本身的变异,因为进入词内而影响词的韵律结构,导致重音移位等,这些一般都不发生在附缀现象中。

弱化形式(weak forms)又称代词的短式。与词缀和附缀相比,弱化形式在语音和形态上不依附于任何其他结构,这一点跟独立代词相似。但弱化形式并不是独立代词的非重读形式;二者在句法分布、语音构成上有所不同。有些语言作为论元的弱化形式是强制性的,而独立代词是非强制性的。有些语言两种形式可以同现,构成复指关系。弱化形式也可能受某些句法限制,比如在有些语言里只能用作主语,在有的语言中不能用做判断句主语等。

独立人称形式和依附性人称形式(尤其是附缀和黏着成分)的句法功能很不相同,对它们的考察角度也有差异。独立代词可以单独充当论元,考察其句法属性主要关注它充当什么句法成分。依附性人称形式本身不能独立充当论元,需要附加在其他词(主要是谓语动词)上,当句中另有同指的名词或独立代词等论元时,依附形式就是一致关系标记,因此对其句法属性的考察主要是看它指向句中什么成分,或者说与什么成分发生一致关系。

独立代词和依附性人称形式与句法成分的相关性表现不同。很多同时有独立代词和依附性人称标记的语言中,独立代词的使用常受限制。与宾语等其他句法成分相比,主语更多用独立代词表示。主语可用独立代词而宾语不能用的情况比较常见,相反的情况几乎没有。另外,有约20%的语言在领属语位置上不用独立代词,领属语的人称由中心名词上所加的人称标记表示。依附性人称标记也表现出对论元种类的敏感,作者将其总结为与论元突出度的相关性。论元突出度表现为"主语 > 宾语1(以受事为原型的直接宾语) > 宾语2(与事等题元角色的间接宾语) > 旁格"的等级序列。本书以丰富实例证明,越靠左的成分越有机会用依附性人称标记表达;一般来说,依附性人称标记能标记(或指向)序列中的一个成分,蕴涵着它也能标记(或指向)其左的所有成分,而不一定标记其右的成分。依附性人称代词同时也存在另一个等级序列,即:零形式 > 黏着成分 > 附缀 > 弱化形式。这两个序列的关系是,大部分语言中,越是靠左的形式(依附性越强)越是用来表达靠左的论元(突出度越高)。当然也有例外存在,如有的语言零形式(最靠左)可以表达宾语,却不能表达主语。可见两个序列还不足以构成绝对的蕴涵共性。

不同语言有不同的形态配置模式,人称标记的句法功能也因此表现出相应的系统性差异。人称代词形式简短,常与所带的格标记或附置词(前置词、后置词)紧密结合甚至产生融合，使人称范畴和格范畴合并在一个形式上，两者的关系因此非常紧密甚至难分难解，还可能造就新的词形，有时就被视为代词格范畴的异干形式，也可能使人称形式与独立名词语在格方面表现有异。比较常见的是，有些格只表现在代词上，名词没有相应的格；相反的情况则少得多。当然，名词代词拥有相同格范畴的语言也不在少数。作者认为，人称代词和独立名词在句法功能的编码模式(或曰论元配置模式)上如表现出差异，是比较有价值的现象。

就单及物结构而言，除了传统上区分的主-宾格和作-通格两种形态配置模式外，本书还列举了中性模式(不及物主语 S、施事 A、受事 P 同格形式)、三分模式(S、A、P 不同格形式)、施事主动非主动模式(按 A 是否有主动性区分格形式)、施受比等级模式(根据 A 和 P 在生命度等方面的等级区分格形式)。以此分类为基础，作者举例说明了名词和代词之间、独立代词和依附性人称形式之间在形态配置模式上的不同。统计表明，主-宾格模式的优势在依附性人称形式中表现得比独立代词中更加显著。这就意味着，有些语言独立代词是非主-宾格模式，而依附性人称形式是主-宾格模式。主动非主动配置模式主要表现于依附性人称标记。值得注意的是，少数语言例外地属于独立代词为主动非主动模式，其中提到台湾邹语(Tsou)和藏语拉萨话两种中国的语言。至少从藏语拉萨话的描写看(如王志敬 1994)，确实会因施事的主动性不同而采用不同的编码方式，只是国内著作的描写未必将之纳入类型学的视角。

参照单及物结构 S、A、P 三元素构成的模式分类系统，双及物结构建立由单及物受事 P、双及物动词客体 T(theme，即国内所说的受事)和与事 R(recipient，接受者)三者构成的 6 种配置模式：中性模式(P、T、R 同格形式)、间接宾语模式(T 与 P 合一，跟 R 相对)、偏向与格模式(R 与 P 合一，与 T 相对)、三分模式(P、T、R 不同格形式)、受事主动被动模式(宾语按主动性强弱分为两类)、两个论元比等级模式(根据动词所支配的两者在人称-生命度等级序列上的地位选择形态标记)。作者分析了不同人称形式在上述模式中的分布及其规律，并对这些规律做出了偏向于功能的解释。例如，名词短语和独立代词都是间接宾语类型占优势，这是因为给予行为常被表达为一个处所性行为，与事被处理为空间方向(**导读者按**：如表示与事的英语 to，古汉语"于"，藏语 -la 本义都表空间)，其余客体被视为单及物的受事 P，自然与 P 同取宾格。

对形态配置模式和人称的相关性，作者注意到，同一语言中的不同配置模式，更常依据人称形式是独立词语还是依附形式来定，而较少按人称不同

（属第几人称）来分。不过，仍有一些语言不同的人称分取不同的形态配置，即所谓分裂式配置，这使配置模式和不同人称的相关性也成为一个有趣的观察角度。例如，在藏缅语族 Hayu 语中，无论是独立代词还是人称词缀，第一人称都取作格配置，而第三人称独立代词取没有形态区别的中性配置，第三人称词缀则取宾格配置。在分裂式配置方面，宾格和作格的组合较具有倾向性，而涉及其他组合的分裂配置时，则看不出明显倾向。例如，有些语言第一第二人称取三分模式，而第三人称单取宾格模式或作格模式。也有些语言恰恰相反，第一第二人称取单纯宾格模式或作格模式，而第三人称取三分模式。

本章最后讨论人称标记的强调形式。形式上，作者主张从严界定人称强调式，只有代词等人称形式带上专用的强调标记才算强调式。假如带的是该语言中广泛采用的强调标记（**导读者按**：如汉语"连他都……"、"是你们……"中的"连"、"是"），则不算人称强调式。句法上，强调式可分论元性的和强化性的。论元强调式像独立名词那样充当各种论元成分（主语、宾语、介词宾语等等），而强化强调式主要帮助同现的非强调人称形式表达强调义。像英语 He himself can do it 中的 himself 就是一个强化强调式。语义上，有些强调式只用于显性的对比性语境，即总是与上下文中的另一对象构成对比；而有些只用于强调，不含明显的对比。强化强调式可以根据其语法功能分为两小类，一类是附名类（adnominal；**导读者按**：约相当于汉语所说的定语性或同位语性），它们和被强调的名词构成一个名词语，如上例中的 He himself；一类是附动类（adverbial；**导读者按**：亦即副词性或状语性的；副词 adverb 在英语字面上就是"附于动词之词"，状语 adverbial 则是附于动词之词所作的成分），如 He can do it himself 中的 himself。根据语义，强化强调式又可以分为包括式和排除式。包括式将强调对象纳入一个更大的集合，相当于"我/你/他也……"等；而排除式将强调对象作为唯一对象，相当于"只有我/你/他……"。作者基于一些语料指出，在某些情况下上述各类之间存有模糊地带，有时需要借助其他标准来判断。例如，有些语言作论元的成分常可省略，这时强化该论元的成分看起来就像是自身单用的论元性强调式了。

另外我们要补充一点，由于强化形式在很多语言里与反身形式同形（作者认为这是因为反身形式常来自强化形式），例如汉语的"自己"、英语的 himself 等都兼有两职，因此国内有些著作不区分两者，如将"他自己去医院"这类强调用法的"自己"也归入反身用法。这种做法不利于调查研究。很多少数民族语言著作在反身代词栏下只列出强化用法而未举反身用法，这也难以判断两者在该语言中是否同形。当然,也有不少语言反身形式和强调形式并不相同,如俄语反身代词是ceбя,强调代词是caм;德语中反身代词是sich,强调代词是selbst。

三、人称聚合的结构

本章从整体上考察不同形式表现的人称标记,把这些人称标记分成不同的聚合(paradigms)逐一讨论,主要涉及人称、数、性等聚合。

3.1节考察人称聚合,即人称系统中三身(三种人称)形式的表现。并非所有语言的人称系统都有三身之别。作者指出,第三身从缺或者其单数取零形式时,三个人称的区别仍旧存在。三身真正无法区分的情况比较少见,一般发生于依附性人称标记。作者归纳了无法区分的4种可能:a.第一、二身同形,区别于第三身;b.第二、三身同形,区别于第一身;c.第一、三身同形,区别于第二身;d.三个人称全部同形。四种可能都已有实例验证。其中,第4种可能以三种人称可依赖其他范畴加以区分为前提。比如,三种人称的单数形式无法相互区分,但复数形式可以。

3.2节考察人称系统的数聚合。Greenberg(1963)曾认为人称范畴存在数的区别是一种语言共性。然而,情况并非如此简单。本书指出,更常见的是,弱化代词不区分数,而独立代词有数的对立(**导读者按**:其实也有连独立代词都不区分数的,如古代汉语)。

就数范畴而言,人称系统的一种表现是存在单、复数的对立,还牵涉到包括式和排除式之别。与单数不同,人称复数形式的理解比较复杂。理论上,第一身复数有4种可能的解读:a.数量超过1的说话人(1+1);b.说话人和听话人(1+2);c.说话人、听话人和第三方(1+2+3);d.说话人和第三方(1+3)。第二身复数有两种可能的解读:a.数量超过1的听话人(2+2);b.听话人和第三方(2+3)。第三身复数只能解读为数量超过1的第三方(3+3)。事实上,第一身复数很少取a解,因为两个或多个人同时发言的情形不多(只有举行仪式等特殊场合可能);在很多语言里,其他三种解读会用形式加以区分,如b和c在形式上与d对立,这也就形成了第一人称复数包括式和排除式的对立。

数范畴在人称系统中的另一种表现是存在双数与大于2的数的形式区别,这样就形成单、双、复数的三元对立。双数的存在势必影响复数的理解,此时复数至少指3个个体。第一人称双数可能区分1+2和1+3两种情况,即包括式对排除式。有的语言仅在双数中有包括、排除式对立,复数中没有;有的语言则相反,如藏缅语族的一些语言复数区分包括式、排除式,而双数不区分。更常见的是,双数、复数对立仅见于包括式而不见于排除式;相反的情况则比较少。由此可见,双数-复数与包括式-排除式互有交叉。

有些语言的人称范畴也区分三数、四数或少量数。四数在使用上的限制比双数、三数要大。作者指出,概括三数或少量数中的包括式和排除式不是件容易的事情。就使用独立人称形式的语言来说,大部分语言的双数、三数/少量数和复数中都有包括式、排除式之分,也有些语言仅在双数、复数中区分二者,三数不区分。另外,作者对"三数蕴涵双数"(即 Greenberg(1963) 共性 34:有双数的语言才有三数)的说法持谨慎态度,因为很多被认为是三数的事实上是少量数。

数范畴在人称系统中的表现受人称等级序列(第一＞第二＞第三人称)的影响。主要体现在三个方面:a. 人称在数的区分上"机会"并不均等。根据人称等级序列,数的对立在第一人称上最常见,在第三人称上最少见。第一、二人称区分数而第三人称不区分的情况在语言中已获广泛验证。当然,也有反例存在,如英语偏偏只有第二人称不区分数。b. 数的具体表现形式不同。作者转引 Dressler & Barbaresi(1994)的观点:如果不同人称上的数形式不同,则第一人称更多使用模糊的形态标注,如异干交替的方式,而第三人称更多使用附加词缀这种明显的屈折形式。本书未就此展开系统研究,但作者根据个人观察指出,在第三人称不是指示词或不与性表达相糅合的语言里,在数的表现方面第三人称比第一、二人称更有规律。c. 第一人称比第二、三人称表现出更多的数对立。比如,有些语言第一人称双数有包括式和排除式之分,但其他涉及两个参与者的组合却没有专门的区分形式。在人称系统的数范畴方面,作者详细介绍了 Ingram(1978)和 Cysouw(2000) 两项研究。二者语种基础(70:265)、统计方法和最后结论都颇为不同。Ingram 归纳出 21 种人称-数模式,其中由三身两数对立构成的 6 人称系统最常见;而 Cysouw 统计的人称-数模式多达 98 种,6 人称系统并不最占优势。作者指出,尽管 Cysouw 有很大进步,但他未将性的变化纳入其中。

3.3 节讨论人称系统的性聚合。跟名词借助一致关系体现性不同(如,阳性名词的修饰或限定成分取阳性形式),人称标记主要通过自身的形式变化反映性。大多数的性的对立是以生理之性为基础的,比如指称男性采用阳性形式,指称女性采用阴性形式。人类(human)-非人类、有生(animate)-无生的对立也与性的区分有一定关系。

人称等级序列对性的区分有很大影响。性的对立在第三人称上的表现最为明显,这一点很容易解释。第一、二人称的性对言语行为参与者来说是不言自明的,而第三人称经常不在交际现场,性的区分就可以为确定该第三方的所指提供线索。作者指出，如果把影响性标注的人称等级序列表示为"第三＞第二＞第一人称"，则存在一些不能解释的例外。相形之下，Greenberg(1963)概括为"第三、二＞第一人称"(共性 44)更加谨慎，作者所知道的唯一反例是 Maká 语。

数范畴对性的区分也有影响，人称的性对立更多体现在单数上。Greenberg(1963)共性 45 云：如果代词的复数有任何性的区别，则单数也会有某种性的区别。作者指出，这条共性事实上可以扩展应用于双数、三数甚至四数等。不过语言中也存在一些这条共性的反例，主要有两种类型：其一，有些语言，非单数人称形式有性对立的比单数形式多；其二，当性的对立不基于生理之性，而基于人类-非人类或有生-无生的对立时，有些语言复数形式有性的对立，而单数反而没有。此外作者还注意到，在有双、复数区分的语言里，基于生理之性的性对立更多见于双数，比如复数是中性与非中性二元对立，而双数是阴、阳、中性三元对立。作者认为，这可能是因为对数量大的群体来说，区分性的难度更大。如果性的区分基于人类-非人类或有生-无生，并且这种性对立并未体现在所有的非单数形式上，那么一般表现在复数形式上，而非双数或三数。此外，如语言有独立形式和依附性形式两套人称标记，独立形式常比依附性形式在性、数等范畴上的区分更多。依附性人称形式最常缺少的是性的区分，其次是包括式、排除式的区别，再次是数的对立。依附性人称形式的内部也有区别，但系统性不强，难以很好地概括。作者指出了其中的两种趋势：不及物主语 S 或及物施事 A 是双数形式、受事 P 不是双数形式的现象，比相反的情况(即 P 是双数形式，S 或 A 不是双数形式)更常见；人称标记的包括式、排除式的对比更常见于 S 或 A。

四、人称一致关系

一致关系(agreement)通常指一个语言单位的语义或形式与另一个语言单位的形式之间的系统共变关系。本书借用 Corbett(2000)的术语，把决定一致关系的语言单位称为"控制项"(controller，如主语)；受控于一致关系的需要形式变化的语言单位称为"目标项"(target，如动词)；发生一致关系的句法环境称为一致关系的"范域"(domain，如小句)；一致关系在目标项上的形式表现(如前缀)称为"一致标记"(agreement marker)，在本书中特指人称一致标记。尽管以上定义暗示一致标记总是附着在目标项上的，但本书的人称一致标记也包括具有相同功能的可分离的标记，如附缀。

4.1 节主要考察人称一致标记与回指代词(anaphoric pronoun)之间的区别。与 1.2 节讨论的人称代词与名词之别一样，从人称一致标记到回指代词也是一个连续统。作者保留了 Bresnan & Mchombo(1987)提出的语法一致关系和回指一致关系的区分,并在此基础上把人称一致标记分为三种类型:a.句法的一致标记(同结构中必须出现显性控制项,如英语的-s),b.两可的(ambiguous)一致标记(同结构中可以出现显性/隐性控制项),c.代词性的一致标记(同结构中不能出现显性控制项)。一致标记与一致关系存在对应关系:代词性的一致标记主要表达回指一致关系,句法的一致标记主要表达语法一致关系,两种一致关系都可以用两可的一致标记表达。

4.2节从目标项的角度考察人称一致关系。跨语言考察显示,人称一致关系的三个主要目标项呈现出"谓词＞被领属名词＞附置词"的等级序列,越靠前(左)的越需要标注一致关系,靠后(右)的标注蕴涵靠前(左)的标注。少量的例外并不影响基于统计的倾向性共性。另外,这三个目标项上标注的一致关系类型有别:谓词上标注的绝大多数是语法一致关系,而被领属名词和附置词上标注的多为回指一致关系。

在不及物谓词内部,人称一致关系标注则呈现出"事件谓词＞属性谓词＞类属谓词、方所谓词"的语义等级序列,靠后(右)的标注蕴涵靠前(左)的标注。至于这四类谓词是否取相同的一致关系标记,则因语言而异。另外,在所有不及物谓词需要标注人称一致关系的语言里,及物谓词也都需要标注这种关系。

领属关系的可让渡性/不可让渡性会影响在被领属名词上体现的人称一致关系,主要表现在:a.不可让渡名词比可让渡名词更需要标注人称一致关系;b.一致标记的位置可能因被领属名词的可让渡性/不可让渡性而不同;c.一致标记的形式因被领属名词的可让渡性/不可让渡性而不同。如 Mohawk 语中,身体部位这种不可让渡领属关系的一致标记与施事标记同形,其他领属关系的一致标记则与受事标记同形。书中以认知语言学理论为依据对可让渡性的对立做了解释,例如不可让渡的关系更紧密,所以在象似性原则影响下,其一致关系标记名词的距离也更近;再如不可让渡的领属者往往有更强的生命度和话题性,所以其一致关系标记有时会与施事一致关系标记同形。

与谓词和被领属名词相比,体现在附置词上的人称一致关系至今尚欠研究。附置词上有人称一致标注的现象在澳大利亚之外的绝大部分语言区域都已有例证,有的涉及所有附置词,有的只涉及部分附置词。作者认为,现在还很难从语义上概括出哪些附置词更需要人称一致标注。此外,有些语言的副词、数词和疑问代词等也会成为人称一致标记附着的对象。

4.3节以控制项为切入点考察人称一致关系。在某些语言里,是否需要表达这种一致关系取决于控制项的属性,即受制于以下等级序列:人称等级序列(第一＞第二＞第三人称)、名词性等级序列(代词＞名词)、生命度等级序列(人类＞有生＞无生＞抽象体)、指称等级序列(有定＞无定实指＞非实指)和焦点等级序列(非焦点＞焦点)。一般而言等级序列左边的项更容易引发一致关系标注,不过也存在少量例外。

4.4节首先讨论人称一致标记的形态音系性质。生成语言学派只将词缀看做潜在的一致标记,附缀和弱化代词是代词性论元、句法投射的核心或算子。功能-类型学派则对人称一致标记的形态-音系形式没有严格的限定。因为形式演变与语义演变被认为是平行的(详见7.2节),所以从代词性一致标记到两可的一致标记、再到句法的一致标记的强制性的增强,就可能体现为一致标记句法独立性和语音形式的弱化。代词性一致标记通常是弱化代词或附缀;句法的一致标记常采取与时、体、式标记相融合的词缀形式;跨语言中最普遍的一致标记是两可的一致标记,一般是词缀形式。另外,强制使用的两可一致标记更容易跟其他语法标记发生融合。作者指出,这些概括都是倾向而非绝对共性,弱化代词也可能是强制使用的。

人称一致标记的位置主要涉及三种语序。其一,一致标记相对于目标项(词干)的位置,即一致标记是前缀还是后缀。与这个问题相关的假设有三个:a. 后缀占优势假设。b. 核心顺序原则(Head Ordering Principle)。该假设预测:"修饰语＞核心"(OV)语言中,一致标记采用后缀形式;"核心＞修饰语"(VO)语言中,一致标记采用前缀形式;c. 历时句法假设(Diachronic Syntax Hypothesis)。该假设预测:在动词居后、领属语前置的语言里,一致标记倾向于用前缀;在动词居前,领属语后置的语言里,一致标记倾向于用后缀;而在动词居中的语言里,一致标记使用前缀后缀的组合形式。作者详细分析了这三条假设在处理人称一致标记问题上的优劣。首先,一致标记的统计数据很难支持第一条假设。其次,相比较而言,核心顺序假设对与施事A相关的一致标记的预测更成功,而历时句法假设则对与受事P相关的一致标记的预测更成功。作者认为,上述三种假设都不足以圆满解释一致标记的位置。其二,一致标记之间的相对位置。一些学者认为,与施事A和受事P相关的两个一致标记的语法化程度会影响它们的相对位置。具体地说,语法化程度高的标记更靠近词干(根据Bybee等(1991)的研究)。本书第7章将会看到,与A相关的一致标记比与P相关的语法化程度更高。这也就意味着,一致标记是前缀时,与P相关的标记在与A相关的标记之前。另一些学者则认为,词缀对词干意义的影响程度会影响词缀的相对位置,影响越大的越靠近词干(根据Bybee(1985)提出的"相关性原则"the principle of relevance)。当 P 比 A 与动词的语义、句法关系更密切时,上述两派观点得出的结论会相反。在考察了更多语言的情况后,作者认为,相关性原则的预测性更强。其三,一致标记相对于其他语法标记的位置。一致标记对词干的语义影响小于时体式标记、变价标记、格标记等,根据相关性原则,一致标记距离词干应比上述其他语法标记更远。然而,例外的情况也并不少见。一些语言学家就此认为,人称一致标记的位置很大程度上是任意的。作者不赞同这种用例外否认已发现倾向性的做法。

本章的分析角度和假设的原则等对中国境内语言的研究富有参考价值。部分藏缅语有谓语动词上的人称一致关系(孙宏开 1994a,b;个别语言如景颇语用句尾词的词形变化表示,见戴庆厦、徐悉艰 1992,戴庆厦 2008),其人称标记多由独立人称代词语法化而来,而其所指向的成分也不像印欧语那样限于主语,而涉及受事宾语、与事宾语甚至领属代词。此外,某些阿尔泰语言有加在被领属成分上的人称一致关系形态(如鄂伦春语,见胡增益 2001:78)。本章内容对深化以上相关现象的研究并以此检验本章的理论会很有帮助。

五、人称形式的功能

本章考察人称形式在话语、句中的分布,运用认知话语分析理论进行解释。

关于人称形式在话语中的功能,有许多不同理论背景的解释,比如"中心化理论"、"话语表征理论"、"新格赖斯语用理论"等。本书的解释主要基于认知话语分析理论。该理论认为,人称形式跟其他直指、回指形式一样,也是说/听者使用的一种话语-模式管理程序,这个程序可以调整或维持话语心理模式中不断发展的所指的认知可及性等级(活跃性或凸显度)。Ariel (1990)提出的名词短语指称的认知可及性等级如下:

零形式＜反身形式＜人称词缀＜人称附缀＜不带重音的代词＜带音的代词＜带重音的代词＋手势＜近指指示词(＋NP)＜远指指示词(＋NP)＜带修饰语的近指指示词(＋NP)＜带修饰语的远指指示词(＋NP)＜名字＜姓氏＜较短的有定性描写＜较长的有定性描写＜全称名词＜带修饰语的全称名词

据此可以预测,采用零形式的指称,其认知可及性比采用反身形式的指称要高,依次类推。Gundel 等(1993,2000)则提出了另一种等级,其解释较倚重语用原则,尤其是格赖斯的"量的准则":

焦点＞激活的＞熟悉的＞唯一可辨认的＞有指的＞类别可辨认的

在上述观点基础上，本书指出，被论及实体的凸显度会影响认知可及性。比如，如果人称标记是连续性的主语话题，则其认知可及性高，那么人称标记就可能通过零形式或动词上的屈折变化表示。如果人称标记是信息焦点（如答句、对比焦点或强调焦点），则影响人称形式选择的不是认知可及性而是信息的性质。另一个影响人称形式选择的是整一性（unity），主要表现在距离和连贯性（cohesion）两方面。如果人称形式的所指与其在话语中上一次出现的距离很小，则影响人称标记选择的就是连贯性。即使话语中没有出现另一个竞争性所指，当相关所指的句间连贯性降低时，就可能会选用独立人称形式，而不使用依附性人称形式。另外，作者不赞同 Ariel 所认为的连贯性的降低必然会造成认知可及性降低的说法。

大多数从认知-心理角度分析人称形式功能的学者主张，影响小句、句内人称形式分布的因素原则上跟话语中的相同；并认为，话语分析中使用的认知可及性已经语法化为句法限制，影响着不同人称形式在句子内部的表现。本书观点也如此。作者用认知可及性对 Chomsky 著名的约束理论（Binding Theory）三原则进行解释，指出反身形式所指的认知可及性比代词的更高，r-表达式（包括专名和有定描述）是中度认知可及性标记。认知可及性受凸显度和整一性的影响。跨语言材料显示，随着先行词凸显度的下降，反身形式跟先行词整一性的降低，使用反身形式的次数也减少。根据认知可及性与形态句法编码之间的关系，如果反身形式比代词的认知可及性高，则其形式应该更简单，然而很多语言的反身形式却比代词形式更复杂。另外，语法化在跨语言中的演变方式和演变速度不同（本书 7.2 节），如果反身形式和代词的句法限制确实是语法化了的认知等级性，那么它们在不同语言中的表现也肯定不同。事实也确实如此。

另外，作者认为 Chomsky(1981) 提出的"避免代词原则"（Avoid Pronoun Principle）是冗余的，不精确的。根据这条原则，能使用不止一种类型的代词（尤其是独立代词和依附性代词）的语法环境优选非显性形式。但正如许多学者指出的，在二者都适用的情况下，选择显性形式并非必然有标记，选择非显性形式也并非必然无标记。究竟选择哪一种人称形式跟其所指的认知可及性相关。

作者考察了视点（point of view）和移情（empathy）这两个影响指称表达的因素。她指出，认知可及性是以听话人为导向的，而视点和移情是以说话人为导向的，即说话人"邀请"听话人从某个他选择的角度（己方或他方）考虑情境或事件。大部分言语都是"自我中心的"，即说话人从个人角度对情境或事件进行描述。从人称、时间的指示形式来看,"小李昨天对我说他今天来看我"是典型的以当前说话人为视点的间接引语,而"小李昨天对我说:'我明天来看你。'"是直接引语。两种引语之间存在三身的转换("他"→"我","我"→"你")。有些语言不采用这种转换人称形式的方式,而使用专门的"视点代词"(logophoricity)。以"她说她途中在 Jos 停留"为例,Mupun 语中第二个"她"用 de 时,两个"她"同指,因为 de 是第三人称阴性视点代词,它反映事件内部参与者的观点;如果第二个"她"用常规的第三人称标记 wa,则两个"她"不同指。换言之,用 de 时,"她途中在 Jos 停留"是间接引语;用 wa 时,则是直接引语。视点代词在句中充当动词的补足语,与动词之间的关联性表现为"交流＞思维＞心理状态＞感知"的等级序列,视点代词最优先跟"说、告诉、报告、宣布"等交流动词搭配,依此类推。从句法功能来看,视点代词在有些语言里只用于主语位置,而在有些语言中可以占据主语、宾语、领属者等一系列句法位置。从形式上看,有些语言的视点代词不因句法功能的变化而改变词形,有些语言则不然。除了跟谓词相关联外,视点代词在有的语言中也表现出与部分结构类型的关联性,如更多出现在目的小句和关系小句中,少见于状语小句。很多语言的长距离反身形式常跟视点代词同形。在与谓词、其他结构类型的关联性上,长距离反身形式也表现出跟视点代词相似的一面。作者未就这两种人称形式的关系展开深入讨论,但她指出,这两个形式的重合及潜在的不同会促进对二者的进一步研究(**导读者按**:已经有人从视点代词的角度来研究汉语"自己"的长距离反身代词问题,如 Huang and Liu 2001)。

移情是与视点密切相关的概念。有些语言学家(如 Kuno 1987)交叉使用这两个概念,不做严格区分。作者认为二者的区别主要在于,移情除了可以反映说者的视点外,还包括说者对人对事的其他形式的确认,包括形容词的使用(**导读者按**:很可能是褒贬中性形容词)、方向动词如"来/去"的选择,主宾语的选择、尊称的使用等,而最重要的就是指称表达的选择。可见,移情概念的范围要比视点更大。大多数学者都主张,与移情相关的指称表达主要体现在人称标记和指示词或其他指称表达的对立分布上。在人称形式只用于指称人类、指示词用于指称非人类的语言里(**导读者按**:如汉语口语指人用"他/她",而指动物通常用"这/那＋量词"),较高级的动物或该文化认同的其他重要动物也可能使用人称形式(如汉语对宠物猫狗使用"它"),这就是移情因素导致的。与此相反,在常规的使用人类指称的场合如果使用了非人类指称,则是缺少移情的反映。比如意大利语中,quello/quella(那一个)或者 questo/questa(这一个)比 lui/lei(他/她)更多用于指称所述故事中不重要的或说话人不赞成的、不喜欢的人，或者在社会或感情上有距离的人。在专名和描述性 NP 代替人称形式方面，各语言表现出很大的区别。

本章最后考察了一种特殊的人称形式，如专用于指称"喜欢散步的人"、"拥有马的人"或"迈克尔·杰克逊的粉丝"等一类人或特定集合的指称表达式。文献中常使用类指(generic)、全称非实指(universal non-specific)、广义无定(generalized indefinite)等术语，作者选用"非人称形式"(impersonal form)这一术语。跨语言考察中发现，复数形式比单数形式更容易成为这类指称的形式标记，其中，最常使用的是第三人称复数形式。

六、人称形式和社会直指语(Social deixis)

正确使用人称形式不仅要了解该语言中有哪几种人称形式、影响人称形式分布的句法、话语-语用规则等，更关键的是要了解这些人称形式所反映的言语行为参与者及第三方之间的社会关系。社会关系主要涉及地位高低、权势强弱、关系亲疏、年龄长幼等等。表现社会关系的语法手段有很多，比如可以通过不同的情态、特殊动词形式、助动词、甚至是分类词和数词来实现，人称形式也是其中的重要手段之一。本章主要讨论人称系统中的尊称。

人称标记通过变化语义范畴实现尊称，这通常会导致人称标记的语义特征与实际话语所指的特征发生错配，如用语法上的复数表示单数个体，用第一人称指称听话人等现象(**导读者按**：汉语口语用"咱"婉指对方时既是复数表单数，又是第一人称指听话人)。

以数的变化表尊称是最常使用的手段，主要表现为非单数形式用做单数的尊称。比如 Tamil 语中，独立人称标记的尊称形式大多是相应的复数形式。而在单-双-复数三分的语言里，复数形式比双数形式更多用做尊称。跨语言材料显示，非单数形式用做尊称在三身人称标记上都有体现。然而，18 世纪的汉语却提供了反例。据 Lee(1999)考察，这一时期的汉语不仅有复数形式用做谦称的现象(即"我们"用做"我"的谦称，"你们"代替"你"指称比自己地位低的单数个体，"他们"代替"他"以表示被论及的单数个体是不重要的、可以忽略的)，还有用单数形式表示复数个体的现象(**导读者按**：这可能是复数体系尚未成熟时沿用不分单复数的早期规则，不同于有了明确单复数系统后以单指复的现象，未必真是反例)。

以人称变化表尊称。有些语言用第三身单数或复数形式指称听者，表明谈话比较正式，或至少暗示了交际双方关系不密切，说者对听者充满敬意。第一身(一般是非单数形式)也可以用做第二身尊称。反身形式用做尊称表示特别的尊敬。Marathi 语中,第二身复数形式可用做尊称,而反身形式用于礼貌、尊敬程度更高的场合。另外,反身形式用做尊称表现出很强的地域性,主要出现在印度次大陆语言中。反身形式用做尊称的原因尚不清楚。

有些语言具有表示社会关系的特定人称标记。也就是说,这些语言的某个/些人称标记甚至整个人称系统本身就有尊称、非尊称甚至更详细的区分。南亚、东南亚地区语言的人称系统相当精密。比如,泰语的第一、二、三人称分别有 27 种、22 种、8 种形式,这些形式可以反映地位高低、关系亲疏,甚至年龄、性别等区别。另外,有些语言不同的人称形式还可以表现说话人顺从、自愿、烦恼、同情等情绪态度,这种区分主要体现在第一人称上。

人称标记的省略也可以反映社会关系,主要有三种方式。一种是人称标记阙如,取零形式。比如日语中,熟识的或地位平等的人之间常常不使用第一第二人称,Tanaka desu(是田中),watasi(我)省略。作者还引介了熊学亮(1998)对现代汉语相关情况的考察结果:在面试、学术提职简介、离职前的告别演说等以谦逊为基调的话语场合中,第一人称通常省略。另一种是使用非实指人称标记,如英语的 one、法语的 on 或汉语的"人"、"人类"等类指名词,或者使用各种不出现具体施事的被动结构,作者称这些结构为"非人称化结构"(impersonalizing constructions)。当然,使用非实指人称标记并不必然是礼貌用法。法语里,对成年人使用 on 表现了对听话人的轻微蔑视或显示说话人的强势地位。第三种方式是使用人名、头衔、亲属称谓等代替人称标记。这种方式主要用于非自称场合。在正式场合或者跟年长于己的人交际时,尽管有多种可供选择的第二人称尊称,有些语言仍会用头衔等指称听话人。汉语中就有这样的现象,我们可以用"大哥、爷爷、叔叔、阿姨"等指称与自己毫无血缘关系的人。

七、历时视角中的人称形式

类型学跟一些强调历时共时区分的学派不同,它常将共时状态与历时演变结合起来研究,注重这两个维度的相关性,尤其是与语法化学说关系密切。所以,毫不奇怪,本书在前文共时考察之后设最后一章专论人称形式的历时演化,包括其来历、演变和去向(直到消失)。由于本书的历时平面主要采纳语法化学说的框架,因此作者先对此学说进行了扼要介绍,包括语法化在语法、语音和语义三方面的主要表现、语法化的机制和动因。

7.1 节讨论人称形式的来源,分为词汇来源和语法来源两个方面,惜乎作者并未明言两类的分野。从所述内容看,词汇来源是指可以直接做人称代词的名词。人称代词语法上是名词性的,所以名词无须改变语法属性就可能直接用作人称代词。语法来源是指需要经过一定的语法化过程演化为人称代词或人称标记的其他词类或语法要素,还包括可以语法化为更虚的人称标记的人称代词或人称标记。

人称形式的词汇来源多已掩埋于历史中无从考溯,不过仍有少数人称形式的词源比较清楚。如东南亚语言常用表示"奴隶"、"仆人"一类自贬自谦之词来表第一人称(**导读者按**:比较古汉语"奴"、"仆"的第一人称用法),用表示"师傅、主人、君王"一类表敬称呼表第二人称(**导读者按**:比较古汉语"君"的第二人称用法)。作为一般倾向,第一第二身代词常来自表示人类关系的词,而第三身代词常来自表示东西/事物、人类、男人、人、身体等义的词(**导读者按**:不过汉语史上"身"曾表第一人称)。有些语言用表示"别人"的词作第三身形式(**导读者按**:汉语"他"的来历相似,见吕叔湘 1940)。有些语言以更具体的名词作为含义更具体的第三身代词,如"神、树、水"。人称代词的另一个来源是分类词(classifier,相当于汉语所说的"量词")。分类词和第三人称代词的一个共同功能是充当回指成分,这使分类词较容易用作第三人称代词。

指示词(特别是远指词)是第三身代词最重要的语法来源。这方面例证极丰(**导读者按**:古汉语有第三身代词作用的"彼(主格)、之(宾格)"原来均为指示词。现代汉语西北地区方言用"那"作第三人称代词及民族语言中的相关情况可参看唐正大 2005)。作者也指出少量反向演化之例,即人称代词成为指示词。两者互变的枢纽是回指功能。指示词和代词都可以用来指代人或者事物。两者的区别点在于,指示词主要用来直指(现场指)而第三人称代词主要用来回指。但指示词也具备回指功能,这就为它演变成代词提供了条件。

依附性人称标记的常见语法来源是独立代词,它往往是代词的某种缩减形式。不过独立代词与其缩减后的依附形式的词形联系,或显豁,或隐晦。有时两者的形式关联只表现在部分人称(通常是第一第二人称)、某些格或某些数(如只表现于非单数)等的人称形式上。此外,作者认为偶有独立代词来自依附人称标记的反向情况,不过她指的是依附性人称标记和某个形态成分或虚词组合成独立人称代词,而不是依附性代词单独变成独立代词——这种由虚到实的演变是违背语法化的单向性原则的,很难出现。

人称代词和其他成分结合乃至并合,可以凝固为新的人称形式。典型例子是分裂句中焦点标记(多来自系词)与人称代词凝固为一个代词。从书中例子看,有些由此形成的代词只是普通代词而不是强调代词。

汉语中也存在来自系词的焦点标记"是"与人称代词合成新代词的现象,《祖堂集》等近代汉语文献中就有"是我、是你、是渠"等式,多用作主语(例见张美兰2001:121),实际上是保留了其分裂句焦点标记的位置;"是"和代词还没有出现语音缩减的情况。而老上海话(现多见于郊区)也有"是/自/实＋我/侬/伊"的代词形式("自"即本地同音的"是","实"则为"是"的弱化促化形式),它们不但已不受句法位置的限制,而且同音字的写法和促化的变异读法表明,其并合程度的深化已使当地人觉察不到其来源。此外还有其他并合形式。例如带有人称形式的助动词可能跟动词并合,从而给动词带去助动词原带的人称形态;再如表示"给予"、"打击"的动词也可能参加到并合导致的人称形式中。

体标记或传信(evidential)标记等虚语素也是人称标记的语法来源之一。

7.2节讨论独立人称标记到句法一致标记的演变。从人称代词到句法一致标记是一个典型的语法化连续统。根据语法化理论,作者将这一演变分解为形式、功能、语义三个维度的连续统,并指出三者之间既有总体平行的一面(即语法化程度基本对应),也有参差之处。对于这些演变的机制及其解释,作者介绍了三种有影响的理论。名词附着说(NP-detachment)由Givón(1976)提出,认为论元话题化的句子变成普通句子,话题变成主语等句法成分,而小句中用来复指话题的代词附着于动词成为与论元保持一致关系的词缀,从而使独立代词完全变成依附性人称一致关系词缀。可及性说(Accessibility Theory)由Ariel(2000)提出,认为可及性越高的成分越会用简化形式表示。人称代词尤其是第一第二人称的所指在交际场合是可及性最高的,表示这些概念的成分可能因此逐步简化弱化并入动词成为人称词缀。频率驱动说(Frequency-driven Morphologization)不是专为人称提出的理论,而是一条解释缩减融合现象的一般性规律。根据这条规律,高频相邻同现的成分容易发生融合,人称代词由于与动词高频相邻同现,所以代词容易融进动词。此外,不同格的代词(主格、宾格、领属格)与动词同现的频率很不相同(统计可证),主格高于领属格许多倍,所以主格更容易融进动词成为人称标记乃至一致关系词缀。作者指出,上述三种理论都不能解释人称标记语法化过程中从两可的一致标记向句法的一致标记发展的阶段。她认为对这一过程的最可能的解释是,独立代词被用来补偿动词上的依附性人称标记因语音混同而产生的歧义。具体地说,动词上的人称标记由于语音弱化脱落等原因,常常导致不同人称或数的标记出现混同,单靠它们已不足以区分论元的人称,于是需要独立代词与依附性人称标记同现以明确人称信息,从而形成人称一致标记。很多现象验证了这一解释的合理性,如有句法一致标记的语言其人称标记往往存在不同人称标记的混同,而某些语言的独立代词只在依附性标记有歧义时出现,这正好体现了一致标记形成过程中的状态。但作者也指出这一看法不足以解释所有现象,可能还有其他原因。如对某些印欧语来说,V2类型(动词出现在句子的第二位置,主语出现在其前或后)要避免动词打头也是促使句首出现独立代词的因素,由句首位置扩散到其他位置便会造成句法性一致关系。

7.3节讨论人称形式历史演变的外部因素,尤其是语言接触带来的借用或影响现象。作者指出,人称形式是否会因语言接触而相互借用,是个见仁见智的问题。有人认为可借,有人认为不可借。观点的取舍会影响对某些语言族群谱系关系的认识,因为有些亲属关系的确立就很依赖人称形式的同源,假如相信人称形式也可以借用,则据此认定谱系就必须谨慎。作者相信人称形式可以借用,同时也承认有不少情况难以确定是借用还是自身的演变。借用大量发生在本身有亲属关系的语言间,也有一些发生在不同语系间。借用的对象除了直接借入独立的或依附性的人称形式个体外,还包括人称范畴的借入(如第一人称复数包括式和排除式的借入),甚至整个人称形态系统的借入。

人称形式的消失有其内部原因和外部原因,有些情况不好分辨;有时甚至难以分辨系统性不强的人称形式是正在形成发展中的人称系统还是正在消亡的系统。书中列举了一些较能确定的因语言接触影响而导致某些范畴甚至整个人称形态系统消失的例子。

导 读 后 语

《人称范畴》一书所在的剑桥语言学教材丛书是一套名著林立的丛书,其中有一批著作是像本书一样以大量的跨语言材料和分析来概述一个语言学范畴的专著,如《时范畴》、《体范畴》、《性范畴》、《数范畴》、《格范畴》等,而本书的语种基础达到了700多种语言,也体现了丛书的一种后出转精。这样的著作对于中国学界来说是非常急需的。传统上,国内语言学界过多地被语种、时代、地域这些界限所分割,某些比较性的研究又常限于个别语言或少数语言的范围,缺少类型学的覆盖力。引进《人称范畴》这类大规模跨语言研究的成果和视角肯定能有力促进国内的相关研究。该丛书中Comrie的《时范畴》、《体范畴》等专著已经引起诸多国内学人的关注,对推动国内相关专题的研究起到了积极的作用。《人称范畴》一书国内原文版的出版为国内读者走近此书提供了更加便利的条件,期待该书能在国内学界发挥更积极的学术作用。

导读引用文献

戴庆厦2008.《景颇语人称标记的多选择性》,《中国语文》第 5 期。
戴庆厦、徐悉艰 1992.《景颇语语法》,中央民族学院出版社。
胡增益 2001.《鄂伦春语研究》,民族出版社。
吕叔湘 1940/1984. The third person pronouns. 原载《华西协合大学中国文化研究所集刊》一卷二期,收入吕叔湘著《汉语语法论文集》,商务印书馆 1984 年。
唐正大 2005.《关中方言第三人称指称形式的类型学研究》,《方言》第 2 期。
孙宏开 1994a.《再论藏缅语中动词的人称范畴》,《民族语文》第 4 期。
——— 1994b.《藏缅语中的代词化问题》,《国外语言学》第 3 期。
王志敬 1994.《藏语拉萨口语语法》,中央民族大学出版社。
张美兰 2001.《近代汉语语言研究》。天津教育出版社。
Huang, C-T James & C.-S. Luther Liu 2001. Logophoricity, Attitudes and ziji at the Interface. In Syntax and Semantics: Long Distance Reflexives. New York: Academic Press.

Preface

This book has two major aims. First of all, it seeks to provide an overview of the various manifestations of the category person in the grammatical system of the world's languages. And secondly it offers a potential account of the principles determining the distribution and form of person markers in utterances. The approach adopted is functional-typological and thus the stress is on the underlying cognitive and discourse basis of person systems and their exponents, on the one hand, and on how these factors are reflected in the existing patterns of cross-linguistic variation, on the other.

While the grammatical category of person is typically associated primarily with that of free personal pronoun, in this book no pride of place is assigned to free as opposed to bound forms or pronouns as compared to agreement markers. A major thread running throughout the discussion is that these different instantiations of the category of person are best viewed as defining both a diachronic and a synchronic cline in regard to their formal and functional properties. Accordingly, no attempt is made to establish universally applicable unique cut-off points on the cline but only to determine the recurring convergences of properties that tend to be found cross-linguistically.

In writing this book I have drawn on the descriptive and analytical insights of numerous scholars. The typological data are taken from over 700 languages. The data originate in the main from reference grammars and grammatical sketches, less frequently from discussions of specific phenomena relating to person marking, both descriptive and theoretical. While I have always made it a point of principle to acknowledge overtly in print each and every source of data or analysis which I have utilized or been inspired by, unfortunately I have not been able to do so in this work. Due to lack of space, I was obliged to eliminate twenty pages of references to the descriptive and theoretical research of my colleagues. Consequently, the list of references at the end of the book contains only the works from which language examples cited in the text are taken and a sub-set of key monographs and articles dealing with various facets of person marking. The full set of publications which I have benefited from is given on my web page http//www.ling.lang.lancs.ac.uk/staff/anna/person/.

Over the four years that I have taken to write this book I have had the opportunity to present various aspects of my ideas to colleagues at conferences, workshops and seminars. I am very grateful for all the comments, observations and data that I received. I would like to thank in particular: Mira Ariel, Dik Bakker,

Delia Bentley, Balthasar Bickel, Kirsti Börjars, Dunstan Brown, Bernard Comrie, Grev Corbett, Bill Croft, Martin Haspelmath, Dick Hudson, Peter Kahrel, Marianne Mithun, Johanna Nichols, Frans Plank, Johan van der Auwera, Robert Van Valin, Nigel Vincent and Anne Wichmann. I am especially indebted to the students of the LOT winter-school in Leiden in 2002 who took my course on Person agreement: synchrony and diachrony, for the lively discussion and challenging data which helped me to fine-tune some of my ideas.

I would also like to acknowledge gratefully the support that I received from the Arts and Humanities Research Council (RLS:APN 13302/AN 7261) and Lancaster University as well as from the Max Plank Institute for Evolutionary Anthropology in Leipzig where I did two months' work of data collection, at the invitation of Bernard Comrie and Martin Haspelmath.

In addition I would like to extend my thanks to the team at Cambridge University Press, especially Andrew Winnard, Jacqueline French and Paul Watt.

Finally I would like to thank my friends and family for their support and patience and especially my husband Dik Bakker for agreeing, much more often than he would like, to take second place.

Abbreviations

A	agentive argument of transitive verb
ABL	ablative case
ABS	absolutive case
ACC	accusative
ACT	actual
ADESS	adessive case
ADVR	adverbializer
AFF	affective
AG	agent, agentive
AGR	agreement
AH	addressee honorific
AL	alienable
ALL	allative case
AN	animate
AOR	aorist
APPL	applicative
ART	article
ASP	aspect
ASRT	assertive
ATTR	attributive
AUX	auxiliary
C	common
CAT	catalyst particle
CAUS	causative
CLF	classifier
CLT	clitic
CMP	completive
CNJ	conjunction
COLL	collective
COMP	complementizer
COND	conditional
CONN	connector
CONT	continuous
COP	copula
CORR	correlative

CP	complementizer phrase
CTR	contrast
DAT	dative
DEC	declarative
DEF	definite
DEM	demonstrative
DES	desiderative
DET	determiner
DETR	detransitivizer
DIR	directional
DIST	distal
DR	direct (as opposed to inverse)
DS	different subject
DSTR	distributive
DU	dual
DUR	durative
EMPH	emphatic
EP	epenthetic (vowel or syllable)
ERG	ergative (case)
EVID	evidential
EXCL	exclusive (of the addressee)
F	feminine gender
FACT	factive
FIN	finite
FOC	focus
FUT	future
GEN	genitive case, possessed
GER	gerund
H	honorific
HAB	habitual
HH	high honorific
HORT	hortative
HUM	human
I	inflection
IMP	imperative
IM.PAST	immediate past
IMPF	imperfective
IMPR	impersonal
INAL	inalienable
INAN	inanimate
INCL	inclusive (of the addressee)
IND	indicative
INDEF	indefinite
INDEP	independent

INESS	inessive
INF	infinitive
INST	instrumental
INT	interrogative
INTR	intransitive
INV	inverse
IO	indirect object
IP	inflection phrase
IPFV	imperfective
IRLS	irrealis
JUS	jussive
LOC	locative
LOG	logophoric
M	masculine gender
MID	middle
MIT	mitigator
MV	main verb
N	noun or nominal
NARR	narrative
NEG	negative element
NF	non-feminine
NFIN	non-finite
NH	non-honorific
NHUM	non-human
NOM	nominative
NP	noun phrase
NPMK	noun phrase marker
NR	nominalizer
NS	nominal suffix
NT	neuter
O	object
OBJ	object
OBL	oblique
OBV	obviative
P	patient argument of transitive verb
PART	participle
PASS	passive
PAST	past
PAT	patient
PAU	paucal
PERF	perfective
PL	plural
PNCT	punctual
POSS	possessive

POT	potential
PP	prepositional phrase
P. PART	past participle
PRED	predicative
PREP	preposition
PRES	present
PRO	pronoun
PROG	progressive
PROX	proximate
PRT	particle
Q	question particle, question word
R	recipient argument of ditransitive verb
REC.PAST	recent past
REDUP	reduplicated form
REFL	reflexive
REL	relative
REM.PAST	remote past
REP	repetitive
RLS	realis
S	single argument of intransitive verb
SEQ	sequential action
SBJ	subject
SG	singular
SPEC	specifier
SS	same subject
STAT	stative
SUBJ	subjunctive
T	theme of ditransitive clause
TAM	tense/aspect/modality marker
TNS	tense
TOP	topic
TRL	trial
TR	transitive
UGR	undergoer
V	verb
VP	verb phrase
1	1st person
2	2nd person
3	3rd person

1 Introduction

The notion of person has been widely discussed in many different fields of study including philosophy, sociology, anthropology, psychology, politics, religion, literature and art. Scholars who have addressed the issue of person within these fields have been concerned with questions such as what is a person, who qualifies as a person, what are the cross-cultural differences in the conceptualization of person, what is the relationship between individual identity and person, how do we identify and reidentify someone other than ourselves, when does a person stop being a person, etc. Though the social and cultural construal of personhood is also a topic of concern within linguistics, particularly sociolinguistics and anthropological linguistics, the notion of person in linguistics is primarily conceived of as a grammatical category, on a par with gender, number, case, tense, etc. Accordingly, it is with person as a category of the grammatical system of languages that this book will be primarily concerned.

1.1 Person as a grammatical category

It is often stated that the grammatical category of person covers the expression of the distinction between the speaker of an utterance, the addressee of that utterance and the party talked about that is neither the speaker nor the addressee. The speaker is said to be the first person, the addressee the second person and the party talked about the third person. This, however, is not quite correct. What is missing from the above characterization is the notion of participant or discourse role. In the case of the first and second persons, the grammatical category of person does not simply express the speaker and addressee respectively, but rather the participant or discourse roles of speaker and addressee.[1] The difference between the two characterizations can be appreciated by comparing the personal pronouns *I* and *you* in (1a) with that of the nominals *mummy* and *Johnny* in (1b).

(1) a.   I will spank you.
    b.   Mummy will spank Johnny.

---

[1] This characterization of the grammatical category person draws on the origin of the term person, i.e. mask. Further, it seeks to provide person forms with a sense as opposed to just a reference.

In certain situational contexts, speakers may refer to themselves and their addressees by their proper names, the relations of kinship that they bear to each other, their titles or occupational roles, etc. Thus in (1b) the word *mummy* could be used by a mother with reference to herself and the name *Johnny* with reference to the child whom she is addressing. In such a case, the words *mummy* and *Johnny* can be said to express the speaker and addressee but they cannot be said to express the discourse roles of speaker and addressee as there is nothing in the words *mummy* and *Johnny* to suggest that they are the speaker and addressee respectively. Conversely, this is precisely what is achieved by the two pronouns *I* and *you* in (1a). *I* is always used to refer to the speaker and you to the addressee.[2] Unlike *mummy* and *Johnny*, the two pronominals cannot have any other referents. Moreover, they do not express anything other than that their referents bear the discourse roles of speaker and addressee respectively. Accordingly, only *I* and *you* and not *mummy* and *Johnny* are expressions of the first and second persons. *Mummy* and *Johnny* are lexical expressions which may be used to refer to the speaker and addressee respectively.

In principle, there is no limit to the nature of the lexical expressions that a speaker may use to refer to herself. By contrast, it would be dysfunctional for languages to have a wide range of expressions to denote the discourse roles of speaker, addressee and third party. And indeed they tend not to. The vast majority of the languages of the world have a closed set of expressions for the identification of the three discourse roles embracing the category of person. The special expressions in question are typically called personal pronouns, or even just pronouns. (The word pronoun without additional qualification is generally interpreted as denoting pronouns expressing person.) In this book, however, we will use the terms *person marker* and *person form* in preference to *pronoun*, as the term pronoun is open to a number of interpretations and even under the most liberal of these, not all grammatical markers of the category person are uncontroversially pronominal. More about the notion of pronoun will be said in section 1.2.

Although the grammatical category of person involves only the three-way distinction of speaker, hearer and third party, this does not mean that languages typically have only three person markers. English, which clearly has many more than three person markers, is by no means exceptional. In fact, despite the array of person markers that English has, it does not qualify as a language rich in person markers. Other languages have many more. For instance, Fijian is said to have as many as 135 person forms. There are also languages with considerably fewer person markers than English. Madurese, an Austronesian language now mainly spoken in Java, has only two, *sengkoq* 'I/me' and *tang* 'my'. For the second and third persons, words meaning 'metaphysical body/spirit' and 'sole/alone' accompanied by a definite marker are used.

---

[2] This is not quite correct. The second-person form *you* in English, and also in many other languages, has an impersonal or generic use, illustrated in (13b) further below and discussed in more detail in chapter six.

The differences in person-marker inventories found cross-linguistically are in part a reflection of the nature of the grammatical categories in addition to person that the person markers encode. Person markers rarely mark person alone. The grammatical category most closely connected with person is that of number. Two other grammatical distinctions regularly expressed together with person are gender and case. Thus, for example, the English *she* encodes third person, singular number, feminine gender and nominative case, that is the case of the subject. Further grammatical categories which may also be marked together with person include definiteness, obviation, tense, aspect, mood and polarity. The last of these is to be found in the person markers of the Australian language Worora, for example, which, as shown in (2), has a distinctive set of forms used in negative utterances.

(2)   Worora (Love 2000:17)

		positive	negative
1SG		ŋaiu	'ŋaui
2SG		ŋundju	'ŋungi
3SG³	M	'indja	'kaui
	F	'nijina	'njuŋgi
	NT	'wuna	'kui
	NT	'mana	'maui

In addition to other grammatical categories, person markers may also encode information pertaining to their referents, for example, the social status of the referent vis-à-vis the speaker, their location relative to the speaker or addressee or, much more rarely, their kin relationship and/or generation level. A celebrated instance of person forms reflecting generation levels comes from Lardil (Hale 1966), another Australian language. In Lardil, in the dual and plural, one set of person forms is used for persons who belong to the same generation level or are two levels apart, and a different set of forms for persons one or three generations apart. Thus the form of the second-person dual 'you two' when used to refer to, say, a brother and sister or a grandparent and their grandchild is *kirri*, but when used to refer to a parent and child or great-grandparent and their grandchild is *nyiinki*. More complex systems involving not only considerations of generation level but also of membership within a given moiety (i.e. a particular set of kin categories) are found in other Australian languages, such as Arabana-Wangkangurru (Hercus 1994:117), Adnyamathanha and Kuyani (Schebeck 1973). In these last two languages there are twelve different sets of person markers to mark the kinship associations of the people to whom the person forms refer and, in some instances, also the speaker's relationship to these people. In contrast to the Australian languages mentioned above, in the Tibeto-Burman language Dhimal (King 2001) there are special person forms just for the first- and second-person singular which are reciprocally used only between two distinct groups, one being the parents of

---

[3] Membership in the two sets of neuter forms in Worora, the *wuna* set and the *mana* set is lexically determined.

a husband and a wife and the other, a man and his wife's senior relatives. In exchanges between these two groups the first-person singular is *kya* which contrasts with the typical *ka*, and the second-person singular is *nya* rather than *na*. Yet another factor, in part relating to referents, which has been noted to be encoded in the person markers of a language is speech style. Jacquesson (2001:123) reports that in several dialects of Tiddim, a Tibeto-Burman language, there are two sets of verbal person markers for all three persons: a prefixal set and a suffixal set. The former is used in narratives, the latter in everyday speech.

The other major source of differences in person-marker inventories is variation in morpho-phonological form. In some languages all the person markers are independent words, while others, in addition to such forms, also have person clitics and/or affixes and/or covert, that is zero forms. Bulgarian, for example, apart from independent forms, which may be used for all syntactic functions, has clitics used for objects, and affixes (fused with tense/aspect) used for subjects. All three forms occur in (3).

(3)   Bulgarian (Dimitrova-Vulchanova & Hellan 1999:490)
            Na Ivana kniga-ta az mu=   ja=   dadox
            to Ivan book-DEF I 3SG:DAT 3SG:ACC give:1SG
            'I gave the book to Ivan.'

1.1.1   Person paradigms

The person markers found in languages do not occur in isolation but rather in closed sets called paradigms. Simplifying somewhat, a paradigm is a set of linguistic expressions that occur in the same syntactic slot in the language. Moreover, each member of a paradigm is in complementary distribution with every other member of the same paradigm. Thus the English person forms *I/you/he/she/it/we/you/they* constitute one paradigm, as each may occur as the subject of an utterance and the use of any one form excludes the possibility of using any of the others (apart from coordinations). The person forms *me/you/him/her/it/us/you/them* belong to another paradigm, since they are employed as objects and complements of prepositions but, crucially, not as subjects. And the forms *my/your/his/her/its/our/your/their* make up a third paradigm used as attributive possessors. In addition to performing the same syntactic function, the members of a single paradigm are also assumed to have the same morpho-phonological form, that is to be all independent forms, or all clitics or affixes, etc.[4] Consequently, independent and clitic forms, such as the Bulgarian third-person masculine object forms *jemu* and *mu*, are seen as belonging to two different paradigms.

While there are languages which have only one paradigm of person markers used for all syntactic and discourse functions, most languages have several. An

---

[4] Occasionally differences in morpho-phonological form are found within what is considered to be a paradigm. For instance, in Fur (Jakobi 1990:28), the dependent object person markers in the singular are suffixes, in the plural clitics or weak forms.

important point to remember is that in those languages which have more than one paradigm of person markers, the structure of the different paradigms need not be the same. The paradigms may differ in regard to the person, number, gender and other distinctions marked. A particularly clear example of such differences between paradigms is presented in (4) from Vinmavis, an Oceanic language spoken on the island of Malakula, in which the independent person markers evince a singular/plural distinction and an inclusive/exclusive one (see section 3.2.1), while the subject prefixes exhibit an opposition between the singular, dual and plural but no inclusive/exclusive contrast.

(4) Vinmavis (Crowley 2002b:640, 644)

Indep form		Subject prefix (non-future)	
1SG	no	1SG	nV- /na-
2SG	gu	2SG	u-
3SG	i	3SG	i-
1PL INCL	get	1DU	er-
1PL EXCL	gemem	2DU	ar-
2PL	gem	3DU	ar-
3PL	ar	1PL	it-
		2PL	at-
		3PL	at-

Although the number of distinct person forms in the two paradigms is actually the same, seven (due to the homophony between the second and third persons in both the dual and plural, in the case of the subject prefixes), they differ radically in their internal structure. The existence of such differences makes it difficult to discuss the person system of a language as a whole. Linguists are often tempted to make general statements about the nature of person marking in a language. Such general statements, however, are possible only for some languages, but definitely not others. This has to be kept in mind while reading this book. Just because a particular language is cited as displaying a particular property or feature in some person paradigm, this does not mean that the same holds for all the person paradigms.

1.1.2   First and second persons vs third person

It is generally acknowledged that "there is a fundamental, and ineradicable, difference between the first and second person, on the one hand, and the third person on the other" (Lyons 1977:638). One manifestation of this difference is that whereas the first and second persons are regularly referred to essentially only by person markers, reference to the third person can be achieved by any lexical expression. It should therefore be unsurprising that languages may have first- and second-person markers but no third-person ones. In many of the languages which lack person markers for the third person, demonstrative pronouns corresponding to the English *this* and *that* are used in lieu of third-person markers. This is the case, for instance, in Basque, Comanche, Imbabura Quechua, Lak,

Lavukaleve and Maricopa. In other languages reference to the third person is achieved only via full nominal expressions. This appears to be so, for instance, in Salt Yui (Irwin 1974:32), a Papuan language, where third person is indicated by a specific noun, such as *yai* 'male' or *al* 'female' followed by a demonstrative. There is no distinction in number. Thus *yai i* denotes 'he' or 'they masculine' and *al i*, 'she' or 'they feminine'. And in yet other languages either full nominal expressions are used or, alternatively, no overt expression at all, the absence of an overt expression being interpreted as denoting third person.

A difference between first and second persons as opposed to the third may also be manifested in languages which have person markers for all three persons. Often the forms of the first and second persons are quite different from that of the third. As (5) illustrates, this may be observed in Nosu, a Tibeto-Burman language belonging to the Northern Yi group, spoken by over two million people in Sichuan and northern Yunnan, China.

(5) Nosu – Northern Yi (Bradley 1993:185)
1SG ŋa^{33}
2SG nɯa^{33}
3SG tsʰz^{33}

There may also be a difference in the order of third-person forms as compared to that of first- and second-person forms. For example, in Takale and Gamale, two dialects of the Tibeto-Burman language Kham (Watters 1993:105), when the agent is first or second person, the agent forms precede the patient forms. But when the agent is third person, the agent forms follow the patient ones. Compare (6a,b) with (6c).

(6) Gamale (Watters 1993:107)
    a. Nə-hnə-kəŋ-khě
       2SG(A)-look-1SG(P)-PAST
       'You looked at me.'
    b. Ye-hnə-rə
       1SG(A)-look-3PL(P)
       'I looked at them.'
    c. Ya-hnə-kəŋ-wo
       PAST-look-1SG(P)-3SG(A)
       'He looked at me.'

Another, not uncommon, difference between first and second persons as opposed to third person involves case marking. Third-person forms may take a different set of case markers than first- and second-person forms. For instance, in the Australian language Wambaya (Nordlinger 1998), there are three separate third-person forms, one for the S (sole argument of an intransitive clause), another for the A (agentive argument of a transitive clause) and a third for the P (patient-like argument of a transitive clause). But there are only two forms for the first and second persons, one for the s and A, and another for the P. Particularly frequent are differences between the first and second persons as compared to the third in regard to number and gender. Number distinctions are often neutralized in the third person, while gender is rarely manifested by second- and hardly ever by first-person forms. (This is discussed in detail in chapter three.)

All of the above differences are typically seen to be a consequence of the fact that first- and second-person forms are inherently deictic expressions, that is their interpretation is dependent on the properties of the extralinguistic context of the utterance in which they occur. Although the first person is always the speaker of the utterance and the second the hearer, the actual identity of each depends on who utters the utterance that contains them to whom, when and where. They belong to the class of expressions often referred to as shifters (Jakobson 1971). Third-person forms, on the other hand, are essentially anaphoric expressions. Their interpretation depends not on the extralinguistic but on the linguistic context of the utterance.[5] The referent of *he* or *she* is typically established by the preceding discourse, as in (7) or, less often, by the following discourse as in (8).

(7) – There's no sign of John.
     – He must have missed his train again.

(8) – She is late again.
     – You mean Sally.
     – Yes.

Third-person forms may be used deictically, as when someone says (pointing to a grinning child who has just been given an enormous ice cream) *He's happy*. Their anaphoric use is, however, the basic one. In fact in some languages, third-person forms can only be used anaphorically, deictic reference being achieved via demonstratives. Much less frequently, in addition to demonstratives there are two sets of third-person forms, one set for deictic reference, and another for anaphoric. This is so in Udihe (Nikolaeva & Tolskaya 2001:753–4), a Tungusic language spoken by about a hundred people in the Russian Far East.

In the linguistic literature, mention is sometimes made not only of the first, second and third persons but of a fourth person. This label is applied to several quite different kinds of categories. For instance, in the French grammatical tradition the term fourth person is often used for the first person plural. In Amerindian studies, especially of Algonkian languages, the label fourth person is used with reference to a less important third person, called an obviative as opposed to a proximate. And in discussions of anaphoric relations across clauses, the term fourth person is used for special third-person forms that indicate coreference, which are also termed logophoric or long-distance reflexives. Under none of the above uses does the fourth person qualify as a bonafide additional discourse category. Therefore, I see no reason for using the term here.

---

[5] In place of the terms deictic and anaphoric, some linguists use the terms exophoric and endophoric.

Whereas some scholars seek to expand the number of categories comprising person from three to four, others seek to reduce it. As mentioned earlier, of the three persons only the first and second persons are actual participants in the speech act realized by the utterance containing them. The third person is a not a participant of the speech act. Some linguists, most notably Benveniste (1971), argue that the grammatical category of person should therefore be seen as embracing only the first and second persons with the third person being a non-person. This is not the view adopted in this book. While fully acknowledging the distinctive nature of the third person relative to the first and second, I see no advantage in excluding the third person from the category of person, particularly in a cross-linguistic study such as this one. In fact, as will become apparent in the course of our discussion, doing so would severely skew our understanding of a number of facets of the category of person.

1.2 The universality of person markers

Despite statements such as the following by Benveniste (1971:225) "A language without the expression of person cannot be imagined", the universality of person as a grammatical category is sometimes called into question. The issue of whether all languages display the grammatical category of person is inherently tied to the issue of whether all languages have the category of personal pronoun. What constitutes a personal pronoun is in turn a matter of considerable controversy. The notion of pronominality has been and continues to be discussed in several different contexts and thus the features taken to be characteristic of pronouns are very much dependent on what they are being compared with or opposed to. Traditionally, personal pronouns have been opposed to nouns or NPs. Within the generative approach, ever since Chomsky's (1981) binding conditions, they have been contrasted primarily with anaphors (reflexives). Another line of inquiry opposes personal pronouns to person agreement markers (e.g. Bresnan & Mchombo 1987). And yet other studies seek to characterize pronouns in terms of a scale of structural deficiency (Cardinaletti & Starke 1999). We will have cause to consider all of the above at various points in our discussion, but for the time being, let us just concentrate on the pronoun vs noun distinction.

Traditionally, a personal pronoun is taken to be a morpho-syntactic category, which may be used to substitute for nouns or rather NPs, but differing from the latter in its morphological and syntactic properties. Under this traditional approach various languages, most notably South-east Asian languages such as Thai, Burmese, Vietnamese and Japanese, have been argued to lack personal pronouns, since the expressions used to indicate person display properties of nouns.[6]

---

[6] Other languages, such as the Salishan Northern Straits Salish (Jelinek 1998) and Halkomelem (Wiltschko 2002) have been argued to possess only bound pronouns. Such languages will be discussed in section 2.1.1.

More recently, however, what constitutes a pronoun has come to be viewed somewhat differently. In the generative literature (e.g. Noguchi 1997, Bresnan 2001b) a pronoun is seen to be not a morpho-syntactic category but rather a feature that sets off certain lexical items from others. The relevant feature is referential dependency; although pronouns are used to refer to individuals and entities, the identity of their referents can be determined only by the extralinguistic context (for first- and second-person forms) or typically the linguistic context (for third-person forms) or inferentially. This referential deficiency distinguishes them from both proper nouns, which are capable of identifying a referent by themselves, and common nouns, which are semantic predicates requiring a determiner to enable them to be used as referential expressions. In terms of this approach, all or some of the South-East Asian languages mentioned above are seen to have pronouns, but differing in syntactic category from the pronouns in, say, English. English pronouns are treated as determiners, and Japanese pronouns as nouns. The morpho-syntactic differences between the relevant forms in the two languages are thus seen to follow from differences in their categorial status but not in their pronominal status.

In the functional literature, in turn, pronouns in the main continue to be viewed as a morpho-syntactic category but often the distinction between pronoun and noun is considered to be not discrete but scalar, with some pronouns exhibiting less prototypically pronominal and more nominal characteristics than others. This position is most clearly articulated by Sugamoto (1989), who posits the characteristics in (9) as representing the pronominal extreme of what she calls the pronominality scale:

(9) a. closed class membership
   b. lack of morphological constancy
   c. lack of specific semantic content
   d. lack of stylistic and sociolinguistic implicative properties
   e. expression of grammatical person
   f. inability to take modifiers
   g. restrictions on reference interpretation

These criteria can be used to place person markers on a pronominality scale both across languages and also within languages. For example, if applied to the personal pronouns in English, Polish, Japanese and Thai, the Polish personal pronouns emerge as more pronominal than the English, both as considerably more pronominal than the Japanese forms, and the Japanese forms as more pronominal than those in Thai, as exemplified on the pronominality scale in (10).

(10)   The pronominality scale
       + Nominal   + Pronominal

       Thai   Japanese   English   Polish

Let us first consider the English personal pronouns.

English personal pronouns have most of the properties in (10). They belong to a closed class and, unlike nouns, are not morphologically transparent as far as number or case is concerned. Whereas number with most nouns is indicated by suffixation of /-(ə)z/ (e.g. *dog* vs *dogs* or *dress* vs *dresses*), with pronouns it is indicated by suppletion of the stem (e.g. *I* vs *we*). And whereas nouns may be marked for the genitive case by /'s/ (e.g. *mother's friend*), pronouns again have separate forms (e.g. *I* vs *my*). Further, pronouns convey no semantic content other than that of the grammatical features which are associated with them and do not vary stylistically, while nouns may do so (e.g. *mother* vs *mummy* vs *mum*). And clearly pronouns distinguish between the first, second and third persons, while nouns are necessarily third person. English personal pronouns can, however, co-occur with some of the modifiers that are found with nouns. The plural forms may be modified by a low numeral (e.g. *us two, we four*), the accusative forms may be modified by certain adjectives, such as *poor, kind, evil, lucky*, (e.g. *poor me, lucky you*) and the nominative forms may be modified by a non-restrictive relative clause, as in *I, who have nothing, he who strives, wins*. As for reference, the personal pronouns are clearly restricted in regard to their referential interpretations in the sense outlined above. While nouns may be used for both definite (e.g. *the book, this book, my book*) and indefinite reference (e.g. *a book, some book*), personal pronouns are (with few exceptions) definite.[7] This is reflected in the fact that they do not normally occur with any of the determiners, i.e. articles (e.g. *the he), demonstratives (e.g. *this she) or genitives (*my he) which transform a noun into a definite referential expression and are normally incompatible with the indefinite article (e.g. *a she). The qualification normally is necessary in view of examples such as those in (11), taken from Noguchi (1997:778–9).

(11) a.   This is not the real me.
     b.   Do you know the real you?
     c.   That's not a he; that's a she.
     d.   It's a he!

The use of the definite article with personal pronouns as in (11a,b) is highly restricted; for most speakers the personal pronoun must be the accusative singular form and, for some, even just the first and second persons (?*This is not the real him.*), and the adjective must be present (**This is not the me.*). The indefinite article is possible only with the third-person nominative (**It's a him*). Such usage thus cannot be seen as actually undermining the essentially definite nature of the personal pronouns.[8] The above notwithstanding, English personal pronouns are not always used strictly referentially, that is to refer to concrete entities or individuals. For example, in (12) *Kate* has no specific person in mind and thus *he* is used non-referentially.

---

[7] For a discussion of reference and definiteness see, e.g., Lyons (1977:177) or Allan (2001:59, 440). The issue will be resumed in sections 4.1 and 4.3.4.
[8] One way in which such atypical co-occurrences of the article and personal pronoun are dealt with is by assuming that a category conversion has taken place, from a pronoun to a noun.

(12)   Kate still wants to marry a Swede. The problem is that he has to be rich and there are not many rich Swedes around.

In (13) the third-person plural form *they* and the second-person form *you* are used for generic or arbitrary reference (i.e. impersonally).

(13) a. They say that time heals all pain.
   b.   You add the eggs to the butter not the other way round.

And in (14) both the personal and possessive forms are bound by the operator *every* and are thus construed as bound variables.

(14) a. Every man thinks that he is clever.
   b.   Everyone loves his mother.

The personal pronouns in Polish, are very much like their English counterparts. They clearly do form a paradigm, are not transparent morphologically, exhibit restricted possibilities in regard to modification, among which modification by a demonstrative is not included. However, they are necessarily definite. Unlike the English forms, they cannot be used non-specifically, generically or construed as bound variables. For example, an overt personal pronoun as in (15a) can be interpreted as coreferential only with some entity outside of the clause, not as bound by the quantified subject NP of the main clause.

(15)   Polish
   a.   Każda kobieta uważa,   że   ona jest   mądra
         every woman considers that she be:3SG:PRES clever
         'Every woman$_i$ thinks that she$_j$ is clever.'

   b.   Każda kobieta uważa,   że   jest   mądra
         every woman considers that be:3SG:PRES clever
         'Every woman$_i$ thinks that she$_i$ is clever.'

A bound variable reading is possible but of the person inflection on the verb, that is in the absence of an overt pronoun, as in (15b).[9] The same holds for a non-specific reading of the Polish equivalent of (12) and a generic interpretation of the Polish version of (13). Both are possible but only in the absence of an overt personal pronoun. Thus if necessary referentiality is viewed as an indicator of greater pronominality, then the Polish personal pronouns are more pronominal than the English ones.[10] The only nominal feature that they do display is the

---

[9] In the generative literature the difference between languages like English and Polish in regard to the bound varible interpretation of overt pronouns is attributed to the Overt Pronoun Constraint which is: overt pronouns cannot receive a bound variable interpretation in situations where a null pronoun could occur.

[10] This need not be the case. For instance, Noguchi (1997) does not view the possibility of being used non-referentially as pertinent to pronominality. For him whether a pronoun can be construed as a bound variable is definitive of its determiner as opposed to noun status. Thus under this analysis, English pronouns are more determiner-like, Polish pronouns more noun-like, counter to the ordering on the pronominality scale in (10).

presence of sociolinguistic implications. Among adults, the third-person forms are considered to be informal (see discussion in ch. 6, section 6.1.2).

Turning to the Japanese personal pronouns, there are quite a few variants used to express each of the three persons, carrying different stylistic and sociocultural implications. Some of the existing forms are presented in (16).

(16) Japanese
1SG watasi, watakusi, ore, temae, boku, etc.
2SG anata, kimi, omae, temae, etc.

Unlike in English and Polish, the pronouns do not differ morphologically from nouns, that is they form the plural by the same means as nouns (*tomodachi-tachi* 'friend-PL', *watashi-tachi* 'I-PL') and take the same postpositional case markers. They also display a greater range of modification possibilities and fewer restrictions on the modifiers that they permit than in the case of English or Polish. They may be modified by any adjective (17a), and significantly be preceded by a possessive pronoun (17b) or a demonstrative pronoun (17c).

(17) Japanese (Noguchi 1997:777)
    a. tiisai/sinsetuna/ookii kare
       small /kind/big   he
       '*small/kind/big he'
    b. watsi-no kare
       I-GEN   he
       '*my he.' (=boyfriend)
    c. kono kare
       this he
       '*this he'

Modification by a restrictive relative clause is allowed as well.

(18) Japanese (Sugamoto 1989:280)
    Nihongo ga   hanas-eru kare wa fuijyuushi-nai
    Japanese NOM speak-can he   TOP inconvenienced-NEG
    'He who can speak Japanese won't feel inconvenienced.'

However, like the Polish forms, the Japanese person forms are necessarily referential. They cannot, for example, be construed as bound variables, as shown by the ungrammaticality of (19b) as compared to (19a).

(19) Japanese (Noguchi 1997:770)
    a. Mary ga   [kanozyo ga   tensai-da   to]   omotte-iru
       Mary NOM she   NOM genius-COP COMP think-PRES
       'Mary$_i$ thinks that she$_i$ is a genius.'
    b. *Dono zyosei-mo [kanozyo ga   tensai-da   to]   omotte-iru
       every woman also she   NOM genius-COP COMP think-PRES
       'Every woman$_i$ thinks that she$_i$ is a genius.'

While this property is a pronominal one, it is outweighed by all the other nominal characteristics that the forms in question display. They are thus placed considerably lower on the pronominality scale in (10) than the English forms.

The expressions used to refer to discourse participants in Thai are even more noun-like than in Japanese. As in Japanese, they do not differ morphologically from nouns (both take no inflectional marking) and exhibit more or less the same modificational possibilities, which include modification by a numeral (20a), demonstrative (20b), quantifier-type expression (20c) and relative clause (20d).

(20)　　Thai (Cooke 1968:10)
  a.　kháw sǎam$_2$ khon$_3$
       3   three   CLF
       'they three'

  b.　phǒm$_1$ nii$_2$
       1:male this
       '*this I'

  c.　raw$_1$ tháŋ$_2$ lǎaj$_3$
       1   all   several
       'we all'

  d.　raw$_1$ sŷŋ$_2$ pen'$_3$ khon$_4$ ruaj$_5$
       1   who   be   rich   persons
       'we who are rich'

Further, even more so than in Japanese, they do not constitute a closed class. The expressions regularly used to designate person include proper names, kin terms and various relational terms such as 'master', 'servant', 'individual crown of the head', etc. Cooke (1968) mentions twenty-seven specialized terms for the first person and twenty-two for the second person. (See ch. 6.) These, however, appear to be only a subset of the available possibilities. And significantly, the forms maintain much of their lexical meaning (similarly to *mummy* and *Johnny* in (1b)), and are highly diverse both stylistically and sociolinguistically. For example, the form *phǒm* 'you' is a general polite form, *tâajtháaw* is used only in highly deferential contexts, when speaking to a superior and *tâajfàa'2la?ɔɔŋ'thúlii'3phrábàad'4*, which literally means 'the one who is holding speaker under the dust of his foot', is employed only when addressing the king. While some or perhaps even most of the many forms that Thai has at its disposal to express person may indeed be fully nominal, the forms that are widely used such as *phǒm* are unlikely to emerge as such at least by virtue of their minimal semantic content.

In the light of the above, I will take the category of personal pronoun, in some sense of the term, to be universal. However, as I prefer to remain agnostic in regard to the nature of the morphological, syntactic and referential properties of personal pronouns, in order to avoid unnecessary confusion, I will refrain from using the term pronoun altogether. As stated earlier, in place of the term pronoun, the terms person form or person marker will be used.

1.3 The nature of this book

The existing similarities and differences in the properties of person markers, in person-marker inventories and in how person markers are deployed constitute a fascinating area of study. They have much to tell us about the human conceptual system and how it is organized. They provide important information about the relationship between the structure of language and the sociocultural and discourse conditions in which it is used. They offer significant insights into the processes of grammaticalization, that is the development, change and disappearance of grammatical categories and grammatical distinctions. And they constitute a source of crucial data for the determination of historical connections between languages, both genetic and areal. Moreover, the pervasiveness of person markers in language raises important questions in regard to their analysis within a theoretical model of grammar. The grammatical category of person manifests itself in both the nominal and the verbal domain and at various syntactic levels: the phrase, the clause, the sentence and even at the level of the text. The study of person thus takes us into each of these domains and levels of language structure and forces us to consider the nature of the relationships obtaining between them and how these should be analysed.

Needless to say, no one monograph devoted to the grammatical category of person can hope to do justice to all the above issues. Nonetheless, in the chapters that follow I hope to provide an overview of the most important concepts, controversies and analyses pertaining to the grammatical category of person, rich enough to constitute a good point of departure for the understanding of more detailed studies of specific issues or the carrying out of further in-depth research, be it synchronic or diachronic, descriptive or theoretical, on the category of person.

The structure of the book is as follows. Chapter 2 presents a typology of person markers from the point of view of the major factors underlying the existence of different person paradigms, namely morpho-phonological form, syntactic function and discourse function. In chapter 3 we turn to a consideration of how person paradigms are structured internally, that is to the nature of the person, number, gender and inclusivity oppositions that they express and how these are distributed in different types of paradigms, in the sense of chapter two. Chapter 4 explores the controversial topic of person agreement. The discussion is structured around the claim that there is no principled basis for distinguishing between anaphoric pronouns and person agreement markers and seeks to bring to light the commonality of the factors underlying the presence of anaphoric and grammatical agreement on different targets and with different controllers. Chapter 5 critically examines the unified account of the function of person markers developed within cognitive discourse analysis and captured in the relationship between relative discourse accessibility and morpho-phonological expression. We will consider to what extent relative cognitive accessibility may be invoked as the major factor underlying not only the inter-sentential but also the intra-sentential distribution of different types of person forms and significantly, first- and second-person forms in addition to third-person ones. Chapter 6 looks at how person markers are utilized in the expression of social relations. The focus of the discussion is not on the specificities of the social relations that induce the use of special person forms, but on the person forms themselves, that is which forms are used and which are not, and which semantic oppositions are exploited in indicating social differences. Finally, chapter 7 seeks to place the preceding considerations in a diachronic context. It reviews the different sources of person markers and outlines the diachronic changes that they may undergo, including their grammaticalization pathways from independent markers to grammaticalized affixes and the factors that may underlie their eventual demise.

The discussion outlined above draws on language data from over 700 languages originating in the main from reference grammars and less frequently from theoretical descriptions of particular phenomena in individual languages or groups of languages. The subset of these languages, namely 402, are included in a computerized database which Dik Bakker and I have been developing for the last ten years. The relevant 402 languages will be referred to as the sample. Unless stated otherwise, the sample is the source of the observations pertaining to the distribution and frequency of particular properties and features of person markers that will be made. Originally the sample was compiled using the sampling methodology outlined in Rijkhoff and Bakker (1998), which aims for maximal genetic diversity. Since then, many languages have been added, even closely related ones. The sample is therefore merely a variety sample. In keeping with the nature of the sample, I have refrained from carrying out any serious statistics on frequencies and distributions and offer numerical data only as an illustration of clear tendencies and evident preferences. The 402 languages in the sample are listed by macro-area in Appendix 1.

2 The typology of person forms

Given the impoverished semantics of person markers and the fact that the range of syntactic and discourse functions that they fulfil cross-linguistically must essentially be the same, the major parameter responsible for the cross-linguistic variation in person markers is morpho-phonological form. Accordingly, this chapter will be concerned with the cross-linguistic formal realization of person markers and how this relates to their syntactic and discourse function.

We will begin our discussion with a review of the existing morpho-phonological types of person markers and their cross-linguistic distribution. Then we will proceed to examine the relationships between the morpho-phonological form of person markers and their syntactic function. This will involve a consideration of, on the one hand, the formal realization of different syntactic functions and, on the other, the alignment possibilities that the different morpho-phonological types of person markers enter into and how these relate to those found with lexical expressions. The last part of the chapter will deal briefly with the existence of person markers for special discourse functions.

2.1 Morpho-phonological form

The basic division of person markers in regard to morpho-phonological form is that between independent and dependent person markers. Other terms used for the independent forms are free, full, self/standing, cardinal, focal, strong, long and disjunctive. The dependent forms are also referred to as reduced, bound, defective, deficient or conjunctive. Typically what is meant by an independent/free/full, etc. person form is a person marker which constitutes a separate word and may take primary word stress, such as the English *I, me, you, she, they*. Dependent forms, by contrast, typically cannot be stressed (though some may receive contrastive stress), are often phonologically reduced relative to the independent forms, and either morphologically dependent on another element in the utterance or at least restricted in distribution relative to the independent forms. Since not all languages have dependent markers and the ones that do virtually always also have independent markers, we will consider the independent markers first.

2.1.1 Independent forms

Above I characterized an independent person marker as a marker which is a separate word and may take primary word stress. The notion of independence invoked is thus that of morphological and prosodic independence. Sometimes, however, what is meant by independent person marker is a syntactically independent form, that is a form capable of constituting a whole utterance all by itself, for instance as an answer to a question, as in (1b), or as an elliptical question, as in (2b).

(1) a. Who are they going to ask?
    b. Me./Her./Us.

(2) a. He said that he would do it?
    b. (Who) him?

Needless to say, syntactically independent person forms are also morphologically and prosodically independent, but the converse is not necessarily the case. For instance, in English the so-called possessive determiners, *my, your, our, their* are considered to be separate words which may be stressed but they cannot be used as utterances in their own right; when unaccompanied by a head noun the corresponding forms *mine, yours, ours*, etc. are employed (but see below). Thus (3b) does not constitute a possible response to (3a), only (3c) does.

(3) a. Who are we going to invite, your mother or my mother?
    b. *My.
    c. Mine.

Nor may the English subject person forms *I, he, she*, etc., in contrast to the object forms, be used in complete isolation, as evidenced by the unacceptability of (4b) as compared to (4c).[1]

(4) a. Who wrote that?
    b. *I/*He/*We
    c. I did./He did./We did.

Yet they, too, are normally viewed as independent person markers. It must be pointed out, that not only certain person markers but also other elements which are normally considered to be words may not be able to constitute a separate utterance. For instance, most adpositions cannot occur alone. The same holds for articles. In view of the above, the ability to occur in complete isolation must be seen as being a too restrictive criterion for independent status. Therefore I will use the term independent form in the morphological and prosodic sense of the term independent, not the syntactic.

There are several diagnostics which may be employed in determining whether a particular person marker is or is not a separate word (see, e.g., Zwicky 1985;

---

[1] A response to (4a) involving a lexical NP, though preferred with the auxiliary *did*, would be possible without the auxiliary.

Dixon & Aikhenvald 2002). The first of these is the ability to be involved in coordinations. Words combine with other words or with phrases. Therefore, if a person marker can be coordinated with another word, particularly a multi-word phrase, it must be a separate word. The English subject and object person markers clearly meet this test as shown in (5).

(5) a. He and Ian's younger brother are doing it.
    b. They selected her and that French woman who we met last week.

So do the possessive forms *mine*, *yours*, *ours* but not the possessive determiners.

(6) a. Sally's mother and mine have turned vegetarian.
    b. *My and Jack's parents are holidaying in France.

Another commonly used criterion for independent word status is the possibility of being deleted under appropriate discourse conditions. One may expect whole words to be subject to deletion but not parts of words. Ellipsis, however, is in most languages constrained both syntactically and pragmatically. Therefore, while the ability to undergo deletion is a reliable diagnostic of word status the inability to do so cannot be thus regarded. And indeed as shown in (7), the English subject person markers may undergo ellipsis but the object markers cannot.

(7) a. She went in and Ø sat down.
    b. *Johni loves herj and Øi trusts Øj.

As for the possessive forms, the possessive determiners may be elided only in NP coordinations, as in (8a), and the headless possessive forms only when used as subject of a coordinate clause (8b).

(8) a. My brother and Ø sister are coming tonight.
    b. Mine rushed in and Ø immediately fell on the food.

A third diagnostic of word status is whether the element in question may be modified by other words. This is a diagnostic that the subject forms, object forms and possessive determiners meet.

(9) a. She alone knows what really happened.
    b. I want just him.
    c. My own brother spied on me.

The possessive forms *mine*, *yours*, *hers*, etc., by contrast cannot be modified. Even when there is no head noun, what precedes *own* is the possessive determiner. E.g.

(10) a. She makes her/(*hers) own, a lot of them.
     b. Here's yours James. You can have your (*yours) own.

As we have just seen, none of the English person markers considered meets all the diagnostics of independent word status. This suggests that tests such as the above should be viewed as convenient heuristics not as necessary and sufficient conditions for word status. And indeed it is thus that they are often regarded. Nonetheless, this is not always so. Consequently, it should come as no surprise that there is some discrepancy in the literature in regard to which person markers should be viewed as independent. For example, in the typology of person forms recently developed by Cardinaletti and Starke (1999), the coordination criterion is taken to be definitive of independent as opposed to dependent person markers (strong vs deficient in their terminology). Accordingly, the English possessive determiners are not considered to be strong forms. More about Cardinaletti and Starke's (1999) approach will be said in section 2.1.2.3.

Another point of controversy in regard to independent person forms is whether or not they are typologically unmarked relative to dependent forms. This is a complex issue which can be explored in detail only within a given approach to markedness and, arguably, within a unified theory of clause structure.[2] Nonetheless, there is one correlate of typological markedness which we can address here. The existence of a typologically marked category, pattern, value or form is taken to entail the existence of the typologically unmarked category, pattern, value or form but not vice versa. Thus if independent person markers are unmarked vis-à-vis dependent person markers, the presence of the latter in a language should necessarily entail the presence of the former. The question that arises is therefore whether all languages which have grammaticalized the category person do indeed have independent person markers?

Contrary to what the previous discussion may lead us to expect, it is not the failure of person markers to meet some or all of the diagnostics of word status that form the basis of most claims pertaining to the lack of independent person markers in a language. It is rather that the words used to denote person do not contain person roots. The relevant words consist of a generic pronominal root, typically invariant across all person-number categories, with person affixes attached. Etymologically the generic pronominal root is often the word for person, body, self or the verb 'to be' or 'exist'. It may, however, be some other form. For instance, in Warekena, an Arawakan language of Brazil, in the case of the first- and second-person and third-person plural, the person prefixes are attached to the emphatic root -*ya* and in the case of the other third-person categories to forms cognate with demonstratives. This is exemplified in (11).

(11) Warekena (Aikhenvald 1998:293, 322)

	Independent	Person prefix
1SG	nu-ya	nu-
2SG	pi-ya	pi-
3SGF	ayu-palu	yu-
3SGNF	e-palu	Ø/i-
1PL	wa-ya	wa-
2PL	ni-ya	ni-
3PL	ni-ya	ni-

---

[2] An excellent discussion of the unmarked nature of independent person forms is presented in the context of Lexical Functional Grammar (LFG) in Bresnan (2001b).

Though in languages such as the above the actual marker of person is a bound as opposed to a free form, the generic root plus person marker function as a semantic unit, just like independent forms in other languages. Accordingly, I see no reason why such languages should be considered as lacking independent expressions of the category person.

Somewhat more problematic are languages in which the generic root to which the person affix is attached appears to continue to function synchronically as the verb 'to be' or 'exist'. One such language is Mbay (Keegan 1997), a Nilo-Saharan language of the Sara group spoken in Chad in which an emphatic form of the verb 'to be' – /īī/ inflected with person prefixes is used in lieu of first- and second-person independent person markers. Some examples are given in (12).

(12)   Mbay (Keegan 1997:66, 75)
   a.   J- īī   kòoń
        1PL-be only
        'It's only us.'

   b.   Ì   m- īī   àí
        it: be 1SG-be NEG
        'It wasn't me.'

   c.   M- īī-ň   àí
        1SG-be-VENTIVE NEG
        'I don't have it.' (Lit. I am with it not.)

Keegan (1997:62) categorically states that Mbay lacks independent person forms. One piece of evidence confirming that the *īī* plus person-prefix combination continues to function as a verbal predicate is that the ventive suffix -*ň* 'with it', which otherwise attaches only to verbs, may be affixed to it, as shown in (12c). On the other hand, the fact that *mīī* can function as a predicate complement of *ì* would argue that it has been reanalysed as a person marker. Since Keegan does not discuss the issue in any detail, it is difficult to know what the final verdict should be.

Even more like predicates bearing person inflection are the so-called emphatic person forms found in North Straits Salish (Lummi) and perhaps also several other Salishan languages. The forms in question together with the subject clitics and object suffixes which the language has are presented in (13).

(13)   North Straits Salish (Jelinek 1998:328–9, 340)

	Emphatic forms	Subject clitics	Object suffixes
1SG	ʔəš	=sən	-oŋəs
2SG	nəkʷə	=sxʷ	-oŋəs
3SG	niɫ	=s/Ø	-Ø
1PL	niŋəɫ	=ɫ	-oŋəɫ
2PL	nəkʷiliyə	=sxʷhelə	?
3PL	nəniɫiyə	=s/Ø	-Ø

Jelinek states that the "emphatic" forms display various properties of predicates including clause-initial position, the possibility of occurring with clitic subjects and object suffixes and the possibility of appearing with a determiner in a determiner phrase. Most importantly, though, the "emphatic" forms are treated syntactically as third person. This is evidenced by the fact that they induce third-person agreement, as shown in (14).

(14) Northern Straits Salish (Jelinek 1998:340)
Leŋ-t-Ø=sən cə nəkʷ
see-TR-3-1SG DET be:2SG
'I saw you.' (Lit. I saw the one that was you.)

If the second-person singular "emphatic" form was an independent person marker one would expect the agreement on the verb to be also second person, that is one should see the suffix -oŋəs on the verb, as in (15).

(15) North Straits Salish
Xči-t- oŋəs-sən
know-TR-2SG-1SG
'I know you.'

Yet the agreement marker on the verb in (14) is Ø, which corresponds to third person. This is even clearer in the irrealis mood exemplified in (16), since then the third-person marker is overt, namely =əs.

(16) North Straits Salish (Jelinek 1998:340)
a. Čte-t-ŋ=sən kʷə nəkʷ-əs
ask-TR-PASS=1SG DET be:2SG-3(SUBJ)
'I was asked if it was you?'

b. Xən-ŋ cə Bill kʷ ʔəs-əs
do/act-MID DET Bill DET be:2SG-3(SUBJ)
'Bill acted for me.' (Lit. acting as if he were me)

Thus if the "emphatic" forms are treated as independent person markers rather than predicates bearing person inflection, they must be considered as highly atypical.[3] If, on the other hand, North Straits Salish is seen to lack independent person markers, it may well be virtually the only language which does so.

Having briefly considered the type of person markers that are found in virtually all languages, let us now turn to the dependent forms which, though highly frequent and widely attested, are definitely not universal.

2.1.2 Dependent person markers

Dependent person markers may be classified on the basis of their decreasing morphological independence and phonological substance into the four types presented in (17).

---

[3] A somewhat different argument for the atypical nature of independent person markers in another Salishan language, Halkomelem, is presented by Wiltschko (2002).

(17)   weak > clitic > bound > zero

For ease of exposition, I will begin the discussion of these four types of person markers with the zero forms.

2.1.2.1 Zero forms

The term zero person marker in (17) is used in the absolute sense of the term, that is for a grammatical person interpretation without any accompanying phonological form of any type be it segmental or suprasegmental. Absence of phonological form may be interpreted as a marker of grammatical person in many languages. The circumstances under which this occurs, however, are typically very restricted. For instance, as illustrated in (18a) and previously in (7a), English has null subjects in coordinate structures, and also in imperatives (18b), non-finite clauses (18c) and occasionally even in finite declarative clauses (18d).

(18) a.   I/you, she came in and Ø sat down.
     b.   Ø go home!
     c.   I/you/she want(s) to Ø come with me.
     d.   (I) didn't recognise that.

The zero forms in (18a) and (18c) may be interpreted as referring to the first, second or third person depending on the person of the subject in the initial conjunct and the main clause respectively. In (18b) the subject is always second person and in (18d) typically the first. English also allows non-subjects to be rendered by zero, but in an even more restricted range of circumstances than subjects, namely in constructions involving VP-ellipsis, as in (19).

(19)   – Why didn't you write to me?
          – I did (write to you).

Similar restricted uses of zero forms are to be found in many other languages which allow for a person interpretation of null structure.

There are, however, languages in which zero person markers are much more widely used. By way of illustration consider the examples in (20) and (21) from Japanese.

(20)   Japanese (Yamamoto 1999:80)
          "... asoko ja rokusuppo Ø   hanashi mo deki nai shi, Ø sangai
              there at property (we) talk   ACC can NEG and (I) third:floor
          no   ongaku kissa o Ø   oshie-toita no"
          CONN music café   ACC her show-PERF CONN
          'But it's too noisy to talk there and (I) told (her) about the coffee shop on the third floor instead.' (Yukiko Mishima, *Hyaku-man Yen Senbei*, translated by Edward G. Seidensticker)

(21) "Gomen-nasai, Ø itokkaidoo no kata desu-ka?"
      forgive:me   (you) Hokkaido CONN person COP-Q
      "Ø Tookyoo desu." To boku wa it-ta   "Ø Tookyoo kara
      (I) Tokyo   cop that I   NOM say-PAST you Tokyo from
      o-tomodachi o   sagashi-ni mie-tan   desu-ne
      friend   ACC to-search come:up-PAST AUX-TAG
      ' "Forgive me. Are (you) from Hokkaido?" "(I'm) from Tokyo," I said.
      "Then (you)'re up here looking for a friend?" ' (Haruki Murakami, *Hitsuji o Megura Booken*, translated by Alfred Birnbaum)

Unlike in English, in Japanese the zero person forms occur regularly in declarative and interrogative clauses both finite and non-finite, main and subordinate and as subjects and non-subjects. Significantly, in contrast to that of the zero form in the English main-clause declarative (18d), corresponding zeroes in Japanese declaratives are not associated with abbreviated or telegraphic colloquial speech. Nor are the clauses in which they occur perceived as being evidently elliptical.

While the possibility of employing zero person forms under certain restricted circumstances in languages such as English is an important aspect of the person system of the language, the notion of zero person marker in the typology of dependent person markers in (17) is to be understood as denoting the Japanese type of zero forms rather than the English.[4]

In all the examples of zero person markers presented above there is absolutely no phonological form corresponding to the person interpretation. This absolute sense of the term zero person marker is to be distinguished from two other uses of the term. The first of these is for an empty syntactic position accompanying person inflection on the verb, as in (22b) as opposed to (22a) taken from Gumawana, an Oceanic language spoken in New Guinea.

(22)   Gumawana (Olson 1992:326)
   a.   Kalitoni i-paisewa
        Kalitoni 3SG-work
        'Kalitoni worked.'

   b.   Ø   i-situ   vada sinae-na
        3SG 3SG-enter house inside-3SG(INAL)
        'He entered the inside of the house.'

Although some linguists consider clauses such as (22b) as having a null subject, under the analysis adopted here the subject of (22b) is not null or zero but rather the person inflection on the verb. (See the discussion in chapter four, section 4.1.) The second use of the term zero person marker to be distinguished from the absolute zero sense of the term is for the zero exponent(s) of a pronominal paradigm. Zero person markers in the absolute sense of the term are open to a first-, second- or third-person interpretation (or any combination of these) depending on the context of utterance. In other words, all the exponents of the paradigm are

---

[4] Further examples are provided in chapter five.

zero forms. By contrast, in the paradigmatic sense of the term zero person marker, there is a combination of overt and zero person forms. Typically the zero form is in the third person, either just the third-person singular as in the Tibetan language Chepang (23) or in the singular and non-singular number as, for example, in the case of the subject prefixes in Seri (24), a language of Mexico.

(23) Chepang (Caughley 1982:54–5)

	SG	DU	PL
1INCL		-ɲe-ce	-ŋ-se
1EXCL	-ŋa	-teyh-c	-teyh-ʔi
2	-naŋ	-naŋ-je	-naŋ-se
3	Ø	-ce	-ʔi/se

(24) Seri (Marlett 1990:514)

	SG	PL
1	ʔ-/ʔp-	ʔa-
2	m-	ma-
3	Ø-	Ø-

In cases such as (24), it is often unclear whether the language should be seen as having zero forms for the third person, as depicted in (24), or as lacking third-person forms altogether. Whatever the interpretation, such zeroes must not be treated on a par with the absolute zeroes in languages such as Japanese.

2.1.2.2 Bound forms and clitics

The second type of dependent person marker in (17) is the bound form. The term bound person marker or pronoun is often used in the literature as a cover term for both person affixes and clitics. Here, however, it designates only person markers expressed by affixes or much less frequently via changes to the stem. The affixes may be prefixes as in Gumawana (22) or Seri (24), suffixes as in Chepang (24) or not so often circumfixes. The example of circumfixes given in (25) is of the perfective subject paradigm in Baale, a Surmic language spoken in the border area between Ethiopia and Sudan. (The symbol -V- stands for an under-specified vowel which is identical to the first vowel of the following verb root.)

(25) Baale (Yigezu & Dimmendaal 1998:302).
1SG kV- . . . -a
2SG V- . . . -u
3SG V- . . . -a
1PL kV- . . . -ta
2PL V- . . . -tu
3PL V- . . . -iða

Person infixes are very rare and do not tend to involve all verbs or nouns. In Au, a Papuan language of the Torricelli phylum, for example, infixes are found with three out of five classes of transitive verbs. One class has third-person subject infixes (26a), another object infixes (26b) and a third benefactive infixes (26c).

(26) Au (Scorza 1985:226)
   a. W-īn-w-atīn   weise
       3SGF-hunt-3SGF-hunts grasshoppers
       'She hunts grasshoppers.'

   b. K-ere-k-ir
       3SGM-hit-3SGM-hit
       'He cuts it.'

   c. K-emit-uwek-pīn
       3SGM-lies-3SGM-lies
       'He lies to him.'

To give another example, in Sorowahá (Dixon 1999:304), an Arawa language of Brazil, the first *o-* and second-person singular *i-* markers are infixes but only with verbs beginning in a consonant; thus *gania* 'see' but *g-o-ania* 'I see' and *sawa* 'wash' but *s-i-awa* 'you wash'. Person marking via changes in the stem is also rare. The following example is from Misantla Totonac, a language spoken in the state of Veracruz in Mexico, where the second-person singular subject marker (with some verbs) is marked by suppletion of the stem.

(27) Misantla Totonac (MacKay 1991:153)
   a. Kit   ?ik-án
       I   1SG-go
       'I go.'

   b. Wš   pin
       you   2SG:go
       'You go.'

   c. ?út   Ø-?án
       (s)he 3SG-go
       '(S)he goes.'

In another language of Mexico, Mazatec (San Jeronimo Tecoatl dialect), most verbs have two stems, one used with first-person singular and third-person subjects and another used with all other subjects. Some examples are given in (28).

(28) Mazatec (Agee & Marlett 1987:60–1)

	1SG and 3	2SG, 1PL, 2PL
see	kocehe	cicehe
cry	khindaya	chindaya
throw	sikathe	nikathe
work	sisa	nisa
talk	ċha	nokhosa
give	cha	?evi
take	?va	ċ?a

A few verbs have three or even four stems depending on person, e.g. the verb 'to say', *sa* 'say:1SG', *co* 'say:3', *si* 'say:2SG' and *viso* 'say:1PL/2PL'. The final type of person marking encompassed by the notion of bound form is via tone. Tonal marking is again uncommon and when it does occur it typically accompanies segmental marking. Pure tonal marking of person is very rare. One case in point is of first- and second-person singular objects in Godie, a Kru language of the Ivory Coast; second-person objects are marked on the finite verb by low tone (29a), first-person objects by a high tone (29b) or, if the preceding tone is low, by a mid tone (29c).

(31) Godie (Marchese 1986:221)
    a.   Ã nì'
         I saw:2SG
         'I saw you.'

    b.   FΛ'   làagɔ yɔku
         take:1SG God side
         'Take me (to see) God.'

    c.   ɔ nî⁻
         He saw:1SG
         'He saw me.'

The third type of dependent person markers in (17) are clitics. Clitics are seen to share properties of both bound forms and independent words.[5] Clitics resemble bound forms in forming a phonological unit with a word (their host) preceding them (enclitics) or following them (proclitics). In fact sometimes they are very difficult to distinguish from bound forms and vice versa. Clitics may also resemble independent words in being written as separate words and being able to take, under some conditions, lexical stress. Therefore person markers which are considered to be clitics by one author may be treated as bound forms or independent forms by another. Following Zwicky (1985), it is customary to distinguish between simple and special clitics. Simple clitics are reduced variants of full forms occurring in the same position as full forms. Their occurrence is governed largely by the dictates of phrasal phonology and may be affected by rate of speech and sociolinguistic factors such as level of formality. The English forms [jə] in (30b) and [em] in (31b) are a case in point.

(30) a.   Bring your friends.
     b.   Bring [jə] friends.

(31) a.   Give them back.
     b.   Give [em] back.

Special clitics, on the other hand, are not just reduced full forms but rather separate allomorphs of full forms displaying their own morpho-syntactic and morpho-phonological properties. In other words, whereas simple clitics conform to the syntax of independent forms, special clitics do not and thus must be dealt with

---

[5] Some tests for distinguishing clitics from affixes are discussed in Zwicky and Pullum (1983) and for distinguishing clitics from separate words in Zwicky (1985).

independently of the principles and rules of non-clitic syntax. We will have nothing further to say about simple clitics here. The term clitic from now on is to be understood as denoting special clitics.

The basic diagnostic distinguishing clitics from bound forms is their relative independence from their hosts. Whereas bound forms attach only to a particular type of stem, for instance to a verb or noun or adposition, clitics are not thus restricted. They attach not to a particular stem but rather to phrases and/or specialized syntactic positions. Thus, for instance, an affixal subject marker will always be bound to the finite verb (lexical or auxiliary), while a clitic subject marker may attach to whatever entity occupies a designated position.

A common position of argument clitics is after the first word or constituent in the utterance, as is the case in Pitjantjatjara, a language of Western Australia. We see in (32) that the subject enclitic is encliticized to an adverb in (32a), a question word in (32b) and an adjective in (32c).

(32) Pitjantjatjara (Eckert & Hudson 1988:143–4)
 a. Mungartji=li pitjangu
     evening-1DU came
     'We two came last evening.'

 b. Nyaaku=ya parari   nyinanyi?
     Why-3PL long way are sitting
     'Why are they sitting a long way off?'

 c. Wati nyara   puḷkangka=ya ma-nyinanyi
     man younder big-with-3PL away are sitting
     'They are sitting with that big man over there.'

In another Australian language, Nganhcara, we find the mirror-image of the type of clitic placement found in Pitjantjatjara; person markers are encliticized to the last element before the verb or to the verb itself. The person clitics may denote the subject, direct or indirect object or even certain oblique constituents. The example in (33) involves indirect object clitics.

(33) Nganhcara (Smith & Johnson 1985:103)
 a. Ku'a nhiŋu pukpe-wu nhila   pama-ŋ=ŋu   waa
     dog 3SG:DAT child-DAT 3SG:NOM man-ERG-3SG:DAT give
     'The man gave a dog to the child.'

 b. Nhila   pama-ŋ nhiŋu   pukpe-wu ku'a=ŋu   waa
     3SG:NOM man-ERG 3SG:DAT child-DAT dog-3SG:DAT give
     'The man gave a dog to the child.'

 c. Nhila   pama-ŋ ku'a nhiŋu   pukpe-wu=ŋu   waa
     3SG:NOM man-ERG dog 3SG:DAT child-DAT-3SG:DAT give
     'The man gave a dog to the child.'

The Pitjantjatjara type of clitics are typically referred to as second-position clitics. The Nganhcara type could be referred to as penultimate clitics. Such placement of clitics is, however, extremely rare and therefore is not often discussed.

Another common clitic position is the beginning of the verb complex. A language manifesting clitics thus located is the Tibetan language Bawm, spoken in Bangladesh, near the border with Burma. We see in (34a) that the subject marker is proclitic to the verb and can be separated from it only by an object clitic (34b) or the direction particle *hwang* (34c).

(34)   Bawm (Reichle 1981:157)
    a.   Aukhawm nih Pathian an= muh dah loh
          nobody   AG God   3PL see ever not
          'Nobody has ever seen God.'

    b.   Na sinah chabu ka= nan= pek
          you to   book 1SG 2SG give
          'I gave the book to you.'

    c.   In   lei a= hwang tlung le
          house at 3SG DIR   arrive PL
          'He arrived home.'

By contrast, in Chalcatongo Mixtec, an Otomanguean language spoken in south-central Mexico, subject markers encliticize to the verb (35a) or any verbal modifiers which follow it, such as the adverbs in (35b) and (35c).

(35)   Chalcatongo Mixtec (Macaulay 1996:141, 142)
    a.   Ni- žéé=rí staà
          CMP-eat-1 tortilla
          'I ate.'

    b.   Ni- žéé šãã-=í staà
          CMP-eat much-1 tortilla
          'I ate a lot / I ate excessively.'

    c.   Ma-kú?ni ni?i=ró
          NEG-tie   tight-2
          'Don't tie it tightly.'

Person clitics may also attach to the beginning or end of the VP. The first of these two locations is illustrated in (36) from Marubo, a Panoan language spoken in a border region between Brazil and Peru.

(36)   Marubo (Romankevicius Costa 1998:66)
    a.   'Wan-tun an='pani-Ø tu'raš-a-ka
          he-ERG 3SG-net-ABS tear-AUX-IM.PAST
          'He has torn the net.'

    b.   I'an ɨn=ka'man-Ø 'win-ai   nɨnu-ma
          I-ERG 1SG-jaguar-ABS see-IM.PAST here-NEG
          'I have seen a jaguar far from here.'

c. ła-Ø in=wi'ša-i-ki
I:ABS 1SG-write-PRES
'I am writing.'

Note that, unlike in Bawm, the person clitics in Marubo may be attached to the object of the verb. Attachment of a person clitic to the end rather than the beginning of the VP is quite exceptional. Most reported instances actually involve cliticization to the verb and not to the VP. However, according to Guirardello (1999) in Trumai, an isolate of Brazil, the third-person clitic attaches to the end of the VP. Unfortunately, all of the examples given involve either the lexical or auxiliary verb (see example (68) in section 2.2.1.2) apart from the following involving a construction with a zero copula, where the third-person enclitic is attached to a plural particle.

(37)   Trumai (Guirardello 1999:70)
       Falti   tak   wan-e
       be: ashamed NEG   PL-3SG
       'They are not ashamed.'

The above locational possibilities of clitics are summarized in the typology in (38), taken from Anderson (1993:74).

(38) a. initial clitics (e.g. as in Marubo)
     b. final clitics (e.g. as in Trumai)
     c. second-position clitics (e.g. as in Pitjantjatjara)
     d. penultimate-position clitics (e.g as in Nganhcara)
     e. pre-head clitics (e.g. as in Bawm)
     f. post-head clitics (e.g. as in Chalcatongo Mixtec)

Anderson argues, however, that a better characterization of the placement of a clitic can be achieved if it is described in terms of the three parameters in (39).

(39) a. Its scope: the nature of the constituent (e.g. clause, VP, NP, PP) which constitutes its domain;
     b. Its anchor: the element of the constituent (first, last, head) relative to which the clitic is located;
     c. Its orientation: whether the clitic precedes or follows its anchor.

Thus, for example, the scope of the Pitjantjatjara clitics is the clause, of the Marubo and Trumai ones the VP and of the Bawm and Mixtec markers a constituent which in the generative literature may be regarded as a projection of the verb, the V'. The anchor of the Pitjantjatjara, Marubo and Bawm clitics is the first element and of the Mixtec and Trumai clitics the last. And while the Mixtec, Pitjantjatjara and Trumai forms are enclitics, the Marubo and Bawm clitics are proclitics. The Nganhcara forms in turn may be characterized as clausal enclitics, attached to the head (the verb) or whatever constituent immediately precedes it.

It is important to note, that while the three parameters in (43) go a long way in characterizing the location of most person clitics, not all three need be relevant.

For instance, in Central Kurdish, according to Fattah (1997:284), subject clitics may attach to any constituent of the VP. In (40a) we see the subject clitic attached to the verbal stem, in (40b) to the negator, in (40c) to the aspect marker and in (40d) to the direct object.

(40) Central Kurdish (Fattah 1997:284, 286)
    a.   Min na:n na:-xo=m
           I   food NEG-eat:PRES-1SG
           'I don't eat food.'

    b.   Min na=m=xwa:r-d
           I   NEG-1SG-eat-PAST
           'I didn't eat.'

    c.   Min da=m=xwa:r-d
           I   ASP-1SG-eat-PAST
           'I was eating.'

    d.   Min na:ni=m xwa:r-d
           I   bread-1SG eat-PAST
           'I ate bread.'

Thus, while the scope and orientation of the clitics is fixed, there is no fixed anchor. To give another example, in various Romance languages, including Sardinian, object clitics are proclitic to a finite verb (41a) and also in the negative imperative (41b) but are enclitic to the verb in the positive imperative (41c).

(41) Sardinian (Jones 1993:83, 28)
    a.   Las=appo   vistas
           3PLF:ACC=have:1SG seen:SG
           'I saw them.'

    b.   Non mi= lu= nies!
           NEG 1SG 3SG tell
           'Do not tell it to me!'

    c.   Nara=mi=lu
           tell-1SG-3SG
           'Tell it to me.'

Thus, in this case, while the scope (arguably) and anchor of the clitic are constant, its orientation is not.[6]

---

[6] Whether person clitics may be seen as having flexible scope depends on how one treats identity of person markers in the verbal and nominal domains. In quite a few languages the person forms used to encode possessors in substantival possession are formally identical to the subject (e.g. Candoshi, Chumash, Dagbani, Retuarã) or alternatively to the object forms (e.g. Anem, Diola-Fogny, Gumawana, Kera). If these forms are clitics and are treated as constituting one paradigm rather than as two homophonous paradigms, then they can be considered as having flexible scope.

The above notwithstanding, there are person clitics which are not easy to characterize in terms of the three parameters in (39). For instance, in Konjo, an Austronesian language of Sulawesi, the absolutive person enclitics attach to the lexical or auxiliary verb (42a) or in the presence of a set of phrase level adverbials that follows the verb, to these adverbials rather than to the verb (42b). Crucially, however, when a location or manner adverbial precedes the verb, the enclitic person marker is attached to it rather than to the verb, as in (42c).

(42)   Konjo (Friberg 1996)
a.   A'-lampa=i Amir
     INTR-go-3SG Amir
     'Amir goes.'

b.   An-jama sarring=a
     TR-work hard-1SG
     'I work really hard.'

c.   Kunjo=a an-jama
     there-1SG TR-work
     'There is where I work.'

Another property of clitics reflecting their relative independence as compared to bound forms is their non-phonological integration with their host. Thus, whereas bound forms often exhibit considerable allomorphic variation dependent on the morpho-phonological properties of the stem, clitics tend not to. The difference in phonological integration is most obvious in languages which have both bound and clitic person forms, as is the case, for example, in the Uto-Aztecan language Cora. Cora has a set of subject prefixes used when the verb precedes its nominal arguments and a corresponding set of subject clitics used when a nominal argument precedes the verb (Casad 1984:171). The two sets of forms are presented in (43).

(43)   Cora (Casad 1984:297)

	Subject prefix	Subject clitic
1SG	n^{y}a-	nu
2SG	pa-	pa
3SG	Ø	pu
1PL	ta-	tu
2PL	sa-/ša-	su
3PL	ma-	mu

The vowel of the subject prefixes is realized as ɛ- before y-initial stems (44b) or consonant-initial stems whose first vowel is i (44c), as u- when it precedes the locative prefix u- 'inside horizontally' (44d) and as zero when the prefix is attached to a following vowel-initial morpheme (44e).

(44) Cora (Casad 1984:324, 178, 324, 325)
    a. N^ya-kuh-mɨ
       1SG-sleep-DES
       'I am sleepy.'

    b. N^yɛ-yáana
       1SG-smoke
       'I'm smoking.'

    c. Tkɨn n^yɛ-t^yí-hí'i-k^wi'i   n^yá'u
       quot 1SG-DSTR-NARR-be sick well
       'He said, "I'm sick, that's all".'

    d. Nú-u-kun
       1SG-inside horizontally-be hollow
       'I have a hole in my ear.'

    e. N-ú-i'ɨwa-n
       1SG-there-bathe-PRT(?)
       'I'm going off to bathe.'

The vowel of the corresponding subject clitics, on the other hand, is invariant.

(45) Cora (Casad 1984:325, 171, 339, 372,)
    a. Ayaa nu=ra-ruu-re
       thus 1SG-DSTR:SG-do-make:APPL
       'That is what I am doing to him.'

    b. M^wán šú=yaana
       you:PL 2PL-smoke
       'You all are smoking.'

    c. N^y-áu-če'e=nú=t^yi'i-k^wa'a-n^yi
       1SG-LOC-CONT-1SG-DSTR-eat-FUT
       'I'm still going to eat.'

    d. Ha'atɨh nú=a-va-tu'a
       someone 1SG=outside-coming-hit
       'I hit someone on the top of the head.'

Bound forms but not clitics may also undergo idiosyncratic suppletive alternations. For example, the Polish first-person subject suffix is either -ę or -m, depending on the conjugation class of the verb. Thus we have *lubi-ę* 'I like' and *prosz-ę* 'I request' but *kocha-m* 'I love' and *rozumie-m* 'I understand'. The object clitics, on the other hand, are the same irrespective of verb class; *lubię cię* 'I like you', *prozse cię* 'I ask you', *kocham cię* 'I love you', *rozumiem cię* 'I understand you'.

Another manifestation of the looser connection of clitics to their hosts than bound forms is that the latter but not the former may induce allomorphic variation of the stem. A interesting instance of this is to be found in Maumere (also called Sikka) an Austronesian language of the Ambon-Timor group of Central Flores,

Indonesia. According to Rosen (1986) Maumere has seven classes of verbs, three of which change their initial consonant or vowel depending on person. In one class the change involves an alternation between voiced and voiceless initial stops, though only of /t/ and /d/ and /p/ and /b/ but not /k/ and /g/. In another class of verbs, person is indicated by an alternation between an initial non-murmured vowel and /g/. And with a third class of verbs there is an alternation between laryngealized and non-laryngealized lateral or median resonants. In each case, the voiceless stops, non-murmured vowel and laryngealized lateral or median resonant is used in the first-person singular and in the first-person inclusive and third-person plural, the voiced stop, /g/ and non-laryngealized forms respectively for the remaining person and number combinations. The examples below illustrate only the voice oppositions.

(46)   Maumere (Rosen 1986:54)
     a.   A.u pano   a
           I   1SG:go   DIR
           'I go.'

     b.   Au bano   a
           you   2SG:go   DIR
           'You go.'

     c.   Nimu bano   a
           (s)he   3SG:go   DIR
           'She/he goes.'

     d.   Ita   pano   a
           we(INCL)   1PL:INCL-go   DIR
           'We (INCL) go.'

As mentioned earlier, bound forms may even trigger suppletion of the stem. Recall, for example, the person marking via stem change in Misantla Totonac and Mazatec illustrated in (27) and (28). Again this does not happen with clitics.

The difference in phonological integration between bound forms and clitics is paralleled at the prosodic level. Whereas bound forms are treated prosodically as part of the word to which they attach, clitics tend not to be. For instance, in Standard Polish, the first- and second-person plural subject clitics -(e)śmy, -(e)ście do not count, so to speak, as far as the placement of word stress is concerned. Word stress in Polish is highly regular, falling on the penultimate syllable. As shown in (47b), the presence of the first-person plural subject clitic does not result in a shift of stress to the right.

(47)   Polish
     a.   MieSZKAli w Warszawie
           lived:3PL   in Warsaw
           'They lived in Warsaw.'

b. MieSZKAli=śmy w Warszawie
   lived-1PL   in Warsaw
   'We lived in Warsaw.'

The situation in Polish with respect to the forms -(e)śmy, -(e)ście contrasts with that in the Tfuya dialect of the Formosan language Tsou, which, like Polish, also has stress on the penultimate syllable. When person suffixes are attached to the noun, the stress shifts from the initial to the second syllable, e.g. ámo 'father' vs amó-to 'our father'.

While many linguists consider the variable host criterion as definitive of the clitic as opposed to bound status of a person form, for some the lack of phonological integration with the stem is sufficient. This is the major reason why a given person marker may be treated as a clitic under one analysis and as bound form under another. In this work, the variable host criterion will be viewed as definitive of clitic status. Thus forms which are always tied to a particular host, be it only loosely, will be treated as bound. This does not, however, include person markers such as those in Djaru (48) and various other Australian languages which are always attached to a special catalyst particle.

(48)   Djaru (Tsunoda 1981:58)
        Ngaju-ngku nga=rna=nyanta   makkarta man-i   yampakina-ngu
        I-ERG   CAT-1SG:NOM-3SG:LOC hat:ABS take-PAST child-ABL
        'I took a hat from a child.'

Such person markers are typically treated by Australianists as clitics and this is also the analysis which I have adopted. The major reason for the clitic as opposed to bound analysis of such person forms is that the catalyst particle is devoid of semantic content and thus functions essentially as a place holder for the person markers. Moreover, the catalyst particle to which the person forms attach is generally located after the first word or constituent of the clause. Thus the person markers may in fact be characterized as occupying a particular location rather than as being attached to an invariable host. They are thus very much like the clitics attached after the first constituents in, for instance, Pitjantjatjara illustrated earlier in (35).

2.1.2.3 Weak forms

The last of the dependent person markers in (17) is the weak form. In contrast to bound forms and clitics, weak forms are not attached, either phonologically or morphologically, to any other constituent. In this sense they are like independent forms. However, they are not just unstressed versions of independent forms but rather differ from them both phonologically and in terms of syntactic distribution. A potential case in point is that of what Sohn (1975) calls subjectives in the Austronesian language Woleaian. As we see in (49) these forms are phonologically distinct from the corresponding independent forms.

(49) Woleaian (Sohn 1975)
	Indep	Subject Subjectives
1SG	gaang	i
2SG	geel	go
3SG	iiy	ye
1EXCL	giish	gai
1INCL	gaaman	si
2PL	gaami	gai
3PL	iir	re

And though they are necessarily preverbal (50) they are not cliticized to the verb. They can be separated from the verb by a negator (50a) or tense/aspect marker (50b,c) to which they are also not attached.

(50)   Woleaian (Sohn 1975:150, 151, 145)
   a.   (Gaang) i   ta   weri-Ø
        I   1SG not see-3SG
        'I did not see it.'

   b.   (Gaami) gai lag!
        you:PL 2PL go
        'You (PL) go!'

   c.   Yaremat laal ye be mas
        man   that 3SG FUT die
        'That man will die.'

As for differences in distribution relative to the independent forms, we see in (51) that the subjectives are obligatory in predicative clauses while the independent forms are not. Conversely, whereas the independent forms may occur in equational clauses (51a), be followed by the focus marker *mele* (51b) and be coordinated (51c), the subjectives cannot.

(51)   Woleaian (Sohn 1975:147, 172)
   a.   Gaang (*i) Tony
        I   Tony
        'I am Tony.'

   b.   Iir mele ie mwali
        they FOC 3PL hid
        'They are the ones who hid.'

   c.   Geel me gaang si   bel lag
        you and I   1PL:INCL will go
        'You and I will go.'

Another language displaying what may be seen to be weak person forms is Sanuma, which belongs to the Yanomami family and is spoken in Brazil and Venezuela. Borgman (1990) calls the weak forms short and the corresponding independent forms long. The two sets of forms are shown in (52).

(52) Sanuma (Borgman 1990:149)

	Indep	Weak
1SG	kamisa	sa
2SG	kawa/kau	wa
3SG	kama	a/te[7]
1PL EXCL	kamisamakö	samako/sama
1PL INCL	kamakö	mako/ma
2PL	kamakö	mako/ma
3DU	kama kökö/tökö	kökö/tökö
3PL	kama pö/töpö	po/töpö

Unlike in Woleaian, the short forms are used not only for subjects (53a) but also for objects (53b), and in predicative clauses are not obligatory; in (53c) there is no overt subject of any type, and in (53d) only a long-form one.

(53) Sanuma (Borgman 1990:27, 29, 151)
    a.   Ipa sai   ha ipa silaka ha sa   kali-palo-ti   kule
        my house at   my arrow on 1SG work-REP-CONT PRES
        'I am working on my arrow at my house.'

    b.   Sama   töpö se kite
        1PL EXCL 3PL hit FUT
        'We will hit them.'

    c.   Ø töpö se kite
          3PL hit FUT
        '(We) will hit them.'

    d.   Kamisa hu pasi-a   ma-ne
        I   go apart-DUR NEG-PRES
        'I am not going.'

Short-form person markers are located in immediate preverbal position with the subject preceding the object and, as we see in (54), may co-occur with the corresponding long forms or a lexical NP.

(54) Sanuma
    Kamisamakö-nö hama sama   töpö se kite
    we-ERG   visitor 1PL:EXCL 3PL hit FUT
    'We will hit the visitors.'

Some other distributional differences between the long and short forms are: the long forms, like lexical NPs, when used as transitive subjects occur with the ergative suffix *-no* (54), but the short forms are unmarked (53a), the long forms but not the short forms are used in declarative identificational clauses and as the complements of the postposition *niha*.

The notion of weak form or weak pronoun is not firmly established in the literature and therefore there is no consensus on the type of properties that weak forms

---

[7] The third-person short forms are the same as the specific and general classifiers, found with nouns.

should display. Bresnan (2001b), for example, imposes no specific requirements on what constitutes a weak person marker other than the general ones presented above. Cardinaletti and Starke (1999), on the other hand, use the term weak pronoun for forms with a very specific set of characteristics. Under their analysis weak pronouns are "mildly deficient pronominals" that cannot be coordinated or modified and do not necessarily refer to human referents. These properties, weak forms are seen to share with clitics which are considered to be "severely deficient pronominals". Unlike clitics, however, they may bear word stress, may be deleted under ellipsis, do not form clusters and cannot be doubled by a full NP (Cardinaletti & Starke 1999:169). The Woleaian subjectives illustrated above do not meet Cardinaletti and Starke's criteria of what constitutes a weak form since although they indeed cannot be coordinated and do not necessarily refer to humans, they are obligatory in verbal predications and are not in complementary distribution with full NPs. The Sanuma short forms also do not qualify as weak forms. They meet the criterion of not being restricted to humans and being eligible to ellipsis, but they too may be doubled up by an independent NP. Thus in Cardinaletti and Starke's terms the relevant person forms would qualify not as weak forms but as clitics. An example of weak form in Cardinaletti and Starke's sense of the term is the French third-person singular masculine unstressed subject person marker *il*, though crucially only when it is located in preverbal (55a) and not in postverbal (55b) position, where it occurs in interrogatives.

(55) French
   a.   Il   part   demain   pour Paris
       3SGM leaves tomorrow for   Paris
       'He leaves tomorrow for Paris.'

   b.   Part-il   demain   pour Paris?
       leaves-3SG tomorrow for   Paris
       'Does he leave for Paris tomorrow?'

French is typically seen as having three sets of person markers, an independent (strong) set (e.g. *moi*) and two unstressed sets, one for subjects (e.g. *je*) and one for objects (e.g. *me*). Although the properties of the unstressed subject and object forms are not identical, both are generally analysed as clitics. Cardinaletti and Starke, however, argue that the preverbal subject markers are weak forms since, unlike the postverbal subject forms and the object forms, they may take lexical word stress and be elided. Compare (56a) with (56b) and (56c).

(56) French
   a.   Il   reviendra   et   Ø verra   Marie
       3SGM will come back and Ø will:see Mary
       'He will come back and will see Mary.'

   b.   *Pierre la= verra   et   Ø saluera
       Peter 3SGF will see and Ø will greet
       'Peter will see her and will greet (her).'

c. *Reviendra-t=il   et Ø verra   Marie
    will come back-3SGM and Ø will:see Mary
    'Will he come back and see Mary?'

Cardinaletti and Starke have not yet applied their typology of deficient pronominals to a wide range of languages. However, given their criteria of what constitutes a weak pronoun as opposed to a clitic, on the one hand, and a strong form, on the other, it is likely that quite a few of the person markers typically considered to be independent forms or clitics will emerge under their analysis as weak.

The dependent person markers most difficult to classify in terms of the four types distinguished in (17) are portmanteau forms combining person and tense/aspect. Such person forms are regularly encountered in Africa, for instance, among the Mande languages (e.g. Boko, Busa, Kono, Kpelle) and also in the Chadic languages (e.g. Mandara, Margi, Podoko) as well as in Austronesia (e.g. Dehu, Iai, Nengone, Tigak). Typically they are the result of the fusion of a subject person marker and a following auxiliary verb. Synchronically, however, it is difficult to know whether they should be treated as auxiliary verbs inflected for person or person markers inflected for tense/aspect or as an atypical clitic cluster of person and tense/aspect. The first of these analyses is not very appealing since in most instances the potential auxiliary verb is rather difficult to identify. This is particularly so when the relevant forms are monosyllabic and consist of just a single vowel with only tonal differentiation, as is quite often the case in Mande languages. By way of illustration, consider some of the subject forms together with the object markers (not inflected for tense/aspect) in Boko, a Mande language spoken in Benin, West Africa.

(57)   Boko (Jones 1998:138, 142)
                    [Subject]   Object

	Perfective	Stative	Subjunctive	
1SG	ma	má	mà	ma
2SG	ŋ	ŋ	ŋ/Ø	ŋ
3SG	á	ā	aà	aà
1PL	wa	wá	wà	wá
2PL	a	á	à	á
3PL	aa	aa	aa	ŋ

Under the second analysis the relevant person markers would be weak forms inflected for tense/aspect (though not weak in Cardinaletti & Starke's 1999 sense of the term as they can be doubled by a lexical NP). Such an analysis seems to be appropriate for languages such as Iai, an Austronesian language spoken on the Loyalty Islands, where as shown in (58), the subject forms look much more like inflected stems.

(58)   Iai (Tryon 1968:46–50, 87)

	[Subject]			Object	Indep
	Present	Future	Past		
1SG	ogeme	ogema	oge	na	iña
2SG	umwe	unwa	uje	u	umwe
3SG	ame	ama	a	Ø	
1INCL	ötine	ötina	ötine		ötin
1EXCL	ömune	ömuna	ömune		ömun
2PL	öbune	öbuna	öbune		öbun
3PL	örine	örina	örine		örin

It is debatable, however, whether the Boko forms should be analysed in the same way. Jones calls the Boko forms both clitics and subject pronouns suffixed or fused with tense/aspect. The motivation for calling the relevant forms clitics is that when followed by an object person marker or an NP modified by a possessive person marker the subject markers form a clitic cluster with the following object or possessive marker. Some examples are given in (59).

(59)   Boko (Jones 1998:131)
   a.   Aa   aà   'è →   aaà 'è
        3PL:PERF 3SG see:PERF
        'They saw him.'

   b.   Wa   á   da   'è →   waá 'è
        1PL:PERF 1SG mother see:PERF
        'We saw our mother.'

However, as shown in (60), the subject person markers are not phonologically attached to a following NP object. Therefore unless the fused subject/tense/aspect forms are themselves treated as a clitic cluster, the inflected weak-form analysis may in fact be preferable. The fact that the subjunctive forms may be elided after aspectual verbs with the same referent (60) may be viewed as an argument in favour of the weak form as opposed to the clitic analysis.

(60)   Boko (Jones 1998:133)
        Má   ye   (mà)   gé
        1SG:STAT want (1SG:SUBJ) go
        'I want to go.'

In the light of the preceding discussion it should be clear that the classification of person forms in terms of their morpho-phonological characteristics is no straightforward matter. Forms that are classified as affixes under one analysis emerge as clitics under another, and vice versa. The same applies to clitics vs weak forms and potentially weak forms and independent ones. What this suggests is that while morpho-phonological form may be a significant parameter of the classification of person markers, it would be unwise to base any syntactic analysis of person forms just on their morpho-phonological properties.

We have seen that the classification of person markers in terms of their morpho-phonological properties is by no means unproblematic. While many person markers are unequivocally affixes or clitics, the status of others depends on which property is taken as definitive of affixes, clitics, weak or independent forms, respectively. This suggests that the distinction between affix, clitic, weak or independent form is not in fact discrete but rather gradual. Such a view of the differences in morpho-phonological form of person markers is in turn fully in line with the assumption that these differences are a reflection of different degrees of the grammaticalization of person markers, an issue which will be discussed in chapter seven.

2.2 Syntactic function

Cross-cutting the morpho-phonological classification of person markers is a classification based on the syntactic functions within the clause that they fulfil. Although person markers may bear the same range of syntactic functions as lexical categories, needless to say, they are much more common with syntactic functions, the referents of which are typically human as opposed to non-human. This holds by definition for first- and second-person forms, but also for third-person forms. Thus person markers are much more common with arguments than with adjuncts, and among the arguments they are more common with subjects than with objects or obliques. As argued by Du Bois (1987), in some languages person markers also clearly favour transitive subjects over intransitive ones. Statistical data from several languages supporting this are presented in Table 2.1. The above holds for all types of person markers. There are, however, interesting differences regarding syntactic functions and the morpho-phonological form of person markers which are worth considering in more detail.

2.2.1 Syntactic function and morpho-phonological form
2.2.1.1 Independent person markers

There appear to be no cross-linguistic restrictions on which syntactic functions may be realized by independent person markers. This is not to say, however, that independent person markers are necessarily available for all syntactic functions. In languages which make much use of dependent person markers it is often the case that independent person markers are employed only in a highly restricted set of circumstances. For instance, according to Miller (1965:174), in Acoma, a Keresan language of New Mexico, the only independent person markers in the language namely *šínumé, hínumé* 'I' and *hísumé* 'you' are used only as single word responses to questions. In all other situations bound forms occur. In the Arawakan language Wari (Everett & Kern 1997:303), spoken in the Rondonia region of Brazil, there is a full paradigm of independent person markers, but they too are never used as verbal arguments. The first- and second-person forms occur

Table 2.1 *Frequency of lexical and pronominal realization of the S, A and P in six languages*

		S (%)	A (%)	P (%)
Sacapultec Mayan oral narrative	lexical	48	6	46
	pronominal	52	94	54
Ch'orti oral narrative	lexical	46	17	38
	pronominal	54	83	62
Yagua oral narrative	lexical	28	19	54
	pronominal	72	81	46
Roviana oral narrative	lexical	33	15	52
	pronominal	67	85	48
Papago oral narrative	lexical	68	16	64
	pronominal	32	84	36
English conversation	lexical	11(K) 22(F)	7	62
	pronominal	81 (K) 78 (F)	93	38

The Sacapultec Mayan data are taken from Du Bois (1987), the Chorti from Quizar (1994), the Yagua from Payne (1990:120–2), the Roviana from Corston (1998:42), the Papago from Payne (1992) and the English from Fox (1995) and Kärkkäinen (1996).

only as single word responses to questions. The third-person forms are used as adnominal emphatics, that is similarly to the English reflexive emphatics found in clauses such as *The queen herself will come* (see the discussion in section 2.3).

Such heavily restricted usage of independent person markers as in Acoma and Wari is highly unusual.[8] Much more commonly, independent person markers are used at least as arguments of some non-verbal predicates and/or in coordinations. This is the case, for instance, in the Austronesian language Kiribatese.

(61) Kiribatese (Groves et al. 1985:64, 104, 87)
    a. Antal ae e oko? Ngala
       who 3SG come he
       'Who came? He did.'

    b. Ngala te beretitenti
       he the president
       'He is the president.'

    c. Ti noora teuaarei ma ngkoe
       1PL see man and you
       'We saw that man and you.'

---

[8] Under the so-called pronominal argument analysis of polysynthetic languages (see ch. 4, section 4.1), the inability of independent person markers to function as verbal arguments is not all that rare since the independent forms are considered to be very much like left-dislocated topics.

We see in (61b) that the non-verbal predicates which occur with independent subject person markers are nominal ones. Subjects of adjectival (62a) and verbal predicates (61c and 62b,c) are indicated by weak person forms, and direct objects (62b) and objects of prepositions (62c) by person suffixes.

(62)   Kiribatese (Groves et al. 1985:106, 86, 111)
- a. Kam baba
 2SG stupid
 'You are stupid.'
- b. E noora-i
 3SG see-1SG
 'He saw me.'
- c. Kam kanakomaia te ika nako-ira
 2SG sent the fish to-1PL
 'You sent the fish to us.'

Significantly, there are no independent person forms for direct objects. Other languages which have independent forms for at least some types of subjects but not for objects are: Anejom, Au, Canela Kraho, Gapun, Geez, Malak Malak, Maranguku, Palikur, Salinan and Sumerian. I am not aware of any languages manifesting the converse situation, that is the possibility of expressing objects by independent person forms but not subjects. Even in languages in which the normal expression of a subject is by a dependent person marker there tend to be special independent forms which may be used at least with non-verbal predicates or for purposes of emphasis, as in Wari, mentioned above.

The impossibility of expressing a verbal argument or adjunct by an independent person marker in preference to, or in conjunction with, a dependent one is not very common as compared to that of the absence of independent possessive person markers in adnominal possessive constructions. There appear to be no independent possessive person markers in 20 per cent of the languages in the sample. Among these languages are: Acehnese, Acoma, Amuesha, Chamorro, Chumash, Evenki, Grand Valley Dani, Hixkaryana, Koasati, Lango, Pipil, Retuarã, Tonkawa, Uma Washo and Yagua. In all, the person of the possessor is expressed by a bound marker or clitic.

2.2.1.2 Dependent person markers and argument prominence

As we have seen, the unavailability of independent person markers to express certain syntactic functions rests on the existence of dependent forms for the rendition of these functions. Nonetheless, complementary distribution in regard to syntactic function between dependent and independent forms must be seen as the exception rather than the norm. In the vast majority of cases dependent person forms have corresponding independent ones. The converse, however, definitely does not hold. Dependent person markers are much more common with arguments than with adjuncts, and among the arguments they are more common

Table 2.2 *Dependent pronominals (as a group) and argument prominence*

Dependent pro.	Subject N=402	Object1 N=402	Object2 N=375	Oblique[i] N=332
No. lgs	330	247	55	20
%	82	67	15	6

[i] The figures pertaining to obliques are only of NP constituents, not adpositional ones.

with subjects than with objects. This is evidenced by the distribution of dependent person markers among the languages in the sample with respect to the four syntactic functions in the argument prominence hierarchy in (63).

(63)   subject > object1 > object2 > oblique

The syntactic functions in (63) are to be understood as follows. The subject corresponds to the A, object1 corresponds to the P and to the argument of a ditransitive clause (either patient or recipient) which has the same person marking as that of the P in monotransitive clauses, object2 corresponds to the other ditransitive object and oblique corresponds to any argument associated with a specific semantic role which is not realized by the subject or object functions. The relevant data are presented in Table 2.2. We see in Table 2.2 that the vast majority of languages have some form of dependent person marking for subjects and just over two thirds for object1. In the case of object2, however, there is a drastic reduction of dependent markers and a similar radical reduction for obliques.

It is not only with respect to cross-linguistic frequency that the distribution of dependent person markers conforms to the hierarchy of argument prominence in (63). With few exceptions the same holds within languages. The availability of dependent person markers for a syntactic function lower on the argument prominence hierarchy entails the availability of dependent person markers for syntactic functions higher on the argument prominence hierarchy. In other words, if a language allows a dependent person marker, say a clitic, to be used for object2, it also allows some type of dependent person marker, be it clitic, bound, weak or zero form to be used for both object1 and subject.

The major group of exceptions to this pattern of distribution comes from languages which have bound or clitic forms for object1 but no dependent subject forms. These include Ani, Barai, Bimoba, Karo-Batak, Nivkh, Noon, Panyjima and Sema.[9] Interestingly enough, in all these languages the dependent object forms are quite restricted. For example, in Panyjima they are found only with the first-person patient or recipient/benefactive. In Sema they occur only in the first- and second-person singular. In the Siberian language Nivkh, the relevant

---

[9] One could also list here the few languages which have person affixes or clitics for the S and P but not the A (and no apparent other reduced pronominals) such as Palikur, and Karitiana.

forms are found only in the imperative. In Ani, there is a full paradigm, but according to Heine (1999:29), it is not used all that frequently. And in Barai the object suffixes occur only with some verbs. Five other exceptional languages are Gude, Kewa, Kolyma Yukaghir, Lepcha and Waskia. According to Hoskinson (1983:110), Gude, a Chadic language spoken in Nigeria and Cameroon, has no dependent person markers for either subject or object1 but does have (in some dialects) a bound object2 form, which is attached to the verb stem between the verb root and the following applicative extension. Compare (64a) with the independent person marker *ci* and (64b) featuring the bound form *nə*.

(64) Gude (Hoskinson 1983:110–11)
a. Kə vii Musa kwaɓa ka ci
    CMP *give Musa money to him*
    'Musa gave money to him.'

b. Kə ka-nə-paa Musa buura
    CMP *set down*-3SGM-APPL *Musa bag*
    'Musa set down the bag for him.'

Kewa, Kolyma Yukaghir and Waskia, in turn, have bound person forms for the subject and in the case of the verb 'give' also for object2. They do not, however, have any dependent forms for object1. The bound forms for object2 are of a special type, that is they involve stem change. Waskia (Ross & Natu 1978:43), a Papuan language of the Ismrud family, for example, has four stems of the verb 'to give' dependent on the person in the singular and number in the plural: *asi* for 1SG; *kisi* for 2SG, *tuw* or *tuiy* for 3SG and *idi* for all persons in the plural. Kolyma Yukaghir and Kewa have only two stem forms, one for third person and another for the first and second persons. This is also the case in the Tibeto-Burman language Lepcha, which like Gude has no other dependent person markers.[10]

If we order the four types of dependent markers discussed in 2.2 in terms of the increase in phonological substance and/or morphological independence as in (65), it is also possible to discern a relationship between argument prominence and the distribution within a language of each of the four types of dependent person markers.

(65) zero bound clitic weak

In the vast majority of languages (89%), more phonologially reduced and/or morphologically dependent forms are used for arguments higher on the argument prominence hierarchy than for those lower on the hierarchy. Among the forty-three languages which exhibit distributions counter to the argument prominence hierarchy, the first group of exceptions involve languages which allow for zero objects but not subjects, as is the case in: Finnish, Kewa, Palauan and Imbabura

---

[10] Further examples of suppletive person marking of recipients with the verb 'give' are provided by Comrie (2001).

Quechua. As one would expect, all the languages in question have bound subjects, as illustrated in (66), on the basis of the Austronesian language spoken on Guam, Chamorro.

(66) Chamorro (Chung 1984:120)
In-bisita Ø q' espitatt
1PL-visit (2SG/3SG/3PL) LOC hospital
'We visited (you, him, them) at the hospital.'

There is also one language which has a zero object2 but does not allow zeroes for object1. This is the previously mentioned Trumai, a genetic isolate of Brazil. Guirardello (1999) documents that person markers in both subject and object2 functions (the latter being rendered by recipients) may have zero realization, given the right pragmatic conditions, but a constituent in object1 function cannot. Compare the use of the dative person marker in (67a) with the examples of zero anaphora in (67b,c).

(67) Trumai (Guirardello (1999:259, 353)
a. Kiki-k atlat-Ø kïṭï hai-tl
man-ERG pan-ABS give I-DAT
'The man gave the pan to me.'

b. Ni'de esak-Ø chi_in kach hai-ts kïṭï ke[11] Ø
this hammock-ABS FOC-TENSE later I-ERG give Ke DAT
'I will give (you) this hammock.'

c. Hai-ts chi(_in) de oke yi-Ø kïṭï Ø
I-ERG FOC-TENSE already medicine YI-ABS give DAT
'I have already given medicine (to her).'

Under the same discourse circumstances an object1 is encoded either by an independent person marker or, in the case of the third person, by the person clitic -n/-e. Recall that the person clitic is attached to the last constituent in the VP, which in (68), in contrast to the example given earlier in (37), is the lexical verb.

(68) Trumai (Guirardello (1999:343)
Ha adif-atl chi_in hai-ta kiti-n
1SG brother-DAT FOC-TNS I-ERG give-3:ABS
'I gave (it/her) to my brother.'

Another distributional pattern which runs counter to the argument prominence hierarchy is the existence of bound objects but weak forms for subjects. This pattern is particularly frequent among the languages of Micronesia. It was illustrated in (62) on the basis of Kiribatese and is also found, for example, in Kusaiean,

---

[11] *Ke* is a morpheme that is placed after the verb whenever the P occurs in any position other than immediately preverbal.

Ponapean, Tigak, Woleaian and Yapese. And finally there are languages that have bound objects, but clitic subjects, as illustrated in (69) from Mundari, an Austro-Asiatic language of India.

(69) Mundari (Cook 1965:239)
      Samu cepeko=e lel-ko-tan-a
      Samu birds-3SG look-3PL-PRES:IND
      'Samu is looking at the birds.'

Some other languages with the same pattern are: Burunge, Halkomelem, Kutenai, Lower Umpqua and South-eastern Tepehuan.

Given the strong tendency for dependent person markers to favour syntactic functions high on the argument prominence hierarchy, the question arises why this should be the case. A promising explanation is suggested by the relationship between morpho-syntactic encoding and the cognitive accessibility of a referent in the memory store of the addressee posited by various scholars within the functional-cognitive paradigm, and most fully articulated by Givón (1983) and Ariel (1990). The notion of cognitive accessibility and the factors underlying it will be discussed in detail in chapter five. For the time being, suffice it to say that high cognitive accessibility is associated with the properties on the left-hand side of the hierarchies in (70) as opposed to those on the right.

(70) a. Speaker > addressee > non-participant (3rd person)
     b. Subject > > object > other
     c. High physical salience > low physical salience
     d. Topic > non-topic
     e. Human > animate > inanimate
     f. Repeated reference > few previous references > first mention
     g. No intervening/competing referents > many intervening/competing referents

Accessibility in turn is viewed as having a direct bearing on formal encoding: the more accessible the referent, the less coding required. Thus, since dependent person markers involve less encoding than independent ones, the expectation is that they should be characteristic of syntactic functions which tend to realize highly accessible referents. And as we have seen, this is indeed so. Dependent person markers are less frequent as one goes down the argument prominence hierarchy, being most common with subjects and least common with obliques. Moreover, accessibility also leads us to expect that the more attenuated of the dependent person markers should favour the syntactic functions which encode the most accessible referents. Language internally, this means that no more attenuated dependent person marker should realize an argument higher on the argument prominence hierarchy than any less attenuated dependent marker. Accordingly, there should be no languages, for example, with weak subject forms but clitic object ones or clitic subject forms but bound object ones, etc. Again, while there are languages in which the dependent person markers that they possess are distributed counter to this expectation, in the overwhelming majority the distribution of dependent person markers is fully in line with accessibility.[12]

2.2.2 The encoding of syntactic function

Person markers may be encoded for syntactic function by morphological case marking and/or order and de facto by their morpho-phonological status. Morpho-phonological status emerges as a means of syntactic function encoding in languages in which independent person markers or, more commonly, person affixes or clitics are available only for particular syntactic functions. When this is not so, either order or morphological case marking may do the job. More often than not, however, order is accompanied by some form of morphological case marking. Accordingly, in what follows we will concentrate on morphological case marking.

2.2.2.1 The expression of morphological case marking

Generally speaking, the expression of case with person forms is the same as that with lexical NPs. The case marking may be analytic via adpositions, synthetic via affixes or very rarely via clitics, suppletive via stem change or suprasegmental via tone or stress. The first of these is essentially restricted to independent person markers.

As with lexical NPs, the more analytic forms of case marking are typical of non-core grammatical functions, the more synthetic of core functions. However, given that person markers tend to be short, monosyllabic or bisyllabic, they more readily fuse with case affixes or adpositions than lexical forms. Thus, for example, while core syntactic functions may be marked by adpositions if expressed by lexical NPs, the corresponding markers with independent person forms may be suffixes. This is the case, for instance, in Awa Pit, a Pazean language of Colombia and Ecuador. As shown in (71), lexical NPs (which are human) are marked for accusative case by the postposition *ta*.

(71) Awa Pit (Curnow 1997:65)
    a.   Na=na Demetrio ta   pyan-tu
          I=TOP Demetrio ACC hit-IMPF
          'I hit Demetrio.'
    b.   Demetrio na-wa pyan-ti-ti-s
          Demetrio I-ACC hit-PAST-LOC-UGR
          'Demetrio hit me.'

The accusative case of independent person markers, on the other hand, is formed by the addition to the nominative forms of suffixes in the singular and clitics in the plural. The nominative and accusative paradigms are presented in (72).

---

[12] Various explanations are available for the exceptional distributions which will be discussed in the context of the development of dependent person markers from independent ones in chapter 7.

(72)   Awa Pit (Curnow 1997:86)
           Nominative   Accusative
    1SG   na   na-wa
    2SG   nu   nu-wa
    3SG   us   us-a
    1PL   au   au ... =mɨza
    2PL   u   u ... =mɨza
    3PL   uspa   uspa ... =tuza

That the first-, second- and third-person plural forms consist of a root plus an enclitic rather than a suffix is evinced by the fact that the plural marker may be attached not to the root but to a numeral as in (73).

(73)   Awa Pit
        au kutnya=mɨza
        we three=1/2:ACC
        'us three'

Owing to phonological factors and frequent use, the combination of person marker and adposition or case suffix may, over time, lead to the complete fusion of the two resulting in the existence of completely different phonological forms of person markers specialized for syntactic function. In such cases the person markers are seen to have different stems. In relation to independent person forms, the marking of all the members of a person paradigm for syntactic function by different stems as in, for example, Teribe (74), a Chibchan language of Costa Rica, is not very common.

(74)   Teribe (Quesada 2000:46)
            Subject   Oblique
    1SG   ta   bor
    2SG   pa   bop
    3SG   Ø   ba
    1EXCL tawa   borwa
    1INCL shi   bi
    2PL   pāy   bomi
    3PL   ebga   ba

Case marking via stem change is typically found with first- and second-person singular subject and object forms, which are the most frequently used person forms in speech. Some languages in which syntactic function by means of stem change is marked only in the first-person singular are: Kusaiean, Kashmiri, Marubo, Roshani and Wappo. Suppletive marking of syntactic function in just the first- and second-person singular is also not uncommon. It is found, for example, in Burji, Mauritian Kreol, Mauwake and Mesalit. Typically the existence of different stems marking syntactic function in the third person or the non-singular implies the presence of such an alternation also in the first and second persons and/or the singular. There are, nonetheless, exceptions to the above. For instance, as shown in (75) in the Adamawa language Koh Lakka, spoken in Chad, the distinction between subject and object is marked by different stems in all persons but for the first and second singular, which exhibit no subject/object contrast.

(75)   Koh Lakka (Glidden 1985:230, 235)

	Subject	Object
1SG	mì	mì
2SG	mù	mù
3SG	ka	ni
1+2SG	ná	
1PL	nári	bburu
2PL	ì	rì
3PL	i	ri

Although in principle there is no limit to the number of oppositions that may be marked by stem change, typically only a two-way distinction is thus marked. In most instances there is one stem for the subject and another for the object, as in Teribe and Koh Lakka. Then one or the other stem is used to mark additional syntactic functions by means of affixes or adpositions. This is generally the object stem, as in English, in which we have, for example, *with me* or *about him* rather than **with I* or **about he*. More rarely, there is one stem for core syntactic functions and another for all others. This is the situation in Coast Tsimshian, a language of north-west USA and Canada. The use of more than two stem forms in the marking of clausal argument functions is not frequently encountered. The example in (76) is from Polish in which there are three different stems in the third-person singular, one for subject *on*, another for direct and indirect object *je-* and a third for prepositional objects *nim*.

(76)   Polish

	1SG	2SG	3SGM	1PL	2PL	3PL
NOM	ja	ty	on	my	wy	oni
ACC	mnie	ciebie	jego	nas	was	ich
DAT	mnie	tobie	jemu	nam	wam	im
LOC	o mnie	o tobie	o nim	o nas	o was	o nich
INST	z mną	z tobą	z nim	z nami	z wami	z nimi

It is often stated that morphological marking of core syntactic functions is more common with independent person forms than with lexical NPs. This is indeed so. Among the languages in the sample there are thirty-three which exhibit morphological case marking with independent person forms but not lexical NPs. In some of these, for instance Koyra Chiini, Kusaiean and Warao the pronominal case marking involves only certain person-number combinations. In others, for instance, Cora, Dutch, English, Italian, Kobon, Rama, Welsh, Yoruba and Zande it involves the whole or most of the paradigm.

The converse situation, that is morphological case marking with lexical NPs but not independent person forms is also attested but in a smaller number of languages, namely in twenty. Some of the languages in question are Acehnese, Coast

Tsimshian, Hunzib, Ika, Iraqw, Kapampangan, Konjo, Labu, Lower Grand Valley Dani, Maisin and Suena. Interestingly enough, in most of these languages the case marking of lexical NPs is either not obligatory or otherwise atypical. For example, in Ika the subject is marked by a postposition only when it is placed immediately before the verb, but not in canonical SOV order. In Acehnese, a preposition (*le*) is used to mark certain subject arguments only when they follow the verb and is moreover optional in the presence of a clitic person marker for the object. In Iraqw, the object appears in the construct rather than the normal form only if it is placed after rather than before what is known as the selector (an auxiliary component featuring also person information). As for atypical case marking, in Capanahua, for example, the marking of the subject involves lengthening of the final syllable. In Waorani, human objects are followed by what Peeke (1994:269) calls affective markers, which are forms of the stative participle inflected for person. And in Coast Tsimshian, the case marking is by means of particles called by Mulder (1994:30) connectives, which combine the role of case markers and determiners and are attached not to the syntactic function that they mark but to the word immediately preceding it.

The above notwithstanding, in the vast majority of languages, either no case marking of core syntactic functions occurs with both independent person markers and lexical NPs, or both exhibit morphological case marking. This is so in 86 per cent of the languages in the sample for which I have the necessary data (N=379). The presence of morphological case marking with both types of nominals (48%) appears to be somewhat more frequent than its absence with both (38%). But this depends in part on areal and genetic affiliation. Morphological case marking is particularly characteristic of languages in Eurasia and Africa and conversely is rather uncommon in the languages of both South-East Asia and Oceania and North America.

The actual means of syntactic function encoding of person markers, be it in relation to lexical NPs or overall, has not been the subject of much typological interest. By contrast, what has aroused considerable curiosity and been considered as a potentially significant typological parameter is the nature of the alignment evinced by person markers as opposed to lexical NPs.

2.2.2.2 Morphological alignment

The term "alignment" when used in regard to syntactic functions denotes how core syntactic functions are organized relative to each other. Up till recently, the major patterns of alignment have been defined exclusively in relation to the arguments of intransitive and monotransitive clauses, that is with respect to the s, A and p. In the last couple of years, the notion of alignment has been extended to cover the patterns defined by the objects of monotransitive and ditransitive clauses. We will first consider the traditional patterns of intransitive and monotransitive alignment of person markers and then compare these to those found in ditransitive alignment.

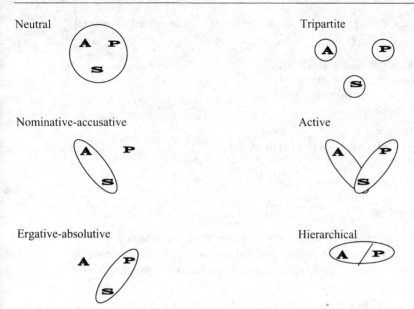

Figure 1 *Morphological alignment types in monotransitive clauses*

2.2.2.2.1 Monotransitive clauses   The alignment patterns found among the s, A and P are shown graphically in Figure 1. Neutral and tripartite alignments, on the one hand, and accusative and ergative, on the other, may be seen as opposites of each other. In a neutral alignment system the s, A and P are all treated identically, in a tripartite system each is distinct. In accusative alignment the s and A are treated alike in opposition to the P, while in ergative alignment it is the s and P that receive the same treatment while the A is distinct. Active alignment may be viewed as a hybrid of accusative and ergative. In active alignment there are two patterns of identification of the s; sometimes it is treated like the A and sometimes like the P. And finally, in hierarchical alignment there is variation in the treatment not of the s but of the A and P. Either one or the other is singled out for special treatment depending on which is higher on the person and/or animacy hierarchies.

The alignment of the s, A and P relative to each other may be determined on the basis of various criteria – morphological marking, syntactic behaviour and semantic properties. We will be considering only morphological marking. It must be pointed out, however, that there is an important difference in the interpretation of what constitutes neutral alignment with respect to morphological marking of dependent as opposed to independent person forms.[13] In the case of independent person forms, lack of phonological distinctiveness of the s, A and P, as illustrated

---

[13] It is important to note that since the dependent person markers used for the core syntactic functions may be of different types, say bound forms and clitics, it is customary to characterize the alignment of dependent person markers as a group rather than separately for bound forms as opposed to clitics or clitics as opposed to weak forms.

in (77) on the basis of the Cushitic language Iraqw, is interpreted as neutral alignment.

(77)   Iraqw (Nordbustad 1988:43, 50)
    a.   Aníng a   huuriim
        I   SELECT:1SG(S) cook:1SG
        'I am cooking.'

    b.   Aníng qaymo a   doósl
        I   field SELECT:1SG(A) cultivate:1SG
        'I am cultivating a field.'

    c.   Kuúng aníng i   atét
        you   me   SELECT:1SG(P) call:2SG
        'You call me.'

In the case of dependent person forms, on the other hand, the notion of neutral alignment is virtually always interpreted as meaning the absence of any type of dependent marking of the S, A or P rather than the presence of dependent person markers which are phonologically non-distinct. Thus, for example, if a language has one set of person clitics or affixes for the S, A and P, but the S/A markers occur in a different location from the P markers, it is typically classified as displaying accusative alignment of dependent person markers rather than neutral. A case in point is Kinyarwanda which, like many other Bantu languages, has phonologically identical S, A and P agreement markers with some classes of nominals. The examples in (78) involve the marker for the third-person plural animate class *ba-* which is located in immediately pre-stem position when it marks the P (78a), but as the first verbal prefix when it marks the S (78b) or A.

(78)   Kinyarwanda (Gary & Keenan 1977:88–9)
    a.   Yohani y-a-ba-kubis-e
        John   3SG-PAST-3PL-strike-ASP
        'John struck them.'

    b.   Abagore ba-a-kubis-w-e   na   Yohani
        women   3PL-PAST-strike-PASS-ASP by John
        'The women were struck by John.'

Whether considerations of location and order should continue to be taken into account in the determination of the alignment of dependent person markers is a controversial issue. The topic will be resumed in chapter 4, section 4.2.1.2. In what follows, I will adhere to standard practice, and identify neutral alignment in the case of dependent person markers with absence of such forms.

The distribution of the six types of alignment in Figure 1 with person markers is by no means uniform and moreover differs significantly with independent as compared to dependent person forms. The relevant data for independent and overt dependent forms among the languages in the sample are presented in Table 2.3. First of all, we see that neutral alignment of independent person markers is much more common cross-linguistically (42%) than with overt dependent person markers (19%). Secondly, though of the non-neutral alignments accusative

Table 2.3 *The alignment of independent and overt dependent person forms*

Alignment type	Independent forms N=386	(%)	Dependent forms N=402	(%)
Neutral	164	42.5	78	19.4
Accusative	165	42.7	231	57.5
Ergative	44	11.4	17	4.2
Active	3	0.8	26	6.5
Tripartite	2	0.5	0	0
Hierarchical	0	0	9	2.2
Split[i]	8	2.1	41	10.2

[i] The row labelled 'split' covers any form of split alignment (e.g. accusative/ ergative, active/tripartite, hierarchical/accusative, etc.) other than that involving neutral and non-neutral (e.g. accusative/neutral), which have been included under the relevant non-neutral alignments.

is the most frequent with both independent and dependent forms, the preference for accusative alignment over the other non-neutral alignments is much stronger with dependent markers than with independent ones. Well over half, 57 per cent, of the languages in the sample exhibit accusative alignment of dependent person markers. The corresponding figure in the case of independent markers is 42 per cent. This means that accusative alignment of dependent markers is favoured not only by languages which exhibit neutral alignment of independent forms but also ergative and other alignments. One such language is Tauya, spoken in the Madang Province, Papua New Guinea. As shown in (79), Tauya has ergative alignment with independent person markers but accusative with dependent ones.

(79)   Tauya (MacDonald 1990:93)
   a.   Ne-ni   na-yau-a-ʔa
        he-ERG 2SG-see-3SG-IND
        'He saw you.'
   b.   Ne   momune-a-ʔa
        he:ABS sit-3SG-IND
        'He sat.'
   c.   Ne   Ø-aʔate-I-ʔa
        he:ABS 3SG-hit-3PL-IND
        'They hit him.'

Note that whereas the bound person markers of the third-person singular S and A are rendered by the suffix -*a*, the P is marked by a prefix which for the third-person singular is zero. Ergative alignment of independent person markers but accusative of dependent ones is also found in various Australian languages, for example Djaru, Malak Malak, Murinypatya, Ngalakan, Ngandi, Pintupi, Rembarnga, Wardaman, Walpiri, Walmathari, Yulparija as well as in Byansi, Copainala Zoque, Hua, Ingush and Una.

Contrary to what is sometimes claimed, the converse split, ergative alignment with bound person markers but accusative with independent forms, does occur, but very rarely. Moreover, the ergativity tends to be manifested only with certain person-number combinations or in certain tenses or aspects. For instance, in Sumerian the ergative alignment of the bound person forms is found only in the "hermit" conjugation and only in the first and second persons. In the third person the alignment is tripartite (see below). Furthermore independent person markers appear to have been used essentially only for the s and A (Thomsen 1984:69). As shown in (80), the s and P are expressed by verbal suffixes and the A by a distinct set of prefixes.

(80)   Sumerian (Thomsen 1984:142–3)
  a.   Sa-e   iku⁴re-en
       you:NOM enter-1/2SG
       'You entered.'

  b.   Za-e   sag   (mu)-e-zig
       you:NOM head (mu)-2SG-raised
       'You raised the head.'

  c.   En-e   I-n-tud-en
       she   ?-3SG-BORNE-1/2SG
       'She has borne me.'

Other languages manifesting ergative alignment of at least some dependent person forms and accusative of independent are Badjiri, Hittite, Munduruku, Narinjari, Sahapatin and Wangaybuwan.

Arguably, the biggest difference between independent and dependent person forms in regard to alignment concerns active alignment. Active alignment with independent person markers is extremely rare. It is illustrated in (81) on the basis of Central Pomo, a language of California.

(81)   Central Pomo (Mithun 1993:122)
  a.   Mu.l   qa-wá-n
       he:AG biting-go-IMPF
       'He is eating.'

  b.   Mú-ṭu   ?ná=ya
       he:PAT mentally hide=wit (evidential)
       'He forgot.'

  c.   Mul   to'   dawáy=ya
       he:AG me:PAT wake=wit (evidential)
       'He woke me up.'

  d.   Mú-ṭu   ?a.   dawáy=la
       he:PAT I:AG wake-PERF
       'I woke him up.'

The only other instances of active alignment with independent person markers that I know of are in several dialects of the Kartvelian language Laz, in Batsbi, Eastern

Pomo, Imonda, Tsou and Lhasa Tibetan. By contrast, with dependent person markers, active alignment is virtually as common as ergative. It is especially frequent in North America (e.g. Acoma, Haida, Koasati, Lakhota, Oneida, Tlingit, Wichita, Yuchi) and South America (e.g. Apurina, Ika, Warekena, Yagua) but also attested in New Ginuea (e.g. Kewa, Nasioi, Yava) and South-East Asia and Oceania (e.g. Acehnese, Bukiyip, Larike, Semelai).

In regard to tripartite alignment there are no significant differences between independent and dependent forms. Tripartite alignment is the least common alignment with both. In the case of independent person forms there are, however, languages in which tripartite is the sole alignment. This is so, for example, in Lower Umpqua (Frachtenberg 1922b:575–6), a Siuslawan language of Oregon, and the Australian language Wangkumara, the tripartite alignment of which is illustrated in (82).

(82)   Wangkumara (Blake 1977:11)
  a.   Palu-ŋa ŋanyi
      die-PAST I:NOM
      'I died.'

  b.   Ngatu ŋaŋa   kalka-ŋa
      I:ERG 3SG:ACC hit-PAST
      'I hit her.'

  c.   Nulu   ŋaŋa kalka-ŋa
      3SG:ERG I:ACC hit-PAST
      'He hit me.'

In the case of dependent person markers, on the other hand, I do not know of any languages where tripartite would be the only alignment.

The last alignment type, hierarchical, is attested only with dependent person markers. It is illustrated in (83) on the basis of Nocte, a Tibetan language spoken in north India.

(83)   Nocte (Das Gupta 1971:21)
  a.   Nga-ma ate   hetho-ang
      I-ERG   I-ERG he:ACC teach-1SG
      'I will teach him.'

  b.   Ate-ma nga-nang hetho-h-ang
      he-ERG I- ACC   teach-INV-1SG
      'He will teach me.'

  c.   Nang-ma nga hetho-h-ang
      you-ERG I   teach-INV-1SG
      'You will teach me.'

We see that in Nocte there is a bound person marker on the verb only for one of the transitive arguments. In (83a) it is the A and in (83b,c) the P. Whether it is the A or the P that is encoded by the bound person marker is determined by which is higher on the person hierarchy of 1 > 2 > 3. If the higher-ranking argument is a P rather than an A, an additional inverse marker occurs on the verb, *h*, in (83b,c). The presence of such an inverse marker is not, however, a feature of all languages with hierarchical alignment. For instance, no inverse marker occurs in the Tupi-Guarani languages, such as Guajajara, Kamaiura or Wayampi or the Carib languages, such as Apalai, Galibi or Waiwai. Nonetheless, hierarchical alignment is often referred to as inverse.

The above differences in the distribution of morphological alignment with independent and dependent person markers are attributable to several factors, the nominal nature of independent person markers as opposed to the typically verbal location of dependent person ones, the difference in the discourse function of the two types of person forms and the semantics of the particular alignment types.

It is typically assumed (see, e.g., Comrie 1981) that the primary function of overt nominal marking is to distinguish and identify the syntactic functions and semantic roles of the verbal arguments and adjuncts. In the case of the S, A and P this may be achieved most economically by marking the P in accusative or A in ergative alignment and least economically by tripartite alignment. Thus the preference for accusative and ergative alignments as compared to tripartite. That accusative alignment should be preferred to ergative may in turn be attributed to the semantics of the two alignment types (e.g. Nichols 1992: 88–93). The former is seen to grammaticalize the subject–object relations, the latter the semantic relations of agent and patient. Semantic role encoding may, however, interfere with the expression of topicality which in most languages is associated primarily with the A and S. Subject–object encoding, on the other hand, does not, since the subject, which is itself typically taken to be a grammaticalized topic (cf., e.g., Comrie 1981:60) is generally unmarked. As for the rarity of active alignment with independent person forms, this may be attributed to the confusing nature of the double marking of the S. Note that given such double marking, on encountering a verbal argument one does not know whether it is an S, A or P until the verb or the second argument is reached. The non-occurrence of hierarchical alignment with independent person markers can be explained even more straightforwardly. Given the semantics of person markers, the marking of referential status on the person markers themselves is simply superfluous. This still leaves us with the relatively high incidence of neutral alignment with independent person markers to be accounted for. The most obvious explanation is that the A may be distinguished from the P not only by morphological marking but also by word order. Therefore one may well expect some languages to opt for the word-order option. Another reason for neutral alignment of independent person markers is that in many languages they are used so infrequently, dependent person markers being preferred, that their coding for syntactic function is not a high priority.

Turning to dependent person markers, as most dependent person markers develop from independent ones (see ch. 7), and the latter favour accusative alignment, so do the dependent forms. What needs to be accounted for independently is the relatively high incidence of active alignment and low incidence of neutral. If one accepts the accessibility explanation for the existence of dependent person markers briefly outlined in section 2.2.1.2, the relative infrequency of neutral alignment is hardly suprising. In fact, the tendency for attenuated encoding of highly accessible discourse referents leads us to expect dependent person markers in most languages. That they should be particularly likely to display accusative alignment follows, in turn, from the higher accessibility of referents expressed by subjects as opposed to no-subjects indicated earlier in (70). Arguably, therefore, it is the absence rather than the presence of dependent person markers that is in need of explanation.

Active alignment has been shown by Mithun (1991) to be dependent on a variety of semantic parameters such as control, instigation, affect, aspect associated with the lexical categorization of verbs. It should therefore be favoured by markers which are bound or otherwise attached to the verb. And this is indeed so. As we have seen in section 2.1.2, the vast majority of dependent person markers are tied to the verb. Interestingly enough, the languages which have active alignment with independent person markers do not have dependent ones bound to the verb.

2.2.2.2.2 Ditransitive clauses

The extension of the notion alignment from monotransitive to ditransitive clauses, as discussed by Dryer (1986), Croft (1990:100–8) and more recently elaborated by Haspelmath (2001), is predicated on the assumption that the analogues of the S, A and P are the P, T and R, respectively, where the P stands for the transitive patient, the T for ditransitive theme (patient) and the R for ditransitive recipient. The postulated correspondences between the S and P, A and T, and P and R respectively, are neither semantic nor morpho-syntactic, but hold at a more abstract level. The parallel between the S and the P is that they are the arguments relative to which the treatment of the A and P in monotransitive clauses, and T and R in ditransitive clauses are compared. The correspondence between the A and T is that each is semantically closer to the S and P respectively, than their co-arguments, the P in monotransitive clauses and R in ditransitive clauses. And by the same token, the P and R, are united by virtue of their dissimilarity to the intransitive S and monotransitive P respectively.

Assuming the above correspondences and adopting a purely formal approach to alignment in terms of the patterns of identification obtaining between three distinct categories of whatever type, the ditransitive counterparts of the major monotransitive alignments are as depicted in Figure 2. We see that each of the three monotransitive alignments corresponds to a ditransitive one. The most obvious is neutral alignment which in the case of monotransitive clauses reflects the identical treatment of the S, A and P, while in the case of ditransitive clauses the identical treatment of the P, T and R. Ditransitive neutral alignment is illustrated in (84) from Spoken Eastern Armenian, where the form of the second-person singular is *kez*, irrespective of whether it is a P (84a), T (84b) or R (84c).

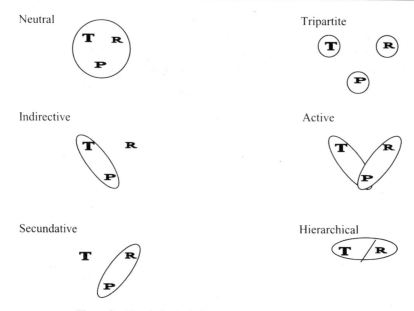

Figure 2 *Morphological alignment types in ditransitive clauses*

(84) Spoken Eastern Armenian (Polinsky 1996:314, 322)
    a. Jes kez t'es-a
        I   you see-AOR:1SG
        'I saw you.'

    b. Jes kez nram t'v-ec-i
        I   you him give-AOR-1SG
        'I gave you to him.'

    c. Jes nram kez t'v-ec-i
        I   him you give-AOR-1SG
        'I gave him to you.'

Corresponding to accusative alignment, which treats the S and A identically in contradistinction to the P, is indirective alignment, which treats the transitive patient P and ditransitive patient T in the same way in contradistinction to the recipient R. An example of indirective alignment of independent person markers is given in (85) from Wolaytta, a West Cushitic language of Ethiopia in which the T is in the accusative case (like the P), and the R is in the dative.

(85) Wolaytta (Lambertii & Sottile 1997:91, 92, 203)
    a. Ali aa   shoc'iis
        Ali him:ACC beat:3SG
        'Ali beat him.'

    b. Aa nee-w   aa   ?efaas^u
        she you-DAT him:ACC took:3SG
        'She took him for you.'

c.   Aa ?aa-w   gutta haatta ehass^u
     she he-DAT some water brought:3SG
     'She brought him some water.'

And corresponding to the identification of the S with the P in contradistinction to the A in ergative alignment is secundative alignment, which groups the transitive patient P with the ditransitive recipient R in opposition to the ditransitive patient T. Secundative alignment of independent person markers is illustrated in (86) from Spanish.

(86)   Spanish
  a.   La vieron   a   ella (pero no a   mi)
       her saw:3PL PREP her but   NEG PREP me
       'They saw her (but not me).'
  b.   Te   lo daran   a   ti, (pero no a   el)
       you him give:3PL PREP you but   NEG PREP him
       'They'll give it to you (but not to him).'
  c.   La lo daran   ella a   Antonia (no mi)
       her her give:3PL   her PREP Antonia NEG me
       'They sent her to Antonia, not me.'

There are also ditransitive versions of the three less common monotransitive alignments. An alignment corresponding to active, that is two patterns of identification of the P, one with the T and one with the R, is found, for instance, in various European languages which have a small class of verbs such as *trust*, *believe*, *help* which take a second argument in the dative case rather than the accusative. Thus the P may be seen as sometimes exhibiting marking corresponding to the T (accusative) and sometimes to the R (dative), as in the examples in (87) from Polish.

(87)   Polish
  a.   Jego   naprawdę kocham
       he:ACC really   love:1SG:PRES
       'Him, I really love.'
  b.   Jemu   naprawdę ufam
       he:DAT really   trust:1SG:PRES
       'Him I really trust.'
  c.   Jego   jej   dam
       he:ACC her:DAT give:1SG:FUT
       'Him, I'll give to her.
  d.   Ją   jemu   dam
       her:ACC he:DAT   give:1SG:FUT
       'Her, I'll give to him.'

Ditransitive tripartite alignment with independent person markers is attested, for example, in Sahaptin, a Native American language currently spoken in Oregon and Washington. As shown in (88), while the first person P in (88a) occurs in the nominative/absolutive case, the T in (88b) takes object marking and the R in (88c) special allative marking.

(88)   Sahaptin (Rude 1993:318, 320)
    a.   I-q'innun-a-aš   iwinš-nɨm inay
         3NOM-see-PAST-1SG man-ERG I:ABS
         'The man saw me.'

    b.   Ináy-naš itayman-a ɨwinš-mí-yaw
         I-OBJ   sell-PAST   man-GEN-ALL
         'He/she sold me to the man.'

    c.   ɨwinš-na pá-ʔtayman-a in-mí-yaw
         man-OBJ INV-sell-PAST I-GEN-ALL
         'He/she sold a man to me.'

Hierarchical alignment is also attested, though again only with respect to dependent person markers. In the Yuman language Jamul Tiipay (Miller 2001:162–3), for example, in transitive clauses there are portmanteau verbal prefixes which indicate the person/number of the A and the P. In ditransitive clauses, whether it is the T or the R that is marked by the portmanteau prefix together with the A depends on which is higher on the person hierarchy of 1 > 2 > 3. Thus in (89b) since the R outranks the T the person prefix marks the R, while in (89c) the T outranks the R, and consequently it is the T that is marked.

(89)   Jamul Tiipay (Miller 2001:141, 162–3)
    a.   Nye-wiiw
         1:2-see
         'I saw you.'

    b.   Xikay ny-iny-ma
         some 1:2-give-FUT
         'I'll give you some.'

    c.   Nyaach maap Goodwill ny-iny-x
         I:SBJ   you Goodwill 1:2-give-IRLS
         'I'm going to give you to Goodwill.'

Reliable data on ditransitive alignment with respect to person markers both independent and dependent are rather difficult to come by. First of all, in languages which have dependent person forms for the T and R, clauses in which the T, in addition to the R, is realized by independent person markers are pragmatically highly restricted. This is suggested in the English translations of the Spanish (86) and Polish (87). Consequently, it is rarely the case that such clauses feature in reference grammars. Another reason why clauses with independent person forms for both the T and the R may be lacking is that it is not uncommon for independent person markers to be restricted to human or animate referents. And as the referents of prototypical Ts are inanimate or at least non-human, the only ditransitive clauses with person referents that we are likely to encounter will feature an overt person referent just for the R, the T being either non-overt or rendered by a dependent person form. The typically inanimate nature of the T may also entail that there is no overt dependent person form for a third-person T. If this is so and if there are no clauses in which the T is a first or second person, then again the nature of the alignment can only be hypothesized on the basis of the marking of the P and R and potentially a lexical T.

The data on the distribution of ditransitive alignment with person markers that I have managed to collect suggest that there are no striking differences in the distribution of active and tripartite alignments between independent person markers and dependent ones. Both are rare.[14] There are, however, significant differences in the distribution of indirective and secundative alignments. With independent person markers, as with lexical NPs, indirective alignment is overwhelmingly dominant. With dependent person forms, on the other hand, both alignments are common, secundative being slightly more frequent than indirective.

The strong preference for indirective alignment with lexical NPs and independent person markers may be attributed to the fact that ditransitive clauses tend to be modelled metaphorically on spatial transfer (move theme to place) in which generally the theme is treated as monotransitive patient (e.g. Blansitt 1988, Heine et al. 1991). Therefore secundative alignment appears to be restricted to languages which have so-called differential case marking of the P, that is where there is either no marking or accusative marking of a non-human or inanimate P, and marking corresponding to that of the R with human or animate NPs. This is so, for example, in Spanish and other Romance languages such as Rumanian or Sardinian, in many Indo-Aryan languages (e.g. Bangala, Hindi) and also in very many Tibeto-Burman languages[15] (e.g. Burmese, Chepang, Copa Moca, Kham, and Kokborok).[16] If the differential case marking is extended to the T, secundative alignment will be found only with non-human or inanimate NPs, if it is suspended, secundative alignment will occur with both human and non-human NPs. With independent person markers, secundative alignment only arises in the latter case since independent person markers are typically necessarily human. Thus it may well be that secundative alignment with independent person markers is even less frequent than with lexical NPs. Whether this is indeed so is impossible to determine as clauses with Ts realized by independent person markers are extremely difficult to find. The only language which without doubt has secundative alignment with independent person markers that I know of is Spanish in which, as shown in (86), the "*a*" marking is suspended for the T. However, it needs to be mentioned that (86c) is a highly atypical construction, reference to

---

[14] With dependent person markers active alignment appears to be always highly restricted. For a detailed discussion of the issue see Siewierska (2003).

[15] LaPolla (1992), after considering 126 Tibeto-Burman languages, identified secundative alignment with lexical NPs in 84, indirective in 20 and neutral in 22.

[16] There are, nonetheless, languages with secundative alignment of lexical NPs in which the P does not exhibit differential case marking such as Comox, Mandak and Southern Sierra Miwok. The relevant structures correspond to the non-prototypical English ditransitives *We presented them with an award* or *We provided them with food*.

a second-person T being normally achieved just by a person clitic. All the other instances of potential secundative alignment of independent person markers that I have come across are based on examples such as (90), from the Papuan language Yessan Mayo, where the T is an inanimate lexical NP.

(90) Yessan Mayo (Foreman 1974:108, 109)
    a. An ti-ni akiye
        I her-ACC/DAT fear:PAST
        'I feared her.'

    b. An ti-ni awes nuwan
        I her-ACC/DAT food gave
        'I gave her food.'

In contrast to independent person markers, dependent forms are just as likely to manifest secundative as indirective alignment. Indirective alignment arises when the attenuated encoding of the P is extended to the T but not to the R. This is particularly likely in languages where the R is adpositionally marked as in the Mayan language Mam, for example.

(91) Mam (England 1983:60, 62,183)
    a. Ma qo-.ok- t-tzeeq'an-a
        REC.PAST 1PL(S/P)- POT-2SG(A)-hit-EXCL
        'You hit us.'

    b. Ma Ø-t-tzuy
        REC.PAST 3SG(S/P)-3SG(A)-grab
        'He grabbed it.'

    c. Ma-a7 Ø-tzaj ky-q'o-7n q-ee
        REC.PAST-EMPH 3SG(S/P)-DIR 3PL(A)-give-DIR 1PL-to
        'They gave it to us.'

Other languages displaying indirective alignment of dependent person markers include Acehnese, Apurina, Bulgarian, Ekari, Guarani, Hungarian, Jacaltec, Mupun, Paamese, Palikur, Coast Tsimshian, Yapese and Yupik. Alternatively, as Rs typically encode more accessible referents than Ts, the attenuated encoding found with highly accessible Ps may be extended to the R rather than to the T, giving rise to secundative alignment. This is most likely in languages in which the ditransitive alignment of lexical NPs and especially independent person forms is neutral, that is where the P, T and R receive the same type of encoding. The Uto-Aztecan language Cora, spoken in the state of Nayari, Mexico, may serve as an example.

(92) Cora (Casad 1984:329, 328, 330)
    a. Ha'ām^{w}a-seih ī ha'atɨ m^{w}ēhmi
        2PL-see ART someone you(PL)
        'Someone sees you (PL).'

b. Pa-ra-a-mʷareh
2SG-3SG-CMP-handle:PAST
'You handled it.'

c. Hāmʷa-a-ta-tíh   mʷēhmi í   ha'atí   i   cuaaša-ri
2PL-CMP-PERF-GIVE you:PL   ART someone ART pipe
'A certain man gave the pipe to you (PL).'

Note that apart for some phonological changes the same person prefix occurs on the verb in both (92a) marking the P and in (92c) marking the R, while there is no third-person prefix for the T corresponding to that of the third-person P in (92b). Some other languages exhibiting secundative alignment of dependent person markers are Cahuilla, Chumash, Kham, Konjo, Kwaza, Lango, Mono Alu, Nyulnyul, Palauan, Tigak, Turkana and Yava.

In the case of independent person markers there are some obvious relationships between the existing monotransitive and ditransitive alignments. Neither neutral nor ergative monotransitive alignment is likely to occur with secundative ditransitive alignment as this would involve marking of the T but not of the P and R. Such marking is found occasionally with lexical NPs (see note 19), but I have not come across any instances involving independent person markers. Accusative alignment, on the other hand, is compatible with both indirective and secundative alignment, though, as stated above, one would expect it to be more common with the former than with the latter. With dependent person markers, there are no obvious incompatibilities as far as the non-neutral alignments are concerned. Accordingly, all the possible combinations of the major monotransitive and ditransitive alignments are attested. However, ergative alignment seems to be more common with indirective (e.g. Abkhaz, Basque, Greenlandic, Jacaltec, Lak, Macushi, Trumai, Coast Tsimshian, Yupik) than with secundative alignment (e.g. Karitiana, Konjo, Limbu, Sierra Popoluca, Uma and Yava). The same holds for active alignment, which occurs together with indirective in, for example, Acehnese, Apurina, Guarani, Kewa, Koasati, Lakhota, Larike, Tonkawa, Warekena and Yuchi and with secundative in, for example, Ika, Nasioi, Oneida, and Tunica. Accusative alignment exhibits no preference for either indirective or secundative.

2.2.2.3 Morphological alignment and person

While there are considerable differences in the patterns of alignment found with independent as compared to dependent person forms, there are no substantial differences between the two with respect to the distribution of alignment relative to person. The relationship between person and alignment is, however, worth a brief look, since it is not as strong as sometimes suggested.

The most widely discussed person-based split in alignment involves accusative and ergative alignments. As discussed by Silverstein (1976) and Comrie (1981), among others, in accusative/ergative splits dependent on person, first and second persons are associated with accusative alignment, the third person with ergative alignment. Such a split in independent person markers is found, for example, in the Australian language Yuwaalaraay and in dependent person markers in Washo and several Salishan languages as well as in another Australian language Ngiyambaa. Although accusative/ergative splits with first person exhibiting ergative alignment were thought not to occur, Bickel (2001) reports precisely such a split in the Tibeto-Burman languages Hayu, Yamphu and Belhare. The split concerns the dependent person markers. The following examples are from Hayu where the first-person ergative s/p suffix is -ŋo (93a,b) in the non-past and -suŋ (93d,e) in the past.

(93)   Hayu (Michailovsky 1988:6–7, 20)
   a.   Gu   bUk-ŋo-m[17]
        I   rise-1SG:NON-PAST-MV
        'I will get up.'

   b.   Mi-ha gu   pUk-ŋo-m
        he-ERG me rouse-1SG:NON-PAST-MV
        'He will get me up.'

   c.   Ga   mi pUŋ-mi
        I:ERG   he rouse-MV
        'I will get him up.'

   d.   Gu   bUk-suŋ
        I   rise-1SG:PAST
        'I got up.'

   e.   Gu   top-sUŋ-ne-m
        me   hit-1SG:PAST-2PL-MV
        'You all hit me.'

   f.   Ga top-kUŋ-me-m
        I   hit-3–3PL-MV
        'I hit them.'

As the examples in (94) show, there is no overt person agreement for a third-person s/A in the past, but accusative agreement with a third-person P is marked by -kU(ŋ)/ko. (See also (93f) above.)

(94)   Hayu (Michailovsky 1988:13, 12, 14)
   a.   BUŋ
        lift
        'He got up.'

   b.   Ga   top-kUŋ-mi
        I:ERG   hit-3SG-MV
        'I hit him.'

   c.   PUk-ko
        lift-3SG
        'You/he got him up.'

---

[17] The final suffix -mi or -m marks the main verb of a declarative sentence in Hayu.

Ergative alignment solely in the first and/or second person has also been observed among independent person markers, though not with accusative alignment but rather with neutral or tripartite. According to Jacquesson (2001) this is the case in several Tibeto-Burman languages of the Naga group. In Khiamnungan, it is the first person that exhibits ergative alignment while the alignment of the second and third persons is neutral. As shown in (95), the first-person absolutive marker is *ni*, while the ergative marker is *ŋo*.

(95)   Khiamnungan (Jacquesson 2001:118–19)
    a.   Ni ší šī
          1SG come CONT
          'I come.'

    b.   Nja ni ep šī
          2SG 1SG see CONT
          'You see me.'

    c.   Ngo nja ep šī
          1SG 2SG see CONT
          'I see you.'

In Chang, ergativity is manifested in both first and second persons, but not in third. And in Konyak, the first person is tripartite, the second ergative.

The other major association between person and alignment is in relation to active alignment. Active alignment favours the first and second persons as opposed to the third. Thus, quite frequently, the first and second persons exhibit active alignment while the third is neutral, as in Koasati, Lakhota or Wichita. More rarely the active alignment of the first and second persons co-occurs with accusative or ergative in the third, as in Batsbi or Semelai.

No clear associations between person and alignment comparable to that involving accusative and ergative can be discerned in relation to splits involving other combinations of alignments. For instance, combinations of accusative and tripartite alignments or ergative and tripartite may involve the tripartite being displayed by the first and second persons, the accusative or ergative by the third, or vice versa. This holds both for independent person forms and for dependent ones. Some relevant patterns involving independent person markers are found in Australia. For instance, Arabana displays tripartite alignment with all persons in the singular, with the third-person plural and second and third dual, but accusative alignment with the first- and second-person non-singular. In the Waalubal dialect of Bandjalang tripartite alignment occurs with all person-number combinations but for the first-person plural, which is accusative. By contrast, in Wagaya, it is only the third-person singular which has tripartite alignment, the remaining forms being accusative. This is also the case in the Amerindian language Nez Perce. And in yet another Australian language Djabugay, tripartite alignment occurs in the first-person singular and in the third person for all numbers, while the first-person non-singular and second person display accusative alignment. A similar plethora of combinations is found with dependent markers. In Yukulta, tripartite alignment is manifested by the first-person singular and non-singular and the second-person singular, accusative alignment by the second-person non-singular and third person. In the Papuan language Yimas, the tripartite alignment is found with the first and second persons, the ergative with the third. Conversely, in the two Salishan languages Comox and Halkomelem, as well as the Australian language Wambaya, the tripartite alignment is confined to the third-person singular, the accusative is found with all other persons and numbers. And in Upper Chinook, tripartite alignment occurs with the third-person dual and plural and ergative with the first, second and third singular.[18]

Person-determined splits in ditransitive alignment are less common than those in monotransitive alignment. They do nonetheless occur. A language manifesting such a split is the previously mentioned Yimas which has secundative alignment of person agreement in the first and second persons but indirective in the third person. As shown in (96), the form of the first-person R marker ŋa- in (96b) is the same as that of the P in (96a).

(96)   Yimas (Foley 1991:206, 208)
   a.   Ma-ŋa-tay
        2SG-1SG-see
        'You saw me.'

   b.   Uraŋ   k- mpu-ŋa-tkam-t
        coconut VI:SG-3PL-1SG-show-PERF
        'They showed me the coconut.'

The form of the third-person R marker -akn in (97b), on the other hand, is quite different from that of the P na- in (96a) and T in (96b).

(97)   Yimas (Foley 1991:201, 212)
   a.   Na-mpu-tay
        3SG-3PL-see
        'They saw him.'

   b.   Na-mpi-tkam-r-akn
        3SG-3DU-show-PERF-3SG
        'They two showed it to him.'

Note also that while the first- and second-person R markers are prefixes, the third-person R markers are suffixes. Moreover, whereas the first- and second-person R forms are subject to the same hierarchical ordering restrictions as those affecting the A and P (see ch. 4, section 4.4.4.2), the third-person R forms are not.

---

[18] Three-way, as opposed to two-way, splits in alignment involving person are quite exceptional, but do occur. In Ilgar (Evans 2000:106), an Australian language of the Iwaidjan family, there is a tripartite split in alignment: first and second and third plural forms follow a tripartite system, third singular forms, an ergative system and the first- and second-person plural forms, an accusative system.

2.3 Discourse function

In contrast to the typologies of person markers based on morphophonological form and syntactic function, the typology of their discourse function is quite underdeveloped and under-investigated. Moreover, in comparison to the other two typologies it is also much more restricted in scope, since only independent markers appear to vary with respect to their discourse function. Dependent person markers invariably encode referents which are highly cognitively accessible and topical within the discourse. There may be different dependent markers for intra- as opposed to inter-sentential antecedents, but there do not appear to be distinct dependent markers solely for different information statuses of their referents within the discourse.[19] This follows largely from the fact that languages tend to have only one type of dependent person marker for a given syntactic function. Thus if a language has bound subjects it tends not to have also clitic or weak ones. And if a language has clitic objects it is unlikely to also have bound ones.[20] In the case of independent person markers, on the other hand, different paradigms for a given syntactic function may exist and may come to be associated with specific discourse functions.

The basic distinction made in regard to the discourse function of independent person forms is between emphatic and non-emphatic person forms. What is generally meant by emphasis is some kind of discourse prominence, typically either contrast (including counter-expectation) and/or intensification, where the latter includes meanings similar to those conveyed by expressions such as *none other than*, *even*, *the very person*, *on one's own*, *alone*, *without help*, *also* and *too*.[21] Both contrast and intensification can be expressed prosodically (via stress, loudness and/or intonation), morphologically (e.g. via the use of adverbials or special particles, clitics or affixes) and/or syntactically (via word order and special cleft or pseudo-cleft constructions). They can also be expressed by special emphatic person forms, used in conjunction with or in preference to, the strategies mentioned above. In English, for example, the *self*-paradigm, *myself*, *yourself*, *herself*, etc., may be used to convey certain types of emphasis, as illustrated in (98).

(98) a. She perceived him soon afterwards looking at herself, and speaking familiarly to her brother.
   b. I knitted it myself.
   c. I do not myself regard it as important.

---

[19] The intra- vs inter-sentential distinction is reflected in some languages by means of special reflexive and logophoric forms to be discussed in chapter 5.
[20] There are some exceptions to this. For example, Cora, Northern Tepehuan, the Northern Italian dialects Fiorentino and Trentino and Polish have both subject bound pronouns and clitics. And Dutch, Italian and Slovak have both clitic and weak object pronouns, at least under some analyses.
[21] Some linguists include under emphasis what others would consider as mere information focus, i.e. the most important or salient information in the clause.

Special emphatic person forms are not, however, a feature of all languages. As mentioned in 2.2.1.1, in some languages all independent person markers are seen to be emphatic.[22] Recall, for instance, the situation in Wari in which independent person forms are not only emphatic but never appear as straightforward verbal arguments. In other languages a given set of person forms may be used both non-emphatically and in emphatic contexts.

If we restrict the term emphatic person marker to a form designated for performing an emphatic function, rather than to a form that may but need not be used emphatically, emphatic person markers do not emerge as very common. This is especially so if we do not consider as special emphatic forms combinations of a person marker with an emphatic suffix (or clitic), such as -(i)y in Kashmiri (99a).

(99) Kashmiri (Wali & Koul 1997:197–8)
 a. Bɨ-y   gatsɨ   dili
     I-EMPH go:FUT   Delhi:ABL
     'I will (myself) go to Delhi.'

 b. Bɨ   chus ra:mɨ
     I   am   Ram
     'I am Ram.'

As (100) illustrates, the same emphatic suffix can be attached to constituents other than person markers.

(100) Kashmiri (Wali & Koul 1997:141)
      Ku:rɨ-y   chanɨ   ja:n
      girl-EMPH   is:not good
      'It's only the girl who is not good.'

Accordingly, Wali and Koul (1997:197) do not view Kashmiri as possessing emphatic person forms. This is the position that I too will adopt. In some languages, however, there are emphatic suffixes or clitics which attach only to person forms. This is the case, for instance, in the Tibetan language Mizo (Murthy & Subbarao 2000:781–2) with respect to the emphatic suffix -maah and the Papuan language Tauya (MacDonald 1990:148) in regard to the suffix -na(si). There is far less consensus in relation to whether such person plus emphatic marker combinations should or should not be considered as special emphatic person forms. For example, Murthy and Subbarao do view the relevant forms as such, while MacDonald does not. In what follows I will treat such combinations as emphatic person markers.

The emphatic person markers found in languages may be seen as comprising two main types: those functioning as arguments and those functioning as

---

[22] However, closer inspection often reveals that the forms in question are used also for referents that are less highly cognitively accessible and not solely for purposes of contrast or intensification. This is the case, for example, in Italian, Spanish, Polish and Kannada.

intensifiers. The argument forms are used as arguments in place of other non-emphatic independent person markers. Some examples of such forms are given in (101a, b) from the Papuan language of the Toricelli phylum Awtuw, in (102c) from the Quechuan language Inga and in (103b) from the Mande language of the Ivory Coast, Yaoure.

(101) Awtuw (Feldman 1986:44)
    a. An   ki-t-ik,   wan-wan æye pa-rokra
        you(DU) IMP-DU-sit 1SG-EMPH food HORT-cook
        'You two sit down, I'll cook the food.'

    b. Nan   də-k owna-y   ræw- ræw-e   kə-ma-puya
        we two FACT-IMPF-sleep-IMPF 3DU-EMPH-OBJ IMP-go-hit
        'We two are lying down, go hit them two.'

(102) Inga (Schwartz 1986:426)
    a. Pi-taca ri-nga
        one-Q go-FUT
        'Who will go?'

    b. Nuca-mi ri-sa
        I-FOC   go-1:FUT
        'I will go.'

    c. Nucaquin-mi ri-sa
        I:EMPH-FOC go-1:FUT
        'I myself will go.'

(103) Yaoure (Hopkins 1986:196)
    a. Ā jā jrà srɔ̄ kógθ
        I be lion near very
        'I am near the lion.'

    b. Mɛ̄ɛ̄ ci jrà srɔ̄ kógò
        I:EMPH be lion near very
        'I am near the lion (I am the one who is nearest the lion).'

As the Awtuw examples suggest, in Awtuw the emphatic markers, which are reduplicated versions of the non-emphatic forms, are mainly used in explicitly contrastive contexts. In Inga, on the other hand, the emphatic forms, which consist of the independent forms plus the morpheme *quin*, cannot be used contrastively. Their use corresponds to that of the English emphatic reflexives such as *I myself* (see below). The semantics of the Yaoure forms, which historically are a fusion of the regular subject marker and the morpheme of identification *bɛ*, is not quite clear. What appears to be involved is prominence on some relevant hierarchy, such as closeness to the lion in (103b).

The emphatic person markers functioning as intensifiers fall into two types, which following König and Siemund's (1999) classification of intensifiers, we will refer to as adnominal and adverbial.[23] In their adnominal use intensifiers combine with NPs to form another NP, e.g. *John himself, I myself* and thus may be seen as adjuncts to NPs. In their adverbial use, intensifiers function not as constituents of an NP but of the VP or clause. Among adverbial intensifiers two main types may be distinguished, which König and Siemund refer to as inclusive and exclusive. Inclusive intensifiers may be paraphrased as *also* or *too* and exclusive intensifiers as *alone, without help*. An example of a person-marked inclusive intensifier is given in (104) from the Papuan language Tauya and of a person-marked exclusive intensifier in (105) from Maale, an Omotic language of Ethiopia.

(104) Tauya (MacDonald 1990:149)
Ya-ʔumana te-amu-nani-ʔa
1SG-too get-1SG:FUT-ASRT-IND
'I too will get one.'

(105) Maale (Amha 2001:90–1)
Táání s'aabb-ó taasi kap-á-ne
1SG:NOM prison-ABS 1SG:alone guard-IMPF-AFF:DEC
'I am guarding the prison alone.'

Whether a given emphatic person form is functioning as an argument or as an intensifier is not always entirely obvious. The distinction between an argument and an adnominal intensifier may be clouded by the possibility of what could be considered to be an intensifier occurring without its head, as in the Turkish (106b) as compared to (106c).

(106)   Turkish (Kornfilt 1997:297)
  a. Bu kitab-i bén yaz-di-m
      this book-ACC I write-PAST-1SG
      'I wrote this book (It was I who wrote this book).'
  b. Bu kitab-i kendí-m yaz-di-m
      this book-ACC self-1SG write-PAST-1SG
      'I myself wrote this book.'
  c. Bu kitab-i ben kendí-m yaz-di-m
      this book-ACC I self-1SG write-PAST-1SG
      'I myself wrote this book.'

Kornfilt suggests that since independent subject forms are regularly omitted in Turkish it is reasonable to view (106b) as a version of (106c) with an elided pronoun. Under such an analysis, *kendím* is an intensifier in both clauses. However, in the absence of (106c), *kendím* in (106b) could well be considered as an emphatic counterpart of *ben* in (106a). In contrast to what happens in Turkish, in Lealao Chinantec, an emphatic person form can combine with a nominal, as in (107a),

---

[23] Intensifiers are often homophonous with reflexives. This is apparently because the latter derive from the former. For some discussion of this diachronic development see König and Siemund (1999).

but not with an independent person marker. Therefore, while in (107a) *ŋiá:*ᴴ qualifies as an intensifier, in (107b) it is difficult to regard it as such, unless one assumes that a pronominal head is obligatorily elided.

(107) Lealao Chinantec (Rupp 1989:82)
    a.   Hąᴹ baᴴ kaᴸ-ziá:ᴴ   ŋiá:ᴴ   ŋí?:ᴴ
        then AFF PAST-arrive REFL:3SG thunder
        'Then Thunder himself arrived.'

    b.   ?iᴴhiá?ᴹ nié:iᴴ hniáᴹ ŋiá:ᴴ
        very   like:3 me   REFL:3SG
        'He himself likes me a lot.'

In Modern English, intensifiers easily combine with subject person forms but not object ones, as evidenced by the unacceptability of the examples in (108).

(108) a.   *I will invite him himself.
     b.   *They should deliver it directly to us ourselves.

The self-forms may, however, occur in object position (in a non-reflexive reading) by themselves, as in (109), taken from Zribi-Hertz (1989:716, 709).

(109) a.   He sat down at the desk and opened the drawers. In the top right-hand one was an envelope addressed to himself.
     b.   And that was exactly it, he really did not care too much what happened to himself.

They thus appear to function here as arguments rather than intensifiers. But again, it could in fact be argued that they are adnominal intensifiers with a missing head.

There may also be problems in determining whether a given emphatic person form is an argument or an adverbial intensifier. This is especially so in languages in which person reference is indicated by verbal inflection and independent person markers are not obligatory, since lack of obligatoriness cannot be used as a factor in distinguishing between argument and adverbial status. Often word order or case marking may help one to decide. For instance, in the Sudanic language Ngiti, the emphatic person markers, which consist of the regular independent forms followed by the compound postposition *-tirɔ*, always occur, either clause initially as in (110a) or clause finally as in (110b).

(110)   Ngiti (Kutsch Lojenga 1994:200)
    a.   Ndɨ-tírɔ k'-ɔzʉ   wɔ-rɨ   bhǔkù
        He-EMPH 3SG-read:PERF:PRES DEM-EMPH book
        'He (himself) has read that book.'

    b.   Ma m-àrà   kòbi   'ɔ   mà- tɨrɔ
        I   1SG-go:PERF:PRES market in:DIR I-EMPH
        'I have gone to the market myself.'

When placed clause initially, as in (110a) the emphatic forms look like arguments, since this is the typical subject position, as we see on the basis of the placement of the regular independent form *ma* in (110b). However, since initial emphatic forms can also be located clause finally which, according to Kutsch Lojenga, is an adjunct position, in both instances, initial and final, they must be seen as adverbial intensifiers rather than arguments. To give another example, the Muskogean language Koasati, in addition to three series of person affixes, has the five sets of independent forms shown in (111).

(111) Koasati (Kimball 1991:417–23)

	simple	emphatic	autonomous	isolative	repetitive
1	anó	ana:bíno	aná:li	aná:łi	ana:kálo
2	isnó	isna:bíno	isná:li	isná:łi	isna:a:kálo
3	ibisnó	ibisna:bíno	ibisna:li	ibisná:łi	ibisna:kálo
1+2	kosnó	kosna:bíno	kosná:li	kosná:łi	kosna:kálo
2+2	hasnó	hasna:bíno	hasná:li	hasná:łi	hasna:kálo

The simple forms are used with the meaning 'too'. The emphatic forms are closest in meaning to the adnominally used English emphatic reflexives, as exemplified in (112).

(112) Ana:bí:no-k ca-ilhó:si-t anó:ka-toho-n am-asilhá:ci-t
       1:EMPH-SBJ 1SG-forget-CONN finish-RLS-SW 1SGDAT-ask-CONN
       akostinní:ci-t cokkó:li-l
       think-SS-CONN sit-1SS
       'I myself had completely forgotten, until he asked me, and I am now sitting and thinking of it.'

They are derived from the simple forms by means of the element *-a:bí:no*, which is related to the noun modifier *bí:no* 'even'. The autonomous forms related to the noun modifier *má:lo* 'one's own' indicate that the person to which the pronoun refers is solely responsible for the ensuing action. The isolative forms, which may be related to the verbal suffix *-máli* 'must', indicate that the person to whom they refer is alone or unaccompanied in the performance of the action involving the relevant person. The repetitive forms are translatable as 'again' and indicate that the action has been done once by the subject, and is being redone in exactly the same way. Examples of the last two uses are given in (113).

(113) Koasati (Kimball 1991:422–3)
   a. Im-aláhka-k   íkso-t   ibisná:ł-o-:si-Vhco-k
      3:POSS-relatives-SBJ non-exist-CONN 3:ALONE-be-DIM-HAB-SS
      at-pa:hókfa-t   á:ta-Vhco-toho-k
      person-live:with-CONN dwell-HAB-RLS-PAST
      'His relatives were no more, and he, completely by himself, lived with people and so used to live.'

   b. Ana:ká:lo-k incá:li-li-t
      1:REP-SBJ   write-1SS-PAST
      'I wrote it again.'

Since the meanings conveyed by some of these forms are clearly adverbial, especially of the isolative as in (113a) and repetitive as in (113b), one may be tempted to treat them as adverbial intensifiers. However, as the above examples reveal, all may be marked for subject by the suffix -*k*, which suggests that they are arguments.

Owing to the controversies surrounding what constitutes an emphatic person marker, it is rather difficult to advance any generalizations regarding their cross-linguistic properties. Nonetheless, my perusal of the literature suggests that intensive emphatics are more common than argument ones.[24] Moreover, of the languages that do have intensive person forms, some, like English, have both adnominal and adverbial ones, but others appear to display only adverbial ones. According to Dol (1999:73), this is so in the Papuan language Maybrat. The emphatic markers consist of the independent forms prefixed by *po-* which is translatable as 'alone' or 'on my/your own'. They are thus exclusive forms in the typology of König and Siemund. The typical use of these markers is as in (114).

(114)   Maybrat (Dol 1999:73)
            M-roh   p-ana   aya
            3UGR-descend EMPH-3PL water
            'They descended to the river on their own.'

Another language in which the only emphatic forms are exclusive ones is the previously mentioned Maale (Amha 2001:90). The relevant forms, illustrated earlier in (105), consist of the first syllable of the subject forms plus the suffix -*si*. There are also languages which appear to have only special forms for inclusive intensification. This is the case in the Malayo-Polynesian language of Sulawesi Padoe. Padoe has three paradigms of independent person markers, an independent set, an irrealis set and an additive set. The irrealis forms are used in the irrealis mood. The independent set are the most comon and occur as answers to questions, as the subject of an equative clause, as the objects of prepositions, in contrastive contexts and, with emphatic particles and clitics, in various emphatic contexts. The additive forms, on the other hand, are very infrequent. They have the meaning of 'too'. E.g.

(115)   Padoe (Vuorinen 1995:102)
    a.   Ku-sue-'iro le'iroda'a
         1SG-see-3PL 3PL:EMPH
         'I saw them too.'

    b.   Umono moema wute ka- no   poN-parenta leda'a
         he   ask   land so that-3SG govern   3SG:EMPH
         'He asked for land so that he too would govern.'

---

[24] It must be mentioned that more often than not intensifiers are not inflected for person. Such is the case, for instance, in Bangala, Dutch, German, Gujarati, Hindi, Japanese, Kashmiri, Korean, Malayalam, Mandarin, Oriya, Polish, Russian, Tamil and Udihe.

While most of the emphatic person forms, of whatever type, that I have come across involve whole paradigms, some languages have special emphatic person forms just for specific person categories. For instance, in Supyire and Ndyuka there are special emphatic person markers only for the third person (just in the singular in Ndyuka). And Basque and Kobon have special emphatic forms only for the first and second persons.

As illustrated most clearly by Koasati, languages may have several paradigms of person markers used for various types of emphasis or discourse prominence. Interestingly though, they do not tend to have distinct forms for degrees of emphasis. This tends to be expressed by whether or not a regular independent person marker is used in addition to the emphatic form, as in the case of the Turkish (106c) as compared to (106b). Alternatively, a higher degree of emphasis may be indicated by the addition of an emphatic particle to a special emphatic person form. This latter option is found, for example, in the Western Grassfields language of Cameroon, Mundani. As shown in (116), Mundani, in addition to a classless paradigm of independent forms, has a paradigm of emphatic forms, most of which still contain traces of the emphatic suffix -a.

(116)   Mundani (Parker 1986:132, 144)
        Classless indep   Emphatic
        1SG   mǎ/N-   m̀mɔ
        2SG   á   àwɔ̀
        3SG   tà   tòà
        1PL   bǎ   báá
        2PL   bǐ   biá
        3PL   bɔ̌   bɔ́bá

A higher degree of emphasis is achieved by adding to the emphatic forms the emphatic particle mbɔŋ, which also occurs in a variety of nominal constructions, or the singular subject pronoun ta followed by mbɔŋ. The second of these two possibilities is confined to elders and people of standing. Thus (117b) is more emphatic than (117a).

(117)   Mundani
    a. È   sú   á   m̀mɔ
        DUMMY   IM.PAST:say   LOC   1SG
        'It has been said by me.'

    b. È   sú   á   m̀mɔ m̀bɔ́ŋ/ m̀mɔ tà m̀bɔ́ŋ
        DUMMY   IM.PAST:say   LOC   1SG /   1SG
        'It has been said by me.'

Significantly, the greater the emphasis, the more encoding there is. Emphatic forms have more phonological substance than non-emphatic forms, and more emphatic forms have greater phonological and morphological substance than less emphatic forms.

3 The structure of person paradigms

In chapter 2 we looked at the major factors underlying the existence of different types of person markers. We concentrated on distinct types of paradigms of person markers as a whole, totally ignoring any differences in the internal structure of paradigms. Now it is time to shift the perspective and consider the type of variation found within person paradigms.

Contrary to what may be supposed, the person paradigms found cross-linguistically differ extensively. By way of illustration, Cysouw (2000) found 98 different paradigmatic structures among the 265 person paradigms that he analysed. This high degree of variation is primarily a reflection of the type of grammatical distinctions in addition to person encoded in the paradigm and of how they are distributed. However, it is also to some extent dependent on the type of assumptions made about paradigmatic structure. The two most common grammatical distinctions encoded together with person are number and gender. Number is by far the more common of the two, and also, in its interaction with person, the more complex. It has therefore constituted the basis of the existing cross-linguistic investigations of person paradigms, most notably those of Forchheimer (1953), Ingram (1978), Greenberg (1988, 1993), and most recently Cysouw (2000). There have been no parallel wide-scale cross-linguistic studies on gender in person paradigms but much is known about the issue from the works of Greenberg (1978), Corbett (1991) and Nichols (1992), among others. In our discussion we will be drawing heavily on the insights stemming from the above investigations. We will first consider paradigms which are defective in the sense that they do not distinguish all three of the grammatical persons from each other. Then we will take a closer look at the interaction of person and number. Next we will discuss the combinations of person and gender. Finally we will see whether there are any interesting relationships between the internal structure of paradigms and the typology of person forms discussed in chapter 2.

3.1 Fewer than three persons

Contrary to what might be expected, a distinction between first, second and third persons is not a feature of all person paradigms. By this I do not mean the absence of a special form for the third person, which is something that occurs fairly regularly in affixal paradigms. In paradigms which lack a third person or in which the third-person singular is expressed by zero, a distinction between the three persons is maintained, though only covertly expressed. A genuine failure to differentiate between the three persons is considerably less frequent and virtually all instances of it that I have come across involve dependent person markers.

The non-differentiation of the three persons may involve one of the four possibilities depicted in (1).

(1) a. 12 vs 3
    b. 1 vs 23
    c. 13 vs 2
    d. 123

The first and second persons may be homophonous and distinguished from the third (1a); the second and third persons may be homophonous and distinguished from the first (1b); the first and third persons may be homophonous and distinguished from the second (1c), and the same form may be used for all three persons (1d). All these possibilities are attested. The first is illustrated in (2) on the basis of the object suffixes in Chai, a Surmic language of the Nilo-Sahran family spoken in south-western Ethiopia.

(2)　　　　Chai (Last & Lucassen 1998:384, 386)
　　　　　Imperfective P suffixes　　Perfective P suffixes
　　　　　1SG -in　　　　　　　　　1SG -n^y
　　　　　2SG -in　　　　　　　　　2SG -n^y
　　　　　3SG -e　　　　　　　　　 3SG -u/-a
　　　　　1PL -ti/-u(n)　　　　　　1PL -(y)i
　　　　　2PL -u(n)　　　　　　　　2PL -y(i)
　　　　　3PL -e　　　　　　　　　 3PL -e

We see that the homophony between the first and second person in the imperfective is confined to the singular, while in the perfective it involves both the singular and non-singular. Some other languages in which this pattern may also be found in regard to the S/A affixes are Au, Burunge, Hamer and Pame in the singular, Barasano both in the singular and plural, Capanahua in the past tense, Tauya in the aorist in both singular and plural, Hunzib in the present tense, Darmiya in the plural of all tenses and, of course, English in the present singular.

The second pattern where the first person is distinguished from the rest is best known from the S/A suffixal paradigm in the singular in Standard Dutch. Quite exceptionally, it is in evidence not only in the suffixal S/A forms but also in the independent person markers in the dual and plural of the Papuan language Amele. The homophony in the independent forms is illustrated in (3).

(3)　　　　Amele (Roberts 1987: 208)
　　　　　　　　SG　　DU　　PL
　　　　　1　ija　　ele　　ege
　　　　　2　hina　 ale　　age
　　　　　3　uqa　　ale　　age

This pattern among the person affixes in the non-singular is quite common in New Guinea. It occurs in the S/A affixal person paradigms, for example, in Bena Bena, Ekari, Fore, Hua, Kapau, Kewa, Kobon, Kuman, Menya and Sentani and in the object affixes of Barai and Gapun. In Gadsup and Wambon, two other languages of New Guinea, the homophony between the second and third person is found in the object prefixes and subject suffixes, respectively, both in the singular and non-singular. In Wambon in the singular the marker for the non-first person is zero. By contrast, in Atakapa, an extinct Amerindian language, the zero form of the second and third persons is confined only to the subject suffixes in the singular. As shown in (4), no comparable reduction in person marking occurs in the object prefixes.

(4) Atakapa (Swanton 1929:125)

	S/A suffixes	P prefixes	
1SG	-ō	1SG	hi-
2SG	-Ø	2SG	n-/na
3SG	-Ø	3SG	ha-
1PL	-tse(l)/-tse	1PL	ic-
2PL	-tem	2PL	nak-
3PL	-ūl/-ti	3PL	cak

Some other languages with person paradigms exhibiting a two-way distinction between the first person vs second and third are Chacobo in the plural of the S suffixes, Chukchee in the S prefixes, Chitimacha in the S/A suffixes, Dime in the singular and plural of the S/A suffixes, Idu in the present and past S/A suffixes, Vinmavis in the dual and plural S/A prefixes and the four Nakh-Dagestanian languages – Akhvakh, Megreb, Tsakhur, Zakatal'.

The third, 13 vs 2, pattern is less common than the other two. It is illustrated in (5) on the basis of the Papuan language Koiari, in which it occurs in the realis mood in the indicative.

(5) Koiari (Dutton 1996:23)

	Present	Past
1SG	-ma	-nu
2SG	-a	-nua
3SG	-ma	-nu
1PL	-a	-nua
2PL	-a	-nua
3PL	-a	-nua

Note that only two forms are used for the whole paradigm (see also the Ekari paradigm, further below). Homophony between the first and third persons also occurs in Spanish, in various tense-aspect-mood inflections, including the "preterito imperfecto", Icelandic, in the preterit inflection of "weak" verbs, Old English, in the inflection of strong verbs and Darmiya, Ika and Kalkatungu in the singular. In the last four, the form of the first- and third-person singular is zero. In the remaining languages with the 13 v 2 pattern, that I know of, the homophony is between the first person and only either the masculine or feminine third-person form. Homophony between the first-person singular and third-person masculine is the less common of the two. It is found in the Arawakan language Apurina, in the case of the P suffixes (6).

(6) Apurina (Facundes 2000:352)
P suffixes

	SG	PL	
1SG	-ru	1PL	-wa
2SG	-i	2PL	-i
3SGM	-ru	3PLM	-ru
3SGF	-ro	3PLF	-ro

Homophony between the first person and the third feminine occurs in the subject affixes of two tenses in the Papuan language Ekari, as illustrated in (7), and in the subject affixes of Cushitic languages such as Oromo, the Jara dialect of Boni and Iraqw.

(7) Ekari (Doble 1987:89)

	Today future	Tomorrow future
1SG	-pig-	-t-
2SG	-pag-	-tag-
3SGM	-pag-	-tag-
3SGF	-pig-	-t-
1PL	-pag-	-tag-
2PL	-pig-	-t-
3PL	-pig-	-t-

In Boni and Iraqw the same form is also used for the second-person plural.

The existence of the last pattern, homophony between all three persons, rests on the assumption that the category of person is distinguished somewhere else in the paradigm, that is that the homophony occurs only within a particular number category, be it singular or non-singular. The only cases of it that I have encountered, however, involve the non-singular, as in the Papuan language Koiari, exemplified in (5) above, as well as in Barai, another Papuan language, in which the homophony occurs with all types of verbs, dependent, medial and final. Only the tense/person suffixes found with final verbs are illustrated in (8).

(8) Barai (Olson 1975:510)

	Present	Imperfect	Past
1SG/123PL	-jo/-vo	-ja/-ve	-i/-e
2SG/3SG	-no/-mo	-ne/-me	-i/-e

Observe that as in Koiari and Ekari only two forms are used for the whole paradigm in the present and imperfect. In the past, there is only one form. The person category has totally disappeared. Homophony between all three person categories is thus a feature of a collapsing person system. It is therefore not surprising that it occurs in earlier stages of the Germanic languages which subsequently lost, or nearly lost, their verbal person markers, such as Old English as well as Old Saxon and Old Frisian. The pattern is still in evidence in present-day English, in which even the 12 vs 3 distinction in the present singular is neutralized in the plural.

3.2 Variation with respect to number

The existence of a number distinction in person paradigms was taken by Greenberg (1963:96) to be universal. Subsequent research has revealed that this is not so. There are languages which exhibit no number oppositions in person paradigms. Such a language is Mura Pirahã, an Amazonian language of Brazil, discussed by Everett (1986). Pirahã has two person paradigms, a paradigm of independent pronouns and a corresponding paradigm of clitics used for all three major grammatical functions s, A and P. As (9) illustrates, neither the independent forms nor the clitics are marked for number.

(9)　　Mura Pirahã (Everett 1986:280–1)
　　　　Independent　　Clitic
　　　　1 ti　　　　　　1 ti
　　　　2 gíxai　　　　 2 gí/gíxa
　　　　3 hiapióxio　　 3 hi/xi/xís

In fact, according to Everett there is no grammatical number in the language at all. The only way to indicate reference to more than one person is by conjunction of person markers, as depicted in (10).

(10)　　Ti gixai pio ahápii
　　　　1　2　　also go
　　　　'You and I will go.' (i.e. we will go)

Note that the conjunction is not overtly expressed. Lack of number marking in any person paradigm is highly exceptional. More commonly, languages lack number marking in reduced pronominals but do display it in independent forms. This is the case in Washo, which has a singular/dual/plural opposition in independent person forms, as illustrated in (11), but no number contrasts in the s/A prefixes. The s/A prefixes are: *le* 'first person', *m-* 'second person' and *ʔ/Ø* 'third person'.

(11)　　Washo (Jacobsen 1979a:146, 148)

	SG	DU	PL
1 INCL		léši	léw
1 EXCL	lé	léšiši	léwhu
2		mí	míší	míw
3		gí	gíší	gíw

The lack of a number opposition in Mura Pirahã and in the person affixes in Washo is quite uncontroversial. However, whether or not a specific person paradigm should be seen as exhibiting a number opposition is not always so straightforward. Particularly problematic in this context is the presence of an inclusive/exclusive distinction, which is something that we will be discussing in detail further below. Another set of problems arises from the morphological expression of number.

Number in person paradigms is typically indicated by suppletive forms (e.g. *I* vs *we*), basically unsegmentable or difficult to segment portmanteau person/number forms or affixation. In the case of affixation, generally the number affixes are attached directly to the markers of person and the two constitute an integral unit, as illustrated in (12) from the Tibeto-Burman language Mizo, where the plural marker is the suffix *-ni*.

(12)   Mizo (Murthy & Subbarao 2000:778)
       SG   PL
     1 kei   1 keni
     2 nang 2 nangni
     3 ani   3 anni

When, however, the markers of person and number are separate, it is not always clear whether the person paradigm should be seen as evincing a number opposition. Consider the situation in Chalcatongo Mixtec, an Otomanguean language spoken in south-central Mexico, for example. Chalcatongo Mixtec has both independent and clitic person forms for the first, second and third persons and for the first-person inclusive. Plural number may be indicated by a variety of morphological and syntactic means including the addition of the prefix *-ka* to the verb, as in (13a) and the use of the plural word *xina?a*, as in (13b) or both, as in (13c).

(13)   Chalcatongo Mixtec (Macaulay 1996:81)
  a.   Ká-xīnū-ro
       PL-run-2
       'You (PL) run.'

  b.   Ndíto-to   xiná?a
       be awake-3 PL
       'They are awake.'

  c.   Ka-xã?ã-Ø xiná?a be?e
       PL-go-3   PL   house
       'They went to (their) house.'

Though number may be expressed with each of the three persons, since this is optional and there is no unique way of doing so, it would be difficult to see number as being part of the person paradigm in this language. The same applies to the verbal person paradigm in the Tibeto-Burman language Limbu, though here number is obligatorily expressed together with person, and not infrequently, several times (see 14c, below). Limbu has an array of number affixes which include the suffix *-i* used to indicate plurality of first- or second-person S (14a) or P (14b), the suffix *-m* which marks plurality of a first- or second-person A (14c), the prefix *me-/m-* used to encode the plurality of a third-person S or A (14d) and the suffix *-si* for indicating the non-singularity of a third-person P (14c).

(14) Limbu (van Driem 1987:95, 99, 85)
    a. Kɛ-ye.-r-Ø-i
         2-laugh-PAST-PL(S)
         'You (PL) laughed.'

    b. Kɛ-Ø-Ø-dum-Ø-i-Ø   Ø-Ø-lɔ?r-ɛ -Ø
         2-3-SG-run into-PAST-PL(P) -PERF 3-SG-say-PAST-PERF
         'She said that she ran into you (PL).'

    c. Kɛ-ghɔnch- Ø-u-m-si-m-Ø
         2-stir-PAST-3(P) -PL(A) -NON-SG(PAT) -PL(P) -PERF
         'You (PL) stirred them.'

    d. Kɛ-Ø-m-hip-Ø-Ø-Ø
         2-3-PL (S/A) -hit-NON-PAST-SG-PERF
         'They'll hit you.'

As we can see in the examples above, while the markers of person, with the exception of the third-person P, occupy the first prefixal slot in the verb, the above four number affixes occupy four different positions. Again, they cannot be considered as belonging to the actual person paradigm. In Pipil, an Uto-Aztecan language of El Salvador, by contrast, although, as shown in (15), the subject person and number markers are discontinuous, there is one number suffix used with each of the three persons, and, as (16) illustrates, it always occurs as the last verbal affix.

(15) Pipil (Campbell 1985:54–6)

	SG	PL
1	ni-	1 ti. .-t
2	ti-	2 an. .-t
3	Ø-	3 Ø. .-t

(16) a. Ti-mitsin-ita-ke-t
         1PL-2PL(P) -see-PAST-PL
         'We saw you (PL).'

    b. Ø-tech-ita-ke-t
         3-1PL(P) -see-PAST-PL
         'They saw us.'

The number suffix is obligatory with non-singular person forms and is exclusive to such forms; it does not mark plurality of NPs. It is thus much more reasonable to treat the number affix as part of the person paradigm.

As extensively discussed and documented by Corbett (2000), number is by no means a simple category. This is nowhere more evident than in its relationship to person. Since the most commonly found number opposition in person paradigms is the singular/plural distinction, let us consider this number opposition first.

3.2.1 More than one person and the inclusive/exclusive distinction

What is typically understood by the singular/plural opposition is a distinction between one and more than one. This distinction is not, however, necessarily interpreted in the same way with respect to person markers as in the case of nouns. A singular noun refers to a single token of the entity denoted by the noun and a plural noun refers to multiple tokens of the relevant entity; thus *books* refers to more than one instance of the class of objects called *book*. Plural third persons are interpreted in an analogous way, that is they refer to third parties consisting of several individuals or items. Plural first-person forms, by contrast, only very rarely refer to more than one speaker. The English *we* may identify several or more speakers in a swearing-in ceremony or some other special occasion when a number of people are actually speaking simultaneously. In all other instances *we* does not identify more than one speaker but rather the speaker and somebody else. This somebody else may be just the addressee, as in (17a), some other individual or group of individuals and the addressee, as in (17b), or some individual or group of individuals among which the addressee is not included, as in (17c).

(17) a. We've got a bond in common, you and I.
 b. You, Anne and I are working ourselves to death.
 c. Me and Sarah Jones, we went up early.

The four possible interpretations of the first-person plural may be depicted schematically as: 1+1, 1+2; 1+2+3 and 1+3 respectively.

The second-person plural is also open to two interpretations. Compare the examples in (18a) and (18b).

(18) a. You ought to be ashamed of yourselves, children.
 b. You and John will have to cook for yourselves.

In (18a) both the forms *you* and *yourselves* refer to an addressee consisting of more than one member, which is made explicit by the NP *children*. In (18b) *yourselves* refers to a singular addressee (you) and a third party, John. The two interpretations can be depicted as 2+2 and 2+3, respectively.

The referential interpretations of plural number with the three persons are summed up in (19).

(19)   1+1   more than one speaker
        1+2   the speaker and addressee
        1+2+3 the speaker, addressee and minimally one other
        1+3   the speaker and other
        2+2   more than one addressee
        2+3   the addressee and minimally one other
        3+3   more than one other

The two interpretations of the second-person plural appear not to be formerly distinguished in languages (see Moravcsik 1978:356; Greenberg 1988:14; Cysouw

2000:71).[1] Nor is the rare 1+1 reading of the first-person plural. By contrast, various combinations of the other three interpretations of the first person frequently are distinguished.

Most commonly, languages have one form for the interpretations which include the addressee, i.e. 1+2 and 1+2+3 and another for the 1+3 interpretation under which the addressee is excluded. Not suprisingly, the two forms of "we" are referred to as inclusive and exclusive. The inclusive/exclusive opposition is exemplified in (20) on the basis of the independent forms in So, an Nilo-Saharan language spoken in north-eastern Uganda.

(20) So (Carlin 1993:79)
      1SG   aya
      2SG   bia
      3SG   ica
      1+2+3/ 1+2 **inia**
      1+3   **isia**
      2PL   bitia
      3PL   itia

There are also languages which have grammaticalized a somewhat different two-way opposition of the first-person complex, namely that of the speaker and hearer 1+2 as opposed to 1+2+3 and 1+3. Such an opposition in independent person markers is found in Hatam, a West Papuan language spoken in Irian Jaya.

(21) Hatam (Reesink 1999:40)
      1SG   da
      2SG   na
      3SG   no(k)
      1+2+3/ 1+3 **nye**
      1+2   sa
      2PL   je
      3PL   yo(k)

Another possible opposition within the first-person plural is between 1+2+3 and a grouping of 1+2 and 1+3, as illustrated in (22) from Yaoure, a Mande language of the Ivory Coast.

(22) Yaoure (Hopkins 1986:192)
      1SG   ā
      2SG   ī
      3SG   ē
      1+2+3   kàà
      1+3   kŪ
      1+2   kŪ
      2PL   kā
      3PL   ō

---

[1] But if a language has a dual just for the second person then second-person dual will be 2+2 and second plural will be 2+3; alternatively second-person dual could be 2+2 and 2+3 while second plural could be 2+2+2 and 2+3+3. This seems to be the case in Nambiquara and Dizi.

Paradigms in which each of the three readings of the first-person plural are expressed by a separate form are attested as well. The independent markers in the Atampaya dialect of Uradhi, an Australian language spoken in Cape York, are a case in point.

(23) Uradhi (Crowley 1983:33)
      1SG   ayu
      2SG   antu
      3SG   ulu
      1+2+3 **ana**
      1+3   **ampu**
      1+2   **ali**
      2PL   ipu
      3PL   ula

Although I have been using the term first-person plural for the three interpretations of "we" introduced in (19), as none actually identifies more than one speaker, the term plural seems to be hardly appropriate. The term plural is particularly misleading in the case of the forms for 1+2 as in Hatam or Uradhi, which, unlike all the other forms of "we", refer to exactly two individuals. Consequently under traditional analyses such forms have been treated as a first-person dual. According to this analysis, Uradhi would have not a singular/plural opposition in the first person, but a three-way number opposition of singular/dual/plural with the 1+2+3 form being a plural inclusive and the 1+3 form a plural exclusive, as shown in (24).

(24)
	SG	DU		PL	
1	ayu	1+2	**ali**	1+2+3	**ana**
2	antu			1+3	**ampu**
3	ulu			2PL	ipu
				3PL	ula

The treatment of the 1+2 forms in languages such as Uradhi as duals is, however, also questionable as the referential value of these forms is not the speaker plus some other individual but rather the speaker and addressee. Some linguists therefore refer to such forms as dual inclusive. This analysis has its drawbacks too, namely it entails recognizing an additional number opposition just for the first person.[2]

An alternative analysis, first suggested by Thomas (1955) for the Philippine language Illocano, is to treat the 1+2 forms as belonging to the same number category as the first-, second- and third-person singular. In view of the fact that

---

[2] As we shall see below, the 1+2 category is treated in two different ways in languages; in some it is morphologically a dual (has the morphology associated with other dual forms in the paradigm) which is also an inclusive in that it includes the addressee, while in other languages it is morphologically an inclusive form which refers to exactly two participants, and thus is only referentially a dual.

paradigms analysed in this way obviously cannot be seen as displaying a singular vs plural number opposition, they are referred to as having a minimal vs augmented distinction. The term *minimal* refers to the smallest number possible given the person specification of the category, while the term *augmented* refers to a number larger than the smallest one otherwise possible, given the person specification of this category. The Uradhi paradigm presented in (23) recast in terms of the minimal/augmented analysis is shown in (25).

(25)
	Minimal	Augmented	
1	ayu	1+3	**ampu**
1+2	**ali**	1+2+3	**ana**
2	antu	2+2	ipu
3	ulu	3+3	ula

Yet another analysis not only of the speaker-addressee dyad in languages such as Uradhi, but of the singular/plural opposition as applied to person has been recently suggested by Cysouw (2000:86). Cysouw contends that the above problems in the interpretation of number with person can be better dealt with if the singular/plural distinction is interpreted as a distinction between single individuals and groups of individuals. Under such an analysis, the 1+2 dyad clearly belongs together with what are traditionally considered to be the first-, second- and third-person plural forms in the group category. In order to distinguish the 1+2 forms from the other first-person forms, Cysouw calls the 1+2 forms minimal inclusive, the 1+2+3 augmented inclusive and the 1+3 exclusive. The group categories together with the singular give us the person system in (26).

(26)
	Singular	Group	
		1+2	minimal inclusive
1		1+2+3	augmented inclusive
		1+3	exclusive
2		2+3	
3		3+3	

The Uradhi paradigm in terms of this analysis is shown in (27).

(27)
	Singular	Group	
1	ayu	1+2	**ali**
		1+2+3	**ana**
		1+3	**ampu**
2	antu	2+2	ipu
3	ulu	3+3	ula

Cysouw suggests that the eight-person distinctions shown in (26), three singular and five group, constitute a much better point of reference for the analysis of person paradigms than the traditional six-way distinction of three persons and two numbers. First of all, the eight-person paradigm makes explicit that what is of relevance for the group categories is not so much the number of participants

Table 3.1 *The subdivision of the first-person complex*

	(a) No we	(b) Unified we	(c) Only incl	(d) Minimal incl	(e) Augmented incl	(f) incl/excl	(g) Minimal/ augmented
1+2	–	A	A	A	A	A	A
1+2+3		A	A	B	B	A	B
1+3		A	–	A	A	B	C

The typology of the first-person complex in this table is a slightly modified version of Cysouw's typology. It is taken from Siewierska and Bakker (forthcoming), where it is discussed in detail.

but their nature. Secondly, it fully integrates the traditional inclusive/exclusive distinction into the structure of person paradigms and thus allows for a unified account of languages which do and do not instantiate this distinction in various ways (see below). And thirdly, by recognizing a group category rather than a plural number, it does away with the problem of the different interpretation of the notion of plurality when applied to person markers as compared to nominals.

An analysis of the first-person complex using Cysouw's approach results in the seven-way typology of the first-person complex illustrated in Table 3.1. The "no we" pattern relates to paradigms in which no distinction is made between "I" and "we", as is the case of the person paradigms in Mura Pirahã, exemplified earlier in (9). The "unified we" pattern covers paradigms in which one form is used for all three of the interpretations of "we" distinguished in (19), as is the case in English, for example. The "only-inclusive" pattern captures paradigms in which there is also just one form of "we", but it does not cover all the three interpretations distinguished in (19). Rather the special form is used only for the interpretations involving the addressee, i.e. 1+2 and 1+2+3. Such a paradigm is illustrated in (28) from Chalcatongo Mixtec.

(28)   Chalcatongo Mixtec (Macaulay 1996:139)
                               1+2   žóʔó
        1   rúʔú   1+2+3   žóʔó
        2   róʔó
        3M   càà
        3F   nāʔā
        3animal   kɨtɨ
        3supernatural íʔa, íža

Note that there is no non-singular form in the paradigm other than that for the only inclusive. In Chalcatongo Mixtec, as in other languages exhibiting the only-inclusive pattern, the exclusive 1+3 combination is expressed by the first-person form accompanied by non-singular number marking, as shown in (29b) and (29c) where -rí is the first-person clitic corresponding to rúʔú.

(29) Chalcatongo Mixtec (Macaulay 1996:139, 81, 114)
  a. Ni- žee-rí
     CMP-eat-1
     'I ate (it).'
  b. Ká-satíũ-rí
     PL-work-1
     'We're working (exclusive of hearer).'
  c. Kúžaa-ri núndua xiná?a-ri
     live-1   Oaxaca PL-1
     'We (exclusive) will live in Oaxaca.'

The remaining patterns have already been illustrated. The minimal inclusive is the pattern found in Hatam independent forms presented earlier in (21). The augmented inclusive pattern covers paradigms such as those in Yaoure, shown in (22). And the minimal augmented covers paradigms such as (23) from Uradhi.

Of the above patterns of encoding of the first-person complex, by far the most common are the "unified we" and the "inclusive/exclusive" ones. Among the independent person paradigms of the languages in the sample, a little over half (55.5%) have a "unified we" and just under a third (32%) the "inclusive/exclusive" pattern. The two patterns thus account for 87 per cent of the independent person paradigms in the sample. Of the remaining patterns, "minimal augmented" is marginally more common than the others occuring in 4 per cent of the languages.[3] Some languages, other than Uradhi, with independent person paradigms manifesting this pattern are Guugu Yimidirr, Malak Malak, Marunguku, Tiwi, Wardaman (all in Australia), Gude, Nivkh, Hatam, Kapampangan, Kawaiisu and Koh Lakka.[4] Next in line in terms of frequency is the "only-inclusive" pattern (2.75%). It occurs in the independent person paradigms of various languages in the Americas such as Aymara, Campa, Canela Kraho, Jaquaru, Kwaza, Wichita and Tarascan. The only instances outside the Americas of such paradigms of independent forms that I have come across are in Chrau, a Mon-Khmer language of Vietnam, and the Austronesian language Imonda. The minimal inclusive pattern exhibits a somewhat more varied geographical distribution. Apart from Hatam it is found in the independent person forms, for example, of Lele, Nigiti (Africa), Tagalog, Uma (Austronesia), Koiari (New Guinea), Lakhota, Mountain Maidu (North America), Pech, Selknam (South America) and in Australia Nyulnyul (the current person

---

[3] I have included under the *min/aug* pattern the famous five "we" paradigms, often called unit augmented, found among some of the non-Pama Nyungan languages of Australia. Under the traditional analysis these paradigms are seen as having an inclusive/exclusive contrast in the dual and plural and an inclusive trial encompassing 1+2+3. Cysouw (2000:265) treats the trial as a special type of dual. Instead of a straightforward inclusive/exclusive opposition in the dual and plural, there is an opposition between an augmented inclusive vs exclusive, and the minimal inclusive 1+2 is undifferentiated.
[4] To this category are likely to belong all paradigms which are classified as having a dual for the first person and have an inclusive/exclusive opposition.

forms) and Tiwi (the emphatic forms).⁵ Even less common than the two inclusive patterns is the "no we" pattern (1.75%). Languages which have no special form for "we" in their independent person markers include Kawesquar, Kiowa, Maricopa, Oneida and Salt Yui. The rarest pattern is the augmented inclusive (1.25%). The languages in the sample, in addition to Yaoure, that display it in their independent person markers are Bunuba, Gooniyandi, Yidin (all three Australian) and Fula.

We will return to this eight-person paradigm in section 3.2.4, but first let us consider the other types of number distinctions that may be in evidence in person paradigms.

3.2.2 Duals and larger numbers

Number distinctions in person markers are not confined to the singular/plural (group) opposition. Many languages in addition to a plural (group) have a dual for sets of exactly two participants. The presence of a dual obviously has an effect on the interpretation of the plural; in the presence of a dual, the plural always denotes at least three participants. As in the case of the plural, the first- and second-person dual are referentially ambiguous. A first-person dual is open to a 1+2 interpretation or a 1+3 reading. A second-person dual may refer to two addressees, 2+2 or an addressee and one other individual 2+3. Again, distinct forms for the two interpretations are only found with respect to the first-person dual. Traditionally the 1+2 reading is referred to as a first-person dual inclusive and the 1+3 reading as a first-person dual exclusive.

The existence of a 1+2 vs 1+3 opposition in the dual typically implies the presence of such an opposition in the plural, as illustrated in (30), from Kunama, a Nilo-Saharan language of Eritrea.

(30)   Kunama (Bender 1996:18)
           SG   DU   PL
                        1+2 kiime   1+2+3 kime
        1 'aba   1+3 'aame   1+3+3 'ame
        2 'ena   2+2 'eeme   2+2+2 'eme
        3 'unu   3+3 'iime   3+3+3 'ime

This is so in thirty-nine of the forty-five languages in the sample that have a dual opposition. They include: languages from the Pacific (e.g. Bali-Vitu, Lavukaleve, Maori, Nakanai, Rapanui, Samoan, Yapese), New Guinea (Tehit, Vanimo, Waskia), Australia (e.g. Ngiyambaa, Nyangumarta, Panyjima, Yulparija, Wambaya), the Americas (e.g. Lower Umpqua, Mohawk, Trumai, Wasco-Wishram, Washo) and South-East Asia (e.g. Akha, Atsi, Maru, Mundari

---

⁵ Greenberg (1988:9) considers the Siouan language Assiniboine to be of this type. However, the distinction between 1+2 vs 1+2+3 and 1+3 in Assiniboine is not actually marked within the pronominal paradigm itself but by the presence vs absence of a plural suffix.

(Austoasiatic), Pola (Burmish), Sani (Lolish) and Sedang. There are, nonetheless, paradigms which have an inclusive/exclusive opposition only in the dual but not in the plural. This is so in Tanimbili, an Oceanic language of the Solomons Islands, with respect to the subject prefixes, which are depicted in (31), and also the possessive suffixes.

(31)   Tanimbili (Tryon 1994:628)

	SG	DU	PL
		1+2 *si-*	1+2+3 **misu-**
1	nyi-	1+3 *me-*	1+3+3 **misu-**
2	nu-	2+2 mwa-	2+3+3 muku-
3	i-	3+3 ŋgi (li)-	3+3+3 ŋgu-

Some other languages with paradigms in which there is an inclusive/exclusive distinction in the dual but not the plural are Biri, Coos, Kinnauri and Wik Munkan. The converse situation, that is the existence of an inclusive/exclusive opposition in the plural but not the dual, as in the Papuan language Yava, appears to be both more common and more widespread.

(32)   Yava (Jones 1986:42)

	SG	DU	PL
		1+2 **ririm-**	1+2+3 *wam-*
1	sy-	1+3 **ririm-**	1+3+3 *ream-*
2	n-	2+2 ip-	2+2+3 wap-
3M	p-	3+3 y-	3+3+3 w-
3F	m-		

Such paradigms occur in the Australian language Gugu-Yalanji and quite a few Tibeto-Burman languages such as Lahu, Nosu, Jiarong, Jinuo and Rawang. Another, highly unusual paradigmatic structure attested in languages diplaying a dual/plural contrast and the inclusive/exclusive distinction is the existence of the dual/plural opposition in the inclusive but not in the exclusive. This paradigmatic structure is displayed in the independent person markers (33), subject proclitics and object suffixes in the Austronesian language Ponapean.

(33)   Ponapean (Rehg 1981:158)

	SG	DU	PL
		1+2 *kita*	1+2+3 *kitail*
1	ngehi	1+3 **kiht**	1+3+3 **kiht**
2	kowe koh	2+2 kumwa	2+2+3 kumwail
3	ih	2+3 ira	3+3+3 irail/ihr

We also find the opposite situation, again rarely, that is a dual/plural contrast in the exclusive but not in the inclusive, as in the Australian languages Burarra and Ngankikurungkurr and Yagua (34), a language of Peru.

(34)   Yagua (Payne 1990:28-9)
          SG   DU   PL
                  1+2 **nayin**   1+2+3 **nayin**
        1 ráy   1+3 *nááy*   1+3+3 *núúy*
        2 jiy   2+2 saadá   2+2+3 jiryéy
        3 nii   3+3 naadá   3+3+3 riy

Further number oppositions in person markers, namely trial and paucal are also attested. Trials refer to groups of three participants and paucals designate several or a few. Though it is not all that rare to come across a language which is said to have a trial in a person paradigm, Corbett (2000:21) cautions that typically the forms in question are in fact paucals. This is sometimes stated outright. For instance, Keesing (1985:27) mentions that in Kwaio, what is morphologically a trial set semantically designates any plurality of higher animate entities. According to Love (2000:10), in the Australian language Worora, the trial number is actually a limited plural rather than denoting precisely three. It may designate three, four and sometimes even five. A language which unquestionably has a genuine trial is Larike, an Austronesian language spoken on Ambon Island, Central Malaku, Indonesia. In Larike the trial occurs not only in the independent person markers, but also in the affixal person markers shown in (35).

(35)   Larike (Laidig 1993:321)
                    SG   DU   TRL   PL
        1 INCL   itua-   itidi-   ite-
          EXCL   au-   arua-   aridu-   ami-
        2   a-/ai- irua-   iridu-   imi-
        3 HUM   mati-
        3 NHUM   i-   iri-

We see that the trial in Larike co-occurs with the dual. It is often stated in the literature that the presence of a trial entails the presence of a dual. However, whether this is indeed so remains to be seen. As mentioned above, most trials are in fact paucals. Paucals, in turn, are attested in paradigms which have no dual. This is the case in Walapai, a Yuman language of Arizona, which has an opposition between singular, paucal and plural in independent person forms, as shown in (36).

(36)   Walapai (Redden 1966:149, 159)
          SG   PAU   PL
        1 ɲá   ɲáč   ɲáčuv
        2 má   máč   máčuv
        3 θá   θáč   θáč

Nonetheless, it is far more common for the paucal to co-occur with the dual, as in Fijian, Loniu, Paamese, Ungarinjin and Yimas (37).

(37)   Yimas (Foley 1991:111)

	SG	DU	PAU	PL
1	ama	kapa	paŋkt	ipa
2	mi	kapwa	paŋkt	ipwa

It may in fact be possible for the paucal to co-occur with both a dual and a trial. Corbett (2000:25) suggests that such a large array of number oppositions in person paradigms may exist in Lihir, an Oceanic language of New Ireland, investigated by Malcolm Ross.

(38)   Lihir

	SG	DU	TRL	PAU	PL
1INCL		kito	kitol	kitahet	giet
1EXCL	yo	gel	getol	gehet	ge
2	wa	gol	gotol	gohet	go
3	e	dul	dietol	diehet	die

The exact interpretation of the paucal differs from language to language. In Loniu (Hamel 1994:52) the paucal may refer to any number more than two but less than ten. In Yimas, the paucal prototypically refers to a class of three to five individuals (Foley 1991:216). And in Fijian, the paucal may denote as many as twenty individuals. Dixon (1988:52) states that there is no fixed boundary between the plural and the paucal, the only condition being that the plural is more than the paucal.

Rather suprisingly, some languages appear to have two paucals, a lesser and a greater paucal. This is the analysis which Corbett (2000:26–9) advances for the Austronesian language Sursurunga which has been analysed by (Hutchisson 1986:5) as possessing quadral number. We see on the basis of the paradigm of emphatic person forms in (39) that Sursurunga has a five-way number opposition.

(39)   Sursurunga (Hutchisson 1986:5)

	SG	DU	TRL	Quadral	PL
1EXCL	iau	giur	gimtul	gimhat	gim
1INCL		gitar	gittul	githat	git
2	iáu	gaur	gamtul	gamhat	gam
3	-i/on/ái	diar	ditul	dihat	di'wuna

The quadral, however, unlike the dual and trial is rather restricted in usage. Hutchisson (1986:10) states that it is mainly used with relationship terms and in oratory discourse.

Given the cross-linguistic uncommonality of trials/paucals, it is difficult to draw any generalizations about the distribution of the inclusive/exclusive distinction in these higher numbers relative to duals and plurals. As far as independent person markers are concerned, among the languages in the sample the majority have an inclusive/exclusive opposition throughout, that is in the dual, trial/paucal and plural, e.g. Anejom, Dehu, Labu, Larike, Paamese, Tigak, Tolai, Ungarinjin and Worora. The languages with an inclusive/exclusive distinction in the dual and plural but not in the trial are Arabana, Mangarayi and Vanimo. There are none with an inclusive/exclusive contrast in the trial or paucal but not in a lower number.

3.2.3 Number and the person hierarchy

In virtually all the languages mentioned so far, the discussed number oppositions are displayed by all the three persons within the relevant person paradigm. This appears to be the cross-linguistic norm. But we do not have to search far to see that this is not always the case; English does not distinguish between singular and plural forms of *you*. The distribution of number within person paradigms is seen to conform to the person hierarchy in (40) being most common with the first person and least common with the third (Corbett 2000:65).

(40)   1 > 2 > 3

Paradigms in which only the first person manifests a distinction in number, such as the one illustrated in (41), are found in Berik, a Papuan language of Irian Jaya, several Papuan languages of the Chimbu family, Kamanugu, Kuman and Salt Yui the Ge language Xerente, the Himalayan language Rangpa and the Omotic language Dimé.

(41)   Kuman (Foley 1986:70)

	SG	PL
1	na	no
2	ene	
3	je	

Traditionally also included in this category are paradigms manifesting an only-inclusive pattern illustrated earlier on the basis of Chalcatongo Mixtec in (28) or paradigms with just an inclusive/exclusive opposition as the one in (42) from the Carib language of Suriname, Tiriyo.

(42)   Tiriyo (Meira 1999:152, 154)

	SG	INCL/EXCL	
1	wï(i)	1+2	kïmë
		1+2+3	kïmë
		+3	**anja**
2	ëmë		
3AN	nërë		
3INAN	irë		

Corbett (2000:65), however, suggests that the presence of an inclusive/exclusive opposition alone is not sufficient to warrant recognizing a number opposition since such forms imply number only secondarily. As we have seen, this is also the view adopted by Cysouw (2000) who treats the inclusive/exclusive distinction as specifying a particular grouping of participants rather than their number. If we follow Corbett and Cysouw, the existence of actual number distinctions only in the first person emerges as being quite uncommon.

By contrast, paradigms in which there is a number distinction in the first and second persons but not the third are widely attested, particularly among dependent person forms. An example of such a paradigm of independent markers is given in (43) from Sentani, a language spoken by a few thousand people in West New Guinea.

(43)   Sentani (Cowan 1965:16)
                SG   PL
         1EXCL   da   me
         1INCL   (e)
         2   wa   ma
         3   na

As evidenced by English independent person markers, the distribution of number within person paradigms does not always conform strictly to the person hierarchy; there is a number distinction in the first and third persons but not the second. Such paradigms also occur in Apurina and the Macro-Jê languages Guató and Xokleng. The mirror-image of English, that is the existence of a number opposition only in the second person but not in the first or third, is found among the person affixes of most dialects of Dargwa, a language of Dagestan, as illustrated in (44).

(44)   Gubden dialect of Dargwa (Helmbrecht 1996b:138)
             SG   PL
         1   -ra   -ra
         2   -de   -da
         3   -Ø   -Ø

Some other paradigms exhibiting a similar pattern are the A prefixes in Classical Ainu, the independent person markers of Tairora, a New Guinea Highland language, and the prefixal, though not suffixal, paradigm in Big Nambas, a language of Vanuatu.

So far we have been looking at the distribution of the presence vs absence of number oppositions among the three persons. Another aspect of the relationship between person and number which is seen as being governed by the person hierarchy is the actual way in which number is expressed (e.g. Forchheimer 1953:64; Dressler & Barbaresi 1994:60–4; Corbett 2000:76). The postulated relationship between the expression of number and the person hierarchy is based on the assumption of the existence of a certain degree of isomorphism between semantic and morphological structure. Thus Dressler and Barbaresi (1994:60–4), for example, argue that the differences in how number is interpreted with the first and second persons as compared to the third, discussed in detail in section 3.2.1, should be echoed in how number oppositions are expressed in the former as opposed to the latter. More specifically, they suggest that if the person forms within a paradigm differ in regard to how number is expressed, more opaque means of morphological marking, in particular cumulative expression and the use of different stem forms, will be used especially in the case of the first person, more transparent inflectional forms of marking via agglutinative affixation, in the case of the third. Thus languages are predicated as displaying suppletive marking in the first person only, as in the case of the nominative forms in Modern Eastern Armenian (45) or in both the first and second persons, as in the nominative forms in Polish (46) or in all three persons, as in the strong forms of Breton (47).

(45) Modern Eastern Armenian (Kozintseva 1995:13)

	SG	PL
1	es	menk'
2	du	duk'
3	na	nrank'

(46) Polish

	SG		PL
1	ja	1	my
2	ty	2	wy
3M	on	3mp	oni
3F	ona	3mnp	one
3NT	ono		

(47) Breton (Stephens 1993:369)

	SG	PL
1	me	1 ni
2	te	2 c'hwi
3M	en	3 int
3F	hi	

The only exceptions to the above that Dressler and Barbaresi have observed involve suppletive marking of number in the second person but not the first, as in various Manchu-Tunguisic languages, such as Buryat and Daur (48).

(48) Daur (Wu 1996:21)

	SG	PL
1	bi:	ba: /bed
2	ši:	ta:
3	in	a:n

I have not investigated this issue systematically myself, but it does seem to be the case that in languages in which the third-person forms are not demonstratives or exhibit irregularities connected with gender, they are the most likely to display regular number marking.

The third way in which the person hierarchy is seen to exert an effect on the relationship between person and number is with respect to the variety of number oppositions exhibited by the three persons. The first person is said to display more number distinctions than the second and the second more than the third. Whether this is indeed so depends on the interpretation of the speaker-addressee dyad 1+2, called traditionally the dual inclusive. Recall from the discussion in section 3.1.1 that there are languages with paradigms which have a special form for the 1+2 but not for any other combination of two participants. If such paradigms are analysed as exhibiting a dual, then the dual may be seen as primarily a number opposition found in the first person. This is the most commonly held view and the view represented by Plank (1989), who has led a longstanding investigation of dual number. According to Corbett and Cysouw, on the other hand, such paradigms do not qualify as displaying a dual. If paradigms in which the only dual form is for the speaker-hearer dyad (1+2) are disregarded, the dual, and also the trial and paucal, are most commonly exhibited by all persons.

The above notwithstanding, there are languages which have a dual only in the first person while the second and third manifest a simple singular/plural contrast. In the Austronesian language of Easter Island Rapanui there are four different forms of "we", two of which refer specifically to two participants, 1+2 and 1+3 respectively. These must be seen as defining a first-person dual inclusive and exclusive, as shown in (49).

(49)   Rapanui (Du Feu 1996:140)
         SG   DU   PL
         1 au   1+3 maua   1+3+3 matou
                   1+2 taua   1+2+3 tatou
         2 koe   2+2(+2) korua
         3 ia   3+3(+3) raua

Dual just in the first and second persons but not the third is also an attested paradigmatic pattern. It is found in the Tibeto-Burman languages Limbu and Chamling, the Australian language Biri and the Papuan language Kâte (50), for example.

(50)   Kâte (Capell 1969a:85)
         SG   DU   PL
         1 -pa?   -pere?   -peneŋ
         2 -me?   -pire?   -pieŋ
         3 -?, -ye?

There are, however, quite a few languages in which the distribution of the dual and other higher numbers is not consistent with the person hierarchy. For instance, as shown in (51), in Tlappanec, a language of Mexico, the independent person paradigm manifests a dual in the third person but not in the first or second.

(51)   Tlappanecan (Radin 1935:53)
         SG   DU   PL
         1 íkú'   íkálú
         2 íká   ìkàlà
         3 ìkà'   iki   ikì

This is also the case in the Nishel dialect of Kham (Watters 2002:162) in regard to the possessive prefixes. The same atypical distribution of person and number may be observed in relation to the trial. We see in (52) that in the independent person forms of the Austronesian language Biak there is a trial in the third person but none in the second or first.

(52) Biak (Plank & Schellinger 1997:63)

	SG	DU	TRL	PL
		1+2 ?u		1+2+3 ?o
1	ai'a	1+3 nu		1+3+3 n?o
2	'au	mu		m?0
3	i	su	s?o	si/na

Some other departures from the person hierarchy include the following. In the independent person forms of the Mon-Khmer language Sedang and the Djapu dialect of the Australian language Dhuwal as well as in the subject suffixes of the West Himalayish language Tinani, there is a dual in the first and third persons but not the second. In Aleut, Ancient Greek and Classical Arabic there is a dual in the second and third persons, but not in the first. In the Omotic language Dizi there is a dual in the second person but not the first or the third.[6] And in Nambiquara there is a dual in the second person, but in the first only an inclusive/exclusive distinction. In fact the exceptions to the person hierarchy in regard to the distribution of the dual are frequent enough to put into question any attempt to see its distribution as being determined by the hierarchy of persons.

3.2.4 Towards a typology of paradigmatic structure

We have seen that person paradigms may exhibit up to five number oppositions. The existing oppositions in number may but need not be evinced by all three persons. And furthermore, in the non-singular numbers there may be various groupings of the first-person complex sensitive to the presence of the addressee, commonly referred to as the inclusive/exclusive distinction. The resulting array of person paradigms is quite bewildering.

A very simple means of classifying the existing variation was presented by Ingram (1978:215–16) who grouped the person paradigms occurring in languages according to the number of "roles or combinations of roles in the speech act that each language considers to be of sufficient importance to mark by a separate lexical form". Such a classification is similar to counting the number of vowels or consonants in a language. Applying this system to the seventy-language sample of Forchheimer (1953), Ingram identified person paradigms containing from four to fifteen lexical items, organized in twenty-one paradigmatic patterns. The four most common of these twenty-one paradigmatic structures, which account for 71 per cent of the paradigms that he considered, are listed in decreasing frequency in (53).

---

[6] Bender (2000:146) considers the dual forms in Dizi dubious.

(53) 6-person system: 123: SG VS PL 19 lgs
11-person system: 123: SG VS DU: INCL/EXCL VS PL: INCL/EXCL 15 lgs
7-person system: 123: SG VS PL: INCL/EXCL 10 lgs
9-person system: 123: SG VS DU VS PL 5 lgs

As (53) reveals, the most common person system identified by Ingram is the 6-person system involving an opposition between three persons and two numbers. The three other most common systems are an elaboration of the 6-person system by the addition of an inclusive/exclusive contrast (7-person system) or the dual (9-person system) or both (11-person system).

These findings are based on a consideration of a selected set of person paradigms from only seventy languages. If we apply the same system of classification to the 265 paradigms investigated by Cysouw (2000), we obtain rather different results. First of all, the number of different paradigmatic structures rises from 21 to 98. Secondly, Ingram's four most common person systems account for only 40 per cent (107/265) of the paradigms. Thirdly, the 6-person system does not emerge as the favoured system; it is just as common as the 7-person one. Each is displayed in thirty-eight (14%) of the paradigms. And finally, the 9-person system is marginally more frequent than the 11-person system, rather than being three times less common, as in Ingram's sample.

A system of classification which results in the recognition of ninety-eight types of person paradigms, is clearly not very revealing as far as paradigmatic structure is concerned. It is therefore rather suprising that the only serious alternative classification that has been suggested is that developed recently by Cysouw (2000). Cysouw's typology of person paradigms is based not on the enumeration of oppositions and listing of lexical contrasts, but rather on the existing patterns of homophony manifested in the paradigm, where by homophony is meant the use of the same form to express two or more independently established categories. Cysouw groups the homophonies occurring in person paradigms into three major types: singular homophonies involving an overlap among the singular categories, vertical homophonies involving overlap among the non-singular categories and horizontal homophonies involving overlap between the singular and non-singular categories.[7] The three types of homophonies are presented in Figure 3, where a horizontal line stands for a conflation of categories. All three types of homophonies have been amply illustrated throughout the chapter, singular and vertical homophonies in section 3.1, and horizontal in section 3.2.3, so there is no need to consider additional examples here.

The major patterns of singular and vertical homophonies are defined with reference to the four oppositions, which, if present, render the 8-person paradigm of three singular categories and five group ones discussed in section 3.2.1. The four oppositions are listed in (54).

---

[7] There are also diagonal homophonies such as between a singular second person and a non-singular third. These are very rare.

Singular homophony

SG	PL
	1
	2
3	3

SG	PL
1	1
	2
	3

Vertical homophony

SG	PL
1	
2	
3	

SG	PL
1	1
2	
3	

Horizontal homophony

SG	PL
1	1
3	3

SG	PL
1	1
2	2

Figure 3 *Singular, vertical and horizontal homophonies in person paradigms*

(54) Major splits
split inclusive: an opposition between minimal inclusive and augmented inclusive, i.e. 1+2 vs 1+2+3
split we: an opposition between inclusive and exclusive, i.e. 1+2 and 1+2+3 vs 1+3
split non-singular: an opposition between the non-singular categories 2+3 vs 3+3 and between each of these and the first-person complex
split singular: an opposition between the three singular categories, 1 vs 2 vs 3.

Table 3.2 *Major singular and vertical homophonies in Cysouw's sample*

Split inclusive	+	−	−	−	−
Split we	+	+	−	−	−
Split non-singular	+	+	+	−	−
Split singular	+	+	+	+	−
Number of cases	26	78	99	20	21
244 (92.1%)					

The pluses in this table, unlike the use in Table 3.3, denote the absence rather than the presence of a distinction.

A consideration of the presence vs absence of these four splits among the 265 person paradigms in Cysouw's sample reveals considerable differences in their frequency of occurrence and co-occurrence. Of the sixteen logical possibilities, only the five combinations in Table 3.2 are common. They account for 92 per cent of the person paradigms in his sample. As we see, these five patterns define a hierarchy which Cysouw calls the Explicitness Hierarchy (EH) presented in (55a) and (55b).

(55) a. Explicitness Hierarchy (rough outline)
totally explicit > less explicit non-singular > less explicit singular

b. Explicitness Hierarchy (middle part)
speaker and addressee > at least speaker > speaker or addressee and other

The EH specifies that explicitness in the non-singular categories tends to be reduced before it is reduced in the singular categories (55a), i.e. that vertical homophonies tend not to imply singular ones. This is confirmed by the paradigms in my sample, among which vertical homophony is quite frequent without singular homophony. In Kobon (56), for example, there is a vertical homophony between the second- and third-person non-singular and the minimal inclusive and exclusive, but none in the singular.

(56) Kobon (Davies 1981:94, 154)
      1   yadi/ad
      2   ne/nɨ
      3   nipe/ne
      1+2   **hol**
      1+2+3   hon
      1+3   **hol**
      2+2(+2) köl/kale
      3+3(+3) köl/kale/ kalɨipe

The EH also specifies (55b) the likelihood of the existence of different types of vertical homophonies. Thus, among the non-singular categories, those involving the speaker and addressee (1+2 & 1+2+3) tend to be combined prior to those involving at least the speaker (1+2 & 1+2+3 & 1+3 or 1+2 & 1+3), and these in turn tend to be combined prior to those involving the speaker or addressee and other (e.g. 1+3 & 2+3 or 2+3 & 3+3). As the figures in Table 3.2 show, the most common paradigms are in the middle part of the hierarchy, that is those with a unified "we" (99 paradigms), followed by those which have an inclusive/exclusive distinction (78 paradigms), while those displaying a minimal augmented distinction (26 paradigms) are far behind. This echoes the distribution of independent person paradigms in the languages in the sample, presented earlier in Table 3.1.

Turning to horizontal homophony, Cysouw observes that of the theoretically possible combinations of singular and non-singular categories, only four are relatively frequent in his sample. These are listed in (57).

(57) 1/1+2+(3): the first-person singular is homophonous with the inclusive
      1/1+3:   the first-person singular is homophonous with the exclusive
      2/2+3:   the second-person singular is homophonous with the second-person plural
      3/3+3:   the third-person singular is homophonous with the third-person plural

Paradigms exhibiting the 2/2+3 homophony (e.g the independent markers of English) or the 3/3+3 homophony (e.g. the independent forms in Malay) and even both (e.g. the independent markers of Kuman) have been illustrated in section 3.2.3. The vast majority of the other two homophonies are in "no we" paradigms, that is there is homophony between the first-person singular and both the inclusive and exclusive. Paradigms with just one or the other of the first two homophonies in (57), that is between the first-person singular and just the inclusive or just the exclusive are extremely rare and have been attested only in dependent person forms. Several paradigms of person suffixes manifesting the former type of homophony exist in the Papuan language Binandere. The paradigm in (58) is of the past II stative suffixes.

(58)   Binandere (Capell 1969b:16–31)
                    1+2   -ana
        1 -ana   1+2+3   -ana
                    1+3   -ara
        2 -ata   2+3   -awa
        3 -evira   3+3   -ara

Homophony between the first-person singular and just the exclusive occurs in the person prefixes of Warrwa, one of the Nyulnyulan languages spoken in West Kimberly, Western Australia. It is illustrated in (59) on the basis of the forms in the future with class I verbs.

Table 3.3 *Major horizontal homophonies in Cysouw's sample*

1/Inclusive	23	–	–	–	–	+
1/Exclusive	41	–	–	–	+	+
2/2+3	63	–	–	+	+	+
3/3+3	101	–	+	+	+	+
Number of cases		136	38	22	18	23
		237 (89.5%)				

(59) Warrwa (McGregor 1994:41)
                  1+2   -ya
        1 **-ka**   1+2+3 -ya
                  1+3   **-ka**
        2 -wa   2+3   -wa
        3 -Ø   3+3   -ku

Again, of the sixteen logically possible combinations of the horizontal homophonies in (57), only five are common. These are shown in Table 3.3. The five combinations again form a hierarchy.

(60) Horizontal Homophony Hierarchy
      no homophony < (3/3+3), (2/2+3), (1/EXCL), (1/INCL)

The Horizontal Homophony Hierarchy accounts for 90 per cent of the horizontal homophonies in Cysouw's sample. The figures in Table 3.3 confirm the relationship between non-singular number and the person hierarchy discussed in section 3.2.3. While the absence of any horizontal homophonies is the most common (136 paradigms), homophonies not involving speaker or addressee (101 paradigms) override those involving just the addressee (63 paradigms), and these override those involving speaker and/or addressee (41).

The plotting of the Horizontal Homophony Hierarchy onto the Explicitness Hierarchy reveals that the amount of horizontal homophony is highest in the middle of the EH, that is in paradigms with either an inclusive/exclusive opposition or a unified we. This in turn suggests that: (a) the paradigms with vertical and/or singular homophony disfavour horizontal homophony; and (b) the paradigms with a division between minimal and augmented inclusive disfavour horizontal homophony. The near complementary distribution between singular or vertical homophony and horizontal homophony may be seen as a way of maintaining a level of explicitness within person paradigms. While the presence of either the first type or the second type of homophony reduces explicitness to some degree, the presence of both does so to a greater extent. Particularly interesting is the virtual absence of horizontal homophony in languages with a minimal augmented distinction. This suggests that the distinction between the minimal inclusive and augmented inclusive is the ultimate addition of a pronominal paradigm. This opposition is found only in paradigms which distinguish all other referential categories as well.

Several further generalizations pertaining to the structure of person paradigms emerge from a consideration of the distribution of the three types of homophonies, singular, vertical and horizontal in paradigms with and without an inclusive/exclusive distinction. Cysouw (2000:187) observes that paradigms with an inclusive/exclusive distinction display no singular homophonies and fewer vertical homophonies than those without such a distinction.[8] Horizontal homophonies, on the other hand, are common. This corroborates the importance of the inclusive/exclusive distinction for the structure of paradigms. The presence of such a distinction severely restricts the nature of the homophonies that occur.

The observations on the structure of person paradigms presented above do not take into account oppositions involving higher numbers, the dual and trial/paucal. A consideration of the person forms involved in such oppositions in terms of the vertical homophonies they display identifies an explicitness hierarchy analogous to the one in (51). Yet again, the most common paradigms are those in the middle of the hierarchy, that is those with a distinction between the second- and third-person dual and minimal differentiation of the first-person complex, that is no inclusive/exclusive distinction (28 paradigms) or just an inclusive/exclusive opposition (25), but no split within the inclusive category. In contrast to the patterns of vertical homophony, those of horizontal homophony do not form a hierarchy. While absence of homophony between any of the dual and plural categories is the norm, its presence, unlike in the case of the singular/plural (group) opposition, does not favour the third person over the second, or the second over the first. This was already suggested in section 3.2.3. As for the relationship between vertical and horizontal homophonies, the same observations can be made as those suggested earlier with respect to the singular and plural; vertical and horizontal homophonies do not co-occur, and the distinction between minimal and augmented inclusive is found only in paradigms displaying all the other distinctions. Further, the presence of the inclusive/exclusive distinction disfavours the presence of vertical homophonies.

Do the three different types of homophonies, singular, vertical and horizontal provide a better point of reference for the classification of the structure of person paradigms than the traditional approach as reflected in Ingram's classification? The following points suggest that they do. First of all, the vast majority of paradigms appear to conform to the patterns captured in the explicitness hierarchies and horizontal homophony hierarchy. Secondly, the separating out of singular and vertical homophonies allows us to see the relationship between

---

[8] Some languages with the inclusive/exclusive distinction with vertical homophonies are: Itonama, Kei and Sanuma in independent forms between the inclusive and the second-person plural; Buma in subject prefixes between the plural and dual exclusive and the second-person dual and plural, Kabana in the subject prefixes between the exclusive and the second-person plural and Labu in the independent forms between the first-person inclusive and the third in the trial.

the two, namely that the former typically imply the latter and thus constitute an indication of advanced degeneration of a person paradigm. Thirdly, the fact that vertical and horizontal homophonies tend to be in complementary distribution strongly suggests that they may be reflections of different principles. This is supported by evidence from diachronic change. Cysouw's investigation of cognate paradigms reveals that while the explicitness hierarchies constitute a viable model of diachronic change, the horizontal hierarchy does not. Further, the integration of the inclusive/exclusive distinction firmly into the person system reveals that it has a delimiting function with respect to possible homophonies, strongly disfavouring vertical and singular ones. Finally, it is only in the absence of any homophonies that the ultimate differentiation of person categories, between the minimal and augmented exclusive, appears to be possible.

While Cysouw's approach to the paradigmatic structure of person systems constitutes a notable advancement relative to previous analyses, it does not take into account variation in gender. It is to this that we now turn.

3.3 Variation in gender

Gender, as defined by Corbett (1991), is a form of classification of nominals, shown by agreement. In the case of person markers, however, gender is shown by the form of the markers themselves. Gender distinctions in personal markers may be based on sex, humanness, animacy and a combination of semantic and formal criteria often referred to as class. Most gender contrasts in person markers are sex based, that is markers used for the referents of males are masculine and those used for females are feminine. The treatment of other referents varies. They may be referred to by a separate set (or sets) of neuter forms, as is the case in English and many other European languages. Alternatively, they may be grouped with the referents of masculine gender (e.g. Amharic) or less commonly with the referents of feminine gender (e.g. Warekena) or split over the masculine and feminine genders in an arbitrary way or according to some semantically based principle (e.g. Garifuna). Sex-based gender may interact with the human/non-human and or animate/inanimate distinction. For instance, there may be masculine and feminine person markers reserved just for humans, a special marker for non-human animates and yet another form for all other referents.

Gender contrasts not involving sex but solely the human/non-human or animate/inanimate distinctions are considerably less common.[9] A distinction between human/non-human is found in the independent person markers of the Kru language Godie (61), and between animate/inanimate in Dagbani (62), a Gur language spoken in northern Ghana.

---

[9] Gender distinctions involving the animate/inanimate or human/non-human distinction are somewhat more common among the languages of Africa, South America and the Solomon Islands.

(61) Godie (Marchese 1986:220)
	SG	PL
1	ʌ	à
2	ʌ̃	a
3 HUM	ɔ	wa
3 NHUM	ɛ/ɯ/a	i

(62) Dagbani (Olawsky 1999:21)
	SG	PL
1	n	ti
2	a	yi
3 AN	o	bɛ
3 INAN	di	di/ŋa

Further gender distinctions in person markers are found in languages with noun classes. In such languages typically there is a third-person marker for humans, which may or may not be differentiated for sex, while non-humans are referred to by a series of so-called noun class markers. These noun class markers are in most cases semantically motivated and reflect distinctions such as animal, plant, utensil, material, etc. For instance, in Swahili, as shown in (63), there are ten third-person non-human independent person markers corresponding to each of the ten noun classes.

(63) Swahili (Ashton 1944:304)

Noun class prefix	3rd person non-human pronoun
M-	uu
MI-	ii
KI-	kiki
VI-	vivi
JI-	lili
MA-	yaya
N-	zizi
U-	uu
KU-	kuku

As suggested by the two sets of forms in (63), the person markers are in fact reduplicated forms of the class prefixes, with some minor modifications.

3.3.1 Gender and the person hierarchy

The examples of gender contrasts given so far all involve the third person. This is not coincidental. Gender oppositions are characteristic of third rather than first or second person. Of the 133 languages in the sample (33%) which have gender in their independent person forms, 129 (97%) have gender in the third person as opposed to 24 (18%) in the second and three in the first (3%). Moreover, gender in the second and first persons much more so than in the third is strongly tied to area or genetic affiliation. Most languages with gender in the second person are from Northern Africa, from the Semitic (e.g. Arabic, Hebrew), Berber (e.g. Tamachek, Tamazight, Tarifit Berber), Cushitic (e.g. Burunge, Iraqw) and Chadic (e.g. Angas, Beja, Koyfar, Lele) families. Some languages outside of this area which have gender in the second person are:[10] Abelam, Boikin, Iatmul, Manambu, Ngala and Yelogu, all belonging to the Ndu family and spoken in New Guinea, Vanimo, another Papuan language but of the Sko family, Tunica, an extinct language formerly spoken in the Gulf of Mexico, Itonama, an isolate language of Bolivia, Abkhaz and Abaza, two Caucasian languages, Poguli, an Indo-Aryan language of Kashmir (only in the absolutive suffixes), Ani, Nama and !Ora, three Khoe languages of southern Africa and Khmu, a Mon-Khmer language spoken in Laos and Thailand. Gender in the first-person singular is very rare. It is found in the previously mentioned Itonama, !Ora and two of the Ndu languages, Manambu and Ngala, the Western Austronesian language Minangkabau, the three Macro-Jê languages, Rikbaktsa, Yate and Karaja and the Tucanoan language of Colombia Cubeo, though only in the person suffixes in the non-recent past and present habitual.

Why third- but not first- and second-person markers should have a gender opposition is not difficult to explain. The genders of the first and second persons are typically self-evident to both of the speech act participants and thus gender marking of the first and second persons is communicatively redundant. The gender of third persons, on the other hand, is not obvious. Though third parties may be present in the extra-linguistic context of the utterance, they need not be and in fact typically are not. Gender marking of the third person therefore helps the interlocutors to keep track of which third-person referent is being talked about.

As in the case of person and number, the relationship between person and gender is often expressed in the form of a typological hierarchy, though with the positions of the first and third persons reversed, as in (64).

(64)　　　3 > 2 > 1

Thus according to (64), languages should have gender either in the third person only, as in English, or in the second and third persons only, as in Hausa (65), or in all three persons, as in Ngala (66).

(65)　　　Hausa (Newman 2000:477)

	SG	PL
1	nī	1 mū
2M	kai	2 kū
2F	kē	
3M	shī	3 sū
3F	ita	

---

[10] If not stated otherwise, the relevant forms are the independent ones or include the independent ones. Only languages with gender in the singular are cited.

(66)   Ngala (Laycock 1965:133)
             SG   DU   PL
         1M wn   1 ʌyn   1 nan
         1F ñən
         2M mən   2 bən   2 gwn
         2F yn
         3M kər   3 (kə) bər 3 rʌr
         3F yn

Though the distribution of gender in most person paradigms is in conformity with the hierarchy in (64), there are some exceptions. For example, gender in the second person but not the third (or first) occurs in the Cushitic languages Iraqw and Burunge, in the Chadic languages Kofyar and Angas and in the Australian language Minangkabau. This unusual distribution of gender is illustrated in (67) on the basis of both the long- and short-form markers in Iraqw.

(67)   Iraqw (Nordbustad 1988:30)
                  Long   Short
         1SG   aníng   án
         2SGM   kúung   kú
         2SGF   kíing   ki
         3SG   inós   ís
         1PL   atén   át
         2PL   kuungá   –
         3PL   ino ín   inín

The converse distribution of gender, in the first and third persons but not the second is found in the emphatic person forms of the Macro-Jê language of Brazil, Karaja, in some of the suffixal person paradigms in the Tucanoan language Cubeo and in the possessor paradigm in the Australian language of the West Torress Straits, Kalaw Kawaw Ya.

(68)   Karaja (Wiesemann 1986b:361)
              Masculine   Feminine
         1   jiarỹ   1 jikarỹ
         2   kai   2 kai
         3   tii   3 tiki

And according to Aikhenvald (2000:253), Maká, a language of the Mataguayo family, has a paradigm in which feminine gender is distinguished just in the first-person inclusive.

A somewhat more cautious view of the relationship between person and gender is formulated by Greenberg (1963:96) in his universal 44: "if a language has gender distinctions in the first person, it always has gender distinctions in the second or third person, or both". Thus universal 44 corresponds to the hierarchy in (69) rather than to the one in (64).

(69)   3, 2 > 1

The only exception to universal 44 that I know of is the Maká paradigm mentioned in Aikhenvald (2000:253).

3.3.2 Gender and number

Gender is not only typical of the third as opposed to the first and second persons but also of singular rather than the non-singular forms. As the gender of single individuals or objects is much easier to establish than of groups of individuals, this is by no means suprising. Of the 133 languages in the sample which have gender in their independent person forms, 84 have gender only in the singular as compared to 48 with gender in the non-singular in addition to the singular and only one in the non-singular but not in the singular. The preference for gender in the singular as opposed to the non-singular is captured in Greenberg's universal 45: "If there are any gender distinctions in the plural of the pronoun, there are gender distinctions in the singular also." Though universal 45 is formulated with reference to the singular/plural distinction, it is typically interpreted as including higher numbers as well. If extended to higher numbers, universal 45 may be seen as covering not only paradigms in which the same gender oppositions (in the same persons) are expressed in all of the number categories within the paradigm, be it singular and plural (e.g. Tarifit Berber), or singular, dual and plural (e.g. Kapau) or even singular, dual, trial and plural, but also those in which gender occurs in only a subset of the non-singular categories in addition to the singular. Interestingly enough, in the last of the cases mentioned above, gender contrasts based on sex, that is involving the masculine/feminine distinction seem to be always marked in the restricted number category, that is the dual but not in the plural, as in the Papuan language of the Solomon Islands, Lavukaleve.

(70)   Lavukaleve[11] (Terrill 2000:156, 159)

	SG	DU	PL
1EXCL	ngai	el	e
1INCL		mel	me
2	inu	imil	imi
3M	fona	fonala	fova
3F	fo	fol	fova
3NT	foga	fogala	fova

This is also the case in Bora, Muinan Witoto, Murui Witoto, Ocaina and Resigaro.[12] In the Australian language Worora, while there is a gender distinction in the plural, it is not sex-based. As shown in (71), the dual and trial, like the singular, display a four-way opposition between masculine, feminine and two

---

[11] In Lavukaleve four degrees of distance are distinguished in the third-person forms. Only the proximal forms are given in (70).
[12] All these languages but for Resigaro, which is Arawakan, belong to the Bora-Witoto family. Aikhenvald (2000:246) suggests that the Resigaro paradigm is modelled on the Bora one.

types of neuter (formally conditioned); in the plural the distinction between masculine and feminine is neutralized resulting presumably in an animate/inanimate or human/non-human distinction.

(71)   Worora[13] (Love 2000:8–10)

	SG	DU	TRL	PL
INCL		ŋarendu	'ŋariŋ'guri	'ŋari
1EXCL	'ŋaiu	a'rendu	'ariŋguri	'ari
2	'ŋundju	nji'rendu	'njiriŋguri	'njiri
3M	'indja	iŋ'gandu	'iŋguri	**'arka**
F	'nijina	njiŋ'gandinja	'njiŋgurinya	**'arka**
NT	'wuna wun	'gandu	'wunguri	'wuna
NT	'mana man	'gandum	'mangurim	'mana

We find a similiar situation in the New Guinean language Au (Scorza 1985:233). In all the person paradigms the gender opposition in the plural is neuter vs non-neuter, while in the dual it is sex based, between masculine, feminine and neuter. Somewhat surprisingly though, in the singular the distinction between masculine and neuter has been collapsed and thus the resulting gender contrast is between feminine and non-feminine. The lack of a sex-based gender distinction in the plural as opposed to its presence in restricted number categories, may be viewed as a reflection of the increasing difficulty of establishing the gender of larger groups of individuals compared to smaller groups. Significantly, when the gender distinction is based on animacy or humanness and it is not reflected in all the non-singular categories, it may well be that it is displayed in the plural but not in the dual (or trial). This is so, for example, in the Austronesian language Larike which in its bound affixes has a human/non-human distinction only in the singular and plural but not in the dual and trial. The relevant paradigm was presented earlier in (35). Additional examples of such paradigms will be provided further below.

There are somewhat more exceptions to universal 45 than to universal 44. One class of exceptions involves paradigms in which the gender in the non-singular involves either all persons or at least two. Some relevant instances with respect to independent forms are: gender in the plural for all persons but only in the second and third singular in Kabylie Berber and several other Berber including Ntifa, Ayt Ndhir and Shilha languages (see Plank & Schellinger 1997:65); gender in the plural of all persons but only in the third person in the singular in Spanish and Tariana; gender in the plural of all persons but only in the second in the singular in Tăhăggart Berber; gender in the dual and plural of all persons but only in the second and third persons in the singular in Ani and Nama; gender in the dual of all persons but only in the third person of the singular and plural in Lithuanian and Murui Witoto; gender in the second- and third-person plural but only the

---

[13] The third-person forms in Worora have proximate, medial and remote variants. Only the proximate forms are given in (71).

second-person singular in Biblical Aramaic. Some of the paradigms mentioned are presented below.

(72)   Kabylie Berber (Chaker 1983:154)
         SG   PL
         1 nK(-i)-(ni)   1M nkʷni
                             1F nkʷnti
         2M kC(-i)-(ni)   2M kunwi
         2F km(-i)-(ni)   2F kuNmti
         3M nT'a   3M nitni/nutnti
         3F nT'at   3F nitnti/nutnti

(73)   Lithuanian (Ambrazas 1997:185)
         SG   DU   PL
         1 àš   1M mùdu   1 mēs
                   1F mùdvi
         2 tù   2M jùdu   2 jū
                   2F jùdvi
         3M jìs   3M juõdu   3M jiē
         3F jì   3F jiẽdvi   3F jõs

(74)   Tăhăggart Berber (Plank & Schellinger 1997:62–5).
         SG   PL
         1 nək   1M nəkkanid̪
                         1F nəkkanetid
         2M kay   2M kawanid
         2F kəm   2F kəmətid
         3 ənta   3M əntanid
                         3F əntanətid

Another class of exceptions to universal 45 are paradigms in which the gender distinction is not based on sex but rather on humanness or animacy. As we see in (75) from Dagaare, a Gur langauge of Ghana, there is a human/non-human distinction in the plural but no such distinction in the singular.

(75)   Dagaare (Bodomo 1997:71)
         SG   PL
         1 maa   1   tenee
         2 foo   2   yɛnee
         3 onɔ   3HUM   bana
                         3NHUM   ana

Similar paradigms may be found in Fur (only of the person prefixes), Kiribatese (only in the object and possessive suffixes), the Sauias dialect of Biak and Wandamen, two South Halmahera languages, Katu, a Mon-Khmer language, and Palauan, an Austronesian language.[14] In Wandamen and Katu, the

[14] The last five of the languages mentioned are cited in Plank and Schellinger (1997:62–5).

relevant paradigms contain also a dual and the Biak paradigm (see (48)) has a dual and a trial. As the earlier discussion of the distribution of sex and non-sex-based genders in higher numbers would lead us to expect, the lack of the animate/inanimate or human/non-human distinction in the singular also holds for the dual and trial. There do not appear to be any exceptions to universal 45 involving only sex-based gender distinctions in the third person, that is the presence of a gender distinction in the plural or dual and lack of such a distinction in the singular.

3.3.3 Gender and the inclusive/exclusive distinction

Whereas gender in the case of third-person forms may but need not directly reflect actual properties of the real-world referents of these forms, gender in the case of the first and second persons is directly tied to the sex of the speaker or addressee. According to Cysouw (2000:321), this difference in the underpinnings of gender between the first and second persons on the one hand and the third person on the other is manifested in person paradigms with respect to the presence vs absence of the inclusive/exclusive distinction. Gender marking in the third person is fully compatible with the marking of the inclusive/exclusive distinction, but gender marking in forms involving the speaker and/or addressee is not. The argument is that the encoding of the intrinsic properties of referents is in conflict with the encoding of their discourse roles as speaker and addressee. And since the inclusive/exclusive distinction introduces extra fine-grained encoding of discourse roles, it should not be found in paradigms which focus on the encoding of the intrinsic properties of referents.

Among the person paradigms that he has considered, Cysouw has noted only a few exceptions to the claim that the inclusive/exclusive distinction and gender marking in forms involving the speaker and addressee do not tend to co-occur. These exceptional paradigms are from the Khoisan language !Xu, the Papuan languages Baniata and Vanimo and the Australian language Ndjébbana. Some further exceptions that I have come across are the Khoekhoe languages Nama and !Ora, the Chadic langauges Kera, the Australian languages Kalaw Kawaw Ya (with respect to possessors) and Nunggubuyu and the isolate spoken in Bolivia, Itonama. In Kera the gender marking involves only the second-person singular (apart from the third singular) and in Kalaw Kawaw Ya the first-person singular. In all the remaining languages both the first and second persons are involved. In Vanimo, Ndjébbana and Nungubbuyu the gender marking in the first and second persons occurs in the dual and in Baniata in the dual and trial, but not in the plural or the singular. In !Xu and Nama the first and second persons display gender marking in both the dual and plural but in the singular there is no gender marking in the first person. Only in Itonama and !Ora is there gender marking of both the first and second persons in the singular. As shown in (76) in Itonama, the gender marking is confined to the singular.

(76) Itonama (Camp & Liccardi 1967:322)

	SG		PL
1F	osni?ka	1EXCL	sihni
1M	osni	1INCL	dihni
2F	ko?ni	2PL	dihni
2M	o?ni	3PL	ohnitʸe
3F	pini		
3M	ohni		

In !Ora, as shown in (77), the gender marking embraces all persons, in all numbers.

(77) !Ora (Güldemann 2001)

		SG		DU		PL
			C	sa-m INCL	C	sa-da
			F	sa-sam	F	sa-se
			M	sa-kham	M	sa-tje
1	F	ti-ta EXCL	C	s-im EXCL	C	csi-da
	M	ti-re	F	si-sam	F	si-se
			M	si-kham	M	si-tje
2	F	sa-s	C	sa-khaoo	C	sa-du
	M	sa-ts	F	sa-saro	F	sa-sao
			M	sa-kharo	M	sa-kao
3	C	ll'ãi-'i	C	ll'ãi-kha	C	ll'ãi-ne
	F	ll'ãi-s	F	ll'ãi-sara	F	ll'ãi-de
	M	ll'ãi-b	M	ll'ãi-khara	M	ll'ãi-ku

The !Ora paradigm is the fullest person/number/gender paradigm that I have come across. It is of interest to note, that in line with what was said above, in the first- and second-person singular there is only a two-way gender contrast between masculine and feminine, while in the other person/number/inclusivity combinations an additional third gender, common, is distinguished. Another observation that needs to be made in relation to !Ora and also Nama is that according to Güldemann (2001), the inclusive/exclusive opposition in these languages is an innovation, a borrowing from the !Ui-Taa languages.

Although the vast majority of paradigms featuring gender marking of the first and second persons (or combinations thereof) indeed do not evince an inclusive/exclusive distinction, it is not yet clear whether an actual dispreference between the two should be posited. As discussed earlier, gender marking in the first and second persons is itself cross-linguistically uncommon. For instance, it occurs in the independent person paradigms of only 24 of the 133 languages (18%) in the sample which display gender marking. Only four of these 24 languages (17%) have an inclusive/exclusive opposition. The inclusive/exclusive distinction is considerably more frequent among the 133 paradigms featuring gender marking per se, i.e. with any person; it occurs in 50 paradigms (38%). While this

100 per cent difference may be seen as lending support to Cysouw's claim, other factors (e.g. areal and genetic) relating to the distribution of the inclusive/exclusive distinction need to be considered before a positive conclusion with respect to the incompatability of this distinction and gender marking in the first and second persons is reached.

3.4 Differences between paradigms

As most languages have more than one paradigm of person markers, there is an enormous potential for differences in paradigmatic structure within languages. And, indeed, during the discussion in this chapter we have repeatedly noted that certain oppositions are found only in some subset of the person paradigms of one language or another. Nonetheless, language-internal differences within paradigmatic structure are the exception rather than the norm. In the vast majority of languages the same person, inclusivity, number and gender distinctions may be observed in all the existing person paradigms. When differences do occur, they typically involve only one of the just-mentioned oppositions, though differences along several dimensions are occasionally to be found as well. The most frequently commented upon differences in paradigmatic structure are those between independent and dependent person paradigms. These will be briefly discussed in section 3.4.1. Then in section 3.4.2 we will consider differences between dependent person forms connected with syntactic function.

3.4.1 Independent vs dependent paradigms

In languages in which the independent and dependent forms differ in paradigmatic structure, it is generally the case that the paradigms of independent markers are richer than those of dependent markers. But, the converse also occurs, be it very infrequently. For instance, as shown in (78), in Chepang there is no inclusive/exclusive distinction in the independent person markers, but the dependent ones do have this distinction.

(78) Chepang (Caughley 1982:54–5)

	Indep		Person suffixes
1SG	ŋa	1SG	-ŋa
2SG	naŋ	2SG	-naŋ
3SG	ʔow?	3SG	Ø
1DU	ŋici	1DU INCL	-ŋə-cə
2DU	niŋji	1DU EXCL	-təyh-cə
3DU	ʔoʔnis	2DU	-naŋ-jə
		3DU	-ce
1PL	ŋi	1PL INCL	-ŋ-sə
2PL	niŋ	1PL EXCL	-təyh-ʔi

In the Papuan language Sentani the subject suffixes in the realis mood evince a dual, while the independent forms have only a singular/plural opposition. This is demonstrated in (79).

(79)   Sentani (Cowan 1965:16, 28, 31)
         Indep   S/A
         1SG da   1SG -a
         2SG wa   2SG -(j)é
         3SG na   3SG Ø-w
         1PL me   1DU -ən, ə(j)
         2PL ma   2DU -əw
         3PL na   3DU -əj
                      1PL -an -a(j)
                      2PL -aw
                      3PL -aj

And in the Austronesian language Larike in the subject, object and possessive affixes there is a human/non-human distinction in the singular and plural, while the independent forms do not display any gender distinctions. Compare the independent forms in Larike in (80) with the dependent forms presented earlier in (35).

(80)   Larike[15] (Laidig 1993:321)

	SG	DU	TRL	PL
1INCL		itua	itidu	ite
1EXCL	a?u	arua	aridu	ami
2	ane	irua	iridu	imi
3	mane	matua	matidu	mati

Among the dependent paradigms with more elaborate paradigmatic structure than the corresponding independent ones the "extra" opposition in the dependent forms is most often the inclusive/exclusive. Such is the case, in addition to Chepang, in Achumawi, Jabêm, Kiowa, Murle, Oneida, Sye, Tauya (in the future) and Yulparija. The presence of an additional number distinction occurs in Kiowa, Kobon, Nambiquara, Oneida and Raga. As for gender, all four instances of gender occurring solely in a dependent paradigm that I am aware of again involve non-sex-based gender. Apart from Larike, they are the possessive prefixes expressing inalienable possession in another Moluccan language Nuaulu, the subject prefixes in Fur and the object and possessive suffixes in Kiribatese.

Impoverished dependent paradigms relative to independent ones are far more common and widely attested. The impoverishment may involve the complete absence of a semantic opposition found in the independent forms or a decrease in the distinctions made. The most common opposition completely absent in dependent forms as compared to their independent counterparts is gender. This

---

[15] The third-person independent forms in Larike are used only for human referents. For non-human referents classifiers are used.

may be observed in many European languages in regard to inflectional subject markers (e.g. Albanian, Dutch, English, German, Latvian, Polish (in the non-past)), as well as in Dehu, Kapau, Lavukaleve, Maale, Marind, Mundari, Nasioi, Nambiquara, Trumai and Witoto. The complete "loss" of gender is illustrated in (81) on the basis of the Papuan language Kapau, in which, somewhat unusually, the loss involves the singular, dual and the plural.

(81) Kapau (Oates & Oates 1968:17, 45)

	Independent		P prefixes
1SG	ni	1SG	n-\ng-
2SG	nti	2SG	qä-\ä-
3SGM	ago	3SG	u-\w-
3SGF	i		
1DU	yäl	1DU	eä-\e – ä
2DU	qi	2DU	qä'-\qä-\ä-
3DUM	aqoä'u	3DU	u-\w-
3DUF	isä'u		
1PL	nai	1PL	nä-
2PL	hai	2PL	he-
3PLM	aqoä	3PL	u-\w-
3PLF	i'yoä		

Lack of any form of the inclusive/exclusive distinction in a dependent paradigm as opposed to its presence in the corresponding independent one is also relatively widely attested, though slightly less so than in the case of gender. Such a situation, illustrated in (82), can be observed in the dependent subject forms in Barasano, Daur, Ju-chen, Kinnauri, Kobon, Koiari, Kusaiean, Lakhota, Nama, Nyulnyul, PaTani, Tarascan, Trumai, Turkana and Vanimo, for example.

(82) Barasano (Jones & Jones 1991:31, 73–4)

	Independent		S/A markers
1SG	yʉ	1SG	-ha
2SG	bʉ	2SG	-ha
3SGM	ī	3SGM	-bō
3SGF	so\sō	3SGF	-bī
3SGIN	ti	3SG INAU	-ha
1INCL	yʉa	1PL	-ha
1EXCL	bādi		
2PL	bʉa	2PL	-ha
3PL	īdā	3PL AN	-bā
		3PL INAN	-Ø

Total absence of all number oppositions in a dependent paradigm in contrast to the presence of number in an independent one is far less frequent than in the case of gender and inclusivity, especially if forms expressing the inclusive/exclusive distinction are treated as involving number. One case in point, namely that of

Washo, was illustrated earlier in (11). Another such language is Jamul Tiipay, a Yuman language of California. As shown in (83) there are singular and plural independent forms for the first and second persons, for the third, demonstratives are used. The dependent forms distinguish between the first, second and third persons, but have no number.

(83) Jamul Tiipay (Miller 2001:150, 135)
      Independent   s/A forms
      1SG nyaach   1 '-/Ø
      2SG maach   2 m-
      1PL nya'wach   3 w-/u-/uu-/Ø
      2PL menya'wach

Some other languages which have no number oppositions in their dependent forms, though they may express number by separate affixes on the verb, are Capanahua, Cree, Indonesian, Kutenai, Limbu, Mataco and Wintun. (Some of these already have reduced number in the dependent person forms. For instance, Nez Perce has only a number distinction in the first person of independent forms.) The last possibility, complete absence of person distinctions, disqualifies the forms in question from being considered as constituting a person paradigm, and is, in that sense, impossible. Minimal encoding of person occurs in paradigms which fail to distinguish between the speaker and addressee, as in English in the case of present-tense inflection and the various other examples of 12 vs 3 paradigms cited in section 3.1.

Impoverishment in dependent paradigms relative to independent ones resulting from a reduction in the number of distinctions made within a particular semantic opposition rather than from the loss of the opposition per se only rarely involves gender. This follows from the fact that most frequently gender is confined to the third-person singular. When only partial loss of gender occurs in a dependent paradigm we may expect the reductions to be in conformity with the person and number hierarchies, that is to favour the first person over the second and/or third (Greenberg's version) and/or non-singular numbers over the singular. That this may indeed be so, at least as far as the person hierarchy is concerned, is suggested by the distribution of gender among the Berber languages, which are exceptionally rich in gender distinctions and exhibit distinct subject, direct object, indirect object and possessive person paradigms. The data on the person paradigms in Berber dialects cited in Plank and Schellinger (1997:65–9) reveal that in six of the dialects the independent markers have gender in all three persons in the plural and in the first and second persons in the singular, as depicted schematically in (84a) and in another five dialects there is gender in the second and third persons both singular and plural, as shown in (84b). In virtually all the dialects the dependent direct object forms have gender marking in the second- and third-person singular and plural, as represented in (84a), the possessive and indirect object dependent markers lack gender in the third singular (85b), while the subject markers lack gender in the second-person singular (85c).

(84) a. SG PL   b. SG PL
         − +   − −
         + +   + +
         + +   + +

(85) a. SG PL   b. SG PL   c. SG PL
         − −   − −   − −
         + +   + +   − +
         + +   − +   + +

The relevant dependent forms are illustrated in (86) from Tarifit, spoken in northeastern Morocco. (Tarifit has independent forms of type (84b).)

(86)   Tarifit Berber of Morocco (McCelland 2000:19, 20, 21, 29)
                 S/A   P   R
         1SG   -g   1SG   -i   1SG   -i
         2SG   t–d   2SGM   -s   2SGM   -k
                          2SGF   -m   2SGF   -m
         3SGM   i-   3SGM   -t   3SG   -s
         3SGF   t-   3SG   -ə
         1PL   n-   1PL   -nəg   1PL   -nəg
         2PLM   t–m   2PLM   -kum   2PLM   -kum
         2PLF   t–nt   2PLF   -səm   2PLF   -kənt
         3PLM   -n   3PLM   -sən   3PLM   -sən
         3PLF   -nt   3PLF   -sənt   3PLF   -sənt

In the six dialects with gender distribution in independent markers as in (84a), the distribution of gender in the dependent direct object forms in (85a) is fully in conformity with expectations, as gender is lost in the first-person plural and not in any other person/number combination. In the paradigms in (85b) and (85c), however, a gender distinction in the singular is lost before all the distinctions in the plural are. This is counter to what the number hierarchy would predict. In the five dialects with gender distribution in the independent forms as in (86b), the gender marking in the direct object forms is the same as in the independent markers. Thus only gender distributions which counter the number hierarchy are found.[16] Of the other languages that I know of which have gender marking in the first person in independent forms, in virtually all either the same gender marking occurs in the dependent forms (e.g. Ani, !Ora, Manambu and Nama) or there is no gender (e.g. Karaja, Lithuanian, Rikbaktsa and Tate). In Itonama, however, it is only the dependent first-person forms that lack gender while the second and third persons do display it. This is again in conformity with the person hierarchy.

A reduction in the distinctions made in dependent forms as compared to independent ones in relation to the inclusive/exclusive distinction occur more frequently than partial reductions in gender distinctions. They may involve a

---

[16] In some dialects, including Tarifit, the possessive forms have gender in the second- and third-person singular but only in the third person in the plural. This distribution is also in conformity with the hierarchy.

difference between, for example, minimal/augmented and augmented inclusive as in Nivkh (87), or minimal augmented and inclusive/exclusive as in Tiwi (88) or inclusive/exclusive and only inclusive as in Tiriyo (89).

(87) Nivkh (Gruzdeva 1998:25–6, 34)

	Indep		Imperative suffixes
1	n'i	1	-nykta/-nyxta
2	či	2	-ja/-j
3	if/i	3	-ĝazo
1+2	**megi/mege**	1+2	**-nyte/-nte**
1+2+3	mer/mir	1+3	**-nyte/-nte**
1+3	n'yṇ	1+2+3	-da
2+2	čyṇ	2+2	-ve/-be/-pe
3+3	imṇ, ivṇ, imɣ	3+3	-ĝazo

(88) Ṭiwi (Osborne 1974:54, 27)

	Indep		P prefixes
1	ŋia	1	məni
2	ŋiṉta	2	məṉi
3M	ŋara	3	Ø
3F	nira		
1+2	mua	1+2	**mani**
1+3	ŋawa	1+3	məwəni-
1+2+3	ŋaya	1+2+3	**mani**
2+2	nua	2+2+3	mani-
3+3	wuta	3+3	wəni

(89) Tiriyo[17] (Meira 1999:152, 245)

	Independent		A/S(A) prefixes
1	wï (i)	1	w-, wi-, wi-
2	ëmë	2	m-, mi-, mi-
	irë	3	n-, ni
3AN	nërë		
1+2	kïmë	1+2	**kit-, kii, k(:)-**
1+2+3	kïmë	1+2+3	**kit-, kii, k(:)-**
1+3	**anja**		

Alternatively, the inclusive/exclusive distinction may be absent only in one of the non-singular categories, as is the case in Tanimbili, in which it is lacking in the plural, though not the dual of subject prefixes, and possessive suffixes, though not the object suffixes. The absence of the inclusive/exclusive distinction in only one of the non-singular numbers is, however, more commonly the result of the loss of the relevant number category and not just of the disappearance of the inclusive/exclusive distinction. This is so, for example, in the dependent person forms in Anejom, Labu, Tehit and Ungarinjin.

---

[17] In the case of both the free forms and the bound ones, a minimal inclusive (1+2) reading is distinguished from the augmented inclusive one (1+2+3) by means of the addition of a collective suffix.

A decrease in non-singular number distinctions in dependent forms owing to the absence of the dual or trial/paucal occurs more frequently than total loss of all number oppositions. In addition to the languages mentioned just above, such a difference between independent and dependent subject forms may be observed in, for example, Bali-Vitu, Byansi, Ekari, Kokota, Maranguku, Mountain Maidu, Navajo, Pech, Rawang, Waskia, Yapese and Yimas. The most common source of a reduction in number distinctions in dependent forms is, however, the existence of horizontal homophonies. These are most common in the third person and least common in the first. While horizontal homophonies, unlike vertical ones, are not notably more frequent in dependent forms than in independent ones, they do not tend to overlap with the homophonies found in independent forms. Among the languages in the sample, out of forty horizontal homophonies in dependent S/A forms, only five were the same as in the independent forms.

3.4.2 Differences between dependent forms

Although the dependent forms used for different syntactic functions may be due to different diachronic developments, on the whole they tend not to differ from each other in terms of paradigmatic structure. The differences that do occur are not very systematic and do not lend themselves to any strong generalizations. Nonetheless, certain tendencies are worth mentioning.

Among the languages in the sample, dual number in S/A forms but not in P forms is more common than the converse, that is dual number in P forms but not in S/A forms. The former is illustrated in (90), the latter in (91).

(90) Chumash (Wash 2001:68, 42)

	Indep	S/A	P
1SG	noʔ	k-	-it
2SG	piʔ	p-	-in
3SG	(DEM)	s-	-Ø
1DU	kiškɨʔ/kiški	k-iš-	–
2DU	piškɨʔ/piški	p-iš-	–
3DU	–	s-iš-	–
1PL	kiykɨʔ/kiyki	k-iy-	-iyuw
2PL	piykɨʔ/piyki	p-iy-	-iyuw
3PL	(DEM)	s-iy-	-wun

(91) Yapese (Jensen 1977:132–42)

	Indep	S/A	P
1	gaeg	**gu**	-eeg
2	guur	mu	-eem
3	qiir	i/Ø	Ø
1+2	gadow	da	-dow
1+3	gamouw	**gu**	-mow
2+2	gimeew	mu	-meew

3+3	yow	ra	-row
1+2+3	gadaed	*da*	-daed
1+3+3	gamaed	**gu**	-maed
2+2+3	gimeed	mu	-meed
3+3+3	yaed	ra	-raed

Lack of the dual in the P forms is found, in addition to Chumash, in Achumawi, Mapuche, Paamese, Tonkawa and Yukulta, while the only language other than Yapese to have a dual in P forms but not S/A forms is Anejom.

Also somewhat more common in S/A forms than in P forms is the inclusive/exclusive distinction. This is the case in Guarani, as illustrated in (92), as well as in Achumawi, Hanis Coos, Mohawk, Murle, Oneida and Tauya.

(92)   Guarani (Gregores & Suarez 1967:131, 141)

	Indep	A/S($_A$)	P/S($_P$)
1	še	a-	če-
2	ne	re-	ne
1+2	**yané**	**ya-**	**yane-**
1+2+3	**yané**	**ya-**	**yane-**
1+3	oré	ro-	**yane-**
2+2	peẽ	pe-	pene-
3		o-	i-/iy-

The opposite situation, that is lack of any form of inclusivity marking in S/A forms coupled with the presence of such marking in the P forms is found in only three of the sample languages, Nyulnyul, Tanimbili and Yapese (91).

In contrast to number and the inclusive/exclusive distinction, gender does not appear to favour, even weakly, either S/A or P forms. Gender in S/A but not in P forms is found, for example, in Boni, Ekari, Ket, Kiowa, Mbay, Quileute, Retuarã and Tiwi. And gender in P forms but not in S/A forms occurs in Greek, Kiribatese, Lavukaleve, Marunguku and Passamaquoddy. Gender may, however, weakly favour possessors. The presence of gender in dependent S/A or P person forms, typically implies gender in dependent possessor forms. But gender on possessor forms but not on S/A or P forms is found, for example, in Mangarai, Nasioi and Paumari.

4 Person agreement

Although several definitions of agreement have been suggested in the literature, for example by Moravcsik (1978), Lehmann (1982:203), Corbett (2000:178), there is no generally accepted definition of the term. What is usually meant by agreement is in the words of Steele (1978:610) "some systematic covariance between a semantic or formal property of one element and a formal property of another". Needless to say, in the case of person agreement, the property in question is the grammatical category of person. The systematic covariance of person features can be observed in (1) from Gumawana, an Oceanic language spoken in the Mine Bay province of New Guinea, which illustrates, arguably, the prototypical instance of person agreement, namely that between the subject and verb.

(1) Gumawana (Olson 1992:326)
    a. Yau a-mwela
        I   1SG-climb
        'I climbed up.'
    b. Komu ku-mwela
        You 2SG-climb
        'You climbed up.'
    c. Kalitoni i-paisewa
        Kalitoni 3SG-work
        'Kalitoni worked.'

Using the terminology introduced by Corbett, I will refer to the element determining the agreement as the **controller** (e.g. the subject) and to the element whose form is determined by the agreement as the **target** (e.g. the verb). The syntactic environment in which agreement occurs will be called the **domain** of agreement (e.g. the clause). And finally, the formal manifestation of the agreement on the target (e.g. by a prefix) will be called the **agreement marker**, in our case the person agreement marker. Though the above terminology suggests that agreement markers are always attached to the target, in line with standard practice we will allow for the possibility of detached markers such as clitics functioning as agreement markers.

In most mainstream work on agreement this notion includes within its scope the determination of the form of independent person markers commonly called anaphoric pronouns. The domain of agreement is therefore not restricted to the clause, or even sentence, but may be a larger discourse unit such as a thematic paragraph. When linguists use the term person agreement, however, what they typically have in mind is a relation involving a controller and target within the domain of the clause. Accordingly, this is what this chapter will be chiefly concerned with. Nonetheless, in section 4.1, we will take a closer look at the distinction between person agreement marker and anaphoric pronoun, as the distinction between the two is by no means always obvious. Then in section 4.2, we will consider person agreement from the perspective of the targets of agreement, concentrating on the effect of the semantic properties of the target on the distribution and nature of the agreement markers. The effect on the presence and obligatoriness of person agreement of the changing properties of controllers will be the subject of section 4.3. Finally, in section 4.4, we will discuss a number of characteristics of person agreement markers such as their order and co-occurrence possibilities.

4.1 Anaphoric pronoun vs person agreement marker

In section 1.2 we briefly discussed person markers in relation to the pronoun vs noun distinction. Recall that nowadays some linguists consider the difference between pronouns and nouns to be not discrete but rather scalar, with person markers, across and within languages, exhibiting different degrees of pronominality. The same essentially applies with respect to the distinction between anaphoric pronoun vs agreement marker. This too constitutes a continuum.

Most scholars working on agreement acknowledge that there is no good basis for differentiating between person agreement markers and anaphoric pronouns. This does not mean, however, that no lines between the two have been drawn, but rather that the distinctions made have been based on theory-internal grounds. Consequently, there is quite some variation in what is considered to be a person agreement marker and what an anaphoric pronoun.

If we restrict our attention to English the distinction between the two seems quite clear. The form *she* in (2b) is an anaphoric pronoun, the antecedent of which is *Anne* in (2a). And *-s* in (2a) is a person agreement marker marking the agreement relation between the subject and verb.

(2) a. Anne leave-s for Cambridge tomorrow.
    b. She will be back for Christmas.

She cannot co-occur with *Anne* in the same clause if the two refer to the same discourse referent and, as shown in (2c), *-s* alone cannot normally be used to refer to *Anne*.

(2) c. *(She) spend-s Christmas Day with us every year.

Given these differences between *she* and *-s* there seems little reason for treating anaphoric pronouns and agreement markers as other than quite distinct. However, in many languages, as exemplified in (3) on the basis of the previously mentioned Gumawana, this is not the case.

(3) Gumawana (Olson 1992:326, 308)
    a.   Kalitoni i-paisewa
           Kalitoni 3SG-work
           'Kalitoni worked.'

    b.   I-situ vada sinae-na
           3SG-enter house inside-3SG(INAL)
           'He entered the inside of the house.'

We see that exactly the same prefix is used both in (3a) to mark the agreement relation between the subject and verb and in (3b) where it functions as an anaphoric pronoun, though, unlike in English, a dependent rather than an independent one. In the case of languages such as Gumawana, the functions of agreement marker and anaphoric pronoun appear to converge in one form. The motivation for treating the markers as realizations of different phenomena is therefore considerably reduced. In fact most linguists do not do so. One view is that both person markers are agreement markers, but involving different domains of agreement, local in which the controller and target belong to the same syntactic constituent, in the case of (3a) and non-local where the controller and target do not belong to the same syntactic constituent in the case of (3b). In the wake of Bresnan and Mchombo (1987), the former is commonly referred to as a marker of grammatical agreement and the latter, of anaphoric agreement.[1] Under the alternative view, held by the proponents of the various versions of Chomsky's generative grammar, both of the person markers are also treated as agreement markers. Interestingly enough, though, both markers are considered to be markers of a local agreement relation. The controller of the agreement prefix *i-* in (3b) is taken to be not the subject of (3a) *Kalitoni*, but rather the covert subject of (3b), which is called *pro*. Thus in terms of this analysis the agreement relation in both clauses is that of subject and verb within a single clause, the only difference being that in (3a) the subject is overt, while in (3b) it is covert.

While most linguists are happy to consider the person marker in (3b) as an agreement marker on a par with the one in (3a) and also the one in (2a), there is less consensus in relation to person markers such as the one in (4b) in the Carib language Macushi.

---

[1] The distinction between grammatical and anaphoric agreement is discussed earlier by Lehmann (1982:219) under the guise of syntactic and anaphoric agreement.

(4) Macushi (Abbott 1991:84)
a. U-yonpa-kon João ko'mamî-'pî miarî
1-relative-COLL John remain-PAST there
'Our relative John stayed there.'

b. Aa-ko'mamî-'pî asakîne wei kaisarî
3-remain-PAST two day up:to
'He remained two days.'

The antecedent of the person prefix *aa-* in (4b) is *João* in the preceding clause (4a). Thus this person prefix appears to be just like the corresponding prefix in the Gumawana (3b). However, unlike the person prefix in Gumawana, the person prefix in Macushi cannot co-occur with an overt subject in the same clause, be it a nominal one or a pronominal one. Both (5a) and (5b) are ungrammatical.

(5) Macushi
a. *João aa-ko'mamî-'pî
John 3-remain-PAST

b. *Mîîkîrî aa-ko'mamî-'pî
He 3-remain-PAST

Can therefore the person prefix in (4b) be considered to be an agreement marker?

For linguists who conceive of agreement as necessarily being a local phenomenon the answer must be no. Note that since the person prefix is in complementary distribution with an overt nominal or pronominal NP, no covert subject can be posited as a local controller, unlike in the case of the person prefix in the Gumawana (3b). If, on the other hand, we allow for non-local agreement, the person prefix *aa-* in Macushi does qualify as an agreement marker, though an anaphoric as opposed to grammatical agreement marker in the terminology introduced by Bresan and Mchombo. There is nothing in this two-way typology of agreement which would suggest that anaphoric agreement markers must also double up as grammatical agreement markers or vice versa.

The treatment of the person prefix in Macushi as an agreement marker, though appealing, raises the question of the status of person forms such as *she* in the English (2b). If the Macushi person prefix is considered to be an agreement marker, shouldn't *she* in (2b) also be viewed as such? It is difficult to see how such a conclusion could be avoided. The form *she* in (1b) differs from the form *aa-* in the Macushi (3b) in that the former is an independent person marker while the latter is a dependent one. The independent/dependent distinction is, however, one of morpho-phonological form and not one of function (pronoun vs agreement marker) and few would argue that the two should simply be equated. Nonetheless, if *she* in (2b) is considered to be an agreement marker, then the same analysis must be extended to all anaphoric pronouns.

There is also another angle to the debate on what is an anaphoric pronoun and what an agreement marker which, if pursued, leads to virtually the converse conclusions. It concerns the issue of argument status. Anaphoric pronouns such as *she* in (2b) are syntactic arguments. Traditionally, agreement markers are not. But unless covert arguments are postulated, anaphoric agreement markers such as the Gumawana *i-* in (3b) and the Macushi *aa-* in (4b) must be treated as arguments. An argument analysis of the Macushi *aa* in (4b) is unproblematic; since it cannot co-occur with a corresponding nominal or pronominal NP in the same clause, it obviously satisfies the argument structure of the verb. The Gumawana person prefix *i-*, on the other hand, can co-occur with a corresponding nominal or pronominal NP, as shown in (3a) and also (1) given earlier. Should it therefore be treated as an agreement marker when it does co-occur with a corresponding NP and the realization of the verbal argument when it does not? This is one possibility. Another is to consider it as always being an argument, that is both in (3b) when it occurs by itself and in (3a) when it is accompanied by a nominal. If such an analysis is adopted, then given the assumption of function-argument bi-uniqueness or the Theta-Criterion (or their equivalents in models of grammar other than LFG and GB), the nominal *Kalitoni* in (3a) cannot also be an argument.[2] It is therefore considered to be an adjunct, in apposition to the person argument on the verb, similar to either a left-dislocated topic, such as *Anne* in (6) or an NP involved in non-restrictive apposition, such as *the doctor* in (7).

(6)   Anne, she'll return for Christmas.

(7)   He, the doctor, told me, the patient, what to do.

Thus under this analysis, known in the literature as the pronominal argument analysis, neither Gumawana nor Macushi display person agreement.[3] Only English does.

In addition to the issues of locality and argument status, there are matters of referentiality which have a bearing on the anaphoric pronoun vs agreement marker distinction. Recall from chapter 1 (section 1.2) that a primary feature of personal pronouns is taken to be necessary referentiality and even definiteness. This is reflected in the fact that personal pronouns typically cannot occur with definite determiners, or indefinite articles, be construed as bound variables or receive a non-specific or generic interpretation. Person agreement markers, on the other hand, need not be so restricted. In fact in most European languages that display it, subject person agreement is obligatory. Consequently, it occurs with all sorts of subjects: indefinite, non-specific, generic, quantified, etc. For instance, in Polish, as exemplified in chapter one (see example (15)), while a third-person independent form can only be interpreted as coreferential with some entity outside the clause, not as bound by the quantified subject NP, the person agreement marker on the verb is open to a bound variable reading or a non-specific or generic interpretation. If the lack of referential restrictions on person

---

[2] The assumption of function-argument bi-uniqueness is: each expressed lexical role must be associated with a unique function and conversely (Bresnan 2001a:311).
[3] The pronominal argument analysis is discussed in detail in Baker (1996) and Evans (2002). Arguments against it are presented in Austin and Bresnan (1996).

agreement markers in languages such as Polish are taken as characteristic of agreement markers, questions arise (e.g. Austin & Bresnan 1996; Evans 2002) with respect to the pronominal vs agreement marker status of person forms in polysynthetic languages. Consider, for instance, the following examples from Bininj Gun-wok, a polysynthetic Australian language.

(8)   Bininj Gun-wok (Evans 2002:30, 28)
  a.   Balanda **bi**- mey
      European 3/3HUM-marry:PAST.PERF
      'She married the white man / a white man.'

  b.   Kakkawarr kaben-ma-ng   birri-wern bininj
      messenger 3/3PL-bring-NON-PAST 3PL-many person
      'The messenger will bring the many people/many people.'

  c.   Munguyh **kaben**-yawa-n   daluk minj **kabi**-marnedjare
      always   3/3PL-look for-NON-PAST woman not 3/3HUM – love-NON-PAST
      daluk bininj na-mekke. **Kabirri**-warnyak daluk
      woman man M-dem   3PL/3-not want   woman
      'He's always looking for women, but there is no woman who loves that man. Women don't want him.'

We see that the person prefix for the P (here a portmanteau form for the A and P) can be used irrespective of whether the referent is definite or indefinite (8a), specific or non-specific (8b) or even generic (8c). The person marker thus exhibits the referential properties associated with agreement marking not with personal pronouns. Yet such languages are prime candidates for a pronominal argument analysis, where the person markers on the verb and not the NPs co-occurring with them are considered to be the verbal arguments. Should therefore, the expectation of necessary referentiality be relaxed with respect to bound pronouns or is in fact the pronominal argument analysis not the optimal one for polysynthetic languages after all?

We have just seen that the attempts to distinguish person agreement markers from anaphoric pronouns so far have met with little success.[4] One set of considerations has resulted in extending the notion of person agreement to cover anaphoric pronouns. Another set has resulted in reducing the scope of person agreement and treating what are traditionally considered to be bona fide agreement markers as anaphoric pronouns. And a third set of deliberations has restored some anaphoric pronouns to the status of agreement markers but also put into question the nature of the referential properties traditionally associated with pronouns. It should therefore come as no surprise that the actual analyses of person agreement within languages are quite varied. The solutions linguists adopt largely depend on the theoretical framework that they work with and the aspects of person agreement that they are interested in. Alternatively, they sidestep the issue of distinguishing

---

[4] A fourth set of considerations in regard to the pronoun vs agreement marker distinction, though essentially only within generative approaches, involves the issue of clitic vs affixal status. See section 4.4.1.

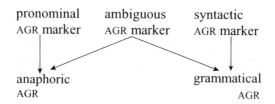

Figure 4 *Relationship between type of agreement markers and type of agreement*

between person agreement markers and anaphoric pronouns and abandon the term person agreement in favour of other terms such as person head marking, person indexation or person cross-referencing. All of these terms refer to some subset of dependent as opposed to independent person markers, the precise definition of which may differ from linguist to linguist. All include within their scope what others call agreement markers, though none is necessarily co-terminous with the notion of person agreement.

In this chapter we will continue to use the term person agreement, despite the problems associated with it. Building on Bresnan and Mchombo's (1987) grammatical vs anaphoric agreement typology, we will distinguish three types of person agreement markers: syntactic, ambiguous and pronominal. We will call a person agreement marker syntactic if it cannot occur without an overt controller in the same construction, as is the case with the English -*s* in (2a). The term ambiguous agreement marker will be used for markers such as the *i*- prefix in Gumawana which occur both in the presence of an overt controller in the same construction, as in (3a), and in the absence of such a controller, as in (3b). And the term pronominal agreement marker will be applied to markers which cannot occur with an overt controller in the same construction, such as the Macushi *aa*- in (4b). In addition to the tripartite typology of syntactic, ambiguous and pronominal agreement markers, we will also use Bresnan and Mchombo's terms grammatical and anaphoric agreement in line with their definitions, that is we will use the term grammatical agreement for agreement with an overt local controller as in the English (2a) and Gumawana (3a), and anaphoric agreement for agreement with a non-local controller as in the Gumawana (3b) and Macushi (4b). The tripartite typology is thus a typology of person agreement markers, the bipartite typology a typology of the type of agreement that the markers may be involved in. This is shown schematically in Figure 4.

We will see in section 4.3 that the distinction between pronominal and ambiguous agreement markers and thus between anaphoric and grammatical agreement is a scalar one. Nonetheless, for the time being we will treat it as discrete, taking the ability of a person marker to co-occur with a local controller under any circumstances as indicative of its ambiguous as opposed to pronominal status. The distinction between ambiguous and syntactic agreement markers, on the other hand, tends to be categorical.[5] The presence of a controller, if not obligatory,

---

[5] The distinction between ambiguous and syntactic agreement corresponds to the infamous pro-drop vs non pro-drop distinction to which a whole generation of generative linguists working within

typically depends on the phonological distinctiveness of the agreement marker rather than on the inherent or contingent properties of the controller or target. We will postpone a consideration of the potential factors underlying the development of syntactic agreement markers till section 7.2.2.[6]

Although the three-way typology of person agreement markers and the two-way typology of agreement are based on the co-occurrence possibilities of person markers and their controllers in the same construction and not on the morpho-phonological form of the person markers, in what follows we will restrict our attention solely to forms, which are morpho-phonologically dependent, in the sense discussed in chapter two. Further, we will consider only overt dependent forms. Thus the following discussion will be restricted to affixes, clitics and weak person markers. This will allow us to relate our observations pertaining to person agreement directly to other research expressed in terms of not only person agreement but also head marking, person indexing or cross-referencing, all of which either explicitly or implicitly involve person affixes, clitics and weak forms.

4.2 The targets of person agreement

The three primary targets of person agreement are predicates, possessed nouns and adpositions. Cross-linguistically, person agreement with predicates is considerably more common than with possessed nouns, and that with possessed nouns is considerably more common than with adpositions. This is captured in the predicate hierarchy in (9).

(9)   The predicate hierarchy
         predicates > possessed nouns > adpositions

Among the languages in the sample 77 per cent exhibit person agreement on intransitive (event) predicates, 62 per cent on possessed nouns and only 28 per cent on adpositions. Also noteworthy is the difference in the type of person agreement found with the three types of targets. Whereas person agreement on predicates is in the vast majority of instances grammatical, both possessed nouns and adpositions strongly favour anaphoric agreement. The relevant data for the languages in the sample is depicted in Table 4.1. We see that while 88 per cent of the person agreement with predicates is grammatical, the corresponding figures for person agreement on possessed nouns is only 44 per cent and for adpositions a mere 21 per cent. As independent person markers in the role of possessors or adpositional complements are in many languages rare or even unattested, the typical pattern is complementary distribution between a nominal and a person agreement marker, as in (10) and (11) from the Carib language Apalai.

---

the Principles and Parameters approach devoted so much attention. As documented in Gilligan (1987), they did not manage to establish the factors underlying this distinction.

[6] It is important to note that what makes a person marker a syntactic agreement marker is not its obligatoriness but the obligatoriness of its controller.

Table 4.1 *Distribution of anaphoric and grammatical agreement with different targets*

	Predicate N=309		Possessed noun N=246		Adposition N=107	
Anaphoric AGR	38	12%	99	40%	84	79%
Grammatical AGR	271	88%	147	60%	23	21%

(10) Apalai (Gildea 1998:85, 99)
   a. i-kyry-ry
      3-thing-POSS
      'her/his possession'

   b. nohpo kyry-ry
      woman thing-POSS
      'the woman's possession'

(11) a. i-pona
      3-to
      'to it'

   b. pata pona
      village to
      'to the village'

The hierarchy in (9) is not only valid cross-linguistically but also language internally. In the vast majority of languages the presence of person agreement on adpositions entails the presence of person agreement on nouns, and the presence of person agreement on nouns entails the presence of person agreement on predicates.[7] The major class of exceptions to this are languages with person agreement on possessed nouns but not on predicates, such as Burmese, Kayah Li, Koh Lakka, Kokborok, Meithei, Paiwan, South Eastern Pomo and Yessan Mayo. In all the relevant languages the person agreement is anaphoric rather than grammatical. Considerably less frequent are languages which have person agreement on adpositions but not on possessed nouns, such as Bari, Chacobo and Fur. These exceptions do not, however, undermine the hierarchy in (9) as a statistical universal.

So far we have been considering whether or not a language displays person agreement with a particular target without taking into account any properties of the target beyond its grammatical category. The presence of person agreement is not, however, solely dependent on the grammatical category of the target. Its presence may be influenced by various characteristics of the target. We will consider some of these below, beginning with predicates.

---

[7] Statistical data in support of the predicate hierarchy were first presented in Nichols (1992:85–6); 95 per cent (95 out of 99) of the languages in her sample that have person agreement with possessed nouns also have person agreement with predicates. There are no clear instances of agreement with adpositions but not possessed nouns.

4.2.1 Predicates

In terms of the number of arguments that they take predicates are typically classified into intransitive, monotransitive and ditransitive. We will begin the discussion with intransitive predicates.

4.2.1.1 Intransitive predicates

The western grammatical tradition distinguished four semantic classes of intransitive predicates: event predicates, property or quality predicates, class predicates and locational predicates. Each of the four semantic classes of predicates is associated with a part-of-speech category, a verb in the case of event predicates, an adjective in the case of property or quality predicates, a noun in the case of class predicates and an adverbial element in the case of locational predicates. This is exemplified in (12).

(12) a. Joanna rides.
　　b. Joanna is strong.
　　c. Joanna is a fine horse-woman.
　　d. Joanna is in the stable.

As has been demonstrated by Stassen (1997) in his extensive cross-linguistic study of the formal encoding of the four semantic classes of predicates, most languages do not encode the four types of predicates in a uniform way.[8] One of the manifestations of the differences in formal encoding is the presence vs absence of person agreement marking. Stassen's investigation reveals that this is not random. There are languages in which person agreement marking occurs only on event predicates, as is the case in English and the New Guinea language Waskia, for example. We see in the examples in (13) that only the event predicate *namer* 'go' exhibits person agreement.

(13)　　Waskia (Ross & Natu Paol 1978:21, 10, 11, 12)
　　a. Inong i namer-iki
　　　　village to go-1SG:FUT
　　　　'I shall go home.'

　　b. Kawam mu ititi
　　　　house ART new:PL
　　　　'The houses are new.'

　　c. Aga bawa taleng-duap
　　　　my brother policeman
　　　　'My brother is a policeman.'

　　d. Kadi mu kawam se bage-so
　　　　man ART house in stay-3SG:PRES
　　　　'The man is in the house.'

---

[8] Stassen (sample 410 languages) discusses a number of different encoding strategies and groups them into nominal vs verbal. There is no space to discuss the details of the typology here.

In other languages such as Guarani (14), person agreement marking is found with two types of predicates, event predicates and property predicates.

(14) Guarani (Gregores & Suarez 1967:131, 107, 158, 163)
    a. A-ma.apó
       1SG(s_A)-work
       'I work.'

    b. Šé-rakú
       1SG(s_p)-warm
       'I am warm.'

    c. Né soldádo
       2SG soldier
       'You are a soldier.'

    d. O-imḗ okḗ mḗ
       3SG-be door at
       'He is at the door.'

There are also languages which have person agreement marking on three types of predicates, event, property and class predicates, as in Coos (15) or event, property and locational predicates, as in Acehnese (16).

(15) Coos (Frachtenberg 1922a:389, 418, 388, 367)
    a. N̥-ła
       1SG-go
       'I go/went.'

    b. N̥-le 'ɣī
       1SG-good
       'I am good.'

    c. N̥i-loxqai'nîs
       1SG-doctor
       'I am a doctor.'

    d. Yîxâ 'wex-ētc lōwa'kats
       house at   3SG:sit:PROG
       'He is at home.'

(16) Acehnese (Durie: 1985:201, 107, 126)
    a. Teungku-Jôhan ka-leupah'-geuh u-keude baroe
       title-Johan   inch-PASS-3   to-town yesterday
       'Teungku Johan went to town yesterday.'

    b. Gopnyan panyang-geuh
       3SG   tall-3SG
       'He is tall.'

    c. Gopnyan guru-'(*geuh)
       3SG   teacher
       'He is a teacher.'

d. Abang di-keude-geuh
elder brother at-town-3SG
'Elder brother is\was in town.'

And finally there are languages with person agreement marking of all four semantic types of predicates. This is illustrated in (17) on the basis of the Salishan language Kalispel.

(17) Kalispel (Vogt 1940:41, 42, 24, 69)
a. Čin-x ís-t
1SG-go-CMP
'I walked/have walked.'

b. Čin-xēs-t
1SG-good-CMP
'I am good.'

c. Čin-ilemíxum
1SG-chief
'I am a chief.'

d. Čin-es-əl'ɛi
1SG-CONT-here
'I am here.'

Stassen's findings are summed up in what he calls the Agreement Universal presented in (18).

(18) If a language has person agreement in intransitive main clauses, this agreement will at least be used in sentences with event predicates. (Stassen 1997:38)

According to this Agreement Universal, languages may display person agreement with any subset of the four semantic classes of predicates provided event predicates are included. Theoretically this allows for the eight possibilities indicated in (19).

(19)

	Event	Property	Class	Locational
1	+	+	+	+
2	+	+	+	−
3	+	+	−	+
4	+	−	+	+
5	+	+	−	−
6	+	−	+	−
7	+	−	−	+
8	+	−	−	−

However, Stassen's data reveal that of these eight patterns, three appear not to occur, namely patterns 5, 6 and 7 in which person agreement is found with class and/or locational predicates but not property ones.[9] Thus the distribution of person agreement with the four semantic classes of predicates may be captured in the semantic predicate hierarchy in (20).

(20) The semantic predicate hierarchy
      event > property > class, locational

As one would expect, in terms of cross-linguistic frequency, person agreement with just event predicates is far more common than with both event and property predicates, and person agreement with all four semantic classes of predicates is the least common. Thus event predicates are particularly favoured in relation to person agreement.

While in some languages the same person agreement markers occur on all the semantic types of predicates which display person agreement (e.g. Acehnese, Coos and Kalispel), this need not be so. In languages in which more than a single set of person markers is employed, it seems to be always the case that one set of person markers is used on event predicates and another on the remaining semantic classes of predicates that display agreement. A relatively common pattern is the one exemplified in (21) from Guarani, that is for the majority of event predicates to feature the same person agreement markers as those used for the As of transitive predicates and for property predicates to display markers characteristic of transitive Ps. Compare (14a,b) with (21a,b).

(21) Guarani
   a. A-gwerú aina
      1SG-bring them
      'I am bringing them now.'

   b. Še-peté
      1SG-hit
      'He hits me.'

The person agreement markers found with property predicates may also be extended to class ones as, for example, in the Siberian language Ket. As shown in (22) the person agreement markers used with verbal predicates (with the exception of a few items meaning 'to know', 'to forget' and 'to fear') are mainly prefixes (or infixes), while those used with property and class prefixes are suffixes fused with tense/aspect.

(22) Ket (Castren 1958 via: Stassen 1997:40)
   a. Dy-fen
      1SG:PRES-stand
      'I am standing.'

---

[9] These three patterns are excluded by two other universals postulated by Stassen (1997:126) which specify a relationship between the encoding of property predicates and class predicates on the one hand, and property predicates and locational predicates on the other.

b. Ul pal-a
water warm-3SGF:PRES
'The water is warm.'

c. Fèmba-di
Tungus-1SG:NON-PAST
'I am a Tungus.'

I am not aware of any clear cases of one set of person agreement markers being used for verbal predicates and another for all three classes of non-verbal ones. Such a situation may have originally existed in the Turkic languages in which a special set of person agreement markers is used with all three classes of non-verbal predicates, though only in the present. However, nowadays, the same set of person agreement markers is also used with verbal predicates in the present as opposed to the past tense. Thus a contrast in the nature of the person agreement markers between verbal and non-verbal predicates can be discerned only if one compares verbal predicates in the past tense with non-verbal ones in the present.[10]

4.2.1.2 Transitive and ditransitive predicates

All languages which exhibit person agreement on intransitive predicates also have person agreement on transitive ones. Where they differ is in regard to the number and nature of the arguments with which the predicate may or must agree. As documented in Table 4.2 among the 283 languages in the sample which display person agreement on verbal predicates, person agreement with both the A and P is favoured over agreement with just one or the other of the monotransitive arguments. This holds irrespective of the nature of the alignment of the person agreement. In languages in which transitive predicates exhibit person agreement only with one or the other of the monotransitive arguments, the relevant argument tends to be the A in accusative alignment and the P in ergative alignment. However, whereas person agreement with the A in preference to the P in accusative alignment is found in numerous languages, person agreement with the P to the exclusion of the A in ergative alignment is considerably less common. The only languages with such a pattern of ergative person agreement that I know of are Karitiana, Kolana, Lak, Palikur, Trumai and potentially Canela Kraho.[11] This atypical realization of ergative person agreement is illustrated in (23) from Karitiana, which is a language belonging to the Arikem family spoken in Brazil.[12]

---

[10] Non-verbal predicates in the past do not carry agreement markers. Person agreement is expressed by the same forms as used on verbs but on a copula.
[11] Person agreement with the (s) P but not the A in ergative alignment, is very often illustrated with examples from Avar or other North-East Caucasian languages. However, the (s) P agreement in Avar is not an instance of person agreement but only of gender and number agreement.
[12] Karitiana (Storto 1999:163) exhibits agreement with the A rather than the P in clauses in which the P is placed in initial position in a focus construction.

Table 4.2 *Person agreement in monotransitive clauses relative to alignment*

Syntactic function	Accusative N=231		Ergative N=17		Active N=26		Hierarchical N=9	
A & P	151	65.4%	14	82%	22	85%	6	67%
A	68	29.4%	0		4	15%	0	
P	12	5.2%	3	18%	0	0%	0	
A or P	0	0%	0	0%	0	0%	3	33%

(23) Karitiana (Storto 1999:157)
   a. Yn a-ta-oky-j   an
       I 2SG-DEC-hurt-IRLS you
       'I will hurt you.'

   b. An y-ta-oky-t   yn
       you 1SG-DEC-hurt-NON-FUT me
       'You will hurt me.'

   c. Y-ta-opiso-t   yn
       1SG-DEC-listen-NON-FUT I
       'I listened.'

   d. A-ta-opiso-i   an
       2SG-DEC-listen-NON-FUT you
       'You listened.'

Interestingly enough, in all the languages mentioned with ergative (S)P agreement but no A agreement with the exception of Lak, the agreement is anaphoric. In contrast to ergative (S)P agreement, accusative agreement solely with the (S)A is rarely anaphoric. Old Egyptian, Maale, Mountain Koiali and Rama constitute four notable exceptions. More commonly, either the S, A and P all exhibit anaphoric agreement (e.g. Berta, Bimoba, Comanche, Dagbani, Indonesian, Retuarã) or only the P does (e.g. Anejom, Kera, Kilivila, Kiribatese, Mbay).

The existence of person agreement with just the A in ergative alignment is even rarer than with just the P. Such ergative agreement occurs in the Austronesian language Chamorro (Cooreman 1988:106–8), in Yanomani (Aikhenvald & Dixon 1999:348), a dialect cluster of northern Brazil and southern Venezuela, and in Teribe (Quesada 2000:60), a Chibchan language of Panama and Costa Rica. In Chamorro the ergative agreement with just the A is, however, confined to the realis mood. In the irrealis, the agreement is accusative rather than ergative. In Yanomani, in addition to the person agreement with the A, there is number agreement with the S and P. And in Teribe, there are a few intransitive verbs which sometimes display person agreement with the S.

In contrast to what we find in ergative alignment, in accusatively aligned person agreement, agreement with the P to the exclusion of the A is not so uncommon, particularly if one considers only person marking on the verb. Verbal person marking of only the P is found in the Austronesian language Muna, the Micronesian languages Anejom, Gilbertese, Kusaiean, Ponapean, Pulo Annian, Puluwat, Tigak, Trukese, Woleaian and Yapese, several Chadic languages (e.g. Daba, Kera, Mandara, Margi, Podoko) and various other African languages such as those of the Boko-Busa language cluster, Bari, Doyayo and Fyem. As mentioned in chapter 2, section 2.2.1.2, most of these languages also have person agreement with the S/A though marked not on the verb but by special weak person forms (e.g. Kusaiean, Pulo Annian, Puluwat, Trukese, Woleaian) or forms which encode person together with tense (e.g. Anejom, Tigak and Fyem).

Active alignment, even more so than accusative and ergative, favours person agreement with both the A and P (and S). There are nonetheless a few languages with active alignment in which only the A and one type of S (S_A) display person agreement, as shown in (24) which is from Marubo, a Panoan language of Brazil spoken in the state of Amazonas.

(24)   Marubo (Romankevicius Costa 1998:60, 66, 68)
    a.   ła-n 'matu-Ø in-ʃu'tun-ai
         I-ERG you:PL-ABS 1SG(A)-push-PRES/IM.PAST
         'I have pushed you.'

    b.   ła-Ø in-wi'ʃa'-i-ki
         I-ABS 1SG(S_A)-write-AUX-PRES/IM.PAST
         'I am writing.'

    c.   ła-Ø ra'ka-ai
         I-ABS lie-PRES/IM.PAST
         'I am lying.'

The other languages which appear to display the same agreement pattern are Bare and Tariana, two Arawakan languages of Brazil, and three Austronesian languages Semelai, Taba and Tsou. The mirror-image pattern of active alignment, that is person agreement with just the P and the SP is, to the best of my knowledge, not attested.

Whereas monotransitive predicates are much more likely to show agreement with both the A and P than with either just one or the other, with ditransitive predicates agreement with both the T (theme) and R (recipient) is disfavoured. Moreover, while there are uncontroversial instances of indirective alignment involving agreement with both the T and R, as in (25) from Ekari, a language of the Ekari-Wodani-Moni family of Irian Jaya, there are no corresponding uncontroversial instances of secundative alignment with both the T and R.

(25)   Ekari (Doble 1987:90, 84)
    a.   Mee wedaba nemouga ne-epeemegai
         people many behind 1PL-follow
         'Many people followed us.'

b. Niya-e-dokai
   1PL-3SG-carry
   'Carry him for us!'

The ditransitive alignment in Ekari is uncontroversially indirective since the marker used for the T *ne-* is phonologically the same as the one used for the P, while the marker of the R *niya-* is distinct. Corresponding instances of secundative alignment where one set of markers is used for the P and R and another phonologically distinct set for the T are unattested. This follows from the fact that while languages may have special dative person forms for the R, they simply do not have special person forms distinct from the P for the T. Consequently, the vast majority of instances of person agreement with both the T and R, other than those which are uncontroversially indirective, involve markers which are phonologically the same. Phonologically identical T and R markers are found, for example, throughout the Bantu languages (e.g. Haya, Kinyarwanda, Nkore-Kiga, Shambala), in Diola Fogny, Doyayo, Wolof, Koromfe, Noon, Classical Arabic, Nahuatl, Chinookan, Slave, Amele, Manam and Kambera.

The nature of the ditransitive alignment of person agreement in the above type of languages depends on the criteria used in the determination of alignment. If only matters of phonological form are taken into account, the alignment must be seen to be neither indirective nor secundative but neutral. If, on the other hand, location and/or order of the markers are taken into account, languages exhibiting the patterns in (26a,b) will emerge as exhibiting indirective alignment (by virtue of the placement of the T and P next to the verb stem) and those displaying the patterns in (26c,d) as displaying secundative alignment (by virtue of the placement of the P and R next to the verb stem).[13]

(26) a. R-T-verb   b. verb-T-R
         P-verb   verb-P
     c. T-R-verb   d. verb-R-T
         P-verb   verb-P

Amele (27) may serve as an example of order-determined indirective alignment (pattern 26b) and Chinookan (28) of order-determined secundative alignment (pattern 26c).

(27)   Amele (Roberts 1987:279-80)
   a.   Hina qet-ih-i-na
        you cut-2SG(P) -PRED-3SG:PRES(A)
        'He is cutting you.'

---

[13] The issue of the nature of the criteria used in the determination of the alignment of person agreement is discussed in more detail in Siewierska (2003). Note that closeness to the stem is not the only way that order can be interpreted. Alignment could also be considered in terms of left-to-right order.

b. Ija sigin eu unan- ad-ih-ig-en
I knife that sharpen-3PL(T) -2SG(R) -1SG(A) -FUT
'I will sharpen those knives for you.'

(28) Chinookan (Silverstein 1976:130)
a. Ga- č - ɬ -u -ɬada
PAST-3SGM(A) - 3NT(P)-DIR-*throw*
'He threw it.'

b. Ga- č -ɬ -aš -l -u-ɬada
PAST -3SGM(A) - 3NT(T) - 3DU(R) - TO-DIR-*throw*
'He threw it at the two of them.'

My investigations suggest that among languages in which the P, T and R are not phonologically distinct, of the four patterns in (26), those in which the R is placed closer to the verbal stem than the T (26c,d) are far more common than those in which the T is closer to the stem than the R (26a,b). Thus if affix order is viewed as a relevant criterion for the determination of alignment, secundative alignment appears to be preferred to indirective among such languages. Nonetheless, since all the languages in which the R markers are phonologically distinct from the T and P ones evince indirective alignment (e.g. Abkhaz, Bulgarian, Ngiyambaa), overall, among the languages which have person agreement with both the T and R, there is no clear preference for either indirective or secundative alignment.

As for person agreement with only either the T or the R, the former is characteristic of indirective alignment, the latter, of secundative alignment. Person agreement with the T but not the R in indirective alignment is widely attested cross-linguistically. It is found in, for example, Acehnese, Apurina, Bororo, Guarani, Lavukaleve, Mizo, Ngiti, Paamese, Palikur, Polish, Tiriyo, Tzutujil and Warekena. The converse pattern of indirective alignment, that is agreement with the R but not the T (or P) is very rare. It is found in the Chadic language Gude (see chapter two, section 2.2.1.2), in the Muskogean language Choctaw (though only in the third person) and in a number of languages in which the agreement with the R involves suppletion of the verb stem such as Enga, Kewa, Kolyma Yukaghir, Lepcha, Malayalam, Tsez and Waskia (all listed in Comrie 2001). The expected secundative alignment of agreement, that is agreement with the R but not the T is very common. In fact, various linguists (e.g. Givón 1984) have argued that this is the preferred cross-linguistic pattern. It is found in Anejom, Anem, Bagirmi, Cahuilla, Chumash, Cora, Daga, Hua, Ika, Mangarayi, Nandi, Nyulnyul, Pech, Sentani, Tauya, Tunica, Wari and Yava. The alternative secundative person agreement with a single argument, that is with the T but not the R (or P) is unattested. This is not very surprising. Most referents of Ts are third-person inanimates while those of Rs are typically human. As person agreement strongly favours humans and particularly speech-act participants, it would be very strange for a language to have developed person agreement with the T but not the R or P.

4.2.2 Possessed nouns

The major factor affecting person agreement between the possessor and possessed in substantival possession is the distinction between alienable and inalienable possession. Inalienable possession is generally seen as involving a fairly stable relation over which possessors have little or no control, alienable possession as comprising a variety of less permanent, more controlled relationships. Whether the relationship between the possessor and possessed is alienable or inalienable depends to some extent on the possessor (only humans and higher animates are typically seen as capable of exerting control) but primarily on the semantic properties of the possessed. We will see further below that there is quite a good deal of cross-linguistic variation in regard to which possessed nouns belong to the inalienable category. Most commonly the inalienable nouns encompass some set of nouns referring to body parts, kinship terms, spatial terms and part-whole relations. The inalienable/alienable distinction has a bearing on person agreement in three ways. First of all it bears on the presence of person agreement. If a language has person agreement with alienable nouns, it also has person agreement with inalienable ones, but not vice versa. This is captured in the possessed noun hierarchy in (29).

(29)   The possessed noun hierarchy
       inalienable > alienable

An example of a language with person agreement just with inalienable nouns is Tauya. Inalienable nouns display anaphoric person agreement by means of a person prefix (30a), while the possessor of an alienable noun (30b) is marked by an independent person marker in the genitive case, typically following the possessed.

(30)   Tauya (MacDonald 1990:129, 131)
   a. ya-neme
       1SG-head
       'my head'

   b. wate ne-pi
       house 3SG-GEN
       'his/her house'

The presence of person agreement with both alienable and inalienable nouns is illustrated in (31) on the basis of Udihe, a Tungus language currently spoken by only a hundred people in north-east Russia.

(31)   Udihe (Nikolaeva & Tolskaya 2001:481)
   a. bi   anda-i
       1SG friend-1SG
       'my friend'

b. nuani ja:-ŋi-ni
    3SG   COW-AL-3SG
    'his cow'

In Udihe the person agreement marker is a suffix. As shown in (31b), alienable nouns have an additional suffix -*ni* which precedes the person agreement suffix. To the best of my knowledge there are no exceptions to the possessed noun hierarchy in (29); there are no languages which display person agreement with alienable nouns but not inalienable ones.

The second way in which the alienable/inalienable distinction may effect person agreement is in regard to the location of the person agreement marker. In some languages person agreement markers may be attached to constituents other than the possessed. Often the relevant constituent is a classifier, as in the following examples from Maricopa (32), a Yuman language of Arizona, and from Paamese (33), an Oceanic language spoken mostly on the island of Paama in the Republic of Vanuatu.

(32)   Maricopa (Gordon 1987:33)
  a.   qwaqt '-ny-hat
       horse 1-AL-CLF
       'my horse'

  b.   snyák   tiiwamtor Ø-ny-wish
       woman   car   3-AL-CLF
       'the woman's car'

(33)   Paamese (Crowley 1996:386, 389)
  a.   ono-m   vakili
       CLF-2SG canoe
       'your canoe'

  b.   ani   emo-n   ēhon
       coconut CLF-3SG   child
       'child's drinking coconut'

Maricopa has only two classifiers in possessive constructions, one *ny-hat* for pets and domestic animals and another *nywish* for general possession. Paamese, on the other hand, has four classifiers reflecting different semantic relations between the possessor and possessed, such as whether the possessed item is to be consumed, whether it has been planted or grown, whether it is especially characteristic of the possessor, etc.[14] Significantly, the classifiers are used only with alienable nouns. Thus in the case of inalienable nouns the same person agreement markers are directly attached to the possessed as shown in (34) and (35) respectively.

---

[14] The classifier in Maricopa is a possessed classifier, the one in Paamese a relational classifier. Relational classifiers express a semantic relation between the possessor and possessed, while possessed classifiers characterize the nature of the possessed item itself. Oceanic languages tend to have relational classifiers. Possessed classifiers are found in Yuman, Uto-Aztecan, Carib and various Papuan languages. See Aikhenvald (2000:ch. 5).

(34) Maricopa (Gordon 1987:30, 31)
   a. '-iishaaly
      1-hand
      'my hand'

   b. m-kpur
      2-hat
      'your hat'

(35) Paamese (Crowley 1996:389, 411)
   a. vati-n ēhon
      head-3SG child
      'child's head'

   b. ue-n atuvoi
      handle-3SG basket
      'handle of the basket'

The constituent to which the person marker attaches may also be an adposition, associative marker or some other linker. The relevant generalization that may be drawn is that if there is a difference in the location of the person agreement marker in adnominal possessive constructions dependent on the alienable/inalienable opposition, it is always the case that the person marker will be located closer to the possessed in inalienable possession than in alienable possession.

A third way in which the alienable/inalienable opposition may reflect on person agreement is in relation to the form of the person agreement markers. In the Iroquaian language Mohawk, for example, person agreement is found in all types of possession. However, with inalienable possession, which typically involves body parts, the person prefixes used are the same as those that mark agents on verbs, while with other types of possession, so-called patient prefixes are used.

(36) Mohawk (Mithun 1996:638)
   a. ke- neri?st-a?-ke
      1SG:AG-navel-NS-LOC
      'my navel'

   b. ake- ?sere
      1SG:PAT-car
      'my car'

In contrast to Mohawk, in Koasati, a Muskogean language of Louisiana, patient prefixes appear on inalienable nouns (37a), while alienable ones take prefixes used to mark recipients (37b).

(37) Koasati (Kimball 1991:433–4)
   a. ca-halkí
      1SG-wife
      'my wife'

b. am-ifá
    1SG-dog
    'my dog'

In Tawala, an Austronesian language spoken in the Milne Bay area of Papua New Guinea, person enclitics attached to the possessed are used in inalienable possession, as shown in (38a). In alienable possession, on the other hand, person agreement is marked by what may be seen to be weak person forms (38b). The person enclitics and independent possessive forms are related though not identical.

(38)   Tawala (Ezard 1997:151, 152)
  a.   koiba-ta
        stomach-1PL:INCL
        'our stomachs'

  b.   tauyai   i   dewa
        1PL:EXCL   1PL:EXCL custom
        'our customs'

Some languages also exhibit different person agreement markers for subtypes of inalienable possession. For instance, in the variety of the Yuman language Diegueno, called Jamul Tiipay, spoken in California there are two series of person prefixes used in adnominal possession. The series in (35a) occurs with a set of kinship terms, and that in (39b) with all other types of possession both alienable and inalienable.

(39)   Jamul Tiipay (Miller 2001:145–6)
  a.   1 Ø   b. Ø
        2 m-   m-
        3 Ø   k-/kw

Compare (40a) with (40b) and (40c).

(40)   Jamul Tiipay (Miller 2001:146–7)
  a.   kwe-sáw
        3-offspring
        'her offspring'

  b.   Ø-nye-wa
        3-AL-house
        'her/his house'

  c.   Ø-llyta
        3-hair
        'her/his hair'

As evidenced by (40b,c), alienable nouns are distinguished from inalienable ones by the use of an additional prefix *ny-*, which is attached to the stem of alienable nouns (40b) but not to inalienable ones (40c). To give another example, in the

Australian language Ndjébbana (McKay 1996), spoken on the north coast of Arnhem Land, there are four different ways of expressing adnominal possession, two of which involve person agreement on the possessed. One of the two is by means of a person suffix, as in (41a), the other is via a person prefix as in (41b).

(41) Ndjébbana McKay (1996:304, 306)
    a. marnákarna-njabba
        rib bone-1SG:POSS
        'my rib bone'
    b. nga-ngardabbámba
        1SG-liver
        'my liver'

We see that both of the person markers are used with body parts, though different body parts.

Two of the three ways in which person agreement is affected by the alienable/inalienable opposition have received a cognitive explanation. Both the preference for person agreement in inalienable over alienable possession and the closer location of person markers to the possessed in inalienable than in alienable constructions is typically attributed to the smaller conceptual distance between an inalienable possession and its possessor than between an alienable possession and its possessor (Seiler 1983:68; Haiman 1985:106; Croft 1990:174–6). This is thus a typical instance of iconic motivation of marking patterns. The use of different person markers for alienable vs inalienable cannot be explained in the same terms. In some languages the inalienable forms are shorter than the alienable. This is the case in the Arauan language Paumari spoken in Brazil, which uses the prefixes in (42a) for alienable possession and the discontinuous prefix and suffix in (42b) for inalienable possession.

(42) Paumari (Chapman & Derbyshire 1991:256–7)

	a.			b.	
	1SG	kodi-		1SG	o- -na
	2SG	kada-		2SG	i- -ni
	3SG	kidi-		3SGF	Ø- -ni
	GEN	ka-		3SGM	Ø- -na
	1PL	akadi-		1PL	a- -na
	2PL	avakadi-		2PL	ava- -ni
	3PL	vakadi-		3PL	va- -na

This may be interpreted as a reflection of the later origin of the alienable forms. But differences in the length of alienable and inalienable forms are by no means characteristic of all languages in which the two are phonologically distinct. For instance, no such differences exist in Mohawk. One would therefore expect there to be some other explanation for why some languages have distinct sets of person agreement markers to mark alienable and inalienable possession. Seiler (1983) argues that the existence of different person agreement markers for inalienable and alienable possession can be attributed to the fact that the former involves a possessor conceived of as an inactive patient, the latter a possessor agent that acquires the possessed. This suggests that there should be formal affinities between the person agreement markers used in inalienable possession and those of the P, on the one hand, and those used in alienable possession and those of the A, on the other. However, there are also good reasons to expect formal affinities between the person agreement markers used in inalienable possession and the A as opposed to the P. Though semantically the possessor in inalienable possession may be more like a patient than an agent, it tends to display the pragmatic properties associated with agentivity, namely humanness and topicality. Accordingly, affinities between possessors involved in inalienable possession and both the A and the P seem to be motivated. And indeed, as documented in Siewierska (1998), while the formal affinities between inalienability and P marking are stronger than those between inalienability and A marking, both types of formal affinities are in fact common cross-linguistically.

So far we have noted that if a language has person agreement in substantival possession it will involve at least inalienable nouns. Is it, however, possible to say anything further about the types of nouns which are likely to be inalienable and thus which will preferentially display person agreement? Several linguists, most notably Seiler (1983:13), Haiman (1985:136), Nichols (1988) and Chappell and McGregor (1996b:26) have suggested that it is. They have sought to capture the relations most likely to be expressed as inalienable in an alienability hierarchy. For example, Nichols (1988:572; 1992:160) has suggested the inalienability hierarchy in (43).[15]

(43) The inalienability hierarchy
      body parts and/or kinship terms > part-whole > spatial
      relations > culturally basic possessed items > other

The inalienability hierarchy is intended as a statement about the semantic classes of nominals comprising the domain of inalienability and not as a statement about the distribution of person agreement with different semantic types of nominals. However, given the predilection for person agreement with inalienable nouns captured in the possessed noun hierarchy in (27), we will consider the inalienability hierarchy in (43) with reference to the domain of person agreement.

The inalienability hierarchy is slightly unusual in that it is headed jointly by two items, body parts and kin terms, connected by both a conjunction and a disjunction. The disjunction is a reflection of the fact that there are languages in which only body parts display person agreement (e.g. Dizi, Paumari, Tauya, Worora) and also languages in which only kin terms do so (e.g. Dongolese Nubian, Mumuye and Wappo). The conjunction, in turn, caters for the languages (e.g. Haida, Maung, Washo and Yuchi) in which person agreement is exclusively with both body parts and kin terms.

---

[15] It needs to be pointed out that unlike some other scholars, Nichols (1988) considers the alienable/inalienable opposition to be lexical rather than semantic.

To the best of my knowledge there are no counter-examples to the placement of body parts and kin terms at the top of the hierarchy.[16] We may therefore posit a universal parallel to Stassen's (1997:38) agreement universal for predicatives, namely:

(44)   If a language has person agreement in substantival possession, this agreement will at least be used with possessed body parts and/or kin terms.

In comparison to the inalienability hierarchy in (43) the universal in (44) is very weak as it covers the presence of person agreement with any combination of nominals provided body parts and/or kin are included. Nonetheless, there are several reasons why it may be preferred to the inalienability hierarchy.

First of all, there appear to be quite some exceptions to the relative ordering on the hierarchy of part-whole relations, spatial relations, culturally basic possessed items and others. For instance, in Sochiapan Chinantec (Foris 2000), a language spoken in the State of Oaxaca in southern Mexico, person agreement occurs with body parts, kinship relations, a few part-whole relations and certain domestic items such as 'clothes', 'cargo', 'firewood' and 'house'. But it does not occur with spatial relations which are treated as alienable. And in the Papuan language Amele (Roberts 1987:171–4) there is person agreement with body parts and kin terms and also a few abstract nouns such as 'wealth', 'bravery', 'presence', 'maturity' and 'voice' but not with part-whole, spatial relations or culturally specific items. Secondly, it is questionable whether the domain of inalienability should in fact be organized in the form of a hierarchy. A crucial fact about the alienable/inalienable distinction, discussed extensively in Chappell and McGregor (1996a), is that in the vast majority of languages only subsets of the relations expressed in the inalienability hierarchy are actually treated as inalienable. This is something which the inalienability hierarchy simply glosses over. The composition of these subsets is in turn often predictable on the basis of language-specific cultural and pragmatic knowledge. For example, according to McGregor (1996a:257), in Nyulnyul only about a third of the body parts are inalienable and display person agreement. These are essentially external parts of the body such as 'hand', 'foot', 'nose'. External coverings of the body such as 'fingernail', 'hair', 'skin' as well as 'genitalia', 'internal organs' and 'bodily products' are all treated as alienable. Thus *nga-marl* 'my hand' vs. *ngay wurrul* 'my fingernail'. McGregor (1996a:286) suggests that the nominals manifesting person agreement are conceived of as belonging to the personal sphere of a human being, that is as inseparable from the individual. The non-agreeing nominals, on the other hand, are those that do not belong to the human being's person sphere and which have independent status as 'thing'. The distinction is therefore clearly semantically motivated though not transparently so. The third argument against

---

[16] A language which would require a different conjunction of nominals at the top of the hierarchy is Ewe (Ameka 1996:795), in which kin terms and spatial relations are treated as inalienable but not body parts. Interestingly enough, Ewe does not display person agreement in substantival possession.

a hierarchical analysis of the relations comprising the category of inalienability is that there are semantic classes of nominals whose treatment as alienable or inalienable appears to be quite independent of the relations expressed in the inalienability hierarchy. According to Chappell and McGregor (1996b:9), this is the case with nominals expressing personal representations, bodily fluids, exuviae and personal attributes.

In the light of the above, universal (44) appears to be a better reflection of the distribution of person agreement with possessed nouns than the inalienability hierarchy.

4.2.3 Adpositions and other targets

In contrast to person agreement on predicates and possessed nouns, person agreement on adpositions has not been extensively studied. Such person agreement, while attested in most areas of the globe apart from Australia, is particularly common among the languages in Meso-America, western North America and Oceania. In some languages all the existing adpositions appear to display person agreement. The Caucasian language Abkhaz, which has a large number of postpositions, is a case in point. Some relevant examples are given in (45).

(45)   Abkhaz (Hewitt 1979:103, 113, 119, 126)
     a.   sarà   s-q'ən t°'
           I/me 1SG-from
           'from me'

     b.   a-j əyas   a-q'niə
           the-river 3SG(INAN) -at
           'at the river'

     c.   axra yə-zə (in)
           Axra 3SGM-for
           'for Axra'

     d.   a-x °ra-k° a   rə-la
           the-wound-PL 3PL-by
           'by (his) wounds'

In other languages person agreement occurs only on a subset of the existing forms. For instance, in Acatec (Penalosa 1987:286), a Mayan language of Guatemala, all the prepositions but for one, *b'ey* 'in', display person agreement. In Burushaski (Tiffou & Pesot 1989:22, 31–2), a language isolate of Pakistan, the postpositions which do and do not display person agreement are approximately equal in number. The first set includes forms such as *pači* 'with', *lji* 'after', *ŋgi* 'opposite', *phatki* 'in the direction of' and *yáte* 'with', the second set forms such as *gandiči* 'because of', *mákuči* 'in the middle of', *iljuwáre* 'around', *it/iti* 'near' and *haráŋ* 'between' do not. Compare (46a) containing a postposition with person agreement and (46b) in which no agreement occurs.

(46) Burushaski
   a. Ja a-pači hurut
      I 1SG-with stay
      'Stay with me.'
   b. Xʊda-ɛ gʌnɛ
      God-GEN for
      'For God's sake!'

What determines the presence of person agreement has not yet been investigated. In the languages of Meso-America, many of which also have a set of adpositions manifesting person agreement and a set that do not, the former often originate from inalienably possessed body-part nouns, where the body part has been reinterpreted as an adposition and the pronominal possessor as the bound pronominal complement of the adposition. In Uto-Aztecan languages even some of the adpositions which currently display no person agreement show traces of once having had it. For instance, in Yaqui many postpositions contain the initial element *be* which is seen to derive etymologically from the third-person singular prefix *pi-* (Langacker 1977:93). Other agreementless adpositions are borrowings from Spanish. And the source of yet others is unknown. Among the languages of Oceania, on the other hand, some adpositions manifesting person agreement appear to originate from person-inflected verbs involved in serial verb constructions (Crowley 2002a:172–6). According to Crowley, the ablative preposition *rani* in Paamese is a case in point. We see in (47b) that it occurs with the same person agreement markers as used for object agreement on the verb (47a).

(47) Paamese
   a. Ni-lesi-ko
      1SG:DIST.FUT-see-2SG
      'I will see you.'
   b. rani-ko
      from-2SG
      'from you'

While in most languages which have person agreement on adpositions the form of the person agreement markers remains the same irrespective of the nature of the adposition, there are some notable exceptions. In the Oceanic language Kusaiean, of the four prepositions that the language has, two, *se* and *ke* (used to express a variety of meanings including instrumental, source, locational), take possessive person agreement markers, and the other two, *nuh* and *liki* (used mainly for direction and location) take object person markers. The same two sets of person agreement markers also occur on prepositions in another Oceanic language, Erromangan (Crowley 1998:151–2), which, somewhat unusually for an Oceanic language, has a large number of prepositions. The two types of marking are more or less evenly distributed among the prepositions. The simple prepositions that take possessive agreement markers are *ira* 'locational/goal', *nisco* 'benefactive', *nompli* '(utterance) about', *nimsi-* 'purposive', *nte(m)pgo* 'accompanitive', *nte(m)pelgo* 'accompanitive' and *ilvucte(ve)* 'between'. The prepositions occurring with object agreement markers, are *pehnur* 'before', *pog* 'dative', *ntovən* 'purposive', *marog* 'ablative', *movog* 'against', *parog* 'adversative/deprivative', *mavel* 'until' and *wog* 'oblique'. In contrast to Erromangan, in the previously mentioned Mayan language Acatec all the prepositions take person agreement markers which are also used as AS and possessors but for one, namely the preposition used to mark indirect objects *e* 'to', which takes the first- and second-person absolutive forms.

As the above examples of adpositions with and without person agreement and with one type of person agreement marker as compared to another suggest, it is difficult to make any generalizations in regard to the semantic nature of the adpositions that are most likely to exhibit person agreement. Nor can any preferences be discerned with respect to the presence or type of person agreement in prepositions as compared to postpositions.[17]

Apart from verbal, adjectival, nominal and locational predicates, possessed nouns and adpositions, occasionally person agreement is found on other targets.[18] For instance, in the Salishan and Wakashan languages of the American Pacific North-West virtually all semantic classes of words take person agreement markers including what in English would be adverbs, numerals and interrogative pronouns. The following examples are from the Nootkan language Makah.

(48) Makah (Jacobsen 1979b:111–12)
    a.   Hu.ʔax̣is   haʔuk'ʷap
        still: IND:1SG eat:CAUS
        'I'm still feeding him.'

    b.   Šučʔi
        five:IND:3
        'There are five.'

    c.   Wa.saʔu.k
        where:PAST:INT:2SG
        'Where were you?'

However, since all the forms in question take not only person agreement but also may be marked for tense, aspect and mood, just like predicates, they are often treated simply as predicates. The same does not apply to certain forms taking person agreement in various Quechuan languages such as Cuzco, illustrated in (49), which according to Muysken (1994) are all quantifiers.

---

[17] Several Uto-Aztecan languages (Langacker 1977:92) and Tawala (Ezard 1997:167), an Austronesian language of New Guinea, have both prepositions and postpositions but person agreement only on the latter. This, however, seems to be due to the more recent origin of the forms manifesting agreement rather than to their postpositional as opposed to prepositional status.

[18] Gender and number agreement occur on a greater variety of targets (e.g. non-finite verbs, adverbs, complementizers) than person agreement. See especially Corbett (1991:106–15; 2000:76, 178).

(49)   Cuzco (Muysken 1994:192)
  a.   Llipi-n-ta   riku-sha-ni
       each-3-ACC   see-PRES-1
       'I see each one.'

  b.   Sapa-yki hamu-nki-chu
       alone-2 come-2-Q
       'Did you come alone?'

  c.   Kiki-y-ta   riku-ku-sha-ni
       self-1-ACC see-REFL-PRES-1
       'I see myself.'

Another language which appears to have rather unusual targets of person agreement is the Oceanic language Manam, spoken in the Madang Province of Papua New Guinea. As shown in (50), adnominal person suffixes are expressed on attributive demonstratives (one class of), adjectives and numerals.[19]

(50)   Manam (Lichtenberk 1983:332, 318, 339)
  a.   áine   ŋé-di
       woman   this-3PL
       'these women'

  b.   maŋ mete?éle-di
       bird tiny-3PL
       'tiny birds'

  c.   níu   te?é-Ø-na-la
       coco-one-3SG-DUMMY-LIMITER
       'only one coconut'

Nonetheless, closer inspection reveals that the forms used with demonstratives and numerals function as number markers, while the relevant adjectives are also open to a predicative reading, and always are interpreted predicatively with first- and second-person suffixes.

4.3 The controllers of person agreement

While in many languages person agreement on a given target and for a given syntactic function is obligatory, in many others it depends on the properties of the controller. Just as in the case of person agreement in gender (Corbett 1991) and number (Corbett 2000), most of the properties in question may be seen as being related in one way or another to the inherent and/or discourse saliency of the controller. This even includes the possibility of agreement with particular

---

[19] Although the form of the person suffixes is the same as that of possessors in adnominal possessive constructions, Lichtenberk (1983:319–21) argues that the constructions in question are not possessive constructions.

syntactic functions if, as suggested in chapter two, section 2.2.1.2, some syntactic functions are taken to encode more salient discourse participants than others.

The factors determining the inherent and discourse saliency of controllers are those comprising the familiar topicality hierarchies (also referred to as person hierarchies or animacy hierarchies or accessibility hierarchies), which for ease of exposition I have decomposed into the following sub-hierarchies.

(51) a. the person hierarchy
1st > 2nd > 3rd

b. the nominal hierarchy
pronoun > noun

c. the animacy hierarchy
human > animate > inanimate > abstract

d. the referential hierarchy
definite > indefinite specific > non-specific

e. the focus hierarchy
not in focus > in focus

All the hierarchies define a preference for person agreement when the controller exhibits the characteristics on the left of > as compared to those on the right of >. Thus the expectation is that if person agreement is not obligatory in a language, it will occur with controllers displaying the characteristics on the left-hand side of the hierarchies rather than with controllers manifesting the characteristics on the right-hand side. We will consider the effect on person agreement of each of the above hierarchies in turn. The effect may relate to the presence vs absence of person agreement, the obligatoriness vs optionality of person agreement, the alignment of person agreement, the order of agreement markers to be discussed in section 4.4 and the type of agreement: anaphoric vs grammatical.

4.3.1 The person hierarchy

In most languages displaying person agreement, the agreement involves all three persons (though not necessarily under the same set of conditions). When less than three persons are involved, the person hierarchy leads us to expect person agreement with just the first person or with just the first and second persons. The former is very uncommon. It is especially rare in relation to the s and A. In fact the only instances of person agreement of the s and A restricted to the first person that I am aware of are those discussed by Helmbrecht (1996b) from East Caucasian languages and concern only certain tenses, aspects or moods or defective verbal paradigms. For instance, Lak exhibits person agreement only in the first person (singular and plural) of the A in the past perfect and of the s and A in the past conditional irrealis and in the future. In Zakatal', a southern dialect of Avar, there is first-person marking of the s and A in the past tense. And in

Tsakhur, a language of the Lezgi group, the first-person agreement is manifested in the present or past. Person agreement involving the P or R confined to the first person is more widely distributed. It is found in, for example, Imbabura Quechua, Panyjima, So and Wintun. As for possessors, possessor agreement just for the first person, occurs, for example, in Dehu, Kayah Li and Timbíra, in the last solely for the first-person inclusive. Also attested is person agreement involving just the first person on adpositions. This is the case in Chacobo, though only in the plural. In the singular there is person agreement for all three persons. Person agreement with just the first and second persons is much more common, particularly if one interprets the lack of person markers for the third person as absence of agreement rather than agreement realized by zero.

Contrary to the person hierarchy, there are quite a few languages which display person agreement just with the third person. Most instances of such person agreement involve the P. This is the case in, for example, the Oceanic language Sursurunga and the Papuan Nanggu, the Carib languages Waura and Parecis, the South American languages Chacobo, Mapuche and Retuarã and many Zapotecan languages. Person agreement just with the third person involving the s and/or A is much less frequent. It is found in a restricted way in English via the -s marking of the verb in the present (e.g. *(S)he come-s*). And ergative s/P agreement only in the third person occurs in the previously mentioned Brazilian language Trumai. Possessor agreement restricted to the third person occurs as well. This is the case in Yukaghir and the Macro-Jê language Karajá. What is also unexpected in relation to the person hierarchy is person agreement with the first and third persons but not the second. The Mixtecan language of Mexico, Copala Trique, for example, has person enclitics, realized by tone and laryngeal replacement, used for the s/A, possessor and object of a preposition only for the first-person singular, the inclusive and the third person. In the Australian language Pitjantjatjara there are clitic possessor agreement forms just for the first-person singular and plural and the third-person singular. And the Macro-Jê language Kipeá displays possessor agreement solely for the inclusive and third-person reflexive. Also noteworthy is the existence of second-person s/A agreement in both the singular and plural but only in the first-person plural in the Tibeto-Burman language Darmiya.

Turning to other effects of the person hierarchy on agreement, arguably the most evident is the existence of hierarchical alignment of agreement in transitive or ditransitive clauses where the identity of the argument manifesting agreement or manifesting one type of agreement as opposed to another is determined by a hierarchy of persons. As illustrated in section 2.2.2.2.1. on the basis of Nocte and in section 2.2.2.2.2 on the basis of Jamul Tiipay, the relevant person hierarchy is typically 1 > 2 > 3. In the Algonquian languages, however, the hierarchy is 2 > 1 > 3, as we see in (52).

(52)   Cree (Wolfart & Carroll 1981:70)
    a.   Ki-wapam-i-n
           2-see-DR-1
           'You see me.'

b. Ki-wapam-iti-n
 2-see-INV-1
 'I see you.'

c. Ki-wapam-ikw-ak
 2-see-INV-3PL
 'They see you.'

In Cree, unlike in Nocte, there is person agreement with both the A and the P. The higher-ranking relation, that is the second person in the examples in (52) is marked by a prefix, the lower by a suffix. Note also that in addition to an inverse marker indicating that the higher-ranking relation is a P rather than the A, there is also a direct marker for when the higher-ranking relation is an A. Yet another ranking of persons used in hierarchical alignment is 1, 2 > 3. This is the case in the Carib of Surinam in which clauses involving two speech-act participants take the invariable prefix *ki-k-* irrespective of which is the A and which the P, as shown in (53c).

(53) Carib of Surinam (Gildea 1994:192–3)
a. S-aroo-ya
 1:DR-take-TNS
 'I take him.'

b. Ay-aaro-ya
 2:INV-take-TNS
 'He takes you.'

c. K-aroo-ya
 1/2-take-TNS
 'I take you / You take me.'

The person hierarchy may also underlie splits in the alignment of person agreement. This, however, has already been discussed in detail in section 2.2.2.3.

4.3.2 The nominal hierarchy

The preference for person agreement with pronouns over nouns captured in the nominal hierarchy is directly reflected in the existence of pronominal as opposed to ambiguous and syntactic agreement markers. Recall from section 4.1 that pronominal agreement markers are markers that cannot co-occur with an overt controller in the same construction. As we discussed in section 4.2, pronominal agreement markers are particularly common on possessed nouns and adpositions. In the case of verbs, they clearly favour Ps over As. This is evidenced by the fact that there appear to be no languages which have pronominal A markers but ambiguous or syntactic P markers. The opposite phenomenon, pronominal P markers and ambiguous or syntactic A markers is, on the other hand, not uncommon. It is found, for instance, in various Bantu languages (e.g. Chichewa, Kinyarwanda), many Austronesian languages (e.g. Anejom, Kilivila, Kiribatese) as well as in Mbay (Nilo-Saharan).

The nominal hierarchy also predicts that there should be instances of person agreement with an independent person marker but not a nominal NP. This does occur but not very frequently. Person agreement in the presence of independent person forms but not nouns is typical of adnominal possessive constructions in the Uralic languages. The example in (54) is from Ostyak which belongs to the Ugric family of Uralic and is spoken in the north-western part of Siberia, along the river Ob.

(54) Ostyak (Nikolaeva 1999:14, 52)
 a. (luw) xo:t-ə-l-na
    he house-EP-3SG-LOC
    'in his house'

 b. Juwan xo:t-na
    John house-LOC
    'in John's house'

A celebrated instance of person agreement with independent person markers but not with nouns is that of Welsh subject-verb agreement. As shown in (55c), in the presence of an overt subject NP the verb is in the default third-person singular form, while it does manifest agreement with an independent person form (55a).

(55) Welsh
 a. Gwel-sant (hwy) y ferch
    see-3PL:PAST they the girl
    'They saw the girl.'

 b. *Gwel-sant y plant y ferch
    sing:COND:3PL the children the girl
    'The children saw the girl.'

 c. Gwel-odd y bachgen/bechgyn y ferch
    see-3SG:PAST the boy/boys the girl
    'The boy/boys saw the girl.'

Roberts (1999:622) notes that the same phenomenon may be observed also with P agreement (56) as well as with agreement with possessed nouns (57) and prepositions (58).

(56) a. Mae Megan wedi ei= weld O
    is Megan after his- see he
    'Megan has seen him.'

 b. *Mae Megan wedi ei= weld Emrys
    is Megan after his- see Emrys
    'Megan has seen Emrys.'

(57) a.   ei=wraig o
          his-wife he
          'his wife'

   b.   *ei=wraig Gwyn
          his-wife Gwyn
          'Gwyn's wife'

(58) a.   arno   fo
          on:3SGM   he
          'on him'

   b.   *arno   y   dyn
          on:3SGM   that man
          'on that man'

The co-occurrence of person agreement markers with pronouns but not with nouns is also found in some Carib languages, though in these languages the phenomenon is sensitive to word order. Consider, for instance, the examples in (59) from Tiriyo.

(59)   Tiriyo (Gildea 1998:64–5)
   a.   Wi   y-ene-Ø
          me   1P-see-TAM
          'She saw me.'

   b.   əmə   k-ənə-Ø
          you   1/2-see-TAM
          'I saw you.'

   c.   Yi-pawana   n-enee-ya-n   pampira-ton
          1-friend   3A:3P-bring-TAM-EVID   book-COLL
          'My friend is bringing all the books.'

   d.   Pampira   Ø-enee-ya-n   yi-pawana
          book   3A-bring-TAM-EVID   1-friend
          'My friend is bringing the book.'

We see that a pronominal prefix can co-occur with an overt first- and second-person P in preverbal position as in (59a,b) and also with a postverbal nominal P as in (59c) but not with a preverbal nominal P (59d). In the Nilotic language of Kenya Dho-Luo (Omondi 1982:36–7), the nominal as opposed to pronominal nature of the controller has a bearing on the obligatoriness of agreement. With independent person markers subject agreement is obligatory, with lexical NPs in the imperfective it is optional. And in the perfective, there is obligatory person agreement with nouns, but the agreement in number is optional.

The opposite situation to that captured in the nominal hierarchy, person agreement with an overt lexical NP but not with an independent person marker also occurs. One case in point is that of the western Austronesian language Palauan, as shown in (60).

(60)   Palauan (Georgopoulos 1991:26)
   a.   Ng-'illebed-ii a bilis (*ngii)
        3SG-hit-3SG   dog   s/he
        'S/he hit the dog.'

   b.   Ng-'illebed-ii a bilis a buik
        3SG-hit-3SG   dog   boy
        'The boy hit the dog.'

Another instance of the above is that of the Pama-Nyungan language of Arnhem Land, Ritharngu (Heath 1978:126). Heath mentions that though the person enclitics of Ritharngu are typically obligatory even in the presence of a corresponding S/A or P NP, they do not co-occur with an independent person marker. Thus (61b) is ungrammatical.

(61)   Ritharngu (Heath 1978:126)
   a.   Ngara ya   wa:n-i gudarpuy
        I   will go   tomorrow
        'I will go tomorrow.'

   b.   *Ngara ya=ra   wa:ni gudarpuy
        I   will-1SG go   tomorrow
        'I will go tomorrow.'

4.3.3   The animacy hierarchy

The preference for person agreement with humans over other animates has already been partially discussed in connection with the person and nominal hierarchies by virtue of the fact that the referents of first- and second-person markers, and in some languages also those of third-person markers, are necessarily human. Here we will confine our attention to the effects on person agreement of animacy distinctions involving third-person referents.

Perhaps the most obvious manifestation of the animacy hierarchy in relation to agreement is the predilection for person agreement between the possessor and possessed with kin terms and body parts discussed in section 4.2.2. The possessors of both are typically human and in some languages are even necessarily so.

As for person agreement with the verbal arguments, the indirect effects of the animacy hierarchy may be discerned in the preference for person agreement with the A over the P in accusative and active alignments and for the R over the T in secundative alignment (see section 4.2.1.2). The A and the R are typically human, the P and particularly the T often not. There is much less evidence, however, of the direct effects of the animacy hierarchy on person agreement with the verbal arguments. Nonetheless, there is some.

Person agreement restricted to humans is found, for example, in the Austronesian language Kusaiean, in two Papuan languages, Hua and Mauwake, and in

Rumanian. In Kusaiean, person agreement is actually displayed only with a subset of human NPs, namely proper names. This holds for both agreement with the A and the P, as (62) demonstrates.

(62) Kusaiean (Lee 1975:101, 126, 335)
  a. Sohn **el** puok-ohl Sah
      John 3SG hit-3SG Sah
      'John is hitting Sah.'

  b. Mwet luo ah (*eltahl) tuhkuh
      man two DET 3PL   come
      'The two men came.'

  c. Kuht sa-akihlen-(*eltahl) mwet forfor ngoh
      1PL NEG-notice-3PL   man distant DEM
      'We did not recognize those men over there.'

In Hua, Mauwake and Rumanian the restriction to humans applies to person agreement with the P. Observe the presence of person agreement in (63a) as opposed to its absence in (63b).[20]

(63) Hua (Haiman 1980:371)
  a. Vedemo **p**-go-e
      men   2/3PL-see:1SG
      'I saw the men.'

  b. Mna-vza-mo   ko-e   (*p-go-e)
      bird-(COLL.) -PL see-1SG (2/3PL-see-1SG)
      'I saw the birds.'

In Acehnese, Gapapaiwa, Kairiru, Mundari and Noon, there is an animacy as opposed to a humanness constraint on person agreement with the P. And in the Australian language Djaru such a constraint operates in regard to person agreement with obliques. There may be person agreement with a human or animate locative, ablative or allative NP but not with an inanimate one. Compare (64a) and (64b). (The agreement is on a catalyst particle not on the verb.)

(64) Djaru (Tsunoda 1981:57)
  a. Ngaju nga-rna-nyanta   yan-an kunyarr-awu
      I:ABS CAT-1SG(NOM) - 3SG(LOC) go-PRES dog-ALL
      'I go to the dog.'

  b. Ngaju nga-rna   yan-an ngurra-ngkawu
      I:ABS CAT-1SG(NOM)   go-PRES dog-ALL
      'I go to the dog.'

---

[20] In Rumanian the human P NP must also be marked by the preposition *pe*.

In the Philippine language Kapampangan, person agreement with the P (by means of an S/P enclitic) can occur with inanimate objects, as in (65a), but according to Mithun (1994:253) generally not with abstractions, as shown in (65b).

(65)   Kapampangan (Mithun 1994:264, 253)
  a.   Pintalan=na=la   reng   mangaragul nang basuraan   Emma
        went to-3SG(A)-3SG(S/P) CLF.PL.ABS   big:PL   her garbage bin Emma
        'He went to Emma's big garbage bins.'
  b.   Tatanggapan=ku   ing   amun   mu
        accepting   1SG(A)   ABS   challenge your
        'I accept your challenge.'

Typically, however, the animacy constraint combines with definiteness, as is the case in many Bantu languages, and also Wanuma and Spanish. This will be discussed below.

4.3.4   The referential hierarchy

The referential hierarchy, like the animacy hierarchy, relates to third-person referents. Unlike the animacy hierarchy, however, it has to do not with the inherent but with the contingent saliency of controllers. It specifies a preference for person agreement with NPs which are definite or at least specific as opposed to non-specific non-referential NPs.

Recall from section 4.1. that whether or not the presence of a person form is sensitive to definiteness or specificity is taken by some scholars to be a major diagnostic of its status as an agreement marker as opposed to bound personal pronoun. Needless to say, given my contention that there is no firm basis for distinguishing between anaphoric pronouns and person agreement, this is not the position adopted here. As stated in section 4.1, the distinction between pronominal and ambiguous person agreement markers is scalar rather than discrete. This has already been demonstrated by the fact that in some languages a given person marker may co-occur in the same construction with a pronominal controller but not a nominal one, or vice versa, or with a proper name but not a common NP, or an animate NP but not an inanimate one. This scalarity may also be expected to be reflected in referential restrictions, which should be strongest for pronominal agreement markers but not necessarily absent from ambiguous agreement markers. And indeed definiteness restrictions on person agreement can be observed quite regularly in relation to pronominal agreement markers, as is the case with respect to P agreement, for example, in various Bantu languages (e.g. Chichewa, Chi-Mwi:ni, Shona) and Persian.

(66)   Persian (Mahootian 1997:255)
  a.   Ketab-o   tæmum-kærd-æm
        book-ACC   finish-did-1SG
        'I finished the book.'

b. Tæmum-es-kærd-æm
   finish-3SG-did-1SG
   'I finished it.'

c. Ye ketab xærid-æm
   one book bought-1SG
   'I bought a book.'

d. #Xærid-æm-es
   bought-1SG-3SG
   'I bought it.'

We see in (66) that the P clitic in Persian is necessarily interpreted as definite. Thus, while it can be used in (66b) with reference to *ketabo in* (66a), it cannot be used in (66d) to refer to the indefinite *ye ketab* in (66c). Definiteness restrictions on ambiguous agreement markers as opposed to pronominal agreement markers are also attested. For instance, in Bulgarian there is optional person agreement with a definite P occurring inside the VP though not with an indefinite P. Note the contrast in (67).

(67) Bulgarian (Dimitrova-Vulchanova & Hellan 1999:487)
  a. Čel sŭm ja knigata
     read AUX 3SG book:DEF
     'I have read that book.'

  b. *Čel sŭm ja kniga
     read AUX 3SG book
     'I have read a book.'

Similar restrictions may be observed in Albanian, Greek, Kambera, Kapampangan, Konjo, Palauan and Spanish.

Ambiguous agreement markers may, however, display a weaker referential restriction, that is they may co-occur with certain indefinite controllers. This is the case in Gela, Mussau, Tinrin, Rumanian, Porteno Spanish and Bawm, for example. In Tinrin the only constraint on person agreement seems to be that the controller be specific. Thus the presence of the subject clitic in (68a) as compared to (68b).

(68) Tinrin (Osumi 1995:215, 246)
  a. Abêêrrî   nrâ= merrò truu môôwi
     Old person 3SG   lie   DUR breathe
     'An old man lay down, taking a rest.'

  b. Hêrrê hôdrô mwâ
     IMPR burn hut
     'Someone burned the hut. / The hut has been burnt down.'

The same holds for object agreement in Gela and Mussau. In Rumanian the controller of the P agreement must be not only specific, but also human and preceded by the preposition *pe*.

(69)   Rumanian (Anagnostopoulou 1999:783)
    a.   O   caut   pe   o secreteră
        3SGF look for:1SG ACC/DAT a secretary
        'I look for a secretary.'

    b.   *Il   caut   pe   un elev   care să știe   englezește
        3SGM look for:1SG ACC/DAT a student which speaks English
        'I look for a student who can speak English.'

In Porteno Spanish agreement is possible also with certain non-specific NPs, namely with a partitive NP (70a) and with an indefinite modified by a relative clause (70b), thought not with a quantified indefinite (70c).

(70)   Porteno Spanish (Anagnostopoulou 1999:763, 784)
    a.   El médico los=examinó   a machos/varios de   los pacientes
        the doctor 3PL=examined:3SG ACC many/several of the patients
        'The doctor examined many/several of the patients.'

    b.   Diariamente la=escuchaba   [a   una mujer que cantaba tangos
        daily   3SGF-listened:3SG ACC a   woman who sang   tangos
        'Every day they listened to a woman who sang tangos.'

    c.   *Los= entrevistaron a   muchos/ varios candidatos por media hora
        3PL=interviewed   ACC many   several candidates for half   hour
        'They interviewed many/several patients for half an hour.'

And finally, in the Tibeto-Burman language Bawm, quantified indefinites also exhibit agreement and so do negative quantifiers. The NP *mipa aumawh* 'some men' in (71a) could potentially be referential but the quantified NPs in (71b) and (71c) clearly are not.

(71)   Bawm (Reichle 1981:157–8)
    a.   Mipâ âumawh an = hwang
        man some   3PL come
        'Some men are coming.'

    b.   Mipâ âutal nih an tangkâ an = khâwi kho
        man any AG 3PL money 3PL save   can
        'Any man can save money.'

    c.   Aukhawm nih Pathian an =muh dah loh
        nobody   AG God   3PL see ever not
        'Nobody has ever seen God.'

As all the examples of grammatical agreement in (67)–(71) feature clitic as opposed to affixal person markers, all would be considered by advocates of the agreement marker vs pronoun distinction as pronouns rather than agreement markers. Yet as we have just seen, they differ in the referential restrictions that they display. Conversely, as pointed out by Evans (2002), and illustrated in section 4.1 on the basis of the Australian language Bininj Gun-wok, some person forms which are by the same scholars standardly considered to be bound pronouns, appear to display no referential restrictions and thus display the characteristics of agreement markers. This, in turn, is suggestive of the fact either that referential restrictions are not pertinent to the pronoun vs agreement marker distinction or that the distinction itself is not a viable one.[21]

4.3.5   The focus hierarchy

Even if person agreement in a language is not dependent on any inherent or referential properties of the controller, the presence vs absence of person agreement may be ultimately determined by the information status of the controller in the utterance. There are two primary information statutes that the elements of an utterance may bear, topic and focus. Both of these notions have been variously defined. Assuming a fairly traditional view, the topic is the entity which the utterance is primarily about and the focus is the most important or salient piece of information in the utterance, as perceived by the speaker. Given this view, the topic and focus are not the converse of each other, that is it is not necessarily the case that what is not topic is focus and vice versa. The topic typically conveys given information, that is previously mentioned or easily recoverable information. The focus, on the other hand, always presents new information, though new relative to the topic, not necessarily new in the discourse.

All the factors favouring agreement in the hierarchies discussed above are associated with topicality. It thus follows that agreement is much more likely to occur with topical controllers than with non-topical ones. However, unless one assumes a bifurcation of the clause into topic and focus, which I do not, this does not imply that person agreement particularly disfavours constituents in focus. Yet in some languages this is indeed so. Therefore, unlike in the case of the other hierarchies discussed above, we will concentrate our attention here on the absence rather than on the presence of agreement.

In terms of the communicative point that the focus is intended to achieve, it is possible to distinguish between contrastive and non-contrastive focus. Non-contrastive focus denotes information that is intended to fill a gap in the pragmatic information of the addressee. Non-contrastive focus may be divided into wh-focus, that is the information sought after by means of a question word in a question, such as *who* in (72a), and completive focus, the supplied missing information, such as *Matthew* in (72b).

---

[21] Mithun (2003) argues against the claim that person markers in polysynthetic languages display properties of agreement markers rather than pronouns. While acknowledging that person markers may co-occur with indefinite or referential expressions, she suggests that reference may be established in these languages somewhat differently than, for example, in English.

(72) a. Who introduced you to Charlotte?
  b. Matthew did.

Contrastive focus, on the other hand, denotes contrastive information in the strict sense of the term, that is information which the speaker assumes to be directly opposed to a restricted range of alternatives deemed to be entertained by the addressee. Contrastive focus may also be further subdivided. Dik (1989:336), for example, distinguished between parallel focus and counter-presuppositional focus. The former involves an explicit contrast of two pieces of information within one linguistic expression, as in (73).

(73) The Afghans play the buzkashi with a goat carcass, the Kazakhs with a sheep carcass.

The latter involves a contrast between the speaker's assertion and the addressee's presupposition, as in (74).

(74) Ken is in Beijing. No he isn't in Beijing, he's in Guangzhou.

In some languages person agreement seems to be absent with all types of focus. This is the case in Konjo, an Austronesian language of South Sulawesi, which displays ergative person agreement by means of A proclitics and s/P enclitics. This is illustrated in (75).

(75) Konjo (Friberg 1996:141)
  a. Na-peppe'-i Amir asung-ku
     3A-hit-3s/P Amir dog-1
     'Amir hit my dog.'
  b. A'-lampa-i Amir
     INTR-go-3SG Amir
     'Amir goes.'

The following examples show that no person agreement clitics occur when the relevant constituent, here the A, is under wh-focus (76a), completive focus (76b) or counter-presuppositional focus (76c).

(76) Konjo (Friberg 1996:146)
  a. Inai ang-kanere-i lamejaha-ku?
     Who TR-ate-3   sweet potatoes-1
     'Who ate my sweet potatoes?'
  b. I-ali[22] ang-kanre-i lamejaha-ta
     A-Ali TR-ate-3s/P sweet potato-2
     'Ali ate your sweet potatoes.'

---

[22] The i-prefix is added to proper names and pronouns, typically for purposes of disambiguation, though this does not appear to be the reason for the use of the prefix in this case.

c. Injo bembe na-kalahakia mana'-mi rua ana'-na
that goat 3A-shepherd.DEF gave birth-3:ASP two child-3
'The goat that he took care of (not some other) gave birth to two kids.'

We find a similar situation in Yagua (Payne 1990:31) and the Arawakan language Apurina (Facundes 2000). In these languages the presence vs absence of person agreement interacts with order. An argument located postverbally displays agreement, while one located preverbally does not. These two facts are easy to reconcile since in both languages preverbal constituents are necessarily focal.[23] In Chalcatongo Mixtec (Macaulay 1996) the focus position is also preverbal and subjects located there fail to display person agreement. Subjects in topic position, which precedes the focus position, on the other hand, co-occur with person clitic markers. Compare (77a), where na?a 'woman' is in topic position with (77b), where it is in focus position.

(77) Chalcatongo Mixtec (Macaulay 1996:140)
    a. Ñā?ā wáā xīnū-ñá
        woman the run-3F
        'The woman is running.'

    b. Ñā?ā wáā xīnū
        woman the run
        'The woman is the one who is running.'

Note also the lack of person clitics under parallel contrastive focus in (78).

(78) Chalcatongo Mixtec (Macaulay 1996:106)
    Rù?ù čí?i itù te máá=de čí?i nduči túú
    I plant corn and EMPH-3M plant bean black
    'I'm planting corn, but he's planting black beans.'

Absence of regular person agreement with constituents in both non-contrastive and contrastive focus can also be observed in another Arawakan language Bare. In Bare, however, wh-focus is accompanied by an indefinite person marker which is prefixed to the verb instead of the person agreement prefix. No such special prefix occurs under contrastive focus; the person agreement markers are simply suppressed. Compare (79a), which exhibits the regular prefixal marking of the A, with (79b) where the A is under wh-focus and with (79c) where the A is in contrastive focus and the verb *muduka* 'kill' occurs with no person marking.

(79) Bare (Aikhenvald 1995:19, 29, 30)
    a. Heñaṛi i-kasa
        man 3SGNF-arrive
        'A man came.'

---

[23] Payne (1990:199, 202, 204) actually gives examples of all the different types of focus mentioned above.

b. Abadi a-diña   nu-yaka-w   iku
    who INDEF-speak 2SG-parent-F with
    'Who spoke to your mother?'

c. Me-hesa   me-wat'u-ka   ada tʃinu i-bara-ka   damakarute diñabu-kua ite
    3PL-want 3PL-beat-DEC that dog   3SGNF-run-DEC   jungle:DIR road-along there
    i-mahasa-ka   wa-kiñaha nu-yakaṛi-minihi   mudukā   kuhū
    3SGNF-disappear-DEC-think 1PL-think 1SG-father-DEFUNCT   kill:PAST he
    'They wanted to beat the dog, (it) ran away to the jungle by the road,
    there it disappeared. We thought my late father killed him.'

4.4   The markers of person agreement

There are two major issues relating to the markers of person agreement, their morpho-phonological status and their location. The first of these will be briefly discussed in section 4.4.1, the second in 4.4.2.

4.4.1   Person agreement and morpho-phonological form

In the generative literature, the morpho-phonological form of person agreement markers has been a subject of discussion mainly in relation to the affix/clitic distinction. The majority view among generativists seems to be that only affixes are potential agreement markers, while clitics and weak forms are pronominal arguments, heads or operators of syntactic projections. In the functional-typological paradigm, on the other hand, no restrictions on the morpho-phonological form of person agreement markers are imposed. Nonetheless, since in the process of grammaticalization morpho-phonological changes and semantic ones are assumed to run in parallel (see ch. 7, section 7.2), one would expect the increase in the obligatoriness of person agreement from pronominal through ambiguous to syntactic to be reflected in a decrease in their syntactic independence and phonological form. And indeed to a large extent this is so.

Pronominal agreement markers are often realized by weak forms or clitics, and syntactic agreement markers are invariably affixes, often fused with tense, aspect or mood. The cross-linguistically most common agreement markers, the ambiguous, while displaying the widest range of formal realizations, tend to be affixes. Moreover, the ambiguous markers that are obligatory are most likely to be fused with other grammatical markers, as is the case with respect to subject agreement markers in, for example, Armenian, Bilin, Burushaski, Greek, Kilivila, Kobon, Latin, Muna, Polish (in the non-past), Sentani, Spanish, Wambon, Wanuma and West Greenlandic. Crucially, however, the above are global tendencies not absolute restrictions. Even weak forms may be obligatory, as is the case in verbal clauses in Woleaian. The examples in (80) illustrate that the weak person forms occur even under completive and wh-focus.

(80)   Woleaian (Sohn 1975:71)
   a.   Iir   mele **re**   mwal
        they FOC   3PL   hid
        'They are the ones who hid.'

   b.   Iteiu mele **ye** buutog?
        Who   FOC   3SG come
        'Who came?'

Obligatory subject clitics are somewhat more common. They are found, for example, in Bawm, Central Kurdish, Konjo, and Taba. We see below that a subject clitic accompanies a generic subject in (81a), an indefinite one in (81b) and a wh-focus in (81c).

(81)   Central Kurdish (Fattah 1997:246, 130, 183)
   a.   Z^in   z^in   na:-xw-**a**:
        woman woman NEG-eat:PRES:3SG
        'A woman does not eat a woman.' (246)

   b.   Z^: nek-u: kur^ek   ha:-t-**in**-a   dare
        woman:INDEF-and boy:INDEF come-PAST-3PL outside
        'A woman and a boy came.'

   c.   Ke- w-   ke ha-t-**in**
        who-and who come-PAST-3PL
        'Who and who came?'

Conversely, affixes may function as pronominal agreement markers. This is so with respect to A markers, for example in Berta, Coptic, Pari, Rama, Retuara, Teribe, Tlingit and Wichita. Affixal P pronominal agreement markers are found, for instance, in Anejom, Beja, Berta, Bimoba, Boni, Candoshi, Chacobo, Geez, Guarani, Jicaque, Kera, Kiribatese, Lele, Mbay, Noon, Paamese, Palikur, Pari, Retuarã, Sema, and Waura. Relevant examples are scattered through out.

4.4.2 The location of person markers

The location of person agreement markers may be considered in relation to three different entities: the target which typically is the verbal, nominal or adpositional stem, other person agreement markers of the same target and other grammatical markers. We will discuss each in turn. We will take into account only person agreement affixes, as clitics, in the sense of the term used here, by definition have a variable location.

4.4.2.1 Prefixes vs suffixes

There are currently three hypotheses relating to affixes which have a direct bearing on the location of person agreement markers relative to the stem.[24] The first hypothesis is that there is a universal preference for suffixes over prefixes. The overall suffixing preference displayed by languages is attributed to three factors (Hawkins & Gilligan 1988; Hall 1988; Bybee et al. 1990): processing ease, the greater likelihood of fusion in post-stem than in pre-stem position and the tendency for the ends of phonological units to be articulated weaker than their beginnings. All three factors are closely interrelated.

The claim that the placing of grammatical material after lexical material enhances processing draws on the results of experimental research which strongly suggests that lexical access is typically achieved on the basis not of a whole word, but rather the initial part of a word. It is therefore argued that the positioning of a stem before an affix facilitates the most rapid possible meaningful interpretation of the input. The assumption that optimally efficient processing is served by stem+affix as opposed to affix+stem order is in turn taken to constitute the underlying reason why free lexical morphemes are more likely to fuse in post-stem than in pre-stem position. The other factor reinforcing the predilection for fusion of post-stem material is that informationally weak or de-emphasized items are prone to both phonetic and semantic reduction. And the phonetic reduction of post-stem material is seen to be enhanced by the tendency for the ends of words to be phonologically less distinct than their beginnings.

The second hypothesis relating to the placement of person markers relative to the stem originates from work in generative morphology (e.g. Williams 1981). It is based on the assumption that the order of affixes, like that of words and phrases, conforms to one of two possible ordering schemas, modifier > head or head > modifier.[25] Person agreement affixes are treated as heads and the targets to which they are attached as modifiers. The prediction thus is that person agreement affixes should be suffixes in modifier > head languages (OV) and prefixes in head > modifier languages (VO). This hypothesis is known as the head ordering principle or HOP.

The third hypothesis pertaining to affix location is the diachronic syntax hypothesis (DSH).[26] The DSH defines a preference for affixes to be located in the positions of the separate words from which the affixes are derived at the time they started being fused together into a single word. The DSH thus predicts a preference for person agreement prefixes in verb-final and genitive-before-noun (GN)

---

[24] There are also various additional theory-internal hypotheses relating to specific types of languages. For instance, Baker (1996) suggests that polysynthetic languages favour person agreement prefixes.

[25] For a discussion of this typology see, for example, Siewierska (1988:16–22) and the references cited there.

[26] According to Robins (1967:101, 157), this principle dates back to the 1500s and has been widely evoked since the 1800s.

Table 4.3 *The distribution of person A prefixes vs suffixes relative to basic monotransitive order*

Form A AGR	V-initial N=25	V-medial N=56	V-final N=99
Prefix	15 60%	41 73%	29 30%
Suffix	10 40%	15 27%	70 70%

Table 4.4 *The distribution of person P prefixes vs suffixes relative to basic monotransitive order*

Form P AGR	V-initial N=28	V-medial N=53	V-final N=73
Prefix	7 33%	19 36%	42 56%
Suffix	21 67%	34 64%	31 42%

languages, person agreement suffixes in verb-initial and genitive-after-noun (NG) languages and a combination of prefixes and suffixes in verb-medial languages.

The existence of a preference for suffixes over prefixes receives support from the ordering of tense, aspect and modality affixes and from the existence of languages which are exclusively suffixing as well as from the lack of languages which are exclusively prefixing (see, e.g., Hawkins & Gilligan 1988). However, it finds only very weak support from the location of person agreement affixes. Among the languages in the sample the markers of A agreement, P agreement and possessor agreement are marginally more often suffixes than prefixes, but the difference is only of 1 to 3 per cent.

The predictions of the HOP and DSH are dependent on the word-order type of a language. For OV languages, that is verb-final ones, the HOP predicts A and P suffixes, and for VO, that is verb-medial and verb-initial ones, A and P prefixes. With the exception of the A prefixes in verb-medial languages, the DSH makes the very opposite predictions. The placement of A and P affixes relative to the verbal stem among the verb-initial, verb-medial and verb-final languages in the sample lends little support to either the HOP or the DSH. The relevant data are presented in Tables 4.3 and 4.4. To simplify matters, only languages in which the person markers in question are either all prefixes or all suffixes and which also have a clear basic order in transitive clauses have been taken into account. We see that the HOP is relatively successful in predicting the location of A markers, and the DSH the location of P markers. Nonetheless, the highest success rate of either hypothesis in regard to the placement of A or P markers in any word-order type is only 73 per cent. In all, the DSH fares somewhat better than the HOP in that in the case of verb-medial AVP languages, it correctly predicts the tendency not only for P suffixes but also A prefixes. Moreover, the DSH can be reconciled with the slight preference for A prefixes as opposed to suffixes in verb-initial languages if it is assumed that the preverbal placement of A person agreement markers is the result of Wackernagel's Law, that is the tendency to place clitics in second position in the utterance coupled with subsequent prefixation of the clitic. However, the preference for A suffixes as opposed to prefixes in verb-final languages is more difficult to account for in terms of the DSH. One possibility, suggested by Givón (1976) for Semitic and Indo-European languages, is that the suffixes were formerly prefixed to a finite verb in a periphrastic construction which subsequently fused with the preceding non-finite verb, as illustrated in (82).

(82) a.   V-non-finite AGR-AUX
    b.   V+AGR-AUX
    c.   V-AGR

Another possibility is, of course, the universal suffixing preference.

In sum, none of the three explanations for the location of person affixes relative to the stem provides a satisfactory account of the data. The coupling of the DSH with the universal suffixing preference fares best but still leaves a considerable amount of data unaccounted for.

4.4.2.2 The order of person agreement affixes relative to each other

The attempts at explaining the order of A and P affixes relative to each other have not been much more successful than those relating to the location of the two types of agreement markers relative to the stem. One line of explanation is based on the degree of grammaticalization of the relevant markers. Diachronically older forms, that is forms that have undergone more development, are expected to occur closer to the stem than younger forms (see, e.g., Bybee et al. 1991:33). Since A markers tend to be more grammaticalized than P markers (see ch. 7), this suggests a preference for P > A order among prefixes, and for A > P order among suffixes, as in (83) and (84), respectively.

(83)   Retuarã (Strom 1992:219)
    Sa-ki-ba?a-ko?o
    3SG(P) -3SG(A) -ate-PAST
    'He ate it.'

(84)   Sentani (Cowan 1965:32)
    Hab-ad-ε
    hit-2SG(A)-1SGF(P)
    'You hit me.'

Another explanation involves the degree to which the meaning of an affix directly affects the meaning of the stem. Affixes which have a greater semantic effect on the stem are expected to be placed closer to the stem than those exerting a smaller effect. This is referred to by Bybee (1985) as the principle of relevance. Assuming that the semantic and syntactic bond between the P and the verb is closer than between the A and the verb, the principle of relevance defines the very opposite

Table 4.5 *The order of the A and P relative to each other in prefixal vs suffixal location*

Form A & P affixes	A > P		P > A	
Prefix N=44	28	64%	16	36%
Suffix N=43	21	49%	22	51%

ordering of affixes than that predicted by the degree of grammaticalization, namely for A > P prefixes, as in (85) and for P > A suffixes, as in (86).

(85) Swahili (Ashton 1944, 1974:42)
Ni- li- mw-ona
1SG(A)-PAST-3SG(P) - see
'I saw him.'

(86) Halkomelem (Wiltschko 2002:165)
Kw'éts-lexw-es   tú-tl'ò thú-tlò
see: TR-3(P) - (3A) DET-3 DET:FEM-3
'He sees her.'

For the eighty-seven languages in the sample in which both the A and P are either prefixes or suffixes and have a discernible and unique order relative to each other the principle of relevance is a slightly better predictor of the existing orders than degree of grammaticalization. The relevant data are depicted in Table 4.5. We see that ordering in line with the principle of relevance, i.e. prefixal A > P order and suffixal P > A order occurs in 57 per cent (50/87) of the cases. This contrasts with a 43 per cent (37/87) success rate for order in line with the assumption that the A grammaticalizes prior to the P.

The success rate of the principle of relevance increases further if it is adjusted to alignment, as suggested in the generative literature by Bitner and Hale (1996) and Baker (1996). Under their analysis, in accusative alignment it is the P that should be placed closer to the verbal stem, and in ergative alignment, the A. The predicted ordering patterns are thus the ones shown in (87).

(87) a.   NOM/ACC A-P-V-P-A
    b.   ABS/ERG P-A-V-A-P

Of the eight languages with the relevant type of ergative alignment of verbal person affixes in the sample (i.e. with overt A and P markers on the same side of the verb), all but one display the predicted order of the A and P. Five languages, Abkhaz, Basque, Jacaltec, Tzutujil and Washo have prefixal P > A order and Greenlandic Eskimo and Kapampangan have suffixal A > P order. The exceptional order of the A and P affixes, namely prefixal A > P order, occurs in the Wasco-Wishram dialect of Chinookan, as shown in (88).

(88) Upper Chinook Wasco-Wishram dialect (Silverstein 1978:239)
Ni-č-d-u-(l)čxm
rem.past-3SGM(A)-3PL(P)-boiled
'He boiled them.'

For the thirty-seven languages in the sample with the relevant type of accusative alignment of verbal person affixes, ordering of the A and P in line with Bitner and Hale's predictions occurs in twenty-four or 65% of the cases. Some languages exhibiting the predicted order are Ainu, Daga, Kanuri, Marind, Ndonga, Pipil, Quileute, Selepet, Swahili, Tarascan and Tiwi. The opposite order, that is where A is closer to the stem than the P, is found, for example, in Amharic, Biri, Cahuilla, Chacobo, Koasati, Mesalit, Murle, Navajo, Retuarã and Sentani. But even so, the principle of relevance, when adjusted to the accusative vs ergative alignment of the A and P, does provide a better account of the ordering of the A and P relative to each other than the unmodified version, 69 per cent vs 57 per cent.

So far we have said nothing about the ordering of the T and R person agreement markers relative to each other in ditransitive clauses. As mentioned in section 4.2.1.2, person agreement with both the T and R is rather uncommon. When it does occur, the two person markers are typically on the same side of the verb. If the ordering of the T and R markers relative to each other, like that of A and P markers, is dependent on alignment, we would expect to see the T placed closer to the verbal stem than the R in indirective alignment, and conversely, in secundative alignment, as shown in (89).

(89) a. indirective R-T-V-T-R
b. secundative T-R-V-R-T

In the case of languages with phonologically distinct T and R markers, all of which evince indirective alignment (see ch. 2, section 2.2.2.2.2), a slight preference can indeed be discerned for positioning the T marker closer to the stem than the R marker. This is so in Bulgarian, Ekari, Kashmiri, Amele and Gooniyandi. The converse order, that is R closer to the stem than T, is found, for example, in Abkhaz (90), Ngiyambaa and Doyayo.

(90) Abkhaz (Hewitt 1979:105)
Sarà a -x̊əč̣'-k°à a- s̊q'- k°à Ø -rə-s-to-yt'
I the-child-PL the-book-PL 3PL(T)-3PL(R)-I-give-FIN
'I give the books to the children.'

By contrast, in languages in which the T and R markers are not phonologically distinct, the R seems to be positioned closer to the stem more frequently than the T. (See section 4.2.1.2.)

While most languages have a unique order of the A and P and/or T and R relative to each other, in some the order of the respective person markers may depend on the position of the referents of the markers on the person and/or animacy hierarchies. This is not uncommon among the languages of Australia (e.g. Gunwinggu, Yukulta, Yulparija). For instance in Yulparija, a Pama-Nyungan language belonging to the Wati subgroup of Western Desert, the person agreement A and P clitics, which are attached to the first word of the sentence, are ordered in line with the person hierarchy of $1 > 2 > 3$. Thus in the first clauses of (91) we have the P preceding the A, and in the second clause, the A preceding the P.

(91) Yulparija (Burridge 1996:51)
Nyuntu-lu-ja-n pu-nganya ngaparrja-rna-nta
you-ERG-1SG:ACC-2SG:NOM hit-FUT in return-1SG:NOM-2SG:ACC
'If you hit me, I'll hit you back.'

In the Papuan language Yimas, the order of A and P prefixes is determined by two hierarchies, a person hierarchy of $1 > 2 > 3$ and a role hierarchy according to which in the case of the first and second persons the P outranks the A, and in the case of the third person, the A outranks the P. The higher-ranking participant is placed closer to the verb stem. Thus when both participants are third person or the A is first or second person and the P third, we have P > A order as in (92).

(92) Yimas (Foley 1991:202, 205)
  a. Pu-n-tay
    3PL-3SG-see
    'He saw them.'

  b. Pu-ka-tay
    3PL-1SG-see
    'I saw them.'

But when the A is third person and the P first or second or the A is second person and the P first, we have A > P order, as in (93).

(93) Yimas (Foley 1991:205–6)
  a. Pu-ŋa-tay
    3PL-1SG-see
    'They saw me.'

  b. Ma-ŋa-tay
    2SG-1SG-see
    'You saw me.'

A conflict between the two hierarchies which arises when there is a first-person A and a second-person P is resolved by means of a portmanteau morpheme *mpan-/kampan*, e.g.

(94) Yimas (Foley 1991:207)
Kampan-tay
1SG:2SG-see
'I saw you.'

A yet more complicated instance of hierarchical ordering of person agreement markers, though this time T and R markers, is found in the Bantu languages

Shambala and Haya. According to Duranti (1979), the order of the T and R markers is determined by a combination of the person, number, humanness and role hierarchies in (95) with the higher-ranked marker being placed immediately before the verbal stem.

(95) a. 1 > 2 > 3
     b. SG > PL
     c. human > non-human
     d. R > T

There are also some additional restrictions on possible combinations of person markers. Shambala does not allow for first- and second-person markers to occur in the same verbal complex, nor for sequences of identical markers. Haya exhibits only the first of these constraints and only in the singular. The two languages also display different strategies in regard to the resolution of conflicts arising from the four parameters in (95). Shambala allows only sequences of T and R markers which differ in a single feature. Thus if the T and R differ only in person or number or humanness or role, they will occur in the orders specified in (95). This is illustrated in (96).

(96)   Shambala (Duranti 1979:36–7)
  a.   A- za- m- ni- et- e- a
       3SG-PAST-him-1SG-bring-APPL-ASP
       '(S)he has brought him to me.'

  b.   A- i- wa- mw- et- e- a
       3SG-PAST-them-him-bring-APPL-ASP
       '(S)he brought them to him.'

  c.   Na-i-mw-itang- i- a
       1SG-it-him- call- APPL-ASP
       'I call it for him.'

  d.   A- ya- i- dik- i- a
       3SG-them-it-cook-APPL-ASP
       '(S)he cooks them for it.'

If, however, there is a discrepancy in, for example, both person and number or person and humanness, then such a sequence of markers is simply ruled out; one of the two must be expressed by an independent NP. In Haya, conflict among the four hierarchies is resolved in favour of person unless both number and role converge in being high on their respective hierarchies. Accordingly, first-person singular will always be placed immediately before the verbal stem, but a first-person plural T may be outranked by a second- or third-person R. Note the ambiguity of (97a,b) as opposed to (97c,d).

(97) Haya (Duranti 1979:40, 42)
a. A- ka- mu- n- leet- ela
3SG-PAST-3SG-1SG-bring-APPL
'He brought him to me / me to him.'

b. A- ka- ku- tu-leet- ela
3SG-PAST-2SG-1PL-bring-APPL
'He brought us to you / you to us.'

c. A- ka- tu- mu-leet- ela
3SG-PAST-1PL-3SG-bring-APPL
'He brought us to him / *him to us.'

d. A- ka- tu- ku-leet-ela
3SG-PAST-1PL-2SG-bring-APPL
'He brought us to you / *you to us.'

Since ditransitive clauses tend to display person agreement with both the T and R much less frequently than transitive clauses do with both the A and P, hierarchically determined affixal T and R order is relatively uncommon. However, it is by no means confined to Bantu languages. It is also attested in, for instance, the Arawakan Campa languages of Peru (Wise 1986:585).

4.4.2.3 The order of person agreement markers relative to other grammatical markers

Since person agreement markers exert less of an effect on the meaning of the stem than do tense, aspect and modality markers (TAM) or valency changing markers or case markers, the principle of relevance predicts that they should be positioned further away from the stem than these other grammatical markers, as in Seri (98) and Biri (99), for example.

(98) Seri (Marlett 1990:525)
Ma-?-si-nip   ?a=?a
2SG(P)-1SG(A)-IRLS-hit AUX=DEC
'I will hit you (with a closed fist).'

(99) Biri (Terrill 1998:26)
Nganhi-gu yinda banhdhu-li-nda-ŋgu bama
why-DAT   you   hit-PAST-2SG(A)-3SG(P) man
'Why did you hit that man?'

This is indeed often so. Nonetheless, the positioning of S or A affixes inside TAM affixes is by no means rare.[27] Two cases in point are illustrated in (100) and (101).

---

[27] Siewierska (2000) documents that the placement of S or A affixes inside TAM affixes is especially common in verb-initial languages. Of the verb-initial languages in her sample 50 per cent displayed such ordering as compared to 22 per cent of the verb-final and 13 per cent of the verb-medial.

(100)   Amele (Roberts 1987:163)
        Silom uga wali-ag   ho-i-a
        Silom 3SG brother-3SG come-3SG-TODAY.PAST
        'Silom's brother came.'

(101)   Upper Chinook, Wasco-Wishram dialect (Silverstein 1978:239)
        Ni-č-d-ulčxm
        rem.past-3SG(A)-3PL(P)-boil
        'He boiled them.'

The fact that person agreement affixes are not necessarily always the outer affixes has led some linguists (e.g. Cinque 1999) to suggest that the location of person affixes is to a large extent arbitrary. In the light of the preferences noted above such a claim seems to be too radical. It is clear that there are no categorical restrictions of any type. But the weak preferences that have been discerned, may be amenable to further refinements which will yield stronger generalizations.

5 The function of person forms

Since person forms are referential expressions, all accounts of their function are based on their distinctiveness relative to other referential expressions. This distinctiveness is seen to lie in their minimal semantic content and attenuated phonological form. In the traditional literature these two characteristics are said to make of person markers convenient substitutes for NPs and thus useful devices for avoiding repetition, redundancy and achieving brevity and clarity of expression. A number of more sophisticated interpretations of the function of person forms have been developed by scholars working in various theoretical frameworks, such as Centering Theory (e.g. Grosz, Weinstein & Joshi 1995), Discourse Representation Theory (e.g. Kamp & Reyle 1993), Neo-Gricean Pragmatic Theory (e.g. Huang 2000) and cognitively oriented discourse analysis (e.g. Ariel 1990; Cornish 1999; Givón 1990; Gundel Hedberg and Zacharski 1993). As it is impossible to give even a brief account of these various approaches here, I will concentrate on one, namely on cognitive discourse analysis.

Section 5.1 will outline the general approach to referential expressions adopted within cognitive discourse analysis and in particular the assumed relationship between the cognitive status of discourse referents in the memory store of the addressee and morpho-syntactic encoding, briefly mentioned in chapter 2 (section 2.2.1.2). In the context of this relationship, person forms emerge as markers of referents which exhibit mid-high to high accessibility. The distribution of different types of person forms in discourse (and, in part, also within sentences) is, in turn, taken to follow from the set of parameters that determine levels of cognitive accessibility. To what extent differences in referent accessibility provide a satisfactory account of the distribution of different types of person forms in discourse will be discussed in section 5.2. In section 5.3 we will move from the level of discourse to that of the sentence and consider whether the factors that operate in discourse can also be viewed as underlying the distribution and interpretation of person forms within sentences. That there is no strict dividing line between discourse and sentence grammar in regard to the distribution of referential expressions and person forms in particular is nowadays widely accepted even by starch syntacticians. What is at issue therefore is whether the rules which are considered to be purely syntactic are indeed such, or whether they are in fact grammaticalized discourse preferences. The dominant syntactic approach to the intra-sentential use of person forms of the last twenty-odd years has been Chomsky's (1981) Binding Theory (BT). The discussion of the intra-sentential use of person forms will therefore concentrate on the range of data that fall within the domain of BT.

The marking of high cognitive accessibility of discourse referents is indisputably the primary function of person forms, but not their only one. The use of a person form over another referential expression may be an indication of speaker empathy or identification. This will be briefly discussed in section 5.4.1. And in section 5.4.2 we will consider the atypical use of person forms as impersonalizing devices.

5.1 Cognitive discourse analysis and referent accessibility

Within the cognitive discourse analysis approach person markers, like other forms of deixis and anaphora, are taken to be discourse-model management procedures used by speakers and hearers to adjust or maintain the accessibility (activation or saliency) level of referents in the evolving mental model of the discourse. Discourse, under this approach, is conceived of not as a text, be it verbal or written, but as a process, that is "a hierarchically structured mentally represented sequences of utterance and indexical acts which the participants are engaging in as the communication unfolds" (Cornish 1999:34). Reference is thus considered to be not a relation between a language expression and an element in the speech context (deictic reference) or discourse context (anaphoric reference) but between a language expression and the current mental representation of the referent denoted by that expression in the mind of the addressee. The morpho-syntactic form or encoding of referential expressions in turn is taken to signal to the addressee where in his/her discourse model the mental representation of the relevant referent is likely to be. Minimum encoding implies that the referent is already in the forefront of the hearer's (and speaker's) consciousness, i.e. that his attention is currently focused on it and therefore that the addressee should not waste time in searching further for the mental representation. Somewhat more encoding suggests that the referent though not currently being attended to has been recently mentioned and is thus activated. It should therefore be easily retrievable from working memory. Yet more elaborate encoding suggests that the relevant discourse referent must be sought deeper in the memory store of the hearer. And highly elaborated encoding indicates that the actual discourse referent is not in the current discourse model and thus there is no point in searching for its discourse representation. Rather, the hearer needs to build up a mental representation on the basis of the information supplied by the speaker. In view of their attenuated phonological form, the primary function of person markers is thus to signal the high level of cognitive accessibility of their referents.

Accessibility is seen to be dependent on a range of factors, the precise nature of which continues to be a topic of some controversy. The most inclusive view of the factors comprising accessibility is that espoused by Ariel (1990). Under Ariel's analysis, accessibility is a function of entity saliency and unity. Entity saliency involves both inherent and discourse saliency. The former may be affected by the personal histories of the interlocutors, their likes and dislikes, past experiences, etc. The latter, though sensitive to the status of referents in the discourse, that is whether they are major or minor characters or props, is mainly a function of how often and how recently they have been mentioned and the amount of competition from other referents that they have encountered. The major factors effecting entity saliency as presented by Ariel (1990) were listed in chapter 2 in the hierarchies in (83) and are repeated below in (1).

(1) a. Speaker > addressee > non-participant (3rd person)
    b. High physical salience > low physical salience
    c. Topic > non-topic
    d. Grammatical subject > non-subject
    e. Human > animate > inanimate
    f. Repeated reference > few previous references > first mention
    g. No intervening/competing referents > many intervening/competing referents

Unity, the second major determinant of accessibility, relates to the distance and degree of cohesion between the units containing the referential expressions of the discourse referents under consideration. By distance is meant whether the referents are embedded in the same clause, sentence, paragraph or frame. In the case of cross-clausal links, of relevance may also be the nature of the clausal linkage, coordination vs subordination and if the latter, the semantic type of subordination involved. Cross-linguistic analyses of clause linkage (e.g. Foley & van Valin 1984:269) suggest that the degree of connectivity between clauses decreases as we proceed from left to right in the hierarchy in (2).

(2) The inter-clausal semantic relation hierarchy causative > modality > psych-action > jussive > direct perception complements > indirect discourse complements > temporal adverbial clauses > conditionals > simultaneous actions > sequential actions (overlapping) > sequential actions (non-overlapping) > action-action (non-specified linkage).

Thus the expectation is that the tighter the linkage between two clauses, the higher the degree of accessibility of a referent expressed in both of them is likely to be. The other correlate of unity is the overall cohesion of the discourse, in particular the temporal, spatial and action continuity between the sentences in which the referents are embedded.

The nature of the relationship between cognitive accessibility and morpho-syntactic encoding is not conceived of in exactly the same way by all adherents of the cognitive discourse analysis approach. Some scholars posit a one-to-one relationship between each level of accessibility and a form of morpho-syntactic encoding, others a one to many. Ariel is the most prominent exponent of the first position, Gundel et al. (1993, 2000) of the second.

The relationship between the morpho-syntactic encoding of discourse referents and their degree of accessibility is captured by Ariel in her accessibility marking scale, given in (3), where accessibility decreases from left to right.

(3) The accessibility marking scale
zero < reflexives < person affixes < person clitics < unstressed pronouns < stressed pronouns < stressed pronoun plus gesture < proximal demonstrative (+NP) < distal demonstrative (+NP) < proximal demonstrative +(NP) + modifier < distal demonstrative (+NP) + modifier < first name < last name < short definite description < long definite description < full name < full name + modifier.

We see that absence of morpho-phonological form, that is zero, is associated with the highest level of accessibility, followed by markers of reflexivity and then the overt person forms. All are viewed as signalling a higher level of accessibility than demonstratives or NPs modified by demonstratives and these as being more accessible than any definite NP. Among the overt person forms, dependent forms, affixes and clitics are considered as higher accessibility coding devices than independent forms, and among the dependent forms affixes are taken to encode higher levels of accessibility than clitics.

The association between level of accessibility and form of morpho-syntactic encoding captured in (3) is assumed to be to some extent language and construction specific in that it depends on the repertoire of encoding devices that a given language has at its disposal. This is particularly evident in the case of person forms, the range of which, as we have seen in chapter two, differs widely from language to language and is heavily dependent on syntactic function. Moreover, there is no expectation that the accessibility levels compatible with a particular form of encoding, say an affixal or clitic form, be necessarily the same across languages. And as we shall see below, indeed they are not. What the accessibility marking scale does predict is that if there are two or more forms of marking available in a language for a given syntactic function in a given construction, the form of encoding higher on the accessibility marking scale will be used for referents that are more cognitively accessible, a form to its right for referents that are less accessible. The form of encoding is thus simultaneously an indication of level of accessibility (relative to syntactic function and the nature of the construction). This is not necessarily the case under the analysis of Gundel et al. (1993, 2000).

Gundel et al. seek to capture the accessibility levels of referents in terms of the six cognitive statuses in the givenness hierarchy in (4).

(4) The givenness hierarchy
in focus > activated > familiar > uniquely identifiable > referential > type identifiable.

Unlike under Ariel's analysis, according to which the various cognitive statuses of a referent are mutually exclusive, the cognitive statuses in (4) are viewed as being implicationally related, each status on the left including all the lower statuses, though not vice versa. Thus a referent that is in focus is necessarily also activated and familiar and uniquely identifiable, etc. This implicational interpretation of the relationship between different cognitive statuses of referents has direct repercussions on matters of morpho-syntactic encoding. If a given level of accessibility entails all lower levels, it follows that the forms of encoding associated with these lower levels of accessibility should be available for the encoding of higher accessibility levels. Thus, under Gundel et al.'s analysis, a given level of accessibility may be encoded by the accessibility marker conventionally associated with that level of accessibility, as well as by all the forms of encoding to its right on the accessibility marking scale. As an example of encoding conventionally associated with a lower level of accessibility than that displayed by the discourse referent in question they cite *these men* in (5).

(5)   As far as the likelihood of Indian women dating American men, my observation is that Indian girls born in America or raised in America from a very young age do not care to date or marry Indian men, for the same reasons mentioned above. They see the double standards Indian men hold on to, even those men that are born and raised here. In a vast majority of cases, **these men** inherit hang-ups from their Indian parents you see.

Gundel et al. (2000:5) point out that since the referent of *these men* must be considered to be activated, having been mentioned three times in the previous two sentences, it could in fact have been encoded by the unstressed person marker *they*. But it also could be encoded by lower accessibility markers such as *those men*, *the men* and even *Indian men* or *Indian men that are born and raised here*.

Given that under Gundel et al.'s analysis there is a one-to many, rather than a one-to-one relationship between accessibility level and form of morpho-syntactic encoding, we need to question what the source of the conventional relationship between the two is. Why is it that highly accessible referents are typically encoded by person forms and not NPs, for example? Gundel et al. argue that the strong association between level of accessibility and a particular form of encoding is due to general pragmatic principles that govern language processing, in particular two Gricean (1975) Maxims of Quantity. The first of these, "Make your contribution as informative as required" is taken to be relevant for pronoun choice, the second, "Do not make your contribution more informative than required" is claimed to underlie the choice of definite determiners. Since higher accessibility markers are more informative in regard to cognitive status than lower ones (the lower being implied by higher but not vice versa), the Maxim of Quantity dictates that, all things being equal, a higher accessibility marker be chosen over a lower one. However, if all things are not equal, a form of encoding associated with a lower level of accessibility may well be used. Accordingly, the referent of, for example, an independent person marker need not be always less accessible than that of the corresponding dependent form.

Implicit in Gundel et al.'s analysis is the assumption that while accessibility exerts a crucial effect on referent encoding, it is not the only factor at play. Ariel's one-to-one view of the relationship between referent encoding and accessibility in turn seeks to subsume all the factors conditioning the distribution of referential expressions in discourse under the notion of accessibility. This carries the danger of depleting the notion of accessibility of its substance. As I will try to show below, the distribution of person forms in discourse clearly favours an account which gives recognition to the effect of factors other than accessibility alone.

5.2 Referent accessibility and the distribution of person forms in discourse

The numerous studies of the distribution of person forms and other referential expressions in discourse carried out over the last twenty odd years have all shown that the referents of all types of person forms typically occur either in the clause immediately preceding the one containing the relevant person form, or one or two clauses back. In other words, the choice of different person forms in discourse is less likely to be determined by unity, at least as reflected in distance, than by entity saliency. We will therefore begin our discussion of the distribution of different types of person forms in discourse with the effect of entity saliency.

5.2.1 Entity saliency

As the accessibility hierarchies in (1) suggest, the circumstances which are most likely to induce the use of the highest accessibility person marking available in a language, inter-sententially, are sequences of clauses in which the same human discourse referent is continuously topic and also subject. The following examples are from Kannada and Japanese where the relevant person marking is by means of verbal inflection and zero, respectively.

(6)   Kannada (Sridhar 1990:115–16)
MaNi nidrisalu eSTo: prayatnisida tale me:le musuku
Mani sleep:INF very much try:PAST:3SGM head on cover
eLedukoNDa nidreya japa ma:Dida. laghu sangi:ta
pull:PAST:REFL:3SGM sleep:GEN recitation do:PAST:3SGM light music
ke:Lida
listen to:PAST:3SGM
'Mani tried very hard to sleep. (He) pulled the cover over his head. (He) repeated the word "sleep" like a mantra. (He) listened to light music.'

(7)   Japanese (Yamamoto 1999:122)
Ø hontoni hinkaku-no-oari-no kata de, fudan wa wagei no
(he) really graceful-H person and, usually TOP speech art of
tatsujin to iwa-rete-irassharu yuumoa tappuri-no
master as call-PASS-AUX:HON humour full of
kata de-irasshai-mashi-ta. Ø hontoni ano, Ø 82-sai
person COP-H-AUX-PAST (he) really well (he) 82-years:old
de o-nakunari-ninaru made geneki de-irasshai-mashi-ta
at die-H until active:service COP-H-AUX-PAST
'(He) was really a graceful person and a person full of humour, usually called a master of speech art. (He) really continued to act until (he) died at the age of 82.'

The number of clauses over which such highly accessible person marking can be sustained differs greatly depending on the form of marking in question, the presence of other participants, the degree of cohesion between the clauses, the nature of the text, etc.

One of the most common discourse contexts leading to the use of a lower rather than a higher accessibility person marker is topic shift, as illustrated in (8) from Udihe, where in the third clause the independent third-person form *bejeti* 'they' rather than just third-person plural verbal inflection is used upon a change of topic.[1]

(8) Udihe (Nikolaeva & Tolskaya 2001:755)
Gida bu-o:ni. E-si-n(i)-de ise loxo **Bejeti**
spear give-PAST:3SG NEG-PAST-3SG-FOC see saber. they
loxo bu-o:-ti
saber give-PAST-3PL
'He gave (them) a spear. He did not see a sabre. They gave (him) a sabre.'

Another common factor underlying the use of a lower as opposed to higher accessibility person marker is competition from other referents. Competition or interference is seen to induce the use of less rather than more attenuated forms of encoding in cases of topic continuity, though it may also increase the likelihood of the use of a lower accessibility person marker upon a change of topic. Most instances of competition involve third person referents which do not differ in regard to animacy and display the same person, gender and number features. In such cases, the use of a lower rather than a higher accessibility person marker may even not be enough to disambiguate the potential referential conflict and additional means of conflict resolution may be used. For instance, in Amharic a topic shift-marker is attached to the independent pronoun, as shown in (9).

(9) Amharic (Gasser 1983:132–3)
(...) Yä-hotel aškär mät't'a-nna säw
of-hotel servant come:3SG(S/A):PAST-and person
indämm-i-fällɨg-aw näggär-äw ɨssu-m
that-3SG(S/A)-want:NON-PAST-3SG(P) tell:PAST-3SG(P) he-TOPIC/SHIFT
kä-ɨngɨda maräfiya bet wärd-o tägänaññ-a
from-guest resting room come=down-3SG(S/A) meet:PAST-3SG(S/A)
'A hotel servant came and told him that someone wanted him. He came down from the lounge and met (the person).'

The use of the independent pronoun *issu* affixed with the topic shift marker *-m* rather than just of verbal inflection indicates that the subject and topic of the fourth clause is not the 'hotel servant' but the 'him' of the object suffix of the preceding clause. If the person inflection alone had been used, which of the two referents is the subject would have been quite unclear. Another means of resolving such referential conflict is via the use of a demonstrative form rather than an actual

---

[1] Switch-reference systems, which are also used for reference tracking, will not be discussed here since they are not sensitive to person.

third-person marker. This form of disambiguation is common in Czech, Slovak, Russian, Dutch and Finnish, for example. In Finnish the use of the demonstrative *tämä* is favoured over that of the third-person form *hän*, in the case of non-subject antecedents, as in (10a) or antecedents expressed by the subjects of subordinate clauses as in (10b).

(10)   Finnish (Kaiser 2000:20, 25–6)
- a. Lammio huusi   Mielosta, ja tämä tuli sisään lähetit
Lammio shouted for Mielonen and this came in   messengers
kannoillaan
heels-on-his
'Lammio called for Mielonene, and he (DEM) came in with the messengers on his heels.'

- b. Vääpeli katseli ajatuksissaan eteiseen, jossa kirjuri kampasi
sergeant looked in thought   vestibule:to where scribe combed
tukkaansa. Tämä ilmehti peilin edessä
hair:3SG this made faces mirror's in front
'Deep in thought the sergeant looked towards the vestibule, where the scribe was combing his hair. He (DEM) was making faces in front of the mirror.'

A preference for non-subject antecedents in the case of demonstratives is also in evidence in Russian, Czech and Slovak. In the last two languages the referent of a demonstrative must be the immediately preceding NP. In Russian this is not necessarily so, as evidenced by (11), where the demonstrative *tot* is separated from its referent in the preceding sentence by the subject of the current sentence *djadja Sandro*.

(11)   Russian (Kibrik 1991:69)
Opjat' na doroge pojavilsja milicioner, Djadja Sandro neskol'ko
again on road   appeared militiaman Uncle Sandro somewhat
podobralsja v ožidanii,   kogda tot poravnjaetsja s   nami
braced:REFL in expectation when that came up   with us
'Again on the road appeared a militiaman$_i$. Uncle Sandro braced himself somewhat in expectation when he$_i$ came up to us.'

Yet another strategy of referent conflict resolution is to use a full referential expression rather than just a form of person marking. According to Subbarao and Murthy, this is the preferred strategy in Telugu, as suggested by the examples in (12).

(12)   Telugu (Subbarao & Murthy 2000:232)
- a. Attagaaru   kooDali   too maatlaaDindi KooDalu   caalaa
mother-in-law daughter-in-law with talked.   Daughter-in-law very
santooSa paDindi
happy felt
'Mother-in-law talked to (her) daughter-in-law. The daughter-in-law felt very happy.'

b. Attagaaru   kooDali   too   maatlaaDindi AawiDa Ø caalaa
    mother-in-law daughter-in-law with talked   she   (she) very
    santooSa paDindi
    happy   felt
    'Mother-in-law₁ talked to (her) daughter-in-law. (She₁) felt very happy.'

Subbarao and Murthy state that when an independent person marker or just verbal person inflection is used, as in (12b), its referent is always interpreted as coreferential with the subject of the preceding clause. Thus in order to ensure disjoint reference a full NP must be employed.

As is often pointed out, competition is not just a matter of the presence of other referents. The referents must be of comparable inherent saliency, that is semantically similar to the current referent and also of comparable importance in the discourse. Moreover, the extent to which other referents constitute competition may be effected by genre or text type. For instance, according to Terrill (2000:436), in Lavukaleve, speakers sometimes use person affixes and zeroes for competing referents even when a lower accessibility marking device is clearly warranted. This happens mainly in the telling of stories, particularly stories which the addressee may be expected to be familiar with. Example (13) may serve as an illustration which comes from a story about a rat and a giant, both of whom are grammatically third-person masculine.

(13)   Lavukaleve (Terrill 2000:439)
        E-o-nege   e-mare   o-vai
        3SGNT(P)-3SG(A)-gave   3SGNT(P)-took   3SG-go out
        'He gave it, then he took it and went down.'

        Vau   a-kui   fi   nga-hourene mele-ngoa- re hide
        Go out   3SGM(P)-burn   3SGNT:FOC   1SG-wait for 2DU-stay-FUT   thus
        o-re
        3SG(S)-say
        '"Once you've cooked it, you two will wait for me," he said.'

        "Ho'bea fi"   hivel
        Good   3SGNT:FOC   do/say
        '"Okay," he said.'

        'He (the giant) gave it (the fire), then he (the rat) took it and went down.
        "Once you've cooked it (the pig), you two wait for me," he (the giant) said.
        "Okay," he (the rat) said.'

Note that there is no indication of the change of subject from the first verb to the second and third nor again with the last verb. The use of an accessibility marker that is higher than the presence of competing referents appears to warrant is also not all that uncommon in English news reporting, particularly in sport commentaries. Consider, for instance, the use of the third-person possessive marker *his* in (14) which is taken from the Lancaster Anaphoric Treebank.

(14)   East German team-mates Bernhard Germeshausen and Meinhard Nehmer
        trailed Schaer by about one-half second, Hans Hilterbrand of Switzerland

was fourth, Americans Rushlaw and Howard Siler ranked fifth and sixth and Austrians Franz Paulweber and Fritz Sperling rounded out a four-nation lock on the top eight spots. The 39-year-old Nehmer won two gold medals in the 1976 Olympics with Germeshausen as his brakeman. To achieve his hopes of a second good run, Schaer has to avoid the hopes of Rushlaw.

There are several competing candidates for the referent of *his* in the last sentence of (14), and *Schaer*, is definitely a less likely candidate than the two mentioned in the previous sentence, *Nehmer* and *Germeshausen*. Yet this evidently ambiguous form of encoding is used rather than a full NP.

The opposite situation to that illustrated in the last two examples above, the use of a lower accessibility marker than what at first sight appears to be warranted, is illustrated in (15) from Gimira, an Omotic language of Ethiopia.

(15) Gimira (Breeze 1986:62–3)
Mat'^{4}n^3 gok^{4}n^3 "sa?^{2}-^{3}k'an^4 yis^{3}i^3 ham^{4}ag^{3}i^5 at^{2}n^{3}ag^{3}uš^{2}n^{3}is^{3}a^2
one   day   forest-LOC   3M-S going-CONT-3M reach-CONT-when-FOC
daw^{3}u^4 ba^{3}i^3 surk'^{2}ns^{4}i^5 yist^{4}n^3 bek'^{3}a^{4}a^2. Daw^{3}u^4 ba^{3}uš^{2}i^3
antelope old-s sleep-PERF-3M be-PAST-DS saw-NARR antelope old-DET-s
surk'^{2}ns^{4}i^5 yist^{4}n^3 ba^3 bek'^{3}uš^{2}am, "yink^{2}a^2 daw^{3}u^4
sleep-PERF-3M be:PAST-DS saw-when there-NPMK antelope old-NPMK
ba^{3}a^2 haš^{2}is^3 tan^{3}a^3 ut'1a^4 yi^5 wot'^{3}a^4 . . . yi^{5}ag^{3}a^2 bet^{3}is^3 ta^3
REFL:3 DET   I-S   seize-1 3M kill-1   3M-GEN skin-o 1
gic'^{4}ns^{3}u^{2}e^3"   mak^{2}i^5 uš^{2}am^4 dont^{2}i^5 daw^{3}u^4 ba^{3}us^{2}is^3 ban^{3}a^3
wear-FUT-I-FIN say-3M then   get up-3M antelope old-DET-O REFL:3
wot'^{3}ns^{3}u^{2}e^3 mak^{2}i^{5}ba^3 ba^3 hank'^{3}a^4 nas^{4}a^2 yink^{2}a^2
kill-FUT-3M-FIN say-3M   REFL:3 go-REFL:3 man-NPMK there-NPMK
daw^{3}u^4 ba^{3}uš^{2}is^3 ut'ie^3 yi^3 mak^{2}ag^{3}uš^{2}n^3 daw^{3}u^4 ba^{3}a^2
antelope old-DET-O seize-JUS 3M say-CONT-when antelope old-NPMK
uš^{2}i^3 . . . at^{2}i^5 yi^5 ut'^{1}ban^{1}e^3 yi^3 mak^{2}ag^{3}uš^{2}n^3 pyaz1ns^{4}i^5
DET-S   reach-3M 3m size-REFL:3-JUS 3m say-CONT-when trip-PERF-3M
dont^{2}i^5 šic^{3}a^{4}a^2. nas^{4}i^3 . . .
get up-3M left-NARR man-s
'One day, when he arrived in the forest, he saw an old antelope sleeping. The old antelope, when he saw him sleeping "This here old antelope I will catch and kill, I will tear his skin," he said, and then said he would kill the old antelope. As he was thinking to catch that there old man antelope, the old antelope came. When he went to catch him, he tripped him up and disappeared . . . The man'

This text is part of a story about a man who went to the forest to hunt antelope. We see that while the protagonist is referred to throughout by person markers, the antelope is referred to seven times by means of an NP. This repeated encoding by means of an NP of a referent which must be assumed to be firmly entrenched in short-term memory is rather suprising. Breeze, however, states that in Gimira discourse, person markers are used for major active participants. Minor participants or important participants who are essentially passive are referred to by full NPs, even if repeatedly mentioned. Note that only in the penultimate sentence when 'the antelope' becomes active is it referred to by a person form. And significantly when 'the man' is reintroduced, it is by means of a full NP. Thus it must be assumed that in Gimira discourse the relative activity vs passivity of discourse referents overrides other parameters of accessibility in relation to referent encoding. A tendency to encode evidently highly accessible but secondary participants by means of full NPs as opposed to person markers is also clearly in evidence in Babungo. In the following extract of a folk story, the main participant, 'the child', is referred to three times by the pronoun *ŋw(e)*, while for the secondary participant, 'her father', the possessive NP *tii wi* is used five times.

(16) Babungo (Schaub 1985:108)
Ngwə fi   ŋɨ   yɔ   gə   kɔ   tɨ tii   wi lāa
she   take:IMPF groundnuts those go: PERF given:PERF to father her that
tii   wi fi   ŋɨ   yɔ   nuŋ   tɨ yi tii   wi fi
father her take groundnuts those keep:PERF for her father her take:IMPF
ŋɨ   yɔ   fwi tii   wi ndɔ   ghɔ   tii wi
groundnuts those heart father her leave:IMPF overcome father her
ndi   ŋɨ   yɔ   kwə ŋwə gəbəŋ jwi   gi
take:IMPF groundnuts those eat she go:IMPF turn back:IMPF say:PERF
lāa tita   ŋwaa ŋɨ   nyaa yi   bə   tii wi laa yi
that father my groundnuts my those where father her that he
kwə   ŋwə lāa tita   ŋwaa ndɔ   ŋɨ   nyaa
eat:PERF she that father my pay:IMP groundnuts my
'She (the child) took the groundnuts, went and gave them to her father and said that her father should take them and keep them for her. Her father took the groundnuts. Her father became greedy. Her father took the groundnuts and ate them. She (the child) went and came back and said, "Father, where are those groundnuts of mine?" Her father said that he had eaten them. She said, "Father, pay my groundnuts!"'.

Under Gundel et al.'s analysis this can be conveniently dealt with in terms of the Maxim of Quality.

A final point that needs to be made in connection with the effect of entity saliency on the choice of different forms of person marking is that there is another type of saliency, independent of accessibility, which has a direct bearing on the selection of person forms, namely information focus. Person markers which constitute the information focus of an utterance, be it the identificational focus (as in answers to a question) or contrastive or emphatic focus (as discussed in ch. 2, section 2.3) are invariably stressed independent forms. Contrast often involves competition and also topic shift as in (8), but arguably it is the informational status of the referents involved rather than their cognitive accessibility which motivates the choice of person form.

5.2.2   Unity

Since the degree of distance between the referent of a person form and its previous mention in the discourse tends to be minimal, the aspect of unity which tends to bear on the choice of one type of person marker as opposed to another is not distance, but cohesion. Even if a given referent is continually present in the discourse and there are no other competing referents, an independent as opposed to a dependent person marker may be used when there is a reduction in the cohesion between the clauses featuring the relevant referent. For instance in (17), from the Australian language Kayardild, an independent as opposed to a zero form is used upon a change in action, signalled in the English translation by 'then'.

(17) Kayardild (Evans 1995:93)
      Barrbiru-tha manharr-iy   kiyarrng-ki kamarr-i wuu-j   bala-tha
      raise-ACT   torch-MODAL.LOC TWO-LOC   stone-LOC put-ACT   hit-ACT
      ngad
      1SG:NOM
      '(I) lifted the torch, put it on two stones, then I hit (the diver birds).'

In (18), from Kolyma Yukaghir, by contrast we have a change in the use of person forms attributable to a switch to and from a background description.

(18) Kolyma Yukaghir (Maslova 1999:628).
      Oqil'l'a qon-gen! Tudel ninge-j   šoromo-gi Oj-l'e.
      pierce   go-IMP:3SG he   [many-ATTR] person-POSS NEG-be(NEG:3SG)
      ča: -je   šoromo-n'-i   tudel qon-gen   a:zu:
      [few:ATTR]   person: PRES.PART-INTR:3SG he   go-IMP-:3SG word
      jannul-gele   joq-to-gen
      message-ACC   arrive-CAUS-IMP:3SG
      'Let the pierce go! He does not have a large family, (he) has a small family. Let him go and bring the message.'

And in (19), from Polish, the use of an independent rather than a dependent person marker is due to the suspension of action, in the fourth clause, and shift in temporal continuity in the fifth, when the speaker switches from the past to the present.

(19) Polish
      [When did you first play truant, who with, where and why?]
      O na takie pytania   się   nie odpowiada, o nie, że   tak powiem
      oh on such questions REFL   not answer,   oh no   that so say:1SG
      byłam,   ale nie pamiętam   kiedy ja byłam,   ja byłam grzecznym
      was:1SG but not remember:1SG   when I was:1SG I was:1SG good
      dzieckiem. Ja na wagarach ostatnio to   jestem   prawie co   drugi
      child   I on truant   recently this am:1SG   nearly every second
      dzień, na takich legalnych ze   zwolnieniem.
      day,   on such   legal   with permission
      'Oh, one doesn't answer such questions, one doesn't. [Actually] (I) will say that (I) have [played truant] but (I) don't remember when. I was, I was a good child. Recently I play truant virtually every second day, but the legal kind, with permission.'

Although Ariel considers reductions in the cohesive links between clauses such as the above as entailing a reduction in the level of accessibility of the discourse referents mentioned, it is by no means clear that this is indeed so. In fact many scholars would argue otherwise. Ariel is forced to interpret reductions in cohesion as reductions in accessibility because of the direct association of each level of accessibility with a given form of morpho-syntactic encoding. Under Gundel et al.'s one-to-many interpretation of the relationship between accessibility and morpho-syntactic encoding, on the other hand, the use of a lower accessibility rather than a higher accessibility marker need not be always attributed to a difference in accessibility. It may be seen simply as a reflection of the workings of some other factors, in this case, a reduction in cohesion. While I would not like to suggest that a reduction in cohesion cannot be a factor contributing to a decrease in the accessibility of a referent, I find it difficult to accept that it necessarily induces a decrease in accessibility.

5.3 Accessibility and the intra-sentential distribution of person forms

Most adherents of the cognitive-psychological view of the functioning of person forms hold that the distribution of person forms within clauses and sentences is in principle attributable to the same range of factors as inter-sententially, that is in discourse. In fact, while acknowledging that some accessibility-based constraints may be grammaticalized, they do not consider the distinction between discourse phenomena and sentential phenomena to be a clear-cut one. That this is indeed so has already been in part illustrated above. Further support for the lack of a clear distinction between discourse-pragmatic principles and syntactic constraints in regard to the distribution of person forms comes from the constantly diminishing range of data that are taken to fall within the domain of pure syntax even by generative syntacticians. One illustration of this is the reduction in the scope of Chomsky's Binding Theory (BT), the dominant syntactic approach to the distribution of person forms. Let us therefore take a closer look at BT.

5.3.1 Chomsky's Binding Theory

BT, as originally formulated, seeks to deal with the patterns of coreference obtaining between the referential expressions found within sentences. Strictly speaking, it encompasses only a subset of the existing coreference possibilities, namely those involving arguments (categories occurring in A-positions) as opposed to adjuncts (categories occupying A'-positions). Thus the referential interpretations in (20) fall outside the scope of BT, as *near him / near Dan* are adjuncts not arguments.

(20) a. Near him, Dan saw a snake.
    b. Near Dan, he saw a snake.

The referential dependencies covered by BT are taken to involve three types of expressions: anaphors, pronominals and r-expressions, each of which may be overt (lexical) or empty. The category of anaphors consists of reflexives and reciprocals, that of pronominals of person forms and that of r-expressions of names and definite descriptions, etc.[2] The basic claim of BT is that while the referential interpretation of r-expressions lies outside the sentence, that of anaphors and pronominals is determined by structural configurations involving dominance and distance relations within sentences. In informal terms, coreference is forbidden when a dependent referential expression is in some sense in a more dominant position than its antecedent and/or is too distant from its antecedent, and is allowed otherwise. The relevant dominance relation is that of c-command, while the relevant distance is expressed in terms of the notion governing category.[3]

The permissible referential dependencies involving anaphors, pronominals and r-expressions are captured by means of the binding conditions in (21), where binding is understood as specified in (22).

(21)   Chomsky's binding conditions
        A. An anaphor is bound within its governing category
        B. A pronominal is free in its governing category
        C. An r-expression is free

(22) α binds β if and only if
        (i) α is in an A-position
        (ii) α c-commands β
        (iii) α and β are co-indexed

The first of the binding conditions, condition A, is intended to account for the fact that the referents of reflexives are highly constrained, that is their antecedents must occur within the same minimal domain as that in which they and their governors occur. The relevant minimal domain is typically the minimal clause, as in (23a,b).

(23) a.   John likes himself.
     b.   John believes that Mary likes herself.
     c.   *John believes that Mary likes himself.

It may, however, be the minimal NP, if the NP contains a specific subject (possessor), as in (24).

(24) a.   John believes any description of himself.
     b.   *John believes Sally's description of himself.
     c.   John believes Sally's description of herself.

---

[2] In discussing BT in this and the following section I will use the terms anaphor and pronominal in the BT sense of the terms.

[3] There are various versions of c-command and of what constitutes a governing category. There is also some indeterminacy in regard to the level of representation at which BT is taken to apply. Formerly the relevant level was S-structure, nowadays it is the interface between syntax and logical form (LF).

And in the case of the subject of a non-finite complement clause, it may be the superordinate clause, provided the subject of the non-finite clause is governed and case marked by the main clause verb, as in (25a).

(25) a.   John believed himself to be discriminated against.
     b.   *John believed that himself was discriminated against.

Moreover, the antecedents of the reflexives must be syntactically more prominent than the reflexives, that is they must c-command them. Thus the ungrammaticality of (26a,c) as opposed to (26b).

(26) a.   *Himself likes John.
     b.   John's sister invited herself.
     c.   *John's sister invited himself.

Condition B specifies that the referential dependencies of pronominals are in complementary distribution to that of anaphors, that is the structural relations which require coreference in the case of anaphors, preclude it in the case of pronominals. Thus the antecedents of pronominals cannot occur in the governing category, i.e. locally, but can be found outside the governing category, non-locally. Accordingly, all the examples in (27) are fine, provided there is no coreference relation between *John* and *him/he* or *Sally* and *her*.

(27) a.   John likes him.
     b.   John believes that Sally likes her.
     c.   John believes any description of him.
     d.   John believes Sally's description of her.
     e.   John believed him to be discriminated against.
     f.   He likes John.
     g.   John's sister invited her.

In the case of the examples in (28), on the other hand, coreference is possible, as the pronominal and its antecedent are not within the same governing category.

(28) a.   John believes that Sally likes him.
     b.   John believes Sally's description of him.
     c.   John believed that he was discriminated against.
     d.   John's sister invited him.

And condition C requires an r-expression to be referentially independent, that is semantically it cannot have an antecedent, and syntactically it cannot be bound, either by another r-expression or a pronominal, not only within the governing category but anywhere within the s. The examples in (29) are therefore ruled out as ungrammatical if there is a coreferential relationship between *John* and *John* or *he* and *John*.

(29) a.   John likes John.
     b.   He likes John.
     c.   He says that John is leaving.
     d.   John thinks that Mary likes John.

Condition C does not, however, preclude coreference between a pronominal and an r-expression if the former does not c-command the latter, as in (30).

(30) a. His sister likes John very much.
 b. A woman he had never met accused John of sexual harassment.
 c. I hired him because John is a good worker.

Thus condition C does not exclude the possibility of cataphora per se.

While the investigations of various languages have provided a good deal of support for BT, they have also revealed numerous exceptions to the predicted patterns of distribution. Violations of all three binding conditions have been observed. One violation of condition A is the existence of so-called long-distance reflexives, that is reflexives that are bound outside their local domain.[4] Such reflexives have been attested in a wide range of languages. In the examples in (31b), from Gujarati, we see that the same anaphor – *pote* – which in (31a) is bound locally, can be bound not only by the embedded subject *Kišor*, as predicted by condition A, but also by the subject of the matrix clause *Raaj*, counter to condition A.

(31) Gujarati (Mistry 2000:351, 353)
 a. Raaj pot-anne vagovše
  Raj self-ACC will humiliate
  'Raj will humiliate himself.'
 b. Raaj kišor kamiTimaa pot-anne nimše em lakhe che
  Raj Kishor committee self-ACC will appoint thus write AUX
  'Raj$_i$ writes that Kishor$_j$ will appoint self$_{ij}$ on the committee.'

Another type of violation of condition A is illustrated in (32) where the anaphor c-commands its antecedent, rather than vice versa.

(32) Greek (Huang 2000:157)
  O eaftos tu   tu   aresi   tu Petru
  the self his:NOM 3SG:DAT like:3SG the Peter:DAT
  'Himself pleases Peter.'

A major class of violations of condition B comes from languages which have no lexical anaphors (reflexivity being indicated by verbal affixation) and which therefore allow their pronominals to receive both disjoint (in accordance with condition B) and coreferential (in contravention of condition B) interpretations in a local domain. This is a rather common phenomenon cross-linguistically. It is illustrated in (33) from the Australian language Gumbaynggir.

(33) Gumbaynggir (Eades 1979:312)
  Gua:du bu:rwang gula:na magayu
  he-ERG paint:PAST he:ABS red paint:INST
  'He$_i$ painted him$_j$/himself$_i$ with red paint.'

Also common is the existence of a special reflexive form, only for the third person. In such languages the first- and second-person forms double up as reflexive

---

[4] Reflexives can also be bound outside the sentence, i.e. in the discourse domain.

anaphors, as shown in (34) on the basis of the Nilo-Saharan language Ngiti, again counter to condition, A and B.

(34) Ngiti (Kutscb Lojenga 1994:199, 225)
    a.   Ma màla   ma
          1SG see:PERF 1SG
          'I have seen myself.'
    b.   Kà rɨ   ma nálă
          he AUX 1SG see:NOM
          'He sees me.'

Another class of violations concerns languages in which anaphors and pronominals may occur in the same structural positions. Given that conditions A and B are mirror-images of each other, they jointly predict that if an anaphor and a pronominal occur in the same position they will receive different readings in regard to their referent. But this is not always so. For instance, Newman (2000:524) mentions that in Hausa, the object of mental sensation verbs may be rendered either by a reflexive anaphor or by a pronominal, as exemplified in (35).

(35) Hausa
    a.   Tàlá tā   gan tà/ ga kântà à madūbîn
          Tala PAST:3SGF see her/ see herself in mirror
          'Tala saw herself in the mirror.'

Even in English there are various contexts where both an anaphor and a pronominal can refer to the same referent. Three such cases involving so-called picture NPs, locative PPs and emphatic reflexives are illustrated in (36).

(36) a.   Patty Smith saw a picture of her/herself in *The Times*.
    b.   They saw a snake near them/themselves.
    d.   Clapton thinks that Dylan is more talented than him/himself.

The lack of complementarity of anaphors and pronominals is particularly common with respect to bound possessive anaphora. While there are languages which under certain circumstances use possessive reflexives, and others which in analogous situations employ pronominal possessives, in yet others, either form may occur with the same referential interpretation, as shown in (37).

(37) Korean (Huang 2000:25)
          John-un   caki / ku   -uy emma-lul hyemohanta
          John-TOP self/ his-GEN   mum-ACC hate
          'John$_i$ hates his$_i$ own/his$_j$ mum.'

As for condition C, it may be seen as consisting of two sub-conditions, one precluding binding of an r-expression by another coreferential r-expression, and the other prohibiting binding of an r-expression by a pronominal. The former seems to be more open to violations than the latter. The presence of bound r-expressions has been observed in, for instance, Thai, Vietnamese, Tamil, Bangala, Gujarati and Malayalam.[5] Thus, for example, in Malayalam a proper name or a

---

[5] Even in English r-expressions may be bound, under certain conditions, as in *Only Churchill remembers Churchill giving the speech about blood, sweat, toil and tears.*

title may be repeated, though as the contrasts in (38) show, only in a non-local domain.

(38) Malayalam (Jayaseelan 2000:163)
 a. Raaman paRaññu siita raaman-e sneehikkunnu ennə
   Raman said Sita Raman-ACC loves   COMP
   'Raman$_i$ said that Sita loves Raman$_i$.'

 b. *Raaman raaman-e pukazhti
   Raman Raman-ACC praised
   'Raman$_i$ praised Raman$_i$.'

But a coreferential pronoun cannot c-command an r-expression. The examples in (39) are ungrammatical.

(39) Malayalam (Jayaseelan 2000:162)
 a. Awan raaman-te amma-ye sneehikkunnu
   he Raman-GEN mother-ACC loves
   'He$_i$ loves Raman*$_i$'s mother.'

 b. Awan wicaariccu peNkuTTikaL raaman-e sneehikkunnu ennə
   he thought girls   Raman-ACC love   COMP
   'He$_i$ thought that the girls love Raman*$_i$.'

However, unlike in the languages mentioned above, in Mandarin the binding of an r-expression by a pronominal is allowed. This is illustrated in (40).

(40) Mandarin (Huang 2000:28)
   Zhexia, Yuan Shikai ke deyi   le, ta yiwei dangjin Zhongguo
   thus Yuan Shikai EMPH complacent ASP 3SG think today China
   zhiyou Yuan Shikai cai shi dang huangdi de liao
   only Yuan Shikai only be act emperor PRT material
   'On that occasion, Yuan Shikai$_i$ was terribly complacent. He$_i$ thought that in today's China only Yuan Shikai$_i$ had got the makings of an emperor.'

The various counter-examples to the binding conditions such as those presented above have over the years led to a number of modifications of BT. The most important of these is the abandonment of condition C, and the reinterpretation of conditions A and B as applying to the marking of reflexivity of predicates (Reinhart & Reuland 1993). Nowadays, condition C has been essentially replaced by Chomsky's general discourse principle, which states that repetition of r-expressions should be avoided, except when conditions warrant it. As for conditions A and B, under Reinhart and Reuland's analysis, they are no longer considered to be mirror-images of each other. The distribution of anaphors is decoupled from that of pronominals and is seen to be dependent on the nature of the anaphor and the type of reflexivity displayed by a given predicate. Two types of anaphors are posited, SE anaphors and SELF anaphors.[6] SE anaphors are taken to occur only with predicates which are marked for reflexivity in the lexicon

---

[6] A more elaborate typology of anaphors within the Chomskian framework has been developed by Everaert (2000) who distinguishes twelve different ways in which anaphors are expressed cross-linguistically.

(intrinsically reflexive), and SELF anaphors only with predicates which are not intrinsically reflexive. Since SELF anaphors mark a non-reflexive predicate as reflexive, they are predicted as being confined to local domains. SE anaphors, on the other hand, may be used in long-distance domains, as in (41b), for example.

(41) Icelandic (Huang 2000:257)
    a.   Jón   elskar sjálfan sig
          John loves   self   self
          'John loves himself.'
    b.   Jón   segir að   Maria elski sig
          John says that Maria loves self
          'John$_I$ says that Maria loves self$_I$ (him).'

Though Reinhart and Reuland's and in particular Everaert's (2000) reinterpretation of BT eliminates some of the major anomalies of the theory, such as the complementarity of anaphors and pronominals, and provides a coherent account of some aspects of the distribution of different types of anaphors, it too makes various incorrect predictions, which are discussed in detail in Huang (2000:159–67). What is of special significance, however, is that if BT is confined to the marking of reflexivity, the distribution of pronominals and r-expressions emerges as being outside the purview of pure syntax and within the realm of discourse pragmatics.

5.3.2 Referent accessibility and BT

The basic insight of BT, when translated into accessibility terminology, is that anaphors constitute higher accessibility markers than pronominals and these, in turn, are higher accessibility markers than r-expressions. This is fully compatible with the accessibility view, as reflected in the accessibility marking scale given earlier in (2). In fact the syntactic configurations which in BT are taken to require and preclude coreference may be seen as grammaticalized accessibility preferences.

Recall that the two major parameters of accessibility are entity saliency and unity. Intra-sententially, entity saliency translates into the grammatical relation hierarchy, with entities expressed by subjects being more salient than those expressed by other syntactic functions, as captured in the accessibility hierarchies in (1). Unity within sentences in turn is reflected in co-argumenthood (or lack thereof) of the same or of different predicates and, in the latter case, in the nature of the linkage between clauses. Sentential complements are more closely linked than adverbial ones and non-finite complements more tightly linked than finite ones. And the tighter the link, the greater the unity. Thus, in the light of the above, if anaphors are higher accessibility markers than pronominals we would expect the former to favour strongly antecedents which are the subject co-argument of the same predicate. By the same token, such contexts should strongly disfavour the use of pronominals. This is precisely what is captured in conditions A and B, though in the form of an absolute constraint, as opposed to that of a preference. As for condition C, proper names and definite descriptions are in accessibility terms, medium accessibility markers. Therefore they should constitute a highly unlikely choice for the encoding of a referent already mentioned in the same sentence, let alone the same clause, particularly if the mention involves a higher accessibility marker. Note, however, that a purely accessibility-based explanation of the binding conditions would involve directionality, that is it would allow for a higher accessibility marker to follow a lower accessibility marker with the same reference but not vice versa. Thus both the examples in (42) and (43) would be predicted as being ungrammatical under a reading where the person form and proper name refer to the same referent, where in fact only (43) are so.

(42) a. I hired him because Sak is a good worker.
b. I saw her before Mary died.

(43) a. I told him$_i$ that she likes Sak$_i$.
b. I convinced him$_i$ that Mary likes Sak$_i$.

The binding conditions, on the other hand, are not directional, being based on hierarchical constituent structure not linear precedence. Thus if the binding conditions are by and large grammaticalized accessibility preferences, grammaticalization must be taken to involve a relaxing of precedence relations in favour of dominance relations and unity. Another point that needs to be mentioned is that if one accepts the one-to-many relationship between accessibility and grammatical encoding of Gundel et al. (1993) sketched earlier, it is not accessibility alone which underlies BT but rather accessibility in conjunction with the pragmatic maxim of quality.

Given that grammaticalization does not proceed exactly in the same way or at the same rate cross-linguistically (see ch. 7, section 7.2), if the syntactic constraints on the distribution of anaphors and pronominals are indeed grammaticalized accessibility preferences, we would not expect the same patterns to be grammaticalized in all languages. And indeed they are not, as the various counterexamples to the binding conditions cited above suggest. What we would expect, though, is for the environments in which anaphors are grammaticalized or even permitted to decrease the less salient the antecedent and the greater the distance between it and the anaphor. To a large extent this is so.

First of all, whereas all languages which have reflexive anaphors require or allow them to be used as verbal arguments coreferential with the most salient antecedent, that is a clause mate subject, only some permit such anaphors to be coreferential with the less grammatically salient object. For example, as shown below, Turkish and Kashmiri (and also English in the translations) do allow the object to be the antecedent of a reflexive anaphor but Mizo and Polish do not.

(44) Turkish (Kornfilt 1997:146)
Hasan   Ayşe-yi   ayna-da   kendin-e   göster-di
Hasan-ACC Ayse-ACC mirror-LOC self-DAT show-PAST
'Hasan showed Ayse$_i$ to herself$_i$ in the mirror.'

(45) Kashmiri (Wali et al. 2000:485)
Aslam-an von me paan-as
Aslam told
'Aslam$_i$ told me$_j$ about self$_{ij}$.'

(46) Mizo (Murthy & Subbarao 2000:796)
Zova-n$_i$ amaah$_{i*j}$ -cuncaang zovi-cu$_j$ a-zooth
Zova-ERG he self about Zovi-ACC 3SG-ask
'Zova$_i$ asked Zovi$_j$ about self$_{i*j\,k}$.'

(47) Polish
Jan opowiedział Piotrowi o sobie
Jan told:3SGM Peter:DAT about self
'John$_i$ told Peter$_j$ about self$_{i*j}$.'

In Mizo, coreference between the complement of the PP and the clausal object is disallowed. In Polish, on the other hand, such coreference is possible (48), but is indicated by means of a lower accessibility marker, i.e. a pronominal not a reflexive anaphor.

(48) Polish
Jan opowiedzial Piotrowi o nim.
John told:3SGM Peter:DAT about him
'John$_i$ told Peter$_j$ about him$_{*ijk}$.'

This may be viewed as consistent with accessibility under the assumption that the grammatical saliency of the subject overrides any considerations of actual physical distance between an antecedent and its referential dependent.

Secondly, there are languages in which reflexive anaphors are required for argument NPs coreferential with a clause mate subject, while coreference of an argument PP with the subject may be indicated either by a reflexive anaphor or by a pronominal. This is the case in Mizo, for example. Compare (49), where the reflexive anaphor *amaah* indicates coreference (49a) and the pronominal *ani* disjoint reference (49b), with (50) where both the anaphor *amaah* and the pronominal *a* may be interepreted as coreferential with the subject.[7]

(49) Mizo (Murthy & Subbarao 2000:793, 807)
a. Zova-n amaah-cu daarTlalaang-ah a-in-hmu
Zova-ERG self-ACC mirror in 3SG-REFL-see
'Zova$_i$ saw self$_{i*j}$ in the mirror.'

b. Zova-n ani-cu a-hmu
Zova-ERG he-ACC 3SG-see
'Zova$_i$ saw him$_{*ij}$.'

---

[7] The possibility of having either an anaphor or a pronominal as the object of a preposition has been accommodated within BT in various ways. One solution suggested by Bresnan (1987) is that the binding domain of pronominals should not contain subjects, which effectively predicts non-complementarity of anaphors and pronominals in categories which lack subjects. Under such an analysis, the binding domain of the object of the preposition is the PP, while that of the anaphor the S. Consequently a pronominal prepositional object satisfies condition B, being free in its domain, while the anaphor prepositional object satisfies condition A, being bound.

(50) Mizo (Murthy & Subbarao 2000:794, 808)
a. Tluaangi-n   zovi-hneena amaah-cungcaang a-hril
   Tluangi-ERG   Zovi-to   self-about   3SG-tell
   'Tluangi$_i$ told Zovi$_j$ about self$_{i*j}$.'

b. Tluaangi-n   zovi-hneena a-cungcaang   a-hril
   Tluangi-ERG   Zovi-to   he-about   3SG-tell
   'Tluangi$_i$ told Zovi$_j$ about him$_{i*jk}$.'

The above difference in distribution may be seen as a reflection of accessibility if an NP argument is taken to be a marker of higher accessibility than that of a PP argument. Significantly, we do not find the opposite situation, that is lack of complementarity with NP arguments but strict complementarity with PP arguments.

Thirdly, while the distance between co-arguments of the same predicate is considered to be close enough to warrant the use of a reflexive anaphor in all languages that have them, that between an adjunct and an argument of the same predicate is variously treated. In Polish, for example, the same reflexive anaphor is used for complements of adjunct PPs coreferential with a clause mate subject as for argument PPs and argument NPs. In Spanish either a reflexive anaphor or a pronominal can be used, as is the case with some adjunct PPs in English. And in Mizo only a pronominal is allowed. These differences are illustrated in (51) through (53).

(51)   Polish
        Basia   odepchneła Janusza od   siebie.
        Barbara pushed:3SGF John:ACC from self
        'Barbara$_i$ pushed John away from her$_i$(self).'

(52)   Spanish (Blackwell 2000:398)
        Bea puso las maletas cerca de ella/si misma
        Bea put   the suitcase near of   her/herself
        'Bea$_i$ put the suitcase near her$_{ij}$/herself.'

(53)   Mizo (Murthy & Subbarao 2000:809)
        Zova-n   leekhabu a-hmaii   a-dah
        Zova-ERG   book   he-front   3SG-keep
        'Zova$_i$ kept the book in front of him$_{ij}$.'

Thus, whereas argument PPs in English require and in Mizo permit a reflexive anaphor when coreferent with the clausal subject, in the case of adjunct PPs such anaphors are only optional in English and impossible in Mizo. Again, the converse situation, that is obligatory use of anaphors with an adjunct PP but optional with a subcategorized one, does not occur.

Similar differences in the use of reflexive anaphors and pronominals can be observed intra-sententially, across clauses. The tighter the dependency between the main and subordinate clause and thus the accessibility of a main-clause antecedent relative to a referential dependent in the subordinate clause, the greater likelihood of a reflexive anaphor being used as opposed to a pronominal. This is captured in the implicational hierarchy in (54) based on Burzio (1998) and Huang (2000:93).[8]

(54) The implicational hierarchy of long-distance reflexivization
small clauses > infinitivals > subjunctives > finite complements > finite adjuncts

Thus, English allows reflexive anaphors in small clauses (55a) and as the subject of a non-finite clause which is governed and case marked by the main clause verb (55b) but not in other types of dependent clauses.

(55) a. John considers himself a good writer.
  b. John believes himself to be superior.

Polish, on the other hand, is somewhat less restrictive in that it permits a main-clause subject to bind a reflexive anaphor in a small clause, and in an infinitival complement clause, though not in a finite embedded clause. Compare (56a,b) and (56c).

(56) Polish
  a. Basia   uważa   siebie za prawdziwą piękność.
      Barbara consider:3SG self   as true   beauty
      'Barbara considers herself a true beauty.'

  b. Renata kazała   Piotowi   zbudować dom   dla siebie/niej/*niego.
      Renata ordered Peter:GEN   build:INF house for self/her/him
      'Renata$_i$ ordered Peter$_j$ to build a house for himself$_j$/herself$_i$/her$_i$/him$_{\cdot jk}$.'

  c. Ala   wie,   że   Joasia kocha   tylko siebie/ją
      Alice knows:3SG that Joanna love:3SG only self/her
      'Alice$_i$ knows that Joanna$_j$ loves only herself$_{\cdot ij}$/her$_{jk}$.'

Observe that the antecedent of the reflexive anaphor in the infinitival clause in (56b) may be either *Renata* or *Piotr*. The overt pronominal in the infinitival clause *niej/niego*, on the other hand, can only be coreferential with the main-clause subject *Renata*, not with the subject of the infinitival clause. Thus, whereas the higher accessibility marker may have a local and a non-local antecedent, the lower accessibility marker requires a non-local antecedent. Even less restrictive than Polish in relation to non-local binding is Icelandic. It allows binding not only into infinitival clauses (57a) but also finite subjunctive ones (57b), though again not into finite indicative clauses.

(57) Icelandic (Halldor: Sigurdsson: pc)
  a. Jón bað   Maríu að   hjálpa sér
      John asked Mary that help.INF self:DAT
      'John$_i$ asked Mary to help him$_i$.'

---

[8] As with all hierarchies, there are languages which exhibit exceptional behaviour. For example, Malayalam allows long-distance reflexives in embedded finite complement clauses but not in small clauses or infinitival ones (Jayaseelan 2000:122, 131).

b. Jón segir að María hjálpi sér
John says that Mary helps:SUBJ self:DAT
'John$_i$ says that Mary helps him$_i$.'

And Telugu sanctions reflexive binding right down the hierarchy, that is into finite indicative complements, as shown in (58b).

(58) Telugu (Subbarao & Murthy 2000:249, 229)
a. Raadha-ki tanu raa-waDam iSTam leedu
Radha-DAT self come-ing pleasing not
'Radha$_i$ does not like self$_i$ (her) coming.'

b. Kamala siita too tanu pariikSa paasu awwagala-du ani ceppindi
Kamala Sita with self examination pass can-3SGF COMP said
'Kamal$_i$ told Sita$_j$ that self$_{ij}$ could pass the exam.'

Such binding is in fact possible even into a finite adjunct clause, as in (59).

(59) Telugu (Subbarao & Murthy 2000:246)
EkkaDki (tanu) weLLinaa kamala kukka-ni tiisi koni weLtundi
wherever self goes Kamala dog-ACC having taken gone
'Wherever Kamala$_i$ goes self$_i$ (she) takes the dog with her.'

Given the decrease in unity between main and finite subordinate clauses as compared to non-finite ones, we would expect reflexive anaphors in finite embedded clauses to be even more strongly subject oriented than in non-finite clauses and within clauses. This appears to be so. In many languages which allow binding into a finite embedded clause the main-clause antecedent can only be the subject. And in the languages which do not exhibit such a constraint, the only other antecedents of a long-distance reflexive anaphor are arguments of a very restricted set of verbs that represent the source of the proposition or the experience of the mental state that is being described. According to Huang (2000:192), the most common types of constructions with non-subject antecedents of long-distance anaphors are those involving the predicate *hear from*, as in (60), or psychological predicates, as in (61).

(60) Mandarin (Huang 2000:192)
Ta ting tongshi shuo ziji tishang le jiaoshou.
3SG hear colleague say self promote ASP professor
'He$_i$ hears from the colleague$_j$ that self$_{ij}$ has been promoted to a professor.'

(61) Kannada (Amritavalli 2000:69)
Taanu phoon maaDuvaaga ii galaaTe raamananna beejaarupaDisitu
self telephoning then this noise Rama-ACC bothered
'The noise bothered Rama$_i$ when (?self$_i$) was telephoning.'

As the examples in (60) and (61) suggest, such antecedents also display features associated with entity saliency, namely humanness, definiteness and individualization, as conveyed by the use of a person form or a proper name.

While the above patterns of distribution of reflexive anaphors and pronominals are consistent with the claim that anaphors are higher accessibility markers than pronominals, the use of the former decreasing together with a decrease in the saliency of the antecedent and the unity between it and the referential dependent, the actual phonological form of reflexive anaphors is often not in line with the assumptions of accessibility. Recall that what underlies the accessibility marking scale is the assumption that the more accessible the referent, the more attenuated its formal encoding. Yet in many languages, reflexive anaphors are not phonologically shorter or less complex than overt pronominals. And in quite a few languages the reflexive anaphors are more complex than pronominals. In Malayalam, for instance, the local reflexive anaphor consists of a personal pronoun or the reflexive pronoun *tann* followed by the emphatic *tanne*, as exemplified in (62).

(62) Malayalam (Jayaseelan 2000:121–2)
      Raaman awan-e tanne/ tann-e tanne sneehikkunnu
      Raman he-ACC EMPH self-ACC EMPH loves
      'Raman$_i$ loves himself$_i$.'

Without the emphatic *tanne* only a disjoint reading would be possible. Moreover, recall that languages may have more than one type of reflexive anaphor. Often in such cases the anaphors differ in complexity. Crucially it tends to be the less complex anaphor, the SE anaphor rather than the SELF anaphor in Reinhart and Reuland's (1993) terms, that is used non-locally, the more complex one locally. This is also the case in Malayalam. When used as a complement of a locative PP or as the subject of a finite complement clause only the reflexive form *tann* is used, without the emphatic *tanne*, as we see in (63).

(63)   Malayalam (Jayaseelan 2000:126, 122)
   a.   Raaman tan-te   munn-il oru aana-ye   kaNDu
        Raman self-GEN front-in one elephant-ACC saw
        'Raman$_i$ saw an elephant in front of self$_i$.'

   b.   Raaman wicaariccu taan mantri aakum   ennə
        Raman thought   self minister will become COMP
        'Raman$_i$ thought that he$_{i \cdot j}$ would become a minister.'

Thus, contrary to what the accessibility marking scale predicts, a more attenuated form of encoding is used for a less accessible antecedent and a less attenuated form of encoding for a more accessible antecedent.

The above suggests that the encoding of anaphors, in the Chomskian sense of the term, cannot be purely a matter of the relative accessibility of their referents. This, however, is not irreconcilable with the basic tenants of the accessibility approach, if it is assumed that anaphors are used to perform a function in addition to that of the marking of the high accessibility of their referents. This function, referred to as empathy or perspective or logophoricity will be discussed in section 5.4.1. Before doing so, a few words need to be said about the intrasentential distribution of independent person markers relative to dependent person markers.

5.3.3 The avoid pronoun constraint

While BT seeks to capture the distribution of pronominals as opposed to anaphors and r-expressions in sentences, it has nothing to say about the conditions determining the use of one type of pronominal over another. Yet, as we have seen, in the vast majority of languages, there are various grammatical contexts in which more than one type of pronominal, typically an independent and a dependent form, is permitted. To deal with instances where the grammar sanctions the occurrence of two alternative person forms Chomsky (1981:65) posits the so-called Avoid Pronoun Principle, which states that whenever there is an option between having and not having an overt pronoun and a non-overt one, the non-overt one is chosen "where possible". The choice of an overt form is thus predicted as being marked and significantly is taken to induce a non-coreferential reading, while the use of a dependent form is seen to induce a coreferential interpretation.

Within the context of the accessibility approach the Avoid Pronoun Principle is both redundant and inaccurate. As pointed out by various scholars, it is not the case that the choice of an overt person form is necessarily marked, that of a dependent form unmarked. The major factor that determines the use of one person form as opposed to another is the relative accessibility of their referents. Just as in discourse, a dependent person form will be favoured if its referent is highly accessible, an independent form if it is less highly accessible. Accordingly, dependent forms tend to be used for referents whose antecedents are topics rather than non-topics, subjects as opposed to non-subjects, humans rather than non-humans, joint rather than split and occur in clauses which are more rather than less tightly linked. Thus, for example, in the following Turkish sentences, as one would expect, the referent of the zero form in the subordinate clause in (64a) is interpreted as corresponding to the more accessible main-clause subject *Erol*, that of the independent person marker in (64b), as coreferential with an antecedent outside the clause.

(64) Turkish (Erguvanli-Taylan 1986:215)
 a. Erol ban-a Ø toplantı-ya gel-mi-yeceğ-in-i söyle-di
    Erol I-DAT (he) meeting-DAT come-NEG.NOM-FUT-3SG:POSS-ACC tell-PAST
    'Erol$_i$ told me that he$_{i,j}$ wouldn't come to the meeting.'
 b. Erol ban-a on-un toplantı-ya gel-mi-yeceğ-in-i
    Erol I-DAT s/he-GEN meeting-DAT come-NEG.NOM-FUT-3SG:POSS-ACC
    söyle-di
    tell-PAST
    'Erol$_i$ told me that he$_{*i,j}$ wouldn't come to the meeting.'

In the Polish example in (65) we have a similar situation. The independent person form *ona* is interpreted as coreferential with the less accessible main-clause object (and potentially with an extra-sentential antecedent). The verbal inflection alone, on the other hand, is open to two interpretations; it may be coreferential with either the matrix subject *Jola* or object *Gosię*. As the accessibility hierarchies predict, the former is favoured, unless the context defines *Gosia* rather than *Jola* as being more topical.

(65)　　Polish
　　　　Jola　　　zaprosi　　　Gosię　　kiedy Ø/(ona) wróci　　　z
　　　　Jola:NOM invite:FUT:3SG Gosia:ACC when (she)　return:FUT:3SG from
　　　　Warszawy
　　　　Warsaw
　　　　'Jola$_i$ will invite Gosia when Ø$_i$ **she**$_j$ returns from Warsaw.'

When the verbal person inflection also features a gender distinction, coreference of the subject of the subordinate clause with the main-clause object may be indicated either by the verbal inflection alone or by an overt form, as in (66).

(66)　　Polish
　　　　Jola　　　zaprosila　　　Jurka　　jak　Ø/on wrocil.　　　z
　　　　Jola:NOM invite:PAST:3SGF Jurek:ACC when he　return:PAST3SGM from
　　　　Warszawy
　　　　Warsaw
　　　　'Jola$_i$ invited Jurek$_j$ when he$_{jk}$ returned from Warsaw.'

In the absence of a discourse context, I cannot discern any clear preference for either the verbal inflection alone or the independent person form. In the case of coordinate clauses, as in (67), however, an independent form is virtually mandatory to indicate coreference with the object, as opposed to the subject, of the previous clause.

(67)　　Polish
　　　　Jola obraziła　　　Jurka i　?Ø/on. ją uderzył
　　　　Jola insult:PAST:3SGF Jurek and he　her hit:PAST:3SGM
　　　　'Jola$_i$ insulted Jurek$_j$ and he$_j$ hit her.'

Thus, while the tighter connection between a main and subordinate clause allows for the possibility of the verbal inflection being interpreted as coreferential with the main-clause object, the looser bond found between two coordinate clauses requires the use of a lower accessibility marker.

In the above examples, the distribution of higher and lower accessibility person forms directly reflects the factors in the accessibility hierarchies in (1). These factors, however, may interact with other factors such as the semantics of the verb, the nature of the discourse in which the given sentence is embedded, the background assumptions and the mutual knowledge of the speakers. And these other factors may override the more typical entity saliency ones. For example, though as illustrated in (64a) above, zero forms in Turkish subordinate clauses are generally interpreted as coreferential with the matrix subject, when a clause such as (68b) is used as an answer to (68a), both a zero form and an overt pronominal in the subordinate clause may be interpreted as coreferential with the subject of the question, rather than with the subject of the matrix clause.

(68)　　　Turkish (Erguvanli-Taylan 1986:223)
　　a.　　Erol yemeg-e　.gel-ecek　mi-ydi?
　　　　　Erol dinner-DAT come-FUT -Q-PAST
　　　　　'Was Erol going to come to dinner?'

b. Nazan ban-a Ø/on-un yedi-de   gel-mi-yeceğ-in-i
    Nazan I-DAT he/s/he-GEN seven-LOC come-NEG.NOM-FUT-3SG:POSS-ACC
    söyle-miş-ti
    tell-PAST-PAST
    'Nazan had told me that he would come at seven.'

In fact Erguvanli-Taylan suggests that in this context a zero is preferred over the independent person marker under the relevant reading. This use of a high accessibility marker for extra-sentential coreference rather than the expected inter-sentential coreference can be handled in accessibility terms, if it is assumed that since *Erol* rather than *Nazan* is the discourse topic, it is the more accessible of the two. A similarly atypical situation where both a zero and an overt form can be used for the same referent is illustrated in (69) from Mandarin.

(69)   Mandarin (Huang 2000:240)
        Yisheng shuo bingren zhidao Ø/te mingtian gei ta kaidao
        surgeon say   patient know 3SG   tomorrow for 3SG operate
        'The surgeon$_i$ says that the patient$_j$ knows that (he$_{ik}$/you/we/they) will operate on him$_j$ tomorrow.'

According to Huang, the use of zero forms in Mandarin reflects a preference for antecedents which are topics over non-topics and subjects over non-subjects. Therefore, we would expect the first pronominal *te* in (69) to be coreferential with an extra-sentential antecedent and not 'the surgeon'. Yet the background assumption that surgeons rather than anyone else operate on patients, appears to determine the coreference with the highest subject, regardless of whether a zero form or an overt form is used. It is not clear whether all such patterns of coreference can be handled directly in terms of accessibility. However, they can be dealt with by accessibility in combination with general pragmatic principles.[9]

5.4   Beyond referent accessibility

In discussing the distribution of different person forms across sentences and within sentences we noted that the choice of one type of person form over another may be influenced by factors which do not necessarily have a direct bearing on the degree of accessibility of their referents, such as lack of action or temporal continuity and relative informativeness, as manifested in contrast or emphasis. Here we will consider another range of factors which may underlie the choice of a particular person marker or of a person marker rather than of an alternative referential expression, namely those involving point of view and empathy. Whereas accessibility is addressee-oriented, point of view and empathy are

---

[9] The neo-pragmatic approach to anaphora (see Huang 2000) seeks to account for all instances of anaphora in pragmatic terms without resorting to accessibility notions. It is not clear to me how successful this approach is in dealing with first- and second-person forms as compared to anaphoric third-person forms.

speaker-oriented; the speaker invites the addressee to consider a given situation or event from the perspective that he has selected, be it his own or that of some other party. We will begin with the so-called logophoric use of lexical anaphors and then review the effects of empathy and perspective on the choice of person forms as opposed to demonstratives and/or NPs.

5.4.1 Long-distance reflexives, logophoricity and point of view

Most utterances in discourse are egocentric, that is the situation or event depicted in the utterance is presented from the point of view of the speaker. In verbatim reports of the utterances of others, as in (70), this normal egocentric point of view shifts from that of the current speaker to that of the speaker of the relevant utterance. This is most readily manifested in the use of deictic expressions, including first- and second-person markers. Thus *I* in (70) refers to *Brian*, not to the current speaker and *you* refers to the current speaker.

(70)   Brian said to me yesterday, "I will see you tomorrow."

In indirect-speech reporting, on the other hand, it is possible to discern the existence of two points of view, that of the current speaker and that of the utterer of the utterance that is being reported. As (71) illustrates, in English the point of view of the current speaker is clearly reflected in the nature of the deictic expressions used; *me* refers to the current speaker and *today* reflects the time of the report of the utterance by the current speaker, not when the utterance was produced.

(71)   Brian said to me yesterday that he would see me today.

The point of view of the utterer can be discerned in the temporality of the verb, *would* as opposed to *will*. Although in English indirect-speech reports, the dominant perspective, especially in regard to deictic forms, is that of the current speaker, there are languages in which the possibility arises of either maintaining such a perspective or changing it to that of the utterer of the utterance being reported. The marking by grammatical means of the perspective of such a secondary ego is called logophoricity, a term introduced by Claude Hagège (1974).[10]

Of the several means of expressing logophoricity, the most common, particularly in Africa, is via the use of special person forms.[11] This is illustrated in (72) from the Chadic language Mupun, where the form *de* is the third-person feminine logophoric marker reflecting the perspective of the internal protagonist and the form *wa* the corresponding "ordinary" third-person one.

---

[10] Within the generative literature the term logophoricity is used slightly differently, namely for any anaphor which cannot be bound within its local domain irrespective of any considerations of point of view, however interpreted. See in particular Reinhart and Reuland (1993).
[11] A good survey of types of logophoric marking is presented in Roncador (1992).

(72) Mupun (Frajzyngier 1993:108)
  a.   Wa sat nə ta de dee n-jos
       she say COMP stop LOG stay PREP-Jos
       'She$_i$ said that she$_i$ stopped over at Jos.'

  b.   Wa sat nə wa ta dee n-jos
       she say COMP she LOG stay PREP-Jos
       'She$_i$ said that she$_j$ stopped over at Jos.'

As one would expect, logophoric person markers are characteristic of the sentential complements of verbs of saying, reporting or implicit reporting. Cross-linguistic investigations reveal that their distribution conforms to the hierarchy in (73), being most favoured with verbs of communication such as *say, tell, report, announce* and least favoured with verbs of perception such as *hear* or *understand*.

(73) Logocentric verb hierarchy (Stirling 1993:259)
      communication > thought > psychological state > perception

When appearing in the sentential complements of the above verbs, the logophoric markers indicate coreference with a core argument of the matrix clause, the "ordinary" forms disjoint reference, as indicated in the Mupun examples in (72) above. The argument in the matrix clause with which the logophoric forms are coreferential is virtually always the subject of the matrix clause, who is the original speaker, or thinker, or experiencer of the reported situation or event. Nonetheless in some languages, as in Tuburi below, the antecedent of the logophoric person marker may also be a non-subject argument representing the source of the proposition, *ja*, in (74a), or the experiencer of the experience being reported in the complement clause, *Pɔl* in (74b).[12]

(74) Tuburi (Wiesemann 1986c:448–9)
  a.   Pɔl laa jág Jaŋ gá sè le'ɛ
       Paul heard from John that LOG fell
       'Paul$_i$ heard from John$_j$ that he$_j$ fell.'

  b.   Heene jɔŋ Pɔl gá sè lέ' cégè
       fear has Paul that LOG fall sick
       'Fear grips Paul$_i$ that he$_i$ will fall sick.'

That the antecedent of the logophoric form should be typically the matrix subject is not surprising, given that people have a strong predilection to talk about themselves rather than others. Coreference with a non-subject, on the other hand, generally entails the report of other parties; *John heard/ learned/ found out/gathered from me that (...)* is far less probable than *I told /informed/divulged/reported (to) John that (...)*.

Turning to the syntactic function of the logophoric form in the complement clause, while in some languages it may be used only in subject function

---

[12] The antecedent of a logophoric person marker may also be the addressee of the matrix clause, as is the case in Mupun (Frajzyngier 1993:112–16) and Mbay (Keegan 1997:163).

(e.g. Igbo), much more commonly it is available for a wider range of functions, at least for subject, object and possessor. The form of the logophoric marker may or may not vary, depending on its function. In Mupun, Tuburi, Boko and Ewe, for example, it does not. In Mbay, on the other hand, the prefix ń- or n- is used for subjects, the suffix -n for all other functions, as illustrated in (75).

(75) Mbay (Keegan 1997:162–4)
 a. Ø-ndìjè-m̄   àn   ké bétə n-à   ń-dān-m̄   wà?
    3SG-asked-1SG said if later LOG-will LOG-accompany-1SG Q
    'He_i asked me if he_i could accompany me.'

 b. Súu èl-á   àn   kə   Ø-àd(ə̄)-n   bik(ə́)
    Suu told-3SG said that 3SG-give-LOG pen
    'Susu_i told him_j to give him_i a pen.'

 c. Súu èl   àn   Ngāró ndà bɔ̄ɔ̄-ń
    Suu spoke said Ngaro hit father-LOG
    'Suu_i said that Ngaro_j had hit his_ij father.'

As for person, logophoric person markers are, with few exceptions, third person. Some languages also use them for second-person referents (e.g. Akɔɔse, Moru, Ngbaka). And two languages, namely Lele (East Chadic) and Yaga Dii (Eastern Adamawa) have been reported to have logophoric marking of all three persons.[13] The strong preference for third-person logophoric markers over second and first is generally attributed to the fact that in indirect speech contexts referential disambiguation is most relevant for third parties. However, as pointed out by Stirling (1993:256–7), some third-person logophoric forms may be better seen not as third-person but as first-person forms which are used when reporting on the speech of anyone but oneself. Under such an interpretation the complement clauses with a logophoric marker would be more like direct than indirect speech, and the logophoric marker would disambiguate between *John* and *I* rather than *John* and some other third party. This would account for the rarity of first-person logophoric forms.[14]

Logophoric marking, while favouring the predicates in the logophoric hierarchy, can in many languages be extended to other constructions, most commonly

---

[13] The existence of logophoric markers for all three persons in Lele suggested by Wiesemann (1986c:445) is not confirmed by Frajzyngier (2001) in his grammar of Lele. The first- and second-person logophoric markers in Lele given by Wiesemann are straightforward combinations of the complementizer *na* and the independent subject pronouns. However, unlike Wiesemann who views the *na* complementizer as an indirect speech introducer, Frajzyngier (2001:374) considers it is a marker of both indirect and direct speech.

[14] It is also worth mentioning that in some languages first- and second-person pronouns can be used in indirect speech contexts to indicate coreference with a third-person subject, as in (i) from Punjabi.

(i) Punjabi (Bhatia 2000:645)
     Gurnek ne   aakhiaa ki   māi jāāvaagaa
     Gurnek ERG said   that I   go:FUT:1MSG
     'Gurnek_i said that I_j/he_i would go.'

purpose clauses (76) and relative clauses (77), less commonly also to adverbial clauses (78).

(76)   Ewe (Clements 1975:160–1)
    a.   Dɛvi-a   xɔ   tohehe   be   wò-a-ga-da alakpa ake   o
        child-DEF receive punishment so that LOG-T-P-tell lie   again NEG
        'The child$_i$ received punishment so that he$_i$ wouldn't tell lies again.'

    b.   Dɛvi-a   xɔ   tohehe   be   yè-a-ga-da alakpa ake   o
        child-DEF receive punishment so that 3SG-T-P-   tell lie again NEG
        'The child$_i$ received punishment so that he$_{i/k}$ wouldn't tell lies again.'

(77)   Tuburi (Huang 2000:226)
    a.   Á Dik tí   māy   mà:gāsɛ kón sú: mònò
        he think of young girl REL LOG see   yesterday CORR
        'He$_i$ is thinking of the young girl he$_i$ saw yesterday.'

    b.   Á Dik tí   māy   mà:gā á kón sú: mònò
        he think of young girl REL   he see yesterday CORR
        'He$_i$ is thinking of the young girl he$_{i/k}$ saw yesterday.'

(78)   Boko (Jones 1998:158)
        Biɔ zɔ́á   dɔ̀   Sàbí wá kɛ́   à   'í   kɔlɛ
        B:o noise emit:PERF Sabi DAT because 3SG water spill:PERF
        wa   yáí
        3SG:DAT:LOG reason
        'Bio rebuked Sabi because he spilt water on him.'

As indicated in the Ewe and Tuburi examples, (76b) and (77b) respectively, unlike in the typical logophoric contexts exemplified earlier, there is no strict complementarity between the use of the logophoric marker and an "ordinary" pronoun. The ordinary pronoun may too be interpreted as coreferential with the main clause subject.[15] Culy (1997) suggests that it is only in cases of such non-complementarity, that the use of a logophoric marker as opposed to a regular person marker is associated with a difference in point of view. In regular logophoric contexts, logophoric markers must be seen not as bearers of the perspective of a secondary ego, but simply as indirect discourse elements bound by an antecedent in the same sentence. As the notion of perspective or point of view is typically predicated on the existence of a choice, and in the case of logophoric predicates no actual choice with respect to the occurrence of a logophoric or ordinary marker is involved, Culy's position has considerable merit. It is supported by the fact that the only illustrations of the existence of a difference in point of view stemming from the use of a logophoric as opposed to a regular person marker cited in the literature involve precisely contexts where the two are not in complementary distribution. Thus, for example, Clements (1975:161), states that whereas the use of

---

[15] According to Jones (1998:167), this is not possible in Boko in which the distribution of logophoric forms is completely grammaticalized.

a normal third-person pronoun in the Ewe (76a) suggests that the child was punished against his will because someone else thought that this would cure him of his lies, the use of the logophoric form in (76b) suggests that the child voluntarily received punishment in the belief that this would cure him of his untruthfulness.

Non-complementarity of logophoric and "ordinary" pronouns is also seen to be a precondition for treating logophoric marking as a form of evidential marking. As pointed out by Banfield (1982), in indirect speech the speaker does not take responsibility for the truth of the propositional content of what someone said only for the fact that the party in question said it. Stirling (1993:266) and Culy (1997) suggest that in languages in which the use of logophoric forms is not completely grammaticalized, the choice between the two may reflect the extent to which the speaker is willing to take responsibility for the veracity of the reported event. The use of a logophoric marker over an ordinary person marker indicates that the speaker does not accept responsibility for the truth of the reported event. The selection of an ordinary person marker, by contrast, indicates that the speaker does accept the truth of the reported event and approves of its content.[16]

It has been repeatedly noted that the use of long-distance reflexives (LDRs) in many languages is strongly reminiscent of logophoric person markers. Although there have been no large-scale cross-linguistic comparisons of LDRs and logophoric person markers, the comparisons that have been carried out reveal that the two tend to occur with the same range of predicates, namely those captured in the hierarchy in (73), exhibit the same range of preferences in regard to the properties of the antecedent in the matrix clause (subjecthood, humanness, definiteness, individuation), are both typically third person and typically can fulfil a number of different grammatical functions. In addition, the use of both may be extended from sentential complements of logophoric predicates to that of other types of constructions. All these properties are clearly in evidence in the examples of LDRs given in section 5.3. Moreover, some instances of the use of LDRs, like that of logophoric markers, appear to be between indirect and direct speech. This is exemplified in (79) where the reflexive *tan* induces first- as opposed to third-person agreement marking in the complement clause.

(79)   Telugu (Subbarao & Murthy 2000:229)
         Kamala siita too   tanu pariikSa paasu awwagala-nu ani   ceppindi
         Kamala Sita with self test   pass can-1SG   COMP said
         'Kama$_i$ told Sita$_j$ that she$_{i*j}$ could pass the test.'

However, the use of LDRs, unlike that of logophoric pronouns, is typically not obligatory. In all of the examples of LDRs found in finite complements given above either an ordinary pronoun or just the person marking on the verb can be used as alternatives to that of the reflexive form. What determines the choice of a reflexive as compared to another type of person marker has been investigated

---

[16] Note that events and states which have been only communicated to the speaker rather than directly observed by him are the most likely to be considered as questionable in regard to their truth value. Consequently, speech predicates are the most likely to feature logophoric marking.

only in a small number of languages. But if (as suggested by Culy 1997) it is the existence of choice which underlies the point of view interpretation of logophoric markers, we would expect differences in point of view to be even more strongly correlated with the use of LDRs than with that of logophoric forms. Whether this is so remains to be seen.

Differences in point of view involving an LDR as compared to a pronominal have been extensively discussed in Japanese, which is arguably the language which has been most thoroughly investigated in regard to the use of LDRs. Nonetheless, again the examples cited tend to involve not LDRs in the complements of verbs of reporting but rather those found in other types of clauses, mainly relative clauses and adjunct clauses. The contrasting pair of sentences in (80) may serve as an illustration.

(80) Japanese (Kuno 1987:254)
a. Yamada wa kare o nikunde iru onna to kekkoniste simatta
Yamada TOP him ACC hating is woman with marrying ended up
'Yamada ended up marrying a woman who hated him.'

b. Yamada wa zibun o nikunde iru onna to kekkoniste simatta
Yamada TOP self ACC hating is woman with marrying ended up
'Yamada ended up marrying a woman who hated him.'

Kuno (1987:254) describes the difference between (80a) with the pronominal *kare* and (80b) with the LDR *zibun* as follows:

> Semantically, these two sentences are different in that while (80a) is a sentence in which the speaker gives an objective description of what happened by placing himself at a distance from *Yamada*, (80b) gives the impression that the speaker is omniscient and has identified himself with *Yamada*. The latter sentence ordinarily implies that *Yamada* knew at the time of the marriage that the woman he married hated him, or that he later came to know it.

According to Kuno (1972), among others, the use of *zibun* is possible in Japanese provided the situation or event represented in the clause can be conceived of from the point of view of the referent of *zibun*. This, in turn, can typically only happen if the referent in question is not only human but also alive and aware of what is or was going on. Hence the contrasts with respect to the occurrence of *zibun* in (81a) and (81b).

(81) Japanese (Kuno 1972:182)
a. John wa zibun ga kommatta toki dake, boku ni denwa o
John TOP self NOM troubled-is when only I to call
kakete-kuru
make
'John$_i$ calls me up only whenever he$_i$ is in trouble.'

b. *John wa zibun ga sinda toki, issen mo motte-imasen desita yo.
John TOP self NOM died when a penny have-not did
'John$_i$ didn't have a penny when he$_i$ died.'

Similar differences have been observed in regard to the use of the Korean LDR *caki*, the Mandarin LDR *ziji* and the LDRs in a number of the South Asian languages mentioned in section 5.3.2 such as Marathi and Telugu.[17] Another language in which the choice of an LDR or a regular person marker has been shown to involve a distinction observed with the use of logophoric forms is Icelandic. The distinction is not so much a matter of point of view or focus of empathy or subject of consciousness, but rather evidentiality. Thráinsson (1991) demonstrates the contrasts in (41) cited in section 5.3.1, that is the combination of an LDR with the subjunctive is used if the speaker is unwilling to take responsibility for the truth of the reported event; the ordinary pronoun and the indicative are used if the speaker considers the report to be reliable.

I will not pursue the issue of the correspondences between LDRs and logophoric markers further. Undoubtedly future studies will reveal significant points of convergence as well as potential differences. What is of relevance in the context of our discussion of accessibility is that in addition to indicating coreference, long-distance reflexives may be viewed as performing a logophoric function. If this is so, then the actual form of the markers may be expected to reflect their dual function rather than just the degree of accessibility of their referents. Accordingly, the fact that a more attenuated form of encoding may be used for a long-distance reflexive than for a reflexive used locally does not constitute a counter-example to the relationship between accessibility and formal encoding captured in the accessibility marking scale in (2). Nor does the fact that the reflexive can alternate with a regular person marker.

5.4.2 Person marker vs other referential expression and speaker empathy

Closely related to the notion of point of view is the notion of empathy. In fact many linguists use the two terms interchangeably. Kuno (1987), who is the linguist who has most extensively written on both notions, considers point of view to be a special case of empathy, which he defines as in (82).

(82)   Empathy is the speaker's identification, which may vary in degree, with a person/thing that participates in the event or state that he describes in a sentence.

In characterizing empathy Kuno uses the analogy of speaker as cameraman who has the option of describing an event involving two participants from the camera angle of participant A, or participant B, or from an objective camera angle. In the examples in (83) in which *John* and *Bill* are brothers, (83a) illustrates the adoption of John's camera angle, (83b) Bill's camera angle and (83c) an objective camera angle.

---

[17] Differences in perspective correlating with the use of reflexives, though emphatic as opposed to pronominal reflexives, can also be observed in English, as discussed in Kuno (1987:120) and Zribi-Hertz (1989:705).

(83) a.   Then John hit his brother.
   b.   Then Bill's brother hit him.
   c.   Then John hit Bill.

Since the description of a situation or event from the camera angle of a participant may take the form of presenting the words, thoughts or feelings of that participant, empathy encompasses point of view, in the "logophoric" sense of the term used in section 5.4.1. Nonetheless, as the examples in (83) suggest, empathy also involves other forms of the identification of the speaker with a person or thing which make it a much broader notion than point of view. These other forms of identification include the use of certain types of adjectives, directional verbs (e.g. *come* vs *go*), the choice of subject and/or object, the use of honorific forms and significantly the selection of referential expressions. While not all scholars who use the term empathy conceive of it exactly in the same way as Kuno does, most agree that among the choices of referential expressions relating to empathy is the choice of person marker vs demonstrative or other referential expression.

It is often noted that in languages in which person forms are used essentially for humans and demonstratives for non-humans, higher animals or otherwise culturally significant animals may be referred to by means of a person form. If the choice between the use of the relevant forms is comparable to that involving the human *s/he* over the non-human *it* in English, then the relevant factor is highly likely to be empathy. In English *s/he* is preferred to *it* by pet owners or animal lovers when speaking about their pets or favourite animals. A rather extreme example of such usage involving even the use of the relative *who* rather than the much more typical *that* (Wales 1996:142) is illustrated in the extract from a story about a cat called Squid cited in Yamamoto (1999:11).

(84)   All we have is a silent Squid, who looks somewhat like a blue-point Siamese, and we can't even ask her if she had other owners before Clay and she met, or how they may have treated her. Surely there had to be someone because Squid was socialized when Clay discovered her in her hour of need. But she makes a game of it, of her relationship with people, and we don't know whether that is a lingering effect of early mistreatment or whether this is her perverse sense of humour. I suspect the latter. I can't believe she isn't laughing at us.

If the use of a person form rather than of a demonstrative for an animal is motivated by empathy, we may expect the converse, the use of a demonstrative rather than of a person form for a human to be an indication of lack of empathy. And indeed there are languages in which this appears to be so.[18] For example, according to Duranti (1984), in Italian conversation the demonstratives *quello/quella* 'that

---

[18] I would not like to suggest that the use of demonstratives with reference to humans is necessarily or even typically non-empathetic. No lack of empathy has been noted in regard to such usage of demonstratives in Russian, Finnish, Dutch, the Tibeto-Burman languages Yamphu or Athpare or the Papuan language Tauya, for example.

one' or *questo/questa* 'this one' are used rather than *lui/lei* for referents which are either unimportant minor characters in a story or for referents whom the speaker disapproves of, dislikes or feels socially or emotionally distant from. The usage of a demonstrative for a minor as opposed to a major character is illustrated in (85) in which *quello* is used to refer to the employee of the factory where the main protagonist (the father) went to have a motor pump repaired.

(85) Italian (Duranti 1984:296)
Non tso che intsomma. Tuo padre pentsa che quando è arrivato
Not know which that is your father think:2SG that when is arrived
là. **Quello** gli ha detto "ritorni domani"
there that to-him has said return tomorrow
'I don't remember what. Your father imagine that, when he arrived there, the guy told him "come back tomorrow".'

In (86), by contrast, the referent of *questo*, a boy called Adamo, is one of the main characters of the story and some of the listeners actually know him. The speaker's use of *questo* to refer to him is an indication of her lack of regard and negative attitude towards him.

(86) Italian (Duranti 1984:305)
Dovevo prendere la macchina. Allora mi ha detto 'guarda
had to:1SG take the car so me:DAT has:3SG said look
sai devo andare all' università te l'ho
know:2SG must:1SG go to:the university you:DAT it have:1SG
spiegato devo pigliare le frequenze." bene allora io ho
explained must:1SG take the attendance good then I have
pensato viene all'università ho detto **questo** c'avra
thought comes:3SG to the university have:1SG said:1SG this must have
la macchina nossignore
the car no way
'I need the car. So he said to me "look y'know I have to go to university, I explained to you I need to get proof of attendance". Good, then I thought he was coming to the university. I thought this guy must have a car. No way.'

That the speaker dislikes Adamo is made quite explicit a few turns later when she says *E scemo* 'he is stupid' and then again *E proprio tonto* 'he is really dumb'. The use of demonstratives in argument positions to refer to humans with whom the speaker has no or little affinity can also be observed in Polish and Czech, New Testament Greek as well as in French, Portuguese, Spanish and Catalan. In the Romance languages, however, the demonstratives appear to convey lack of empathy only when used deictically not anaphorically. It needs to be noted that not all uses of demonstratives in place of person forms are depreciative. Head (1978:183) suggests that in Latin the demonstrative *ille* came to indicate respect or admiration. And in Nkore-Kiga (Taylor 1985:128) the use of the demonstratives *ogu/ogowo* 'this/that' rather than of the third-person singular *we* 'he/she' is considered to be more polite.

Languages differ considerably in the extent to which they allow names and descriptive NPs to be used in place of person forms. For example, according to Nichols (1985:181), in Russian prose, names and descriptions such as *starik* 'old man', *zenscina* 'woman' often appear where in English one would have a person form. A similar observation is made by Yamamoto in relation to Japanese and Sohn (1994:141) in relation to Korean. Nichols suggests that in Russian the use of most types of names rather than of person markers indicates speaker empathy, that of descriptions, lack of empathy. The positive associations springing from the use of a personal name extend to Japanese, Korean and also English. But the use of a description, particularly of a role term, is so prevalent in Japanese that it is better described as neutral rather than positively lacking in empathy.

Empathy verges on issues of politeness, which will be discussed in chapter 6. This also applies to impersonalization about which a few remarks will be presented below.

5.5 Person markers and impersonalization

Among the person-marker inventories of many languages there are often forms which are used to refer not to a specific individual or group of individuals but to people in general or a loosely specified collective, such as people who like walking or people who have horses or any fan of Keith Richards, etc. Various terms are used to refer to such forms in the literature: universal non-specific, generic, generalized human, generalized indefinite, referentially arbitrary and impersonal. I will use the last of these. Impersonal forms may be quite distinct from the person forms which are used to denote specific referents or groups of referents, and therefore qualify as person forms only in the sense that they necessarily denote persons, i.e. humans. The English *one*, French *on*, Romance *uno*, Germanic *man/men*, Udmurt *odig*, Hausa *a/an*, Lele *ge*, Somali *la*, Tinrin *hêrrê* belong to this category.[19] Alternatively, the impersonal forms may simply correspond to one or more of the regular person forms, as in the case of the English *we*, *you* and *they*, which can all be used impersonally. E.g.

(87) a. We routinely lie.
  b. Money can't buy you love.
  c. They don't allow pets.

It is only with this second type of impersonal forms that we will be concerned here.

---

[19] Some of these forms, for example the English *one* may be used strictly referentially, as in (ii) taken from Wales (1996:82).

  (i)   It was a sad moment leaving one's family on the tarmac, waving one goodbye. (Prince Charles, BBC, 26 July 1981)

More about the use of these forms will be said in chapter 6.

Given that impersonal forms denote the general body of humans or some loosely specified group, we would expect plural person markers to more commonly acquire impersonalizing uses than singular markers. This is indeed so. The most common person form which is used impersonally cross-linguistically is the third-person plural, as in (88) from the Papuan language Amele.

(88) Amele (Roberts 1987:208)
Aluh   gemo   na   b-i-me-b   cudun oso   age jain
mountain middle at   come up-PRED.-SS-3SG place INDEF 3PL rest
mud-i-me-ig   meci-egi-na   eu na ono ege na sab
make-PRED.-SS-3PL see-3PL-PRES that at there 1PL of food
j-om
eat-1PL-REM.PAST
'We came up to the middle of the mountain and at the place where they stop to rest and take in the view we ate our food.'

Impersonal uses of the third-person plural are found in, for example, the Germanic, Romance and Slavonic languages, in Greek, Kashmiri, Persian, the Finno-Ugric languages (e.g. Erzya Mordvin, Hungarian, Komi, Mari (Chermis), Nenets, Udmurt), the Turkic languages (e.g. Turkish), the Dravidian languages (e.g. Tamil), some African languages (e.g. Babungo, Godie, Koromfe, Mundani, Nkore-Kiga), some Papuan languages (e.g. Amele, Kombon), some Austronesian languages (e.g. Tawala). Whereas impersonal third-person plural forms exclude both speaker and addressee, in the impersonal use of first-person non-singular forms, as in (89) from the Austronesian language Tuvaluan, for instance, the speaker and addressee are included within the set of possible referents.

(89) Tuvaluan (Besnier 2000:391)
Kaafai e   iita   taatou   maa kkau ki fiafiaga   a te
if   NON-PAST displeased 1PL:INCL COMP join to celebration of the
fenua,   e   ttele fua taatou   keaattea
island-community NON-PAST run just 1PL:INCL away
'If you don't feel like partaking in island festivities, you just leave.'

First-person non-singular impersonal forms, however, do not appear to be very common outside of Europe. The only other non-European languages that I have come across that use the first-person non-singular impersonally are Canela Kraho, Hishkaryana, Macushi, Kaingan, Kilivila, some Kiranti languages, Kurdish and Tukang Besi.[20] Unlike, the third- and first-person non-singular, the second-person non-singular tends not to be used impersonally. One reason for this may be that the second-person non-singular is often used as a polite form of singular address. This will be discussed in more detail in chapter 6.

---

[20] Mithun (1999:71) mentions the opposite phenomenon, the use of impersonal or indefinite forms for the plural inclusive, in some languages of North America, one of them being Caddo. The replacement of first-person non-singular forms by impersonal forms is also to be observed in the Tibeto-Burman Kiranti languages, such as Limbu, Athpare, Belhare and, of course, French.

The second-person singular, in contrast to the non-singular, is a common means of impersonalization throughout Europe. It is used in the Germanic, Romance and Slavonic languages, in Hungarian, Estonian, Komi, Turkish and Abkhaz. In none of these, however, is it as frequent as in English, though according to some authors its use appears to be on the increase, under the influence of English.[21] Outside of Europe the impersonal use of the second-person singular occurs in, for example, Godie, Gulf Arabic, Hindi, Kashmiri, Koromfe, Koyra Chin, Kurdish, Mandarin, Marathi, Mauwake, Maybrat, Macushi, Modern Hebrew, Mundani, Nkore-Kiga and Tuvaluan. As (90) suggests, the second-person singular, like the first-person non-singular, when used impersonally, includes both speaker and addressee among the set of potential referents.

(90) Mauwake (Järvinen 1991:76)
No waaya mik-ap inasina unuma me unuf-inan-na mua
2SGNM pig spear-SS .SEQ spirit name not call-FUT:2SG-if man
oko-ke nainiw mik-ap nefar aaw-inon
other-CTR.FOC again spear-SS.SEQ 2SG:DAT take:FUT:3SG
'If you don't call your spirit name after spearing a pig, another man will spear it again and take it from you.'

While the speaker is included among the set of referents, the emphasis is on the addressee, who is directly invited to imagine himself in the situation or event expressed by the speaker and thus share in the world-view being presented or entertained. The second-person singular is thus an appropriate impersonalizing strategy only in the case of neutral or inoffensive situations or events which the addressee can imagine himself being involved in. In some languages, for instance Godie and Mundani, it is therefore restricted to procedural discourse. In others, for example Polish and Hungarian it is primarily a feature of discourse among friends or intimates.

Considerably less frequent than the second-person singular is the impersonal use of the third-person singular. Moreover, in contrast to the impersonal uses of the first- and third-person non-singular and second-person singular, which may be instantiated by means of weak independent forms or verbal inflections, the only instances of impersonal third-person usage that I have come across involve either verbal inflections, as in Finnish (91), Gothic and Syrian Arabic or zero forms, as in Tuvaluan (92), Mandarin and Malayalam.

(91) Finnish (Sulkala & Karjalainen 1992)
Suomessa kuolee ikävään
Finland:INESS die:3SG boredom-ill
'Finland makes you die of boredom.'

---

[21] In the case of French, the increase in the impersonal use of *tu* has also been attributed to the strong tendency to use *on* as a first-person plural form and thus the need to create a "new" impersonal pronoun. See Blondeau (2001) and the references therein.

(92) Tuvaluan (Besnier 2000:390)
Te vaegaa atu teenaa e see tii maua Ø i gaauta,
the kind-of bonito that NON-PAST see often get 3SG at landward
kae maua Ø i te vasa eiloa
but get 3SG in the deep-sea indeed
'That kind of bonito (you) don't catch near the shore, (but) (you) catch it in the deep waters.'

Presumably the reason why overt third-person singular forms tend not to be used impersonally is that they would be too likely to be interpreted as pertaining to a specific referent. Unlike in the case of second-person forms, the addressee is not in a position to disambiguate.

As mentioned in chapter 1 and chapter 4, in so-called pro-drop languages, the impersonal interpretations of first-, second- or third-person forms obtain only in the absence of a corresponding independent person marker. This is so, for example, in Rumanian, Italian, Sardinian, Iberian Spanish, the Slavic languages, the Finno-Ugric ones, Greek and Tarifit Berber. Nonetheless, in Latin American Spanish an overt person form is regularly used. Thus the impersonal reading cannot be restricted to the absence of an independent person form even in pro-drop languages.

In this chapter we have reviewed the referent tracking function of person forms concentrating on the cognitive status of the referents of different types of person markers within the discourse and the extent to which speakers identify or empathize with these referents. What yet remains to be considered is the social dimension of the use of person forms.

6 Person forms and social deixis

The correct use of person markers in a language requires knowledge not only of the existing person forms and the syntactic and discourse-pragmatic rules governing their distribution but crucially also of the social relations obtaining between the speech-act participants and the third parties that they invoke. As formulated by Mühlhäusler and Harré (1990:207), "pronominal grammar provides a window to the relationship between selves and the outside world".

In much of the earlier research on the social factors underlying variation in the use of person markers, particularly that inspired by the seminal work of Brown and Gilman (1960), the relationship between speaker and addressee (and/or other) was analysed in terms of the dimensions of power (or status) and solidarity (intimacy). The claim was that in asymmetrical relationships the more powerful of the two interlocutors uses a non-deferential T person marker and receives, in return, the deferential v form. In symmetrical relationships, reciprocal forms of address are used; in the higher echelons often v forms, in the lower typically T forms. This, however, also depends on whether speakers wish to express solidarity with their addressees (because of common sex, age, profession, city or region of origin, etc.) in which case they will use T forms, or conversely seek to stress their lack of solidarity, which will result in the use of v forms. Subsequent investigations have revealed that the use of just the two dimensions, power and solidarity, to characterize correct social usage of person forms is not enough. Mühlhäusler and Harré (1990: 132), for example, suggest that at least the following dimensions are required: rank, status, office, generation, formality, informality, public discourse, private discourse, intimacy, social distance and high degree of emotional excitement. There is a wealth of literature documenting the relevance of these dimensions in the selection of person markers in a wide variety of languages (e.g. Head 1976; Brown & Levinson 1987; Braun 1988). We, however, will be concerned not so much with the precise details of the social situations underlying variation in the use of person forms but rather in the formal manifestations of the existing variation.

Social deixis may be expressed in the person system of a language in a variety of ways. The most common way seems to be via the manipulation of the semantic distinctions reflected in a given person paradigm, such as person, number, inclusivity and gender. In chapter 3 these distinctions were discussed in the context of the paradigmatic structure of person paradigms. A consideration of how they are actually used by speakers reveals that there may be considerable mismatches between the semantic features of person forms and the characteristics of their discourse referents. In English, for example, given the appropriate situational context, the person form *we*, which grammatically is the first-person plural, may be used to denote any of the three persons in any number combination, as illustrated in (1).

(1) a. 1 We are not interested in the possibility of defeat. (Queen Victoria on the Boer War, 1899)
   b. 2 We want to eat our din dins now. (Carer talking to patient)
   c. 3 We had wet panties again in playgroup. (Mother talking about her child)
   d. 1 + 1 We solemnly swear . . .
   e. 1 + 2 Shall we book for just the two of us then?
   f. 1 + 3 We will join you the moment Dik arrives.
   g. 1 + 3 + 3 We are underpaid and overworked.
   h. 2 + 2 + 2 We will hear in this presentation . . .
   i. 3 + 3 We won the First World War.

Such mismatches between the grammatical form of a person marker and its referential value as indicators of social deixis will the topic of section 7.1. Another way of expressing social relations via the person system is through the use of special person forms called honorifics which are directly associated with status, rank or social standing. Such special forms are typically found for the second person, though they may also exist for the first person and even for the third. The distribution and use of honorific person forms will be considered in section 7.2. A third possibility, to be discussed in section 7.3, is to avoid the use of certain person markers or combinations of person markers by substituting them with NPs or, in the case of bound forms, "obscuring" the form of the markers.

Before we proceed, it must be mentioned that while the person system is one of the chief grammatical means of indicating social distance in language, it is hardly the only one. Social deixis may be signalled among others by the use of different modalities, the presence of diminutives and augmentatives, the choice of classifier, the selection of particular verbal forms, the choice of auxiliary and the use of number distinctions with nouns. As for the lexical encoding of social deixis, this may range from the use of titles, kinship terms, first names, surnames, nicknames (and the combinations of these), through the use of euphemisms and dysphemisms and/or of special lexicon to the use of speech levels (as in Javanese) or even of particular "languages" such as the mother-in-law languages of Australia (see, e.g., Foley 1997).

6.1   Alternation in semantic categories

A cross-linguistic investigation of how semantic distinctions encoded in person paradigms are used to indicate social deixis has been carried out by Head

(1978). His analysis of over one hundred languages revealed that the semantic distinction most widely employed for this purpose is that of number. Let us therefore consider alternations in number first.

6.1.1 Variation in number

When oppositions in the grammatical category of number are used to signal social deixis, non-singular number is typically associated with greater social distance, status, or respect than the singular number. We see this clearly in the Dravidian language Tamil (2) in which most of the so-called honorific forms of the independent person markers are in fact just the plural forms.

(2) Tamil (Asher 1982:143–5)

		Singular	Plural	Honorific
1	INCL		**naampa/naama**	**naama** (royal)
	EXCL	naan	**naanga**	
2		nii	**niinga**	**niinga/niir**
PROX 3M		ivan	ivanga	ivaru
	F	iva	**ivanga**	**ivanga**
	N	idu		
DIST 3M		avan	avanga	avaru
	F	ava	**avanga**	**avanga**
	N	adu		

As Tamil illustrates, variations in number to signal social deixis may be used for self-reference, when addressing the hearer and when referring to third parties. The use of the first-person plural for self-reference is restricted to royalty (see below). The use of the plural forms for address and in discussing third parties is an integral feature of everyday speech. According to Asher, the normal honorific second-person form of address is the plural form *niinga*, the form *niir* being used only very rarely. For singular honorific third-person reference the plural third-person forms are available in all dialects and can be used with reference to a male or a female. The special non-plural forms *avaru* and *ivaru*, on the other hand, are used only with reference to males. The Tamil use of honorific person forms is non-reciprocal, that is the form used by one person when speaking to another need not be used by that other person when addressing the former speaker.

In Europe, the use of non-singular number for respectful singular reference has been attributed to cultural diffusion, especially the influence of French in which the second-person singular *tu* is used to express intimacy or more rarely condescension, and the second-person plural *vous* to convey social distance or respect. For example, the appearance of such a contrast in English dates to after the Norman Conquest and its disappearance coincides with the waning of French influence. In earlier stages of English *thou* was the second-person singular form and *you* the second-person plural form. After the Norman Conquest the second-person plural *you* began to be used for polite singular reference, the second singular form *thou* when speaking to subordinates or as a sign of intimacy. The following examples are from Chaucer's Book of the Duchess.[1]

(3) a. "Go bet," quod Juno, to Morpheus "Thou knowest hym wel..."
        'Go quickly said Juno to Morpheus – you know him well.'

   b.   "Ye shul me never on lyve yse."
        'You shall never see me alive (again).'

In (3a) *thou* is uttered by Queen Juno to her subordinate. In (3b) Morpheus, the God of Sleep is addressing his wife Alcione. Though they are husband and wife, Alcione is also a Goddess and thus his use of *you* as opposed to *thou* as a sign of respect. In English, this usage never became firmly entrenched (see, e.g., Wales 1996:75) and over time gave way to the general use of *you* and disappearance of *thou* (but for certain religious contexts). In most of the Slavonic languages (e.g. Upper Sorbian, Russian, Czech), some of the Germanic (e.g. Danish, Swedish) and Romance (e.g. Rumanian), in Greek, Modern Eastern Armenian, Finnish and Latvian, on the other hand, the French pattern became the norm, and is used to this day.

The above diffusional explanation for the use of non-singular number for polite singular reference does not, of course, provide an account of the existence of the same pattern in a wide variety of genetically and areally unrelated languages. Some non-European languages which display such variation in the second person are Africa: Amharic, Gbaya, Harari, Koromfe, Mande, Ndyuka, Sango, Shona, Welamo, Yoruba; in South and South-East Asia: Bengali, Fijian, Indonesian, Kapampangan, Khasi, Malayalam, Nepali, Pangasinan, Persian, Telugu, Tukang Besi; in the Americas: Eastern Pomo, Navajo, Silacayoapan Mixtec and in Australia: Djaru, Ngarluma, Ngiyambaa. This suggests that deeper cognitive factors are likely to be involved. One possible explanation offered by Brown (1965:54) is that plurality is a natural metaphor for social power, as in "United we stand, divided we fall". In the light of subsequent research on cognitive metaphors (e.g. More is better; Good is Up) and the metaphorical basis of grammar (e.g. Lakoff 1987), this explanation is more appealing than when it was originally advanced. Another possible explanation is offered by Brown and Levinson (1987:198) who consider the use of plural forms for singular address to be a means of redressing the negative face wants of the addressee. Their theory of politeness is based on a contrast between positive face, the individual's desire to be appreciated, esteemed and approved of, and negative face, the desire to be not imposed upon, to be unimpeded, to be able to act without constraint. Brown and Levinson argue that if as part of a group one is less obligated to act or respond than if one is singled out as an individual, the use of a plural form of address is less face threatening than that of the singular. Thus they see the use of second-person plural forms for address as a type of impersonalizing device.

---

[1] This example is taken from Hock (1986:249).

Variation in number to show deference or degree of social distance, though most common in address, that is with the second person, is also regularly found in speaking about third parties. The following example is from the Dravidian language Malayalam in which, as in the previously mentioned Tamil, the non-singular is used as a respect form both in direct reference and in address.

(4) Malayalam (Asher & Kumari 1997:259)
     Avar   oru prasiddha kalaakaari aalnə
     she:PL a   famous   artist   be:PRES
     'She is a famous artist.'

The use of the third-person plural form *avar* in (4) contrasts with that of the third-person singular feminine *aval*, as in (5).

(5) Malayalam (Asher & Kumari 1997:275)
     Aval   caaya aarri
     she: SG tea   cool:PAST
     'She cooled the tea.'

Turning to self-reference, the use of non-singular number for first-person reference is well attested in Indo-European languages. Two types of usage are traditionally distinguished: the plural of majesty or "royal we", as in (6) and the plural of modesty, nowadays primarily associated with the "editorial we", as in (7).[2]

(6) Danish (Allan, Holmes & Lundskaer-Nielson 1995:146)
     Vi alene vide (attributed to King Fredrick VI)
     we alone know
     'We alone know . . .'

(7) French
     C'est encore une étude que nous présenter-ons ici . . .
     it-is another a   study that we   present-1PL   here
     'This is yet another study that we present here . . .'

The former is maximally distancing since the speaker by making himself plural precludes the possibility of a normal reciprocal relationship. The latter, on the other hand, is seen to originate in the desire to detract attention from self and to suggest joint rather than single authorship and thus modesty of achievement. As pointed out by Wales (1996:64), in English the royal we is hardly used by the current royal family, but can be occasionally discerned in the speech of politicians, as in Margaret Thatcher's (8).

(8) We are happy we are leaving the UK in a very, very much better state than when we came here eleven and a half years ago. (*Guardian*, 29 November 1990: on her deposition from premiership)

---

[2] A royal we *naam* was also formerly used in Malayalam (Jayaseelan 2000:113) and is still in use in Telugu (Subbarao & Murthy 2000:217).

Given the situational context in which (8) was uttered, it is difficult to interpret the *we* in (8) as referring to anybody other than Margaret Thatcher alone. The editorial we, by contrast, is still relatively common. Interestingly enough, though, it tends to be perceived as rather formal and old fashioned, even pompous, rather than as a sign of modesty. The same seems to apply to the editorial we in other European languages.

A real plural of modesty seems to have been used in eighteenth-century Chinese. Lee (1999) states that in classic Chinese novels an individual of inferior status, typically women, servants or children, employs the first-person plural for self-reference when conversing with someone of superior status. For instance, in *The Story of Stone* (vol. I, p. 168) a maid uses the first-person plural pronoun *women* when conversing with a prominent member of the Mandarin family. Unfortunately, Leng does not provide a transliteration of the Chinese characters, just the English translation which is in (9).

(9) "What was this prescription Miss? If you will tell me, we (I) shall try to remember it so that [I] can pass it on to others."

Similar usage is mentioned by Corbett (2000:22) in nineteenth-century Russian and by Head (1978:166) in a number of African languages such as Hausa, Zande and Nyamwezi. The Mixtecan so-called first-person respect forms, as in Ocotepec Mixtec (Alexander 1988:263), may also be of this type. Most Mixtecan languages do not encode number in their person systems. However, the distinction between respectful and familiar is considered to have originated in a number opposition with the plural number developing into the respect form. Since the first-person respect forms are considered as conveying respect to the addressee (as opposed to the speaker) presumably they express self-effacement or self-denigration on the part of the speaker. The first-person plural is also used to show a higher degree of respect than the second-person plural in Tukang Besi (Donohue 1999:114). In contrast to the languages just mentioned, in Sierra Popoloca (Krumholz et al. 1995:300) the first-person plural inclusive is claimed to be the normal form of polite self-reference, the first-person singular being considered as authoritarian. As it is the inclusive form rather than the exclusive that is viewed as polite, this cannot be a form of self-humbling in the same sense as in Chinese, but perhaps is more comparable to the editorial we.

What is unusual about eighteenth-century Chinese, as compared to the other languages just mentioned, is that the plural as a denigrating device is extended to the second and third persons. Lee documents that in the classical novels that he examined the second-person plural *nimen* occurs in place of *ni* for singular address when people of the Mandarin family reprimand individual servants, or when higher-ranking servants address lower-ranking ones. The third-person plural form *tamen* in place of the third-person singular *ta*, in turn, is employed to indicate that the referent is negligible or of little importance. For instance, in (10) Old Mrs Lai, a servant refers to her grandson, who has just been promoted to officialdom, by means of a third-person plural form when speaking to a member of the Mandarin family.

(10) "When will he be leaving to take up his post?" said Li Wan. Old Mrs Lai sighed . . . "Oh, I don't concern myself with their (his) affairs. I just let them (him) get on with it."

Leng argues that by the use of the third-person plural form, Old Mrs Lai is suggesting that her grandson, whom she is obviously very proud of, is in fact unimportant and negligible. In humbling her own family, she is simultaneously showing respect to her employer. I am not aware of any other such denigrating uses of the second- or third-person plural.

In languages which exhibit more than one set of non-singular person markers, for instance, a dual and a plural, it is typically the plural that is used for honorific singular address rather than the dual. Some notable exceptions are found among the Oceanic languages. Besnier (2000:389) mentions three in which the dual is used in preference to the plural, namely Tuvaluan, Tikopia and Mota. In Tuvaluan, which belongs to the Polynesian branch of Oceanic, the dual is in fact used to address singular, dual and plural entities. An example of the use of the dual when addressing a group is given in (11).

(11) Tuvaluan (Besnier 2000:389)
Koo see mafai o tauloto a te uke o taimi mo te lasi o
INC NEG can COMP learn CNJ the many of time and the large of
te alofa   teelaa ne fakaasi nee **koulua**
the empathy that PAST reveal ERG you:DU
'[One] cannot enumerate the number of times and the extent to which you have displayed your generosity.'

Moreover, the dual is used for honorific purposes not only in the second person but also in the first and even the third. Besnier characterizes the use of the dual in Tuvaluan as follows: "use the dual number with pronouns of all persons, but particularly the second person, in social contexts where the social identity of participants is given greater prominence than their personal identity". The use of the dual in Tuvaluan is not therefore so much determined by the relative status of the speaker and addressee but rather by the situational context. It is particularly favoured in oratory.[3] Occasionally both the dual and the plural may be used though for different types of referents. Osumi (1995:140) mentions that in traditional Tinrin,[4] an Austronesian language spoken in southern New Caledonia, the use of second-person forms within the family is dependent on the nature of the relationship between the speaker and addressee. The second-person singular is used to address parents, grandparents, grandchildren, aunts and uncles, between

---

[3] Some other languages which use the dual or paucal rather than the plural when addressing a crowd, mentioned in Corbett (2000:224–5), are Paamese, Sursurunga and Djambarrpuyngu.
[4] However, nowadays this usage is disappearing and many people simply use the French *tu* form for second-person, apart from when addressing non-Kanal people.

husband and wife and when addressing young female siblings or cousins. The second-person dual is employed when speaking to one's daughter, niece, younger brother or cousin or elder sister or cousin. And the second-person plural is the appropriate form of addressing a son, nephew or elder brother or cousin. In Santali (MacPhail 1953:23), an Austroasiatic language spoken in Bihar and West Bengali, the second-person dual forms are used by a mother and father-in-law when addressing their son or daughter-in-law, while second-person plural forms are used between the parents of a husband and wife. A similar situation, though involving not only address but also third-person reference, has been reported by Davies (1981:153–4) in the Papuan language Kobon. The plural is used for certain female and male relatives by marriage, for instance a mother-in-law, and the dual for certain male relatives, such as the father-in-law. This contrast is illustrated in (12); it is in evidence only in the verbal person markers, as the independent forms for the third-person dual and plural are homophonous.

(12)   Kobon (Davies 1981:153–4)
  a.   Gamai   yam   kale   au-ab-öl
       wife's mother group:3DU/PL come-PRES-3PL
       'My mother-in-law is coming.'

  b.   Bama   kale   au-ab-il
       wife's father 3DU/PL   come-PRES-3DU
       'My father-in-law is coming.'

Interestingly enough, though in languages in which the plural is used to signal deference one would expect it to be thus used for both singular and dual addressees, Corbett (2000:226) points out that this is not always so. Apparently in Slovene, the second-person plural can replace the second-person singular but not the second-person dual. Note the use of the plural form in (13a) but the dual in (13b).

(13)   Slovene
  a.   Ali se   boste   (Vi)   used-l-i?
       Q   REFL AUX: FUT:2PL (you:PL)   sit-PART-PL.M
       'Would you like to sit down? (Polite to one person).'

  b.   Ali se   bosta   (Vidva)   used-l-a?
       Q   REFL AUX:FUT:2DU (you:DU)   sit-PART-DU.M
       'Would you like to sit down?' (Polite to two persons, no change)

In all the above examples of alternations in number to indicate social deixis, the unequal social relationship is indicated by the use of a grammatically non-singular person marker for singular reference. The only instance of the converse, that is the use of singular number for non-singular reference that I have come across is again from eighteenth-century Chinese. Lee argues that such usage is characteristic of speakers of high social status discussing referents of inferior social position, whom they consider as unimportant.

6.1.2 Variation in person

As in the case of number, the signalling of social deixis via variation in person is most frequently found in relation to the addressee. The use of third person for address is typically an indication of formality or at least lack of familiarity, or of deference towards the addressee. This is reflected in the contrast between (14a) and (14b).

(14)   Danish (Allan et al. 1995:149)
   a.   Har de kjolen i en anden farve?
        have 3PL dress in an other colour
        'Have you got the dress in a different colour?'

   b.   Farr, kan du låne mig en tie
        Daddy can 2SG lend me a tenner
        'Daddy, can you lend me ten kroner?'

In languages in which there are several deferential forms of address within the person system, the use of third-person markers as address forms appears to be associated with the highest level of deference. This is so in French, for example, in which the use of *il* or *elle* for address (rather than *vous*) as in (15) occurs only in "certain somewhat exaggerated situations of politeness" (Judge & Healey 1985:70).

(15)   French
   a.   Et monsieur, qu'est-ce qu'il désire?
        Sir   what-is-this what-he want:3SG
        'What would you like, sir?'

   b.   Votre Altesse, que désire-t-elle?
        your Majesty what want-t-she
        'Your Majesty, what would you like?'

Another case in point is the Meulaboh dialect of Acehnese (Durie 1985:116–17) in which four degrees of politeness are distinguished in the second person. The polite third-person clitic *geu* has become the normal most polite second-person form.[5] In Standard Swedish, however, according to Holmes and Hinchliffe (1993:134), addressing an individual by means of *han* (he) or *hon* (she), as in (16), is considered to be a little derogatory.

(16)   Swedish (Holmes & Hinchliffe 1993:134)
        Han kan gora som han vill, jag fått haft nog!
        he can do COMP he want I received had enough
        'You can do as you please, I've had enough.'

Nor is deference involved in the use of third-person forms for direct address in English baby-talk, as in (17), cited in Wales (1996:56).

---

[5] A diachronic connection between the third person and the reverential (as opposed to polite and familiar) second-person marker *droel' neu(h)* may also be discerned in Standard Acehnese.

(17) a. Diddums! Did he hurt himself?
  b. Timmy must be a good boy and eat his dinner.

The above is very reminiscent of the effect achieved by the use of first-person forms for second-person address, which in various European languages is associated with doctors addressing patients or caretakers addressing small children or the elderly. Some examples are provided below.

(18)   Upper Sorbian (Schuster-Šewc 1996:119)
       Kak so   nam wjedže?
       how are 1:PL doing
       'How are we today?'

(19)   Dutch
       Waarom hebben we   nog steeds niet gegeten?
       why   have   1:PL still   not eaten
       'Why have we still not eaten?'

In certain varieties of Malay, however, the use of the first-person plural inclusive for address is deferential or expresses solidarity. This is also the case in several other Austronesian languages such as Fehan Tetun, Karo Batak, Toba Batak and Tuvaluan as well as in Ainu and the Australian language Gurindji.

The alternation of third person for second person may or may not be accompanied by an alternation in number. For instance, in Italian, Kashmiri, Sotho and Swedish third-person singular forms are used. In Amharic, Bemba, Danish Eastern Pomo, Fijian, French, German, Norwegian, and Tagalog third-person plural forms are employed. In contrast to the above, the first-person forms used for second-person reference seem to always be non-singular ones.

Closely connected to the honorific use of third-person person markers for second-person reference is the use of so-called pronominalized nouns, that is former nouns, typically titles which have become so grammaticalized that they currently function on a par with person markers. Their third-person status is, however, reflected in the agreement pattern which is third person. The best-known instance of this phenomenon is that of the Polish *Pan/Pani/Państwo* which are used as alternatives for the second-person independent markers *ty* (singular) and *wy* (plural). The form *Pan* originates from the expression *wasza miłość moj miłościwy Pan* – 'Your mercy, my merciful lord' introduced by the Polish gentry around the seventeenth century. The rules governing the choice of a pronominalized noun or second-person pronoun in urban Polish after the Second World War used to be relatively straightforward; any adult who was not an actual intimate and who one did not know well enough to address by their title, profession or name was addressed as *Pan* (male), *Pani* (female) or *Państwo* (plural), virtually irrespective of the situational context, as the examples in (20) attempt to suggest.

(20) Polish
   a.   Pani powinna się wstydzić.
       you should:3SGF REFL ashamed
       'You should be ashamed of yourself.'

   b.   Pan chyba zwariował.
       you perhaps mad:3SGM
       'You must be mad.'

The use of *Pan/Pani* was therefore more neutral than deferential, that of the person forms *ty/wy*, familiar. Currently, the system is undergoing change; the range of contexts in which the person forms rather than the *Pan/Pani* ones appear is clearly on the increase. For example, one even hears *ty* or *wy* being used in both television and radio interviews, though not with government ministers. The *Pan/Pani* forms may thus turn into actual highly deferential forms or alternatively simply disappear. Another language which uses pronominalized nouns as polite second-person pronouns is Brazilian Portuguese (Head 1976). The forms are *o senhor* (male) and *a senhora* (female), which contrast with the familiar *você* or *tu*.[6]

The use of truncated titles (and third-person agreement) for deferential second-person address is also a feature of other European languages such as Dutch, Portuguese and Spanish. In contrast with Brazilian Portuguese and Polish, however, what has remained of the truncated titles is not an original noun but a second-person plural possessive person marker. The Spanish *Vuestra Merced* and Portuguese *Vossa Mercê* which translate as 'your grace' have given rise to the polite second-person markers *usted* and *você*, respectively. Analogously, the Dutch expression *Uwe Edelheid* 'your nobility' has been shortened and generalized to give the second-person polite form *U*.

In certain types of discourse, namely autobiography and baby-talk, third-person forms may even be used for the speaker. In both instances the third-person pronominal form is introduced into self-reference through substitution of nominal forms, proper names, common nouns, etc. Such usage, however, is not motivated by politeness, but rather by a desire for objectivity, in the case of autobiography and perhaps playfulness in baby-talk.

6.1.3 The use of reflexives

In section 5.3.2 we noted that in various languages reflexives are associated with empathy. In some they are also used as honorifics. As observed by Head (1978) this is a common feature of the Dravidian and, to a lesser extent, the Indo-Aryan languages of India. In the languages which have other honorific forms, the reflexive is typically considered to be especially respectful and deferential. This is so in Kannada in relation to the reflexive *taavu* (in the plural), the usage

---

[6] According to Head (1976:338), in most of the country either *você* or *tu* is used but not both. For example, *você* is used in Rio de Janeiro, Salvador and São Paulo, and *tu* in Porto Alegre.

of which Sridhar describes as second-person ultra-honorific. An example is given in (21).

(21)   Kannada (Sridhar 1990:124)
       Taavu ii   kaDe banni
       self this side come:H
       'Please come to this side.'

The reflexive *aapaN* is also considered to be more polite and deferential than the second-person plural from *tumhii* in Marathi. Pandharipande (1997:383) states that it is essentially used when addressing priests, teachers, in-laws or other persons of high authority. E.g.

(22)   Marathi (Wali 2000:515)
       Mem-saheb, aap-laa vicaar   kaay aahe?
       Madam   self   thought what is
       'Madam, what do you wish to do?'

The same holds for the Maithili *apane*, which according to Jhaa (1958:398) is a stronger means of honorification than the normal honorific *aha*. What is interesting is that in contrast to the other languages mentioned, when *apane* is used, the verb is not in the third person but in the first person.

In Punjabi, unlike in Kannada, Marathi and Maithili, there are no separate honorific person forms. However, the ordinary reflexive *aap* appended by the honorific particle *-jii* may be used as a polite second singular or plural address form. It may also be used as a polite third-person singular form, though apparently only in formal introductions, to introduce an important personality, as in (23).

(23)   Punjabi (Bhatia 2000:648)
       Aap vaDDe   netaa ne
       self big:PL leader are(H:SG)
       'He is a great leader.'

In Kashmiri (Wali & Koul 1997:38, 41) politeness is expressed mainly by means of several polite markers, which loosely translate as 'sir', such as *s(e), jina:b, ha* and *ma;hra* as well as by plural forms of the verb and special vocative forms. Nonetheless, the simple reflexive *pani* may also be used as a means of a second-person respectful address, as exemplified in (24).

(24)   Kashmiri (Wali & Koul 1997:129)
       Pa: nas   si:th' di   me pakni
       self-DAT with   allow me walk
       'Allow me to go with you.'

Whereas, in all the languages mentioned above, the reflexive is used as means of honorification, in Malayalam, according to Jayaseelan (2000:116), the reflexive *taan* – 'self' is used with second-person reference to refer to the addressee with whom one is on equal or familiar terms. This is the only instance of such usage that I have come across.

Outside of the Indian subcontinent, the use of reflexives as a polite or respectful form of address is not particularly common. Two languages where such usage is attested are Hungarian and Turkish. In Turkish the reflexive *kendi*, appended with the third-person *si* is used as a third-person singular and plural honorific.[7] E.g.

(25) Turkish (Kornfilt 1997:305)
      Kendi-si opera-ya git-ti
      self-3SG opera-DAT go-PAST
      'He (respectful) has gone to the opera.'

In Hungarian the nominals *ön* or *maga* in the singular and *önök* and *maguk* in the plural are used to express politeness. The less formal of the two, *maga/maguk* corresponds to the third-person singular and plural reflexive *orm*.

(26) Hungarian (Kenesei et al. 1998:266–7)
      Magu-uk   tanár-ok?
      you (formal) teacher-PL
      'Are you (formal) teachers?'

A diachronic relationship between a second-person honorific *kiki* and an emphatic reflexive has also been noted in Imbabura Quechua. And in Tetelcingo Nahuatl, the prefix *mo-* derived from the third-person reflexive is used in conjunction with the second-person prefix as an honorific marker (27a,b) and a third-person prefix, as a high honorific marker (27c).

(27) Tetelcingo Nahuatl (Tuggy 1979:95)
  a. Ti-hti-li-a[8]
      2SG-see-APPL-PRES
      'You see him.'

  b. To-mo-hti-li-a
      2SG-H-see-APPL-PRES
      'You (H) see him.'

  c. To-mo-tie-mo-hti-li-li-a
      2SG-H-3SG-H.H-see-APPL-APPL-PRES
      'You (H) see him (HH).'

Extra-high honorification in reference can be achieved by using *mo* without an additional third-person marker, as in (28).

(28) Tetelcingo Nahuatl (Tuggy 1979:102)
      Nieč-mo-čiwi-li-li-a
      1SG-H-do-APPL-APPL-PRES
      'He (extra HH) does it to me.'

---

[7] Recall from chapter 2 that the reflexive in Turkish is also used as an intensifier and emphatic pronoun in certain cases.

[8] When a the third-person P is a non-honorific form, its presence is signalled only by the applicative marker, as shown in (27a,b). In (27c), the P high-honorific prefix follows the A prefix.

Tuggy mentions that such forms are used only with reference to a deity, or the president of the republic. There is also a special reflexive honorific marker *-cinow* used in the case of second-person honorific reflexives.

(29)   Tetelcingo Nahuatl (Tuggy 1979:96)
   a.   Ti-mo-kokow-a
       2SG-REFL-hurt-PRES
       'You are sick.'

   b.   To-mo-kokoh-cinow-a
       2SG-REFL-hurt-REFL:H-PRES
       'You (H) are sick.'

What underlies the honorific use of reflexive forms is not quite clear. Shibatani (1985:837) suggests that the connection between the two lies in agent defocusing. His argument is as follows. Honorific speech is characterized by the avoidance of the singling out of an agent, be it the speaker, addressee or third party. The defocusing of an agent is also involved in medio-passives, which typically express spontaneous events and states. Such constructions in turn may be morphologically marked by means of a reflexive (by virtue of its valency decreasing function), as is the case in Romance and Slavonic languages, for example.[9] The marking of the absence of an agent in the spontaneous construction may therefore be adopted for the agent defocusing in honorification. While this constitutes a potential explanation for the honorific use of verbal reflexives, as in Tetelcingo Nahuatl, it is by no means obvious that it also holds for the honorific use of pronominal reflexives, as in the Dravidian and Indo-Aryan languages, for example. There is nonetheless a possible connection between spontaneous constructions, pronominal reflexives and honorification, namely via the use of person-marked reflexives as intensifiers or emphatic pronouns. Recall from chapter 2 (section 2.3) that in many languages reflexives double up as emphatics and may be open to an "alone" or "without any assistance" reading, as in *I prefer to go there by myself* or *He did it himself*. If used with inanimate subjects, such reflexive pronouns may produce a reading whereby the event has come about effortlessly or spontaneously. Such is the case in English. Significantly, as shown in (30), this is also the case in Punjabi, in which the reflexive *aap* is sometimes used as an honorific.

(30)   Punjabi (Bhatia 2000:648)
       Kam   aap hoiaa
       work:M:SG self be:PAST:M:SG
       'The work happened on its own. / The work was completed painlessly.'

This spontaneous reading of the pronominal reflexive would thus allow for the extension to the agent defocusing or impersonalizing interpretation, which underlies much honorific usage. It is of interest to note in this context, that the pronominal

---

[9] I am assuming here that reflexivity is not inherently associated with spontaneity. I may be wrong.

reflexives in some of the Dravidian and Indo-Aryan languages may receive an impersonal/generic interpretation, as in the example below.

(31) Marathi (Wali 2000:517)
Phakta aap-lyaa-purta pahaava
only self-about see
'One should only worry about oneself.'

6.2   Special honorific person markers

Rather than utilizing alternations in number or person or substituting person markers from one paradigm with another, languages may indicate distinctions of social deixis via additional person forms. Such additional person forms may exist just for an individual person or several persons or for the whole person paradigm.

The area of the world most known for its elaborate systems of person honorifics is South and South-East Asia. Arguably the most extensive system of person honorifics is the one found in Thai, as discussed in Cooke (1968). Recall from chapter 1 (section 1.2) that in Thai there are 27 forms used for the first person, 22 for the second and 8 for the third. The various forms reflect a range of parameters chiefly status, level of intimacy and what Cooke calls non-restraint, that is the possibility of not conforming to the accepted standards but within prescribed limits. They also reflect deference, assertiveness, age, sex and kinship. Some forms used for the first and second persons are presented in (32).

(32)   Some terms for self-reference and address in Thai
   a.   first person
khâa'1phraphúd'thacâaw''2 (lit. 'Lord Buddha's servant' or '(your) Majesty's servant') – used by ordinary citizen, addressing the king and highest ranks of royalty
klâaw1kraphŏm' (lit. 'hair of the head') – a highly deferential term used by males when addressing high-ranking non-royalty
phŏm' (lit. 'hair') – a general polite term used by males speaking to equals and superiors
dichăn' – a non-intimate deferential term used by females speaking to superiors or formally to equals
chăn' – used by adult or adolesent male speaking to inferior or to female intimate
khăw' – used by child or young women speaking to intimate; often endearing

   b.   second person
tâajltàa'2la?ɔɔŋ'3phrá4bàad'5 (lit. 'dust underneath sole of royal foot') – used speaking to high royalty (though not the king)
tâaj 1thàaw'2 (lit. 'underneath foot') – used when addressing high-ranking superiors

tua' (lit. 'body, self') – affectionate or intimate, used when speaking to equal or inferior not older than the speaker, especially between female friends or to one's spouse

khun' (probably related to noun meaning 'virtue, merit') – general polite term used chiefly to equals and superiors

We see that many of the first-person forms literally refer to the head or hair. The deferential second-person forms in turn refer to the "sole of the foot" or "underneath the foot". Cooke states that these expressions originate from a situation in which the inferior person places the sole of the superior person's foot on a par with his head or hair, the head being the highest and most respected part of the body. While the status of the above forms as person markers and also pronouns (see the discussion in section 1.2) is quite controversial, we will see below that the type of social distinctions that they express are reflected in the person systems of other languages, though not all in any one person system.

A language with a rich system of honorific person markers is Nepali. As shown in (33), there are five levels of respect in the second person and three in the third.

(33)   Nepali (Acharya 1991:108)

			SG	PL
1			ma	hāmī-haru
2	low respect		tā	timī-haru
	equal		timī	timī-haru
	high (informal)		tapāī	tapāī-haru
	high (formal)		yahă	yahă-haru
	honorific		hajūr	hajūr-haru
	royal honorific		sarkār	sarkār-haru
3	low respect		tyo	tinī-haru
	equal		tinī	tinī-haru
	high		wahă	wahă-haru
	royal honorific		sarkār	sarkār-haru, mauaūph-haru

The form used when addressing or speaking about a member of the royal family, *sarkār* is a noun in origin meaning 'government'. And the two formal high respect forms *yahă* and *wahă* are the proximate and distal locative demonstratives 'here' and 'there'. The factors determining the usage of the above forms are less complicated than in Thai; according to Acharya they are essentially caste and age. As in other societies in which Hinduism is the dominant religion, there are four castes: the religious leaders (*Brāhmaṇas*), the administrators and warriors (*Ksatriyas*), the traders and craft workers (*Vaiśyas*) and the ordinary workers (*Sūdras*). A fifth class, called the *achut* 'Untouchables' is outside the caste system. The appropriate honorific level in address dependent on caste and age of speaker and addressee is depicted in Table 6.1.

We see that apart from the royal *sarkār*, there is only one form, which uniquely identifies caste and age of addressee, *tā* used for persons younger than the speaker belonging to the lowest caste.

Table 6.1 *Second-person pronoun usage by caste and age in Nepali*

Speaker's caste	Addressee's caste	Addressee's age (relative to speaker)	Pronoun
Brahman	Brahman	peer	tapāī
		senior	yahă
		junior	timī
Brahman	Ksatriya	same as Brahman	
Brahman	Vaiśyas	peer	timī
		senior	tapāī
		junior	timī
Brahman	Sūdras	peer	timī
		senior	timī
		junior	tā
Brahman	Royal family	all ages	sarkār
Vaiśyas	Brahman	all ages	hajur
Sūdras	Brahman	all ages	hajur

Another language known for its honorific person markers is Javanese. In contrast with Thai, the forms in question are typically considered to be actual pronouns. What is particularly interesting about the Javanese person markers is that they are part of a tripartite speech-level system of the language comprising many hundreds of lexical items. In traditional Javanese society there was a contrast between three speech levels: *ngoko, madya* and *krama*. Ngoko was the basic level used among intimate or familiar equals or in non-reciprocal usage by the speaker of higher rank. Krama was the standard polite level employed among non-intimates or by a person of lower rank to a person of higher rank. And madya was the middle level used mainly by lower castes who had no knowledge of krama, in place of krama. The person markers belonging to each of the three speech levels are presented in (34).

(34)　　Javanese (Uhlenbeck 1978:212)
　　　　basic (ngoko)　middle (madya)　high (krama)
　　1　aku　　　　　　　　　　　　　　kula
　　　　　　　　　　　　　　　　　　　ingsun (ruler)
　　2　kowe　　　　　　dikka,　　　　　sampeyan
　　　　slirane (H)　　　samang
　　　　sliramu (H)　　　　　　　　　　pañjěnengan (H)
　　3　dewege　　　　　piyambaqe　　　piyambaqipun
　　　　deweqne　　　　kiyambaqe　　　kiyambaqipun

The question *Will you take that much rice?* in the three speech levels is exemplified in (35) adapted from Foley (1997:323–4).

(35)　　Javanese
　　a.　Ngoko:Apa　kowé　njupuk　sega　semono
　　b.　Madya:Napa　dikka　njupuk　sega　semonten

c. Krama:Menapa sampeyan mendhet sekul semanten
Q   you   take   rice   that much
'Will you take that much rice?"

In addition to the distinct person markers of each level, in the case of the second person, honorific distinctions were made both within ngoko and krama, *slirane* and *sliramu* being more polite than *kowe* in ngoko, and *panjenengan* being more polite than *sampeyan* in krama. As pointed out by Uhlenbeck (1978:216), the use of *kowe* when *slirane* or *sliramu* was expected was considered to be inappropriate, even insulting. The same held for *sampeyan* as compared to *panjenengan*. In social situations which called for greater deference than that stemming from the use of krama and honorific forms, special nominal expressions were used in place of the person forms. These were in the case of the first person *abdidalěm/ adalěm/ dalěm* literally 'your servant' and for the second person *pakěnira*, from *tělapakěnira* literally 'soles of your feet', as in Thai.

A three-tier system of person markers is also found in Classical Tibetan in which a distinction is made between unmarked person forms, honorific ones and so-called elegant ones, as shown in (36).

(36)   Classical Tibetan (Beyer 1992:208)
        unmarked   honorific   elegant
    1   ña   ñed   bdag
    2   khyod   khyed   ñid
    3   kho   khoñ

The person forms in (36) are the singular forms. The plural is indicated by adding the suffix *tšag*. As in Javanese, the honorific person forms are part of an honorific speech level. The second- and third-person honorific forms are used to address or refer to persons of higher social or spiritual rank, relative to the speaker or addressee. The first-person honorific forms in turn express that the speaker is honoured by some relationship with a superior. They are thus self-humbling terms.

In Korean (Sohn 1994:8–10; 281–91, 358) there are six speech levels distinguished on the basis of the addressee's age, kinship and social status relative to the speaker. The six speech levels are plain, intimate, familiar, blunt, polite and deferential. The plain level is used to children, or to one's younger siblings, children or grandchildren independent of age, as well as between adults who have known each other since childhood. The intimate level is used by children of pre-school age, when addressing or speaking about their family members or between close friends who have known each other since adolescence. The familiar level is slightly more formal than the intimate and tends to be used by adult males when addressing adolescents or between long-standing friends. The blunt, polite and deferential levels are used only between adults. The first of these is virtually obsolete, but may be used by persons of superior social position to an underling. These six speech levels are encoded in a number of ways, which include inflectional suffixes on verbal and adjectival predicates (called enders), independent

Table 6.2 *Korean person markers*

	1st person		2nd person		3rd person	
	SG	PL	SG	PL	SG	PL
I	ce/cey	ce-huy-(tul)	tayk[i]	tayk-tul	D pwun D elun	D pwun-tul D elun-tul
II	na	wuli-(tul)	tangsin Caki	tangsin-tul	D i ku ku nye	Di-tul D-tul ku nye-tul
III	na/nay	wuli-(tul)	caney	caney-tul	D salam ku	D salam D salam-tul D-tul
IV	na/nay	wuli-(tul)	ne/ney	ne-huy-(tul)	D ai/ay	D ai/ay-tul

[i] Sohn (1994:287) states that the second-person singular category I form (deferential and polite) is used only to strangers, not to in-group members.

person markers and honorific subject and addressee verbal markers.[10] There are verbal enders corresponding to each of the six levels but only four categories of person markers. Category I forms belong to the deferential and polite levels. Category II forms are used in the blunt level. The forms in category III involve the familiar and intimate levels, and those in category IV, the plain level. The list of person forms in the four categories is given in Table 6.2. Note that the third person consists of one of the following demonstratives *i* 'this' (close to the speaker), *ku* 'that' (close to the addressee), *ce* 'that over there', indicated in Table 6.2 by D, and a defective noun indicating person. When the subject is a second- or third-person form of category I, a special subject-honorific suffix *-(u)si* (or *-sey*) obligatorily occurs on the verb. Observe the presence of the subject honorific in (37a) where the form of the third person *ku pwun* and the verbal ender *eyo* identify the speech level as polite, and the absence of the honorific in (37b), which is in the familiar/intimate level indicated by the third-person *ku-tul* form and the verbal ender *-ta*.

(37)   Korean (Sohn 1994:105, 142)
   a.   Ku pwun-un   sahoycek-ulo ne-li   hwaltongha-si-eyo
        the person-TOP.CTR social-in   widely   work-SBJ.H-DEC:POLITE
        'He leads a socially active life.'

   b.   Ku-tul-un   cengmal chakhan haksayng-tul i-ess-ta
        they-TOP.CTR   indeed good   student-PL   be-PAST-DEC:PLAIN
        'They were really good students.'

Such a suffix may also surface with second- and third-person subjects of category II, but in this case it is optional. There is also an addressee honorific *-(su)p*, which is an integral part of the verbal enders, used in the deferential speech level. It

[10] The independent person markers in Korean, as in Japanese (see section 1.2), behave both morphologically and syntactically like nouns.

is used for the addressee irrespective of whether the addressee is (38a) or is not (38b), overtly expressed.

(38) Korean (Sohn 1994:288, 346)
    a.   Tayk-un   eti-se   o-si-ess-up-ni-kka?
        You-TOP.CTR where-from come-SBJ.H-PAST-AH-IND-Q(DEF)
        'Where did you come from?'

    b.   Cey-ka ha-keyss-sup-ni-ta
        I-NOM do-will-AH-IND-DEC(DEF)
        'I will do it.'

Note the absence of the addressee honorific in the examples in (39), which are in the blunt, familiar and plain styles, respectively, as reflected in the person forms and verbal enders.

(39) Korean (Sohn 1994:288)
    a.   Tangsin-un eti-se   w-ass-so
        you-TOP.CTR where-from come-PAST-Q(BLUNT)
        'Where did you come from?'

    b.   Caney-nun eti-se   w-ass-nun-ka
        you-TOP.CTR where-from come-PAST-IND-Q(FAMILIAR)
        'Where did you come from?'

    c.   Ne-nun   eti-se   w-ass-ni
        you-TOP.CTR where-from come-PAST-Q(PLAIN)
        'Where did you come from?'

The existence of a complete paradigm of separate honorific person forms is rather rare. Several languages exhibiting such extra honorific paradigms have been noted in Austronesia such as Nengone, Kusaiean and Dehu. The paradigm in (40) is from Nengone, a language belonging to the Loyalty group, spoken on the island of Mare.

(40) Nengone (Tryon 1967:65)

		Normal	Honorific
1SG		inu	inuŋo
2SG		bo, eme	bua, buaŋo
3SG		bɔn	bɔnɛŋo
	(formal)	nubɔn	nubɔnɛŋo
	(trivial)	ič	
1DU	INCL	eθew	eθewɛ ŋo
	EXCL	eṇe	eṇeŋo
2DU		m̥eŋo	bum̥eŋo
3DU	(trivial)	bušew	bušeŋoneŋo
1PL	INCL	εje	ejeŋo
1PL	EXCL	eṇiǰ	eṇiǰeo
2PL		buṇiǰ	buṇiǰeŋo
3PL		buič	buičeŋo

Unfortunately, Tryon does not provide any characterization of the conditions under which the honorific forms are used. (The same holds for Kusaiean and Dehu.)

Considerably more information is available about the social relations reflected in the person paradigms among the Zapotecan and Chinatecan languages of Meso-America. Consider, for instance, the paradigm of person clitics in San Lucas Zapotecan.

(41) San Lucas Zapotecan (Munro & Lopez 1999:14)

	SG	PL
1	-a'	-ënn
2 informal	-ùu'	-ad
2 formal	-yuu	-yùad
3 formal	-ëb	-rëb
3 animal	-ëmm	-rëmm
3 respectful	-ahzh	-rahzh
3 reverential	-iny/-ni'	-riny
3 prox	-ëng	-rëng
3 distal	-ih	-rih

There are no honorific forms for the first person and in the second only a formal vs informal distinction is made. In the third person, however, there is a five-way distinction reflecting age, affiliation with the community and social status. Animal forms are used for animals, babies and children and for young people until marriageable age. They may also be used jokingly or derogatorily to refer to adults. Respectful forms are used when speaking about adults belonging to the community, including all married people. Formal markers are employed with reference to parents, elders and persons holding positions of status such as priests, high officials and teachers. Reverential forms refer to God, holy entities, religious artefacts and certain relatives such as elderly grandparents. And the proximate and distal forms are used for non-Zapotecs (apart from priests and teachers).

Somewhat other distinctions are expressed in the person markers of Sochiapan Chinantec (Foris 2000:167–8). In addition to social deixis, the person system of Sochiapan Chinantec encodes a range of emotional attitudes of the speaker such as compliance, reluctance, annoyance, sympathy and pity. Not surprisingly these are encoded in the first-person markers. There are thus eight first-person singular forms: $hná^{HL}$ 'neutral in social situations', $ná^H$ 'reticence, deferential', $ná^L$ 'compliance, reluctance, annoyance', nia^{MH} 'familiarity, intimacy, ingratiating, self-pity', $hná^{LM}$ 'emphatic, contrastively with irony', $niá$ 'superiority, familiarity with resentment', $hnia^{LM}$ 'familiarity, confident, warm relationship' and na^L 'compliance with pity'. The second-person forms reflect just a two-way distinction but not of formal/informal as in Zapotec, but rather neutral vs. familiar. No actual social distinctions are expressed via the third-person forms.

Much more common than a full paradigm of honorific person forms is the presence of a special form, (other than the non-singular or the third person) just for the addressee. This is the case, for example, in Basque, Copola Trique, Gahri, Imbabura Quechua, Karo Batak, Khasi, Konjo and PaTani.

6.3 Omission of person markers

An alternative to using special person markers to indicate deference and/or respect is the avoidance of overt person forms altogether. This may involve a preference for the use of zero forms, the use of impersonalizing forms or the use of names, kinship terms or titles.

The first of these strategies is favoured in referring to oneself or potentially addressing a familiar or equal-in-status addressee. This is so in Japanese, as exemplified in (42).

(42)   Japanese (Yamamoto 1999:80)
"Gomen-nasai,   Ø Hokkaidoo no kata   desu-ka?" "Ø Tookyoo desu."
forgive:me (you)   Hokkaido LK person COP-Q   (I) Tokyo   COP
To boku wa it-ta   "Ø Tookyoo kara o-tomodachi o   sagashi-ni
that I   NOM say-PAST you Tokyo from friend   ACC to-search
mie-tan   desu-ne
come:UP-PAST AUX-TAG
'"Forgive me. Are (you) from Hokkaido?"
"(I'm) from Tokyo," I said.
"Then (you)'re up here looking for a friend?"' (Haruki Murakami, *Hitsuji o Megura Booken*, translated by Alfred Birnbaum)

The same preference is noted by van Staden (2000:97) in Tidore. Interestingly, absence of an independent person marker is also typically accompanied by absence of person marking on the verb. The use of person markers on the verb without an independent person form is possible but is considered to be highly informal. Van Staden suggests that it is appropriate for addressing only peers and people of lower rank. Thus (43a) without any person marking is polite, (43b) with just the person clitic, very informal.

(43)   Tidore (van Staden 2000:97)
  a.   Tagi ma!
        Go   MIT
        'We/I/you just go.'
  b.   Tosi   rasi
        1SG(s_A)-pee first
        'I've got to pee first.'

The use of zero for deferential self-reference is also a feature of certain types of discourse in Mandarin Chinese. Xiong (1998) states that in modesty-oriented discourse such as job interviews, academic promotion briefings, spontaneous valedictory speeches made by retiring workers, etc. there is an extraordinary high percentage of zeros for self-reference. According to Cooke (1968:10), even in

Thai most speakers prefer the use of zero rather than one of the many first- or second-person forms when interacting with high-ranking royalty.

The second strategy for avoiding person markers is via the use of impersonalizing constructions involving non-specific person markers such as the English *one* or French *on*, German *man* or generic nouns such as 'person', 'human' or various types of passive constructions (without a specified agent). Though, as discussed in section 5.4, such constructions are typically used to invoke the general body of humans, among whom the speaker and/or hearer may be included, they may also be used with reference to specific individuals. For instance, Chafe (1990:64) mentions that in Caddo, a language spoken in Oklahoma, until recently it was obligatory to use an impersonal prefix when referring to or addressing a person related by marriage.[11] Thus, rather than using (44a) with the second-person prefix *-yah?*, (44b) with the prefix *yi-* would be used.

(44)   Caddo (Chafe 1990:64)
  a.   Dikat-yah?-?a=?nih-hah
       what-2(S_A)-do-HAB
       'What are you doing?'

  b.   Dikat-yi-?a=?nih-hah
       what-IMPR(S_A)-do-HAB
       'What are you doing?'

The English *one* may also be sometimes employed as a means of avoiding direct reference to self, as in the examples below, taken from Wales (1996:57, 81)

(45) a.   One hesitates to use such a trite word as delighted, but of course one is delighted. (Hardy Amies on receiving his knighthood, *Guardian*, 19 June 1989)

    b.   I enjoy it and it's a great challenge . . . but it also does sort of make one slightly nervous and very open to doubts as to whether you've made the right decision.

The Germanic *man/men* and French *on* may also be used for self-reference, as in (46) and (47), respectively.

(48)   Swedish (Holmes & Hinchliffe 1993:191)
       Hur   länge behöver man   stå   här   och   vänta
       How   long   need   (I)   stand   here   and   waiting
       'How long do I have to stand waiting here?' (polite but mildly ironical)

(49)   French
       On (=je)   vous epousera, toute fiere   que   l'on (=vous) est
       (I)   you   marry   all   proud   that (you)   be
       'I'll be proud to marry you.'

---

[11] The same set of prefixes is also used for discourse participants in whom the speaker has no interest. Therefore Chafe (1990) calls them defocusing prefixes rather than impersonal ones.

Such usage is not, however, necessarily perceived as being polite. The use of *one* in (45a) or (45b) may be motivated by a desire to detract attention from self, and thus not to impose oneself on the addressee. Nonetheless, owing to the negative and class associations that many speakers have in regard to *one*, its use in (45a) or (45b) may in fact be considered as arrogant or pompous. In Swedish, on the other hand, the use of *man* for self-reference, though formal and polite is considered to be slightly ironical. And in French, according to Judge and Healey (1985:70), *on* when used to an adult addressee expresses slight contempt for the addressee or a powerful position of the speaker. In this latter usage it is like the English royal we.

An interesting variant of avoiding direct reference to self and/or one's addressee has been observed by Heath (1991) among the languages of Australia and by both Heath (1996) and Helmbrecht (1996a) among the languages in the Americas. As is well known, many of these languages have verbal person marking for both the A and P. This marking is not always transparent, that is it is not always obvious which element corresponds to the A and which to the P. Heath states that while irregularities in the marking of the A and P are found with all different person-number combinations, they are exceptionally frequent in combinations involving speech-act participants, that is when the first person acts on the second (1 > 2) or the second person on the first (2 > 1). Heath suggests that this may be a form of redressing the pragmatically sensitive nature of situations and events involving first- and second-person participants. In Brown and Levinson's (1987) terms such interactions are potentially face threatening and consequently speakers may adopt various means of reducing the degree of face threat involved. One of the means of doing so appears to be deflecting attention from the speaker–addressee relationship by masking the transparency of the person forms corresponding to the speaker and addressee.

Heath's analyses of the encoding of 1 > 2 and 2 > 1 combinations reveal that similar masking strategies are employed in language after language. These are listed in (46).

(46) a. marker disguised by partial phonological distortion
    b. one of the two markers expressed by isolated suppletive allomorph
    c. one of the two markers (elsewhere non-zero) expressed by zero
    d. number neutralization, sometimes including use of plural for semantic singular
    e. 1st or 2nd marker merged (or replaced by) 3rd-person marker
    f. entire combination expressed by unanalysable portmanteau
    g. entire combination expressed by zero (special case of portmanteau)
    h. inclusive (+2) marker replaces 1st or 2nd marker, or entire combination
    i. merged 1/2 marker is part of both 1 <->2 and 2<-> 1 combination
    j. subject and object markers compete for a single slot
    k. co-occurring 1st and 2nd markers are widely separated
    l. combinations with identical segments differ in tone

Strategy (a) can be illustrated on the basis of the Australian language Ngandi in which the form *gura* is used for 1SG > 2PL and *gurna* for 1PL > 2SG/PL. In Ngandi, in all 1 > 2 combinations, the P marker is formally plural irrespective of its real-world number. And if the P is plural, then the A must also be plural, again irrespective of its real/world number. The regular form of a first-person plural A is *ñar-*, of a second-person singular P *nu-* and of second person plural P *na-*. Thus the expected form of 1SG > 2PL or 1PL > 2PL should be *ñar-na* and of 1PL > 2SG should be *ñar-nu*. Yet in both cases we have the segment *gur*, which is a special allomorph found only in these 1 > 2 combinations. Strategy (b) is one of the strategies used in the encoding of 1 > 2 combinations in Chinookan. In Chinookan there are regular prefix slots for the A and the P, in this order, apart from the combinations of 1 > 2. In such combinations, instead of 1SG *n-* there is a suppletive prefix *ya-*. Thus 1SG > 2SG is *ya-m*; 1SG > 2DU is *ya-m-t* and 1SG > 2PL is *ya-m-c*. Strategy (c) is utilized in the Aymaran language Jaqaru. The transitive suffixes, some of which are preceded by an onset vowel, are fused in such a way that it is not always clear which is the A and which the P. The second-person P is, however, clearly associated with the suffix *-ma*. As shown in (47), the combinations of 1 > 2, be it in the present, future or desiderative tense, consist of various allomorphs of the second-person but contain no discernible first-person marker.

(47)   Jaqaru (Hardman 2000:57)
  a.   Ill.-k-ima   I see you   1SG > 2SG
  b.   Ill.-k-tma   She sees you   3SG > 2SG
  c.   Ill.-k-t"a   I see him   1SG > 3SG
  d.   Ill.-mama   I will see you   1SG > 2SG
  e.   Ill.-matma   She will see you   3SG > 2SG
  f   Ill.-anha   I will see him   1SG > 3SG
  g.   Ill.-shtama   I should see you   1SG > 2SG
  h.   Ill.-masma   She should see you   3SG > 2SG
  i.   Ill.-sa   I should see him   1SG > 3SG

Neutralization of number, strategy (d), is a feature of 1 > 2 and 2 > 1 combinations in Coos. In the relevant combinations the number (singular, dual or plural) of the A is neutralized and instead of the normal prefixes, a portmanteau suffix is used *-amî* for 1 > 2 and *-aîs* for 2 > 1. Recall also the neutralization of number mentioned above in Ngandi. Strategy (e) is in evidence in the Siouan language Biloxi. The combinations 2 > 1 and 3 > 1 are homophonous both being realized by the prefix *ya-*. Thus *ya-xtedi* 'you/he hit me'. Strategy (f), the use of a portmanteau form for a situation involving speech-act participants, has already been exemplified on the basis of the two suffixes *-amî* and *-aîs* in Coos. Another instance is found in Caddo. A second-person A acting on a first-person P is transparently coded by a combination of the second-person A prefix *yah?-* and the first-person P prefix *ku-*. A first-person A acting on a second-person P is encoded by the portmanteau prefix *t'a* rather than a combination of the first-person A *ci* and second-person P *si*. Compare (48a) and (48b).

(48)   Caddo (Chafe 1976:67)
   a.   Yah-ku-yibahw-nah
          2(A)-1(P)-see-PAST
          'You saw me.'

   b.   T'a-yibahw-nah
          1(A:2P)-see-PAST
          'I saw you.'

The zero expression of a complete transitive combination, strategy (g), occurs in the Australian language Gunwinggu. Whereas both the first- and second-person singular are elsewhere expressed by non-zero morphemes, the combination of 1SG > 2SG/PL is simply zero. Strategy (h) is attested in some other Australian languages Jawony, Nunggubuyu, Anindilyakwa and Alawa. In Anindilyakwa, for example, the marker for 2SG > 1SG/PL is homophonous with the first-person dual inclusive s prefix -*y(e)*; and the marker for 1SG/PL > 2PL is homophonous with the first-person plural inclusive s prefix *ŋar-*. In Alawa the same form is used for 1SG > 2SG as for the first-person dual inclusive s, namely *ñar-*. Strategy (j), the merger, of 1 > 2 and 2 > 1, is found in the Salishan language Lummi. The suffix -*oŋ(e)s* occurs in all combinations where the first person acts on the second, or the second on the first. This marker is positioned just before the A marker and following the transitive marker, as shown in (49).

(49)   Lummi (Jelinek & Demers 1983:168)
   a.   X̌či-t-oŋəs-sən
          know-TR-1/2–1SG
          'I know you.'

   b.   X̌či-t-oŋəs-sx^w
          know-TR-1/2–2SG
          'You know me.'

Strategy (j), a type of hierarchically determined agreement, should need no additional illustration, as it has been discussed in both section 2.2.3.1 and section 4.3.1. Strategy (k), separation of person markers, can be exemplified on the basis of the Salishan language Kalispel. In this language several strategies are utilized which prevent first-person plural and second-person markers from occurring close to each other. This is most evident in the case of predicate possessed nouns such as 'X (is) father of Y'. Consider the examples in (50).

(50)   Kalispel (Heath 1996:91)
   a.   K^u-p.oxút
          2SG-father
          'You (SG) are our father.'

b. P-p.oxut
 2PL-parent
 'You (PL) are our parents.'

c. Qe'-p.oxut
 1PL-father
 'He is our father.'

d. Qe'-p.oxut-l(e)l-t
 1PL-parents-1PL-2
 'We are your parents.'

In both (50a,b) there are only surface prefixes corresponding to the subject markers, k^u- 'second-person singular' and p- 'second-person plural', respectively and none corresponding to the first-person plural possessor. In (50c), on the other hand, there is a first-person plural possessor prefix qe'-. Given that both the subject and possessor prefixes may be overt, we may expect both to occur in (50d). Yet what we find is the first-person plural prefix qe'- and a rather strange second-person suffix, possibly segmentable into first-person plural and second person. Thus, instead of a second-person prefix, there is a suffix resulting in separation of the two forms. The final strategy (l) is found in Popoloca; 2 > 1 is distinguished from 3 > 1, and 1 > 2 is distinguished from 3 > 2 only by the tone of the suffixes.

Whereas Heath sees all these strategies as a means of playing down the speaker-addressee relationship, Helmbrecht considers them as being primarily driven by the speaker's desire to avoid self-reference. He suggests that the use of evident first-person forms runs the risk of drawing too much attention to self and thus offending the addressee. Speakers therefore innovate with respect to first-person reference much more so than in the case of the second person. And indeed, most of the masking of transitive forms exemplified above involved especially the first person. Nonetheless, Heath also cites languages in which it is the second-person which is opaque, the first essentially transparent. This is the case in Tuscarora in which in none of the 1 > 2 combinations is there an identifiable second-person marker, though the regular first-person marker, the prefix k-, is used in 1SG > 2SG and 1DU/PL > 2. In any case, given that the avoidance of self-reference results in defocusing of the speaker–addressee relationship, the two explanations offered above for the opaque nature of transitive combinations involving speech-act participants may be seen as variations on a theme. Crucially, they reinforce rather than contradict each other.

As one would expect, the strategies of masking the speaker > hearer relationship observed by Heath and Helmbrecht are also in evidence in languages outside Australia and the Americas. Particularly worth mentioning in this context are the Tibeto-Burman languages, many of which exhibit various conflations of the speaker and hearer categories marked on the verb. In Limbu (van Driem 1987:78), for example, in 2 > 1 combinations the first-person singular a- is often dropped and replaced by the word *na.pmi*, as in (51a), which immediately precedes the verb. This word also occurs with the meaning 'someone else'.

(51) Limbu (van Driem 1987:78)
 a. Na.pmi kɛ-dɔ-Ø-ba-i.?
   ? 2-insult-NON-PAST-IMPF-Q
  'Are you insulting me?'

 b. A-gɛ-dɔ-Ø-ba-i.?
  2-insult-NON-PAST-IMPF-Q
  'Are you insulting me/us?'

To give another example, in Chamling (Ebert 1990:60–1) in 1 > 2 combinations the form of the second-person singular is *-na*, but in all other combinations 2 > 1 or 2 > 3 or 3 > 2 the form of the second-person singular is *ta-*.

Of special interest in relation to person-masking strategies is Maithili, an Indo-Aryan language spoken by about 30 million people in India and Nepal. Maithili is the only language that I have come across in which not only the form but also the presence of person marking on the verb may be seen to be determined by matters of social deixis. Let us therefore take a closer look at the person agreement system of this language.

Like various other languages in the region discussed earlier, Maithili has special honorific independent person forms both in the second and third persons, though no number distinction. In the second person there are four forms: neutral, mid-honorific, honorific and high honorific. In the third person, there is only a two-way honorific distinction, honorific non-honorific and a proximal vs distal distinction. In the verbal person marking an extra distinction between honorific and high honorific is made in the third person. The verb may agree with up to three participants, as indicated in the verbal template in (52).

(52) stem (-aspect) (aspectual AUX) (AUX)-tense-AGR1 (-AGR2-AGR3)

The first agreement slot AGR1 may be controlled by a nominative participant (intransitive or transitive subject) or a non-nominative one, that is a participant in the dative, ablative, genitive or locative case. The other two agreement slots, AGR2 and AGR3, are controlled only by non-nominative participants, and if they are filled, AGR1 must be controlled by a nominative.

Bickel, Bisang and Yadava (1999) argue that both the form of the various person agreement markers in Maithili and the conditions under which they occur can be accounted for with reference to considerations of face and empathy. The four constraints that they posited are listed in (53).

(53) a. Avoid specific reference to the speaker.
  c. Avoid specific reference to the addressee if s/he has higher social status than yourself.
  d. Mention a third person only if s/he has higher social status than another participant.
  e. Mark a referent if it has an increased degree of empathy.

The first three constraints are familiar from our previous considerations and can be seen to be motivated by the desire to mitigate threats to negative face. The fourth constraint draws on the notion of empathy as developed by Kuno (1987) and discussed in chapter 5 (section 5.4.2). The major manifestation of the first constraint in Maithili is that there is no distinct first-person verbal marker. First persons are always encoded by the same marker as used for honorific second persons, namely *auh* (past), *-i* (present or past) *and -a* (future). For non-honorific and mid-honorific second persons, on the other hand, there are distinct markers. Compare (54a,b) with (54c,d).

(54)   Maithili (Bickel et al. 1999:483)
- a.   (Ham)/ (ahā̃)   daur-l-aūh
  I:NOM you(H) :NOM   run-PAST-1/2H
  'I / you (H) ran.'

- b.   (Ham)/ (ahā̃)   daur- l   rah-a-b
  I:NOM/you(H) :NOM   run-IMPF AUX-1/2H-FUT
  'I / you (H) will be running.'

- c.   Tū   daur-l-æ
  you(NH) :NOM run-PAST-2NH
  'You (NH) ran.'

- d.   Tū   daur-ait   rah-b-æ
  you(NH) :NOM run-IMPF AUX-FUT–2NH
  'You (NH) will be running.'

The homophony between first person and second-person honorific also reflects the second constraint. In the absence of an independent person marker, whether or not the speaker or an honorific hearer is involved can only be deduced from the context of the situation. Thanks to this indeterminacy, the honorific addressee cannot consider himself directly imposed upon. In the case of a high-honorific addressee, a somewhat different avoidance strategy is used, namely indirect address via the use of a third-person form. According to Bickel et al. (1999), the second-person high-honorific verbal marker is structurally a third-person passive-like formation. This is illustrated in (55).

(55)   Maithili (Bickel et al. 1999:498)
- a.   Apne   paṛh-al   je-t-aik
  you(HH) :NOM read-PART AUX:PASS-FUT-3
  'You (HH) will be reading.'

- b.   Apne-sā   i   kitāb paṛh-al   je-t-aik
  you(HH)-ABL this book read-PART AUX:PASS-FUT-3
  'This book will be read by you (HH).'

Another manifestation of the first two constraints is that there is no object marking for either the first person or a second-person honorific. By contrast, non-honorific and mid-honorific second-person objects are always marked on the verb. Compare (56a) with (56b).

(56)   Maithili (Bickel et al. 1999:498, 502)
  a.   Dekh-l-i
      see-PAST-1/2H
      'I saw you (H). / You (H) saw me.'

  c.   Dekh-l-ak-auk
      see-PAST-3-2NH
      'He (NH) saw you (NH).'

Accordingly, owing to the homophony between the first-person and the second-person honorific, transitive clauses involving the two are simply ambiguous; the direction of action between the first- and second-person honorific is blurred.

The marking of third-person participants depends in part on their honorific status, as captured in the third constraint in (53), but also on the person of the subject. If the subject is a speech-act participant, a third-person object may be marked on the verb irrespective of whether it is (57a) or is not (57b) honorific.

(57)   Maithili (Bickel et al. 1999:503)
  a.   Dekh-l-i-ainh
      see-PAST-1/2H-3H
      'I/you (H) saw him (H).'

  b.   Dekh-l-i-aik
      see-PAST-1/2H-3NH
      'I/you (H) saw him (NH).'

With third-person subjects, on the other hand, a third-person object receives no marking (58a,b), unless it is higher in status than the subject (58c) or unless it is in focus (58d).

(58)   Maithili (Bickel et al. 1999:503, 507, 505)
  a.   Dekh-l-ak
      see-PAST-3NH
      'He (NH) saw him.'

  b.   Dekh-l-aith
      see-PAST-3H
      'He (H) saw him.'

  c.   U   hunkā   dekh-ak-ainh
      he(NH) :NOM he(H) :DAT see-PAST-3NH-3H
      'He (NH) saw him (H).'

  d.   Hunke   o   dekha-l-k-ainh
      he:DAT:FOC he (H.REM) :NOM see-PAST-3(NH)-3H
      'He (NH) saw him (H).'

Bickel et al. suggest that the marking of third-person objects irrespective of their honorificity in clauses in which the subject is a speech-act participant may be attributed to the higher degree of empathy that is felt in such scenarios relative to scenarios involving only third-person participants. It is also an increase in empathy, which underlies the obligatory verbal person marking of third-person objects, which are in focus. This is what is captured in the fourth of the constraints in (53).

Since it is generally accepted that the person with whom the speaker empathizes most is himself and the addressee is next in line, in the case of speech-act participants, the face and empathy constraints in (53) are in conflict. The face constraints require the marking of first- and second-person honorifics to be suppressed, the empathy constraint that these participants should receive overt marking. Bickel et al. suggest that this conflict may be resolved by assuming that in Maithili, the face constraints outrank the empathy constraint, face >> empathy. This ranking of the two sets of constraints is also reflected in the verbal person marking of non-nominative (e.g. dative) arguments in intransitive clauses and in the verbal person marking of non-arguments. It is thus applicable to the whole verbal person-marking system of the language.

The last of the person avoidance strategies is the use of names, titles or kinship terms, as opposed to person markers. This is a politeness strategy typically employed in address or reference but generally not for self-reference. Readers may recall from childhood admonishments of parents such as "what she" or "Mrs she" or "Mr X to you" in response to the use of a person marker rather than of a more appropriate nominal substitute. The use of person markers in formal contexts is particularly disfavoured. For instance, Durie (1985:121) mentions that in Acehnese in more formal situations and towards people of an older generation, it is far more polite to avoid the use of any of the three-second person markers and use titles instead. This is also the case in Indonesian, in which in such situations, in preference to second-person markers, pronominal substitutes such as *saudara* 'male sibling', *saudari* 'female sibling', *tuan* 'you Sir' are used. In Korean (Sohn 1994:286, 290), kin terms and professional titles (e.g. *sensayng-nim* 'sir, teacher', *sacang-nim* 'company president', *paksa-nim* 'PhD') are particularly frequent in address in deferential and polite speech styles, since, despite the many second-person forms, there is no form for socially superior or senior persons, who are not strangers. In Kannada (Sridhar 1990:207), third-person expressions are used in preference to the honorific second- and third-person markers only in contexts requiring extreme deference, for instance when addressing a judge or some other important official, formerly the Maharaja. The relevant expressions are *buddhiyavaru, kha:vandaru* 'the lord/boss (H)', *nya:ya: dhi:s'aru* 'the judge (H)' and *doregaLu* 'the king plural'.

In other languages the use of nominal substitutes is more widespread. In colloquial Afrikaans (Donaldson 1993:124), for example, the use of third-person forms instead of the second-person polite *U* is highly common. The third-person forms used are kin terms and titles, such as *Pa, Ma, Oupa* 'grandfather', *Tanni* 'auntie', *meneer*, 'sir' *Dokter, Professor*. The use of these terms is independent of the actual blood relations between the persons involved. In Amele (Roberts

1987:208) kinship terms such as *mei* 'father' or *au* 'mother' or *asi* 'grandparent' as well as *wali/ coti* 'brother friend' are used when addressing adults. Even terms such as *starik* 'old man' can be used in an affectionate or polite way, as is the case in Russian or Polish.

An understanding of how person forms are used to mark social relations is not only of interest in regard to the nature of societies and the factors governing them but also has a bearing on the diachronic changes that person forms may undergo. It is to this topic that we now turn.

7 Person forms in a diachronic perspective

Although person markers are often seen as belonging to the more stable parts of a language, like all other grammatical markers they too are subject to change. In this chapter we will consider the diachronic changes that person markers undergo and the factors underlying these changes. We will first discuss the origins of person markers, then some of the ways in which they may change and finally how they are lost. Central to our considerations of the historical development in person markers will be the notion of grammaticalization, that is the change from lexical item to grammatical marker or from less grammaticalized to more grammaticalized marker.[1] Grammaticalization is a complex phenomenon involving a number of changes – phonological, morpho-syntactic and semantico-pragmatic. (Lehmann 1982:234–41; 1995; Heine & Reh 1984:16–46 and Croft 2000:157–65). The phonological changes involve reduction or loss of phonological material resulting in shorter forms and ultimately in the disappearance of forms altogether. The morpho-syntactic changes are reflected in the rigidification of the syntactic position of a form and, subsequently, loss of independent word status, cliticization and affixation, typically accompanied by increasing obligatoriness of the relevant form. And the semantico-pragmatic changes relate to loss of specific semantic content and acquisition of more general, often more abstract, meanings. These changes are conceived of not as discrete, but rather as gradual transitions which together "form a natural pathway along which forms evolve" (Hopper & Traugott 1993:6). This is typically referred to as a grammaticalization cline.

Person markers, like most other grammatical markers, are taken to originate from lexical items. And like other grammatical markers, they may be plotted along a grammaticalization cline, dependent on the degree of grammaticalization that they display. Grammaticalization thus is a notion that spans the whole lifecycle of a person marker from its initial development from a lexical item, through its subsequent morpho-phonological realizations and semantic changes, to its potential disappearance.

Grammaticalization is one of the mechanisms of language change. In discussions of language change it is traditional to consider not only mechanisms of change but also causes of change. These are traditionally divided into

---

[1] There is an enormous literature on grammaticalization. Interesting accessible discussions can be found in Traugott and Heine (1991) and Hopper and Traugott (1993).

language-internal causes and language-external ones, that is changes resulting from contact with other languages. In practice, however, the two are often difficult to tease apart, as external factors may enhance or conversely impede internally driven changes. Therefore, in our presentation we will not attempt to make a strict separation between internally and externally motivated instances of change.

7.1 The sources of person markers

The sources of person markers fall into two types: lexical and grammatical. What little is known about the former will be discussed in section 7.1.1. The grammatical sources of person markers are quite varied. A major grammatical source of independent person markers are demonstratives. The demonstrative origins of person markers will be reviewed in section 7.1.2. The other major grammatical source of person markers are other person markers. In the process of grammaticalization, independent person markers give rise to various phonologically reduced and morphologically dependent forms. Conversely, dependent person markers may be used as the basis for the development of new independent forms. Moreover, dependent person markers may evolve from other dependent person markers via extension or the grammaticalization of periphrastic constructions, especially those featuring conjugated verbal forms. The development of person markers from other person markers will be considered in section 7.1.3 and from conjugated verbal forms in 7.1.4. Various other grammatical sources of person markers, mainly of person affixes, such as number and/or gender markers, classifiers, tense and aspect markers and evidentiality markers will be briefly discussed in section 7.1.5

7.1.1 Lexical sources

In most languages the lexical origins of person markers are buried in history. In some, however, the expressions used to denote person are transparently related to, or even homophonous with, nominals denoting various types of human relationships, kinship or titles. As discussed in chapter 6 (section 6.2), this is most obviously so in some South-East Asian languages such as Thai, Burmese and Vietnamese, which are by some linguists considered as lacking a true class of person markers. Recall that in these languages the forms used to refer to the first person tend to be related to nominals which belittle the self such as 'slave' or 'servant'. Those used to refer to the second person, on the other hand, tend to be related to nominals that aggrandize or honour their referent such as 'master', 'lord' or 'king'. Similar nominal expressions underlie person forms in other languages. For example, the expressions *ulon* 'slave' and *tuwan* 'lord' are used for polite first-person address in Acehnese (Durie 1985:116–17). The word 'slave' or 'servant' is one of the forms for the first-person singular in Khmer, *khɲum*, and a number of dialects of Malay, Standard Malay, *saya*, *sahaya*, Jakarta

Malay, *sayè*, *ayè* and Banjarese Malay *ulun*. Forms etymologically related to 'lord', 'master', 'sovereign' are used for the second person in Tidore (van Staden 2000:77). There are also other denominal sources of first- and/or second-person markers. For instance, in Kayah Li (Solnit 1997:184), a Tibeto-Burman language spoken in Thailand, the form for the second-person plural *si* also means 'and the rest, and things like that'. Recall also the grammaticalization of possessive modifiers into the polite second-person markers *usted* and *você* and *U* in Spanish, Portuguese and Dutch, respectively.

Whereas the known sources of first- and second-person markers tend to be nominals denoting human relationships, those of the third person are typically words such as 'thing', 'human', 'man', 'person' or 'body'. As shown in (1), this is the case in Zande, a Niger-Congo language of the Ubangi group spoken mainly in the Sudan. The etymologies of the third-person forms are those proposed by Heine and Reh (1984).

(1) Zande (Heine & Reh 1984:222–4)
 3SGM   kɔ́   (<*ko* 'man, male'; Zande *ku-mba/ko-mba*)
 3 HUM INDEF nɪ   (<*ni* 'person')
 3PL AN S/A àmí   (<a general plural marker of nouns plus *mɪ* 'flesh, meat, animal')
 3 INAN P   (h)ɛ   < *hɛ* 'thing')

The words for person *'ba* and **madi* respectively are also used for the third person in some of the central Sudanic languages, such as Keliko, Lugbara and Logo and in the Madi dialects of the Arawá family. In Avukaya the expression 'that man' *gÚlá* denotes third person. In Acehnese the third-person polite form *gopnyan* derives from *gop* 'other person' and the demonstrative *nyan* 'that'. Several different adnominal sources are quite transparent in the case of the third-person clitics (there are no third-person independent forms) in the Mixtecan languages. The examples in (2) are from Ocotepec Mixtec, spoken in the district of Tlaxiaco, Oaxaca, Mexico.

(2) Ocotepec Mixtec (Alexander 1988:264–5)
 masculine de   (< tee 'man')
 feminine   ñā   (< nahan 'woman')
 general   xin (?)
 animal   ti   (< kiti 'animal')
 deity   ya   (< yaa 'deity')
 wood   tu   (< nutun 'tree')
 liquid   de   (< ndute 'water')

A likely diachronic pathway for the development of such third-person forms is via a stage where their nominal sources function as generic classifiers. Classifiers of all types are regularly used as anaphoric devices (see, e.g., Aikhenvald 2000:329) and generic ones are prime candidates for being reanalysed as third-person forms owing to their frequency of occurrence. In the Mayan languages, for example, the generic noun classifiers are used both as classifiers, as in (3a), and in lieu of independent third-person markers, as in (3b).

(3) Jacaltec (Craig 1977:140, 148)
a. Xil naj pel no' txitam
saw CLF:MAN Peter CLF:ANIMAL pig
'Peter saw the pig.'
b. Xil na no'
saw CLF:MAN CLF:ANIMAL
'He saw it.'

Helmbrecht (2001) offers some evidence that the Mixtec third-person markers have undergone such a development. Whether the same can be said for Zande or some of the other languages which display a denominal origin of third-person markers is unclear.

While relational terms are typically the source of first- or second-person markers rather than third, they do occasionally develop into third-person forms. This is so, for example, in the Nilo-Saharan language Ngiti (Kutsch Lojenga 1994:195). Two of the third-person forms *àbadhi* and *iyàdhiyà* consist of the stems for 'father' and 'mother' respectively plus the morpheme *-dhi* which originally indicated possession. Thus the two terms could be translated as 'owner masculine' and 'owner feminine'.

7.1.2 Demonstratives

Although suggestions have been made in the literature regarding the demonstrative origin of some first- and second-person markers (see Blake 1934), demonstratives are primarily the source of third-person forms. The use of demonstratives in place of third-person independent markers is widely attested cross-linguistically.[2] In some languages (e.g. Basque, Comanche, Kawaiisu, Lavukaleve, Tiriyo) any demonstrative can be used for the third person. This is illustrated in (5) on the basis of Kawaiisu, a Numic language of California, which has three definite demonstratives, *si-ʔi-* 'proximate', *sa-ma-* 'neutral' and *su-ʔu-* 'distal', all of which can be used in the singular with the suffix *-na* and the plural with the suffix *-mɨ*.

(4) Kawaiisu (Zigmond, Booth & Munro 1990:48, 76, 83)
a. Suʔumɨ kahni-paa-yu capugwiʔi-dɨ-mɨ
they house-in-ss sew-NMR-PL
'They're in the house sewing.'
b. Siʔimɨ winɨ-dɨ-mɨ
they stand-SG-NMR-PL
'They two are standing.'

---

[2] A detailed discussion of the relationship between third-person markers and demonstratives is presented in Bhatt (forthcoming). Some of the observations below are in part based on his work.

c. Hanaʔoko samamɨ ko-kwee-ka-dɨ-mɨ
    When they   REDUP-go-REALIZED-NMR-PL
    'When did they go?'

In other languages only one of the demonstratives is singled out for third-person usage; as exemplified in (5), this is typically, though not invariably, the remote or distal form, as opposed to the proximate or medial.

(5) | Language | Third-person marker | Demonstrative |
     |---|---|---|
     | Achuar | áu | áu (medial) |
     | Jamul Tiipay | puu | puu (distal) |
     | Kashmiri | su[3] | su (distal) |
     | Malayalam | awan | awan (distal) |
     | Peró | tè | tèejè (distal) |
     | Turkish | o | o (distal) |
     | Warao | tai | tai (medial) |

In yet other languages the relationship between third-person markers and demonstratives is only evinced by the third-person forms used for non-humans or non-animates. Some cases in point are illustrated in (6).

(6) | Language | Third-person marker | | Demonstrative |
     |---|---|---|---|
     | | HUM/AN | NHUM/INAN | |
     | Jaqaru | upa | aka/uka | aka (proximate) |
     | | | | uka (remote) |
     | Mauwake | (w)o | nain | nain (remote) |
     | Sema | pa/li | hi | hi (proximate) |
     | Slave | ʔdi | ʔeyi | ʔeyi (remote) |
     | SS-Miwok | ʔis.ak | ʔi–ʔok/neh–ʔok | neh(promimate)/ʔi (remote) |
     | Udihe | nuati/bueti | ute/uti/ti/tei | ute/uti/ti/tei (remote) |

The existence of a relationship between third-person markers and demonstratives is not always as transparent as in the examples given above. For instance, as we see in (7), in the Arawakan language Asheninca person markers and demonstratives share the stem *ir-* and gender inflection, but are not identical.

(7) Asheninca (Reed & Payne 1986:324, 330)

	3rd person	Demonstratives		
		Proximate	Medial	Remote
Masculine	irirori	irika	irinta	irintó
Feminine	iroori	iroka	ironta	irontó

It is also of interest to note that though typically it is the demonstrative that is the source of the third-person marker, sometimes the direction of derivation is the reverse. Bhatt (forthcoming:132) mentions several languages in which the demonstrative forms consist of a deictic element and a third-person marker. One

---

[3] In languages in which there is a distinction in gender and/or number such as Kashmiri and Malayalam I have given only the third-person masculine forms.

of these is Khasi. The demonstrative is derived by adding to the third-person markers *u* 'third masculine singular', *ka* 'third feminine singular' and *ki* 'third plural' the deictic suffixes *-ne* 'proximate', *-to* 'remote, not very far', *-tay* 'remote, visible', *-ta* 'remote invisible', *-tey* 'up' and *-thie* 'down'.

The synchronic and diachronic relationships between third-person markers and demonstratives are attributable to the functional similarities between the two. Though demonstratives are primarily used deictically to identify a referent in the spatial context and third-person pronoun anaphorically, as we have seen in chapter five, anaphoric usage of the former, even in languages in which the two are quite distinct, is by no means uncommon. In Polish, for example, there are five third-person pronouns, and ten corresponding demonstratives, five proximal and five distal. Both the proximal and distal demonstratives are regularly used anaphorically albeit with a colloquial and expressive flavour. In English, demonstratives cannot be used anaphorically if the antecedent is a concrete individual or object. They are, however, used as anaphors in the case of higher-order entities, that is events, propositions or speech acts, as illustrated in (8), for example.

(8) a.   (i) I've finally managed to sell my car.
      (ii) That's good.

   b.   (i) Your friend is an extremely good liar.
      (ii) Yes, that's true, I'm afraid.

   c.   (i) Can I see you for a moment?
      (ii) Is that a request or an order?

Thus, given the anaphoric potential of demonstratives, all that is required in order for them to develop into third-person markers is that they should lose their deictic force.

7.1.3   Other person markers

While everyone acknowledges that person clitics and affixes typically evolve from independent person markers, synchronic phonological similarity between the two types of forms is by no means always in evidence. And identity of forms must be viewed as quite exceptional. This is hardly suprising. Many person affixes are considered to be of considerable antiquity and thus the forms that gave rise to them are no longer available. Alternatively, the person affixes may have undergone such extensive grammaticalization that they are no longer recognizable as having derived from the existing independent forms. Nonetheless, given that grammaticalization is seen to be a continuous process on-going in all languages in all times, we should be able to find uncontroversial examples of the more recent development of dependent from independent person markers, where the two types of markers are clearly phonologically similar and perhaps even identical. And indeed we do.

Phonological identity of all the dependent markers in a paradigm with their independent counterparts is rather rare. Such identity may be observed, for example, in the Oceanic language Asumboa between the independent forms and the S/A markers, in the Tibeto-Burman language Mao Naga between the independent forms and both the verbal and nominal prefixes, and in the West Chadic language Mupun between the independent emphatic forms and the object suffixes. Much more common are dependent forms which though not identical to the independent are transparently derived from them. Two cases in point are illustrated in (9) and (10) from Wambaya, a non-Pama-Nyungan Australian language of the Northern Territory, and Pari, a Western Nilotic language of the Sudan.

(9) Wambaya (Nordlinger 1998:86:ch. 4 and ch. 5)

	Indep	S/A
1SG	ngawurniji	ngi-
2SG	nyamirnji	nyi-
1PL INCL	ngurruwani	ngurru-
1PL EXCL	ngirriyani	ngirri-
2PL	girriyani	girri-
3PL	irriyani	irri-
1DU INCL	mirndiyani	mirndi-
1DU EXCL	ngurluwani	ngurlu-
2DU	gurluwani	gurlu-
3DU	wurluwani	wurlu-

(10) Pari (Andersen 1988:297)

	Indep	S/P
1SG	ʔáaní	á-
2SG	ʔínní	i-/ɨ
3SG	yíní	yí-
1PL INCL	ʔɔɔní	(ʔɔɔni)
1PL EXCL	wání	wá
2PL	ʔúunú	ú-
3PL	gíní	gi-

In Wambaya the S and A enclitics correspond to the first two syllables of the stem of the independent markers in the case of the non-singular forms, and to the first syllable in the case of the singular forms (plus a vowel change from /a/ to /i/ in the latter). There are no third-person independent forms. In Pari the S/P proclitics are equal to either the first syllable or the first vowel of the independent forms. There is no corresponding clitic for the first-person plural inclusive. Some other languages in which the dependent person markers transparently correspond to the first part of the stem of the independent forms are the Nilotic language So (Carlin 1993:79) in the case of the possessive suffixes, the Omotic languages Koré and Zaysé (Bender 2000:50–1) and the Tibeto-Burman languages Tangut, Mikir and Sgaw Karen (LaPolla 1994), all in the case of the S/A prefixes.

In all of the examples cited above, the phonological relationship between the independent and dependent forms is the same throughout the paradigm. Sometimes, however, phonological similarities or identities obtain only in a subset of the paradigm. Among the Austronesian languages, for example, identities or similarities between independent and dependent person markers are quite commonly manifested only among the non-singular forms. This is so, for example, in Anejom and Ponapean in regard to the object suffixes, in Paamese and Southwest Tanna in the case of possessive suffixes and in Palauan, Yapese, Reefs Ayiwo and Tanimbili with respect to both object and possessive suffixes. Such a pattern of similarities, illustrated in (11) on the basis of Tanimbili, arises because the singular forms typically date back to Proto-Oceanic or Proto-Austronesian, while the non-singular forms are later developments based on numerals.

(11)   Tanimbili (Tryon 1994:628)

	Indep	S/A	POSS	P
1SG	inyo	nyi-	-ŋgu	-ŋgu
2SG	inu	nu-	-mo	-mo
3SG	ŋgingi	i-	-Ø	-Ø
1PL INCL	mite	misu-	-mite	-mite
1PL EXCL	mitekene	misu-	-mitekene	-mite
2PL	mokwe	muku-	-mokwe	-mokwe
3PL	ŋgokwo	ŋgu-	-ŋgokwo	-ŋgokwo
1DU INCL	si	si-	-si	-si
1DU EXCL	me	me-	-me	-me
2DU	mwe	mwa-	-mwe	-mwe
3DU	ŋgola	ŋgi(li)-	-ŋgolo	-ŋgolo

The similarities between independent and dependent forms may be confined only to certain persons. Typically they involve the first and second persons but not the third, as in Basque (12), in which the third-person independent forms are based on the demonstrative.

(12)   Basque (Saltarelli 1988:208, 239)

		Indep	S/P	
1SG		ni	n-	
2SG	formal	zu	z-	
	informal	hi	h-	
3SG	proximate	hau	d-	
	medial	hori		
	distal	hura		
1PL		gu	g-	
2PL		zuek	z-	-te
3PL	proximate	hauek	d-	-te
	medial	horiek		
	distal	haiek		

Although clear phonological resemblance between independent and dependent person markers is typically the result of the latter being derived from the former, the reverse may also be the case. As mentioned in chapter two, there are languages (e.g. Bare, Jacaltec, Koasati, Mundari, Nama, Sentani, Tigak, Waorani, Warekena) in which the current independent forms are built on the dependent forms plus a generic pronominal root, which may be the word for 'person', 'body' or 'self', a deictic form or an emphatic form. For instance, in Mundari, an Austro-Asiatic language spoken in northern India, as shown in (13), the independent person markers consist of the S/A suffixes plus the invariant particle *a*.

(13)   Mundari (Cook 1965:130–1)

	Indep	S/A
1SG	a-ing	-ing
2SG	a-m	-m
3SG	a-e	-e
1DU INCL	a-lang	-lang
1DU EXCL	a-ling	-ling
2DU	a-ben	-ben
3DU	a-king	-king
1PL INCL	a-bu	-bu
1PL EXCL	a-le	-le
2PL	a-pe	-pe
3PL	a-ko	-ko

In the Oceanic language Tigak, the independent person markers are built of a pronominal article *na-* plus the weak person forms of the subject. As we see in (14), this is quite transparent in the case of the non-singular forms, less so in the singular markers.

(14)   Tigak (Beaumont 1979:97–8)

	Indep	Weak subject forms (present tense)
1SG	na-nau	nak
2SG	na-nu	nuk
3SG	na-ne	gi
1DU INCL	na-karak	karak
1DU EXCL	na-mek	mek
2DU	na-muk	muk
3DU	na-rek	rek
1TR INCL	na-karatul	karatul
1TR EXCL	na-memtul	memtul
2TR	na-mitul	miktul
3TR	na-ritul	riktul
etc.		

And in Jacaltec the first- and second-person independent forms are composed of the absolutive proclitics and the particle *ha'*.

Somewhat less commonly the independent person markers are replaced by some set of dependent ones without any additional generic particles. This, according to Thurston (1994:597), is what seems to have taken place in Kabana, an Oceanic language of New Britain. Kabana belongs to the Bariari group of Oceanic languages which also includes Lusi and Kove. Thurston suggests that Proto-Bariari had four sets of person markers: independent forms, subject prefixes, object suffixes and possessive suffixes. This system is still in evidence in Lusi and Kove. In Kabana, however, the independent forms have been largely substituted by the object suffixes. The independent forms and object suffixes in the three languages are presented in (15).

(15) Thurston (1994:596)

	[Lusi]		[Kove]		[Kabana]	
	Indep	P	Indep	P	Indep	P
1SG	viau	-gau	iau	-gau	gau	-gau
2SG	veao	-go	veao	-go	eao	-go
3SG	eai	Ø	veai	Ø	ei	Ø
1PL INCL	teita	-gita	taita	-gita	gita	-gita
1PL EXCL	viai	-gai	iai	-gai	gai	-gai
2PL	amiu	-gimi	amiu	-gimi	gimi	-gimi
3PL	asizi	-zi	asizi	-zi	gid	-gid

Instances of the replacement of one set of person markers by another are by no means infrequent. Typically, however, they are the result of structural changes such as the collapsing of periphrastic constructions. For example, the reanalysis of nominalized verbs with possessive affixes as main verbs has in various languages (e.g. the Altaic, Uto-Aztecan, and Carib) led to the extension of possessive person affixes into the verbal domain. Particularly interesting are changes in person markers which involve not only the displacement of one marker by another, but the actual creation of at least partially new markers. This is often so when conjugated verbal forms are reanalysed.

7.1.4 Conjugated verbal forms

There are a number of ways in which conjugated verbal forms may give rise to new person markers. Arguably, the simplest is via the reanalysis of a cleft construction. In many languages cleft constructions such as *It is I who ...* etc. are a common means of focalizing a first, second or third person. It is not difficult to imagine that over time the person marker plus copula combination may be reanalysed as an emphatic form. One language in which this appears to have taken place is Bokobaru (Jones 1998), a Mande language of West Africa. Bokobaru has a set of emphatic independent subject person forms, shown in (16), which consist of a subject person marker (in the stative aspect), a nasal connective and an emphatic marker *bé*.

(16)   Bokobaru (Jones 1998:141)
         SG   PL
     1   ma+m+bé   wá+m+bé
     2   m+bé   á+m+bé
     3   à+m+bé   áɔ́ɔ́+m+bé

In the related language Boko the corresponding emphatic marker *mɛ* is still a separate form, which Jones suggests may once have been a copula verb. Assuming that this was indeed so, and that it also holds for the Bokobaru *bé*, the current Bokobaru emphatic subject forms may be seen as a fusion of a person marker plus a copula.

Considerably less tentative is such a source of the independent person markers in several branches of the Omotic languages (Bender 2000:199). According to Bender, in the Mao group of languages the former copula is still in evidence throughout the person paradigms. As (17) demonstrates, in some of the languages the copula was *ga*, in others *še*.

(17)   Mao languages (Bender 2000:183)
             Hozo   Sezo
     1SG   dɛŋ+ga   haa+ šɛ
     2sg   hɪɪŋ+ga   hɪn+šɛ
     3sg   aŋ+ga   nam+šɛ
     1pl   nuŋ+ga   dul+šɛ
     2pl   dun+ga   ukke
     3pl   metʸa   nam+šɛ

In the Ardoid languages the copula, which was *ta*, is manifested in the first-person singular and in all persons in the plural, but not in the second- and third-person singular. This may be observed in (18) on the basis of the languages Ari and Galila.

(18)   Aroid Languages (Bender 2000:163)
              Ari   Galila
     1SG   ʔitá   itá
     2SG   aaná   yiná
     3SGM   nó(o)   nu(o)
     3SGF   náa   naa
     1PL   wo(o)tá   wəta
     2PL   yetá   yetá
     3PL   ketá   kɛtá

And in the Ometo group it is found only in the first-person singular. In fact, as shown in (19), the first-person singular is the former copula, without any additional person marking.

(19)   Ometo Languages (Bender 2000:77)

	Koré	Basketo	Maale
1SG	ta	ta	ta
2SG	ne	ne	ne
3SGM	izi	ʔiy	izi
3SGF	iza	iza	iza
1PL	nu	nu	nu
2PL	inte	yinti	intsi
3PL	eti, etc.	inti	iy/zata

The above phenomenon is by no means restricted to the languages of Africa. Other languages which exhibit independent person markers built on copula verbs include Ainu, Alamblak and Wichita.

Another not uncommon way in which new person markers may develop is from conjugated auxiliary verbs in periphrastic constructions. A conjugated form of the verb *to be* is a known source of person suffixes in the Cushitic languages (Hetzron 1976:27). The current past tense in Cushitic is seen to have developed from a former periphrastic construction consisting of a participle followed by the auxiliary *aɣ/ak* 'to be' manifesting subject person prefixes. According to Hetzron, the original form of this inflected auxiliary is still reflected in the definite past forms of the verb in one of the Cushitic languages of the Agaw group, namely Awngi. This is depicted in (20) which also features the corresponding person markers from two other of the Agaw languages, Bilin and Kemat.

(20)   (Hetzron 1976:23)

	Awngi[4]	Bilin	Kemat
1SG	-ɣʷà	-xʷən	-ə́ɣʷ
2SG	-tə́ɣʷà	-rəxʷ	-yə́ɣʷ
3SGM	-ɣʷà	-əxʷ	-ə́ɣʷ
3SGF	-tə̀ɣʷà	-ti	-ti
1PL	-nə́ɣʷà	-nəxʷən	-nə́ɣʷ
2PL	-túnà	-dənəx	-inə́ɣʷ
3PL	-únà	-nəkʷ	-nə́ɣʷ

When the participle and auxiliary fused, the inflected auxiliary was reinterpreted as a person affix. In Kemat and Bilin, as well as in various other languages of the group, the consonant of the stem of the former auxiliary was transferred to word-final position. Thus, for example, the original first-person singular form -àɣʷ became -ɣʷà and subsequently, owing to vowel reduction, -əɣʷ.

An analogous development produced the current past tense enclitic person forms in Polish and other West Slavic languages. Polish inherited from Proto-Slavic a periphrastic past tense consisting of the active past participle, displaying gender agreement with the subject, and the present form of the verb 'be', the root

---

[4] The person prefixes on the auxiliary in Awngi are those of the Afro-Asiatic prefixal conjugation.

of which was *jes*, inflected for person and number. From around the fourteenth century (Długosz-Kurczabowa & Dubisz 1999:305) this construction began to give way to a synthetic one. In the third-person singular and plural the auxiliary was simply lost. In the other persons various reductions of the auxiliary took place, as shown in (21).

(21)   Polish (Długosz-Kurczabowa & Dubisz 1999:292)
      1SG jeśm   -eśm/śm
      2SG jeś   -eś/ś
      3sg jeść, jest, je -Ø
      1PL jesmy   -smy (later -śmy)
      2PL jeście   -ście
      3PL są   -Ø

The reduced forms of the auxiliary became enclitic to either the participle, as in (22a,b) or an element preceding it as in (22c,d).

(22)   Polish
  a. Padł   jesm   → padł-eśm (later padłem)
      fall:PPART be:1SG   fall:PAST-1SG

  b. Przysiągł jeś   → przysiągł-eś
      swear:PPART be:2SG   swear:PAST-2SG

  c. Gdy jeśm   szedł   → gdy-śm szedł
      when be:1SG walk:PPART

  d. Jakoz jeś   przysiągł → jakoześ-eś przysiągł
      as   be:2SG swear:PPART

In current Polish these person enclitics strongly favour attachment to the verb and are thus very much on the way to being reinterpreted as suffixes. Nonetheless, one still comes across instances where they are attached to other clause-initial constituents, such as the question particle in (23a), the complementizer in (23b) or even a corresponding stressed person marker (23c).

(23)   Polish
  a. Czy-ś ty nie zwariował?
      Q-2SG you not to go crazy:P.PART:F:SG
      'You must be crazy!' (Lit. Aren't you crazy?)

  b. Żeby-m cię   tu   więcej nie widział!
      so-that-1SG you:DAT here more not see:P.PART:M:SG
      'Don't dare to come here again.' (Lit. I don't want to see you here again.)

  c. My-śmy widzieli   ją wczoraj.
      We-1PL see.P.PART:PL her yesterday
      'We saw her yesterday.'

Yet another group of languages which are taken to manifest person markers originating from a conjugated auxiliary are the Muskogean languages Alabama, Choctaw, Creek, Hitchiti and Koasati (Haas 1977). Haas argues that the correspondences in the person markers found in these languages can be accounted for if it is assumed that the extra elements occurring in some of the paradigms are remnants of old auxiliary verb stems. According to Haas, Proto-Muskogean, in addition to a synthetic verbal paradigm with the person prefixes in (24), also had two periphrastic paradigms, one with the transitive auxiliary *li and the other with the intransitive auxiliary *ka, both conjugated with the person prefixes in (24).

(24)   Proto-Muskogean
       1SG   li
       2SG   is
       3SG   Ø
       1PL   ili
       2PL   has

The transitive and intransitive auxiliary paradigms can still be discerned in current Koasati. They are illustrated in (25) with the verbs *kalas.li* 'to scratch' and *imfi.ki* 'to pay'.

(25)   Koasati
       1SG   kalas li   -li   imfi.ki   -li"
       2SG   kalas   -ci   imfi.   -hiska
       3SG   kalas li   -Ø   imfi.ki   -Ø
       1PL   kalas -hili   -hili   imfi   -hilka
       2PL   kalas   -haci   imfi   -haska

In Hitchiti and Creek, on the other hand, only the intransitive paradigm is currently in evidence. Each of the two languages possesses only one active person paradigm shown in (26) on the basis of the verb *patapli* 'to hit' in Hitchiti and the verb *wanay* 'to tie' in Creek. (The suffix *-s/is* is the indicative marker.)

(26)   Hitchiti   Creek
       1SG   patapli   -li   -s   wana.y   -ay   -s
       2SG   patapli   -icka-s   wana.y   -ick   -is
       3SG   patapli   -s   wana.y   -is
       1PL   patapl-   -i.ka-s   wana.y   -iy/i   -is
       2PL   patapl   -a.cka-s   wana.y   -a.ck   -is

We see that the intransitive auxiliary is transparent in Hitchiti but much less so in Creek. Haas suggests that the Creek forms have undergone the following changes: loss of *k-* and *ka-* in the first-person singular and plural respectively, and loss of final *a* in the second person.

In all the above examples the source of the new person marker was a reanalysed auxiliary verb. Such reanalysis may also involve other types of verbs. Capell (1969a:85–6) has observed the use of conjugated forms of the verbs 'hit' and 'give' as object person markers in several Papuan languages of the Huon Peninsula, such as Dani, Kâte, Kombai and Ono. In contrast to the previous cases of reanalyses that we discussed, the person markers in question are those of the object not the subject. In these languages regular person marking of the object is found with only a limited number of verbs. In Kâte, for example, it occurs with only six verbs and takes the form of changing the first consonant of the stem, thus, for example, *nu* 'hit me', *gu* 'hit you' and *ke* 'hit him/her/it'. The marking of other verbs for object is achieved by suffixing to the verb the inflected verbs 'hit' (for direct object) or 'give' (for indirect object) as in (27).

(27)   Kâte (Capell 1969a:85–6)
       Mi hone-*gu*-kopa?
       not see-you-I:PRES:RLS
       'I don't see you.' (Lit. I see-he hits you)

This is the only instance of the use of such verbs as person markers that I am aware of.

A final class of conjugated verbs that may be reanalysed as person markers, though as possessive rather than personal ones, are the verbs 'to own' and 'to have'. In Larike, for example, the possessive root *na* inflected with subject prefixes is an alternative possessive pronoun.

7.1.5   Other grammatical markers

In the literature one occasionally comes across statements specifying some non-person origin of one person marker or another. For instance, Hofling (2000:36, note 4) notes that the third-person absolutive suffix -*ij* in Itzaj Maya historically was a perfective marker. Robertson (1999) provides an elaborate argument for treating the /t/ in the fused person markers of transitive verbs in another Mayan language, Huastec, as originating from a preposition *t*+V. Burquest (1986:73) suggests that the third-person singular suffix in the completive aspect in Angas -*kə* is a remnant of the Chadic completive aspect marker. And Chafe (1977) documents that the third-person subject person prefixes in Iroquoian developed from number markers and indefinite pronouns. The situations leading to such localized instances of reanalysis are highly varied. One type of scenario that most readily springs to mind is the filling in of a gap in the bound person paradigm by a grammatical marker co-occurring with person, say a tense, aspect, mood, number or gender marker. One can envisage that a number or tense marker, for example, could be reinterpreted as a third-person marker if its phonological transparency to other number or tense markers is destroyed as a result of a phonological change. Another possible scenario is first fusion of a person and tense or aspect marker and then the subsequent erosion or disappearance of the person part leaving just the tense or aspect marker, in some shape or form.

A yet unmentioned grammatical source of person marking is that of evidentials, especially egophoric evidentials, that is markers which indicate that the speaker is directly involved in the state of affairs expressed in the predication and is also the party responsible for the veracity of the information presented. Egophoric evidentials are primarily linked with the first person. They may, however, also occur with the second person, namely in questions when the addressee is required to specify information that he is responsible for. Egophoric evidentials appear to have given rise to first- and second-person forms in a number of varieties of Tibetan and Newari and possibly in some South American languages such as Awa Pit and Tuyuca. The primary characteristic of a person system stemming from egophoric evidential marking is the distinction between locutor and non-locutor. In statements the locutor is the first person and the non-locutor the second and third. In questions, on the other hand, the locutor is the second person and the non-locutor the first and third. This is shown schematically in (28).

(28)
	Statement	Question
1st person	Locutor	Non-locutor
2nd person	Non-locutor	Locutor
3rd person	Non-locutor	Non-locutor

In Awa Pit, for example, in the non-past tense the locutor is marked by the suffix -s, as in (29), the non-locutor by the suffix -y, as in (30).

(29)   Awa Pit (Curnow 1997:190)
  a. Na-na pala ku-mtu-s
      I:NOM plantain eat:IMPF:Locutor
      'I am eating plantains.'

  b. Shi-ma nu-na   ki-mtu-s
      what-Q 2SG:NOM:TOP-ACC do-IMPF-Locutor
      'What are you doing?'

(30) a. Nu-na   pala   u-mtu-y
        you:NOM plantain eat:IMPF:Non-locutor
        'You are eating plantains.'

  b. Min-a-ma na-na   ashap-tu-y?
      Who-ACC-Q 1SG-NOM annoy-IMPF-Non-locutor
      'Whom am I annoying?'

As argued by Curnow, this marking system can be explained if it is assumed that what was originally being marked is the participant who is a source of knowledge for the event, or has the epistemic authority to make a claim about an event.

7.2 From independent person marker to syntactic agreement marker

Like all grammaticalization processes, the grammaticalization of person markers proceeds along several dimensions – formal, functional and semantic. The formal dimension, first introduced in chapter two, involves the change from independent person marker to affix, the degree of fusion of the affix with the stem and finally its disappearance, as shown in (31).

(31)   independent person marker > weak from > clitic > agglutinative affix > fusional form > Ø

The functional dimension, presented in chapter four, relates to the change from a pronoun, that is a referential expression with deictic or anaphoric force to a syntactic agreement marker, i.e. a form with no referential potential which only redundantly expresses (some) person features. This is depicted in (32).

(32)   pronominal agreement marker > ambiguous agreement marker > syntactic agreement marker

And the semantic dimension, discussed in chapters three and six, pertains to the reduction and potentially loss of information about the referential identity of the person markers, such as whether or not they clearly distinguish the speaker from the hearer, whether they specify that the hearer is or is not included and whether there is an indication of the number of the referents, their gender and social status. This is shown schematically in (33).

(33)   many semantic distinctions > fewer semantic distinctions
         1st vs 2nd vs 3rd   1st & 2nd vs 3rd
         inclusive/exclusive   no distinction
         singular/plural   no number
         masculine/feminine   no gender
         honorific markers   no honorific markers

In the main, the grammaticalization of person markers along these three dimensions runs in parallel. This is sometimes referred to as the parallel paths hypothesis. Nonetheless, the three types of changes do not always coincide. For example, as we have seen in chapter four, both clitics and affixes may function as pronominal and ambiguous agreement markers. And in languages which have both clitics and affixes it is not always the case that the clitics express more semantic distinctions than the affixes.

In the preceding chapters we have provided plenty of examples of person markers at different stages of grammaticalization. Now it is time to consider how these different stages of grammaticalization come about.

Three explanations have been advanced for the grammaticalization of person markers. Two of these, namely frequency-driven morphologization (FDM) and Ariel's (2000) accessibility-theory explanation (AT) focus primarily on the formal dimension of the grammaticalization of person markers. The third is the widely accepted NP-detachment analysis primarily associated with the name of Givón (1976), which focuses on the functional dimension of grammaticalization, in particular on the change from pronominal to ambiguous agreement marker. The three explanations for the grammaticalization of person markers will be considered in section 7.2.1. As we shall see, none of these accounts of the grammaticalization of person markers deals explicitly with the latter stages of grammaticalization, that is with the change from ambiguous to syntactic agreement marker. The factors underlying the emergence of syntactic person agreement will be considered in section 7.2.2.

7.2.1 Three accounts of the early stages of the grammaticalization of person markers

Since the functional and morpho-phonological dimensions of grammaticalization need not always coincide, the three explanations for the early stages of the grammaticalization of person markers do not cover exactly the same range of markers. Nor, however, are they fully complementary. This will become clearer below. We will begin the presentation with the most well known of the three explanations, namely the NP-detachment analysis.

7.2.1.1 NP detachment

The NP-detachment analysis essentially seeks to provide an account of the development of grammatical, as opposed to anaphoric, person agreement between the subject and verb. It seeks to explain in one swoop, so to speak, the presence of a person clitic or affix on the verb and the co-occurrence of this affix with a corresponding NP subject. According to the NP-detachment analysis, this comes about as follows. The person affix or clitic originates as an independent anaphoric person marker in topic-shifted, left- or right-detached construction, such as those in (34).

(34) a. Sally, she came early.
 b. She came early, Sally.

As a result of overuse, such topic-shifted constructions become reanalysed as neutral clauses; the left- or right-detached topic becomes the subject and the anaphoric person marker, becomes attached to the verb as in (34c).

(34) c. Sally she-came early.

The NP-detachment analysis does not deal with the subsequent grammaticalization of the person marker. However, the assumption is that the person marker on the verb gradually loses its referential force and becomes a form that only redundantly expresses person and number and/or gender. Subsequently, owing to phonological erosion, it may be lost altogether.

Though the NP-detachment analysis has been developed in the context of subject person agreement, it is considered to be equally valid for object agreement, both direct and indirect. In fact, most of the synchronic evidence for the NP-detachment analysis comes from object agreement rather than subject agreement. Assuming that person agreement may bear traces of its origin, and the more recent the origin the more traces there may be, what we would expect to find in the case of the NP-detachment origin of person markers are restrictions on agreement connected with topicality. And indeed, recall from chapter 4 that in many languages the presence of object agreement is conditioned by the inherent and discourse saliency of the referents of the person markers, being present with topical referents but not with focal ones. Such restrictions are also exhibited in the case of subject agreement, but much less frequently, presumably because subject agreement tends to be further on the grammaticalization path than object agreement.

The NP-detachment analysis can also be extended to person agreement between the possessor and possessed. The syntactic relationship between the possessor and possessed in adnominal possessive constructions is frequently likened to that between the subject and verb. Moreover, as documented by many studies, particularly those conducted within the framework of Givón (1983), the inherent and discourse properties of possessors and subjects, especially transitive subjects, are very similar. Both are typically human, definite and highly topical. Subjects typically function as clausal topics, and possessors perform a similar function within the NP, that is they facilitate the identification of the possessed referent via the identification of the possessor. Furthermore, structures resembling the NP-detachment ones with person markers placed between a possessor and possessed such as *John his book* are found in various languages. All this suggests that the source of (35c) could be a detached possessor NP as in (35a).

(35) a. John, his car
 b. John his car
 c. John his-car

Given that the NP-detachment analysis has been developed to account for grammatical agreement, it is not suprising that it has nothing to say about the emergence of anaphoric agreement. Under the NP-detachment analysis, anaphoric agreement must be assumed to be either a phenomenon completely independent of grammatical agreement or to constitute the input to grammatical agreement. Note that a right- or left-detached topic may be just as well resumed within the main clause by a dependent person marker (e.g. *Sally, she-came early*) as by an independent one (e.g. *Sally, she came early*).

7.2.1.2 Accessibility Theory

Like the NP-detachment analysis, the AT analysis is also concerned primarily with person agreement between the subject and verb. In contrast to NP-detachment, however, the person agreement that it is concerned with is anaphoric rather than grammatical agreement. Under the AT analysis of Ariel (2000) the development of anaphoric agreement takes place not in topic-shifted constructions, but rather in simple clauses with first- or second-person subjects such as those in (36), and gives rise to clauses such as those in (37).

(36) a. I arrived late.
     b. You won.

(37) a. I-arrived late.
     b. You-won.

The bounding of the subject person marker to the verb is taken to be motivated by the high accessibility of the discourse referent of the subject person marker.

Recall from chapter five that AT posits a close relationship between morphological encoding of discourse referents and speakers' assumptions as to the degree of accessibility of the referents in the memory store of the addressee. The more accessible the referent the less coding required. Person affixes are considered to be high accessibility coding devices, second only to zero and reflexives. Clitics are viewed as encoding also high, but nonetheless slightly less accessible, discourse referents, unstressed pronouns still somewhat less accessible referents, stressed pronouns even less accessible referents and so on.

Although this is not immediately obvious, the scope of Ariel's AT account of the development of anaphoric person agreement is actually quite narrow. According to accessibility theory the speaker and hearer are inherently more highly accessible than third parties (see the accessibility hierarchies in section 5.2.1). Ariel therefore sees AT as providing an account of the development of primarily bound first- and second-person markers not third. Although she does not view the development of third-person forms as incompatible with AT, she considers the development of third-person forms to be much less likely than of first- and second-person forms and also potentially motivated by factors other than high accessibility. Moreover, unlike Givón in the case of grammatical agreement, Ariel is hesitant to extend her AT analysis of the development of anaphoric agreement to person markers other than subject ones. This is rather surprising, as it is precisely objects and particularly possessors which exhibit anaphoric as compared to grammatical agreement (see section 4.2).

Anaphoric possessor agreement is an especially good candidate for an AT analysis owing to the high accessibility of possessors. For instance, in Taylor's (1996) corpus of written English, 76 per cent of the attributive possessors denote referents mentioned either in the same clause or in the immediately preceding one. If only pronominal possessors are considered, the figure is even higher, 92 per cent. If, as suggested by Brown's (1983) data, the average look back of possessors is lower than that of subjects, first- and second-person possessors should in fact be even more likely to undergo cliticization and affixation than first- and second-person subjects. Interestingly enough while there are many languages which have grammatical subject agreement but no possessor agreement, I do not know of any which have anaphoric subject agreement but no corresponding possessor agreement.

As for anaphoric object agreement, in terms of the saliency hierarchies (see section 5.1), objects encode inherently less accessible referents than subjects. Therefore, in order for Ariel's AT analysis of the rise of anaphoric person agreement to be extended to objects, the accessibility conditions underlying clitic and affixal encoding have to be relaxed. To put it differently clitics and affixes must be seen not as devices for encoding only the highest levels of accessibility but also of slightly lower levels of accessibility as well. If one is not prepared to extend the range of accessibility statuses compatible with clitic and affixal encoding, then anaphoric object agreement must be assumed not to be AT driven.

Although the AT analysis deals with the emergence of anaphoric agreement, it can accommodate certain instances of grammatical agreement as possible later stages of development (Ariel 2000:207–8). Since according to AT, the more attenuated the encoding, the higher the degree of accessibility of the referent that the person marker encodes, further phonological reduction of a person affix entails even higher accessibility of its referent. Person affixes, like all other affixes, are subject to phonological pressures and may over time fuse with the stem or with other affixes. When this happens, the number of contexts in which their referents are so highly accessible as to warrant such attenuated encoding become very restricted. Consequently, independent arguments start co-occurring alongside the now even more reduced person markers, which results in grammatical agreement. This account of the development of grammatical from anaphoric agreement, while plausible, rests on the high degree of fusion between the person marker and the verb or other affix. Only those person markers of grammatical agreement which exhibit a high degree of fusion potentially qualify as having an AT origin. What constitutes a high degree of fusion is of course not unproblematic. One reflection of high fusion could be the innermost location of a series of affixes relative to the stem. Another, could be conflation with TAM affixes. In any case, grammatical person agreement in languages with agglutinative outer person affixes which clearly manifest no fusion let alone a high degree of fusion, cannot be attributed to AT.

7.2.1.3 Frequency-driven morphologization

FDM, like AT, attempts to account for the rise of anaphoric person agreement.[5] Also like AT, it is not conceived of with person agreement in mind, but rather as a general principle of morphological change. FDM specifies that forms which occur adjacent to each other with a high degree of frequency are likely to undergo morphological fusion. This, in turn, is motivated by the yet more general principle of economy, that is the tendency to shorten linguistic expressions that are used most commonly (see, e.g., Haiman 1985; Croft 1990). Thus in terms of the FDM, anaphoric person agreement is just one of the manifestations of the fusion of frequently occurring forms and ultimately a reflection of the principle

---

[5] In contrast to both the NP-detachment and AT-based explanations for the rise of person agreement, the FDM account, while implicit in many discussions of person agreement, is rarely explicitly considered. Ariel (2000), who directly contrasts her AT analysis with the FDM one, is a notable exception.

Table 7.1 *Frequency of first- and third-person pronouns in English according to text type, per million words, based on Biber et al.'s (1999) 40-million-word corpus*

Person	Conversation	Fiction	News	Academic
I	38 000	17000	5000	2000
he	11 000	17000	7000	1000
she	8 000	10000	2000	500<
me	4 000	4000	1000	500<
him	2 000	5000	1000	500<
her	1 000	3000	1000	500<
my	2 500	3500	1000	500
his	1 500	9000	5500	250<
her	1 000	5000	2000	500

of economy, one of the fundamental cognitive principles underlying language structure.

In contrast to both the NP-detachment and AT accounts of the rise of person agreement, FDM is not especially tuned to the development of subject agreement. All types of person markers are assumed to be equally susceptible to fusion with the verb, noun or adposition provided that they occur frequently enough adjacent to each other to warrant such fusion. Needless to say, what constitutes the appropriate level of frequency for fusion to occur is impossible to specify. This is the major point of criticism that has been levelled at the FDM, most recently by Ariel (2000) who sees her AT analysis as a significant improvement over the FDM one.

As is well known, the frequency with which person markers are used differs enormously depending on grammatical function (e.g. argument vs adjunct, A vs S, P vs R), text type (e.g. expository prose vs natural conversation) and the category of person (first vs second vs third). By way of illustration consider the data in Table 7.1 which presents the frequency of subject, object and possessive singular person forms in English in four types of texts. (Only the first- and third-person forms are given due to the difficulty in distinguishing between the different functions of *you*.). We see that in conversations first-person forms are nearly ten times more common as subjects than as objects and over fifteen times more common than possessive forms. There are also considerable differences in the frequency of occurrence of first- as opposed to third-person forms within each of the syntactic functions. For instance, in conversation, first-person subjects are over three times as frequent as third-person singular masculine ones. In the case of possessives, the relevant difference is somewhat smaller, only 1.5 to 1. Not surprisingly, however, outside of conversational texts each of the possessive third-person forms is considerably more frequent than the first-person ones.

Assuming that comparably large differences in the frequency of particular person markers obtain in other languages, one wonders what sort of expectations in regard to the potential fusion of the person markers with their targets we should have. For example, should the just-mentioned fifteenfold difference in frequency be interpreted in terms of the FDM as suggestive of the unlikelihood of first-person possessives as compared to first-person subjects ever fusing with the possessed? How should the tenfold difference in frequency between first-person subjects and objects be considered? Do such differences in relative frequency play a role at all or is what counts the absolute frequency of a given person marker? If the latter is the case, how does 11,000 per million words compare with 38,000 per million words in relation to high frequency within the context of the FDM? What if grammaticalization is strongly lexically driven? Perhaps it is not the frequency of just the person markers that we should be looking at but rather at the frequency of occurrence of a particular person marker and verb or noun combination.

While there is every reason to consider frequency as a major factor underlying grammaticalization (see Bybee & Hopper 2001), unanswered questions such as the above considerably undermine the explanatory power of any purely frequency-based account of the development of person agreement such as FDM. The FDM as it stands is simply too general to enable one to use it in a discriminatory way, for example as a predictor of the development of person agreement in one category as opposed to another.

7.2.2 Syntactic agreement markers

Recall from chapter four that syntactic agreement markers, that is person markers which cannot occur without an accompanying NP argument, are cross-linguistically very uncommon. They are extremely well represented among the languages of Western Europe being found in Dutch, English, Faroese, Frisian, Icelandic, Standard German, Swiss German, Romansch (partially), Russian (partially), Standard French and some of the Rhaeto-Romance dialects. Outside Europe, however, I have come across only sporadic instances of syntactic person agreement markers, namely in four Papuan languages – Au, Ekari, Koiari and Vanimo – and three Oceanic ones – Anejom, Fehan and Labu. Moreover, all the person markers in question are markers of the s and A.

The most obvious explanation for the further grammaticalization of an ambiguous to a syntactic agreement marker is phonological erosion. In the course of time, person markers may undergo attrition. This is particularly likely if they are obligatory and thus occur with every verb. If phonological erosion results in the merging of some paradigmatic distinctions, that is in the appearance of homophonous forms, independent person markers may begin to be used for purposes of disambiguation or to mark distinctions not present in the verbal person forms. The use of the independent person markers may then spread from occurrence with just the homophonous forms to occurrence with all forms. This may cause further phonological erosion of the agreement markers because of their lack of functionality, thus reinforcing the need for independent forms.

There is considerable support for the above account of the development of syntactic agreement markers from ambiguous agreement markers. Most of the languages currently exhibiting syntactic person agreement display considerable homophony of the person forms. In Dutch, the second- and third-person singular forms of the indicative of weak verbs are homophonous, as are also all the persons in the plural. In Standard French, only the first- and second-person plural are now phonetically distinct. In English, where the person agreement system is most reduced being confined only to the present, there is homophony between the first and second persons in the singular and between all the persons in the plural. Extensive homophony of person forms is also found in languages with syntactic agreement outside Europe. In Koiari (Dutton 1996:23), one form is used for the first- and third-person singular and another for all the remaining person and number combinations both in the case of the imperfect and perfect person suffixes. (See example (5) in ch. 3, section 3.1.) In Ekari there are only two forms for the whole paradigm, one for the first- and third-person singular feminine and second- and third-person plural and another for the remaining person/number combinations. (See example (7) in ch. 3, section 3.1.) In Anejom, as shown in (38), the S/A forms, which are fused with TAM markers, are homophonous in the aorist non-singular, and nearly homophonous in the past indicative and subjunctive. There is also homophony between the second- and third-person singular in the past indicative.

(38)   Anejom (Lynch 1982:117–18)

	Aorist	Past indicative	Subjunctive
1SG	ek/k	kis/is	ki
2SG	nei/na	is	ni
3SG	et/t	is	iniyi/yi
1PL INCL	ekra/era/rai	kis/is	ri
1PL EXCL	ekra/era/rai	is	ri
2PL	ekra/era/rai	ekris/is	ri/ra
3PL	ekra/era/rai	ekris/is	ri/ra

According to Lynch, the person markers in (38) represent a considerable simplification of the original person system which was not only non-syncretic but manifested a dual and trial in addition to the plural. In Vanimo person marking of the verb is indicated by changes of the initial consonant of the stem. There appear to be four basic paradigms corresponding to the four places of articulation of Vanimo consonants: bilabial, alveolar, alveo-palatal and glottal.[6] Since the last two have been found only with five verbs, (39) illustrates only the bilabial and alveolar paradigms.

---

[6] Ross (1980:94) suggests that the different paradigms derive from the fusion of a subject prefix, originating from the independent person markers, with verb stems featuring different consonants, the manner of articulation of which was neutralized.

(39)   Vanimo (Ross 1980:94–5)
         Bilabial   Alveolar
         sit   fly   do, make   pull
1SG   ve   vé   le   lu
2SG   pe   pé   ble   blu
3SGM   hve   hvé   hle   hlu
3SGF   se   sé   pli   plu
1PL   hve   hvé   de   du
2PL   ve   vé   le   lu
3PL   hve   hvé   di   hlu

We see that in the bilabial paradigm there is homophony of the first-person singular and second-person plural as well as of the third-person masculine singular and first- and third-person plural. In the alveolar paradigm there is homophony between the first-person singular and second plural and, with some verbs, also between the third-person masculine and the third plural. There is less homophony in the person markers of Labu, but it does exist. In Labu, as in Koiari and Anejom, the subject prefix is sensitive to TAM distinctions, namely to tense (past vs non-past) and modality, though only in the singular, and in the case of modality only for the second and third persons. The forms of the person prefixes are shown in (40), where V stands for vowel.

(40)   Labu (Siegel 1984:98–9)
         Irrealis   Realis   Past
1SG   ndV-   ndV-   yV-
2SG   nô-   ŋô-   ô-
3SG   vV-   ŋV-   Ø
1PL INCL lV-
1PL EXCL mV-
2PL   mô-
3PL   sV-

The realization of the vowel in the subject prefix depends on verb class. In one class of verbs the vowel is /ô/ in the second-person singular and plural, and otherwise assimilates to the first vowel of the stem. In this class of verbs in which the initial vowel of the stem is /ô/, the second- and third-person singular in the non-past (both realis and irrealis) and the second- and third-person plural are homophonous. In the other class of verbs, the vowel in the second person is again /ô/ except for the non-past in which case it is /a/. Thus with this class of verbs there is homophony between the second- and third-person non-past in verbs featuring an /a/ vowel.

In the languages mentioned above all the agreement markers are syntactic. One cannot therefore actually see that the co-occurrence of the dependent and independent forms is driven by the need for disambiguation. That this may indeed be so is evidenced by languages such as Maricopa. Gordon (1987:17, 61) states that in Maricopa, the first-person prefix '- is often omitted from verbs beginning with a consonant. As a result, first-person verbs are homophonous with third-person ones, which lack any prefix. Independent person markers are therefore used to disambiguate both in the case of intransitive clauses (41) and transitive ones with third-person objects (42).

(41) Maricopa (Gordon 1987:17, 61, 17, 19)
    a. Nyaa hmii-k
       I   tall-RLS
       'I am tall.'

    b. Hmii-k
       tall-RLS
       'He is tall.'

(42) a. Nyaa wik-k
       I   help-RLS
       'I helped him.'

    b. Wik-k
       helped-RLS
       'He helped him.'

A particularly interesting instance of the use of independent pronouns caused by the homophony of verbal person forms is that observed in the Austronesian language Kisar. According to Blood (1992:3), the language has three sets of subject person forms: subject prefixes, short pronoun subjects and complex pronoun subjects. These are listed in (43).

(43) Kisar (Blood 1992:3)

Subject	Prefix	Short subject	Complex subject
1SG	'-/'u-	ya-	ya'u
1PL EXCL	m-	ai	aim
1PL INCL	k-	i-	ik
2SG	m-	o	om
2PL	m-	mi	mim
3SG	n-	ai	ain
3PL	r-	hi	hir

A look at the subject prefixes reveals that the second-person singular and plural as well as the first-person exclusive forms are homophonous. There is also some homophony in the short subject pronouns, namely of the first-person exclusive and the third-person singular. However, when both the subject prefixes and the short subject pronouns co-occur, all the forms are disambiguated. Not surprisingly, therefore, Blood states that clauses with first- and second-person subjects nearly always feature, in addition to the subject prefix, either a short or a complex subject pronoun. The use of the short or complex form of the pronoun depends on whether the verb is vowel or consonant initial. Vowel-initial verbs co-occur with short pronouns, as in (44a) and consonant-initial ones with complex pronouns, as in (44b).

(44) Kisar
  a. Ya-'amaka   riuk wolimanoho-ro-ropo
     I-1SG-awaken strike five island-REDUP-before dawn
     'I wake up at five o'clock in the morning.'
  b. Ya'u hamlinu
     I   forget
     'I forget.'

As the forms in (44) illustrate, the complex forms are a combination of the short forms and the subject prefixes. Blood argues that because of a syllable structure constraint which prohibits complex syllable onsets, in the case of consonant-initial verbs the subject prefixes attach to the immediately preceding pronoun rather than to the verb. Thus, while the homophony of the person prefixes has induced the use of overt pronouns, the syllable structure constraint has produced a separate set of such pronouns. Note also that the first-person singular and plural exclusive short subject pronouns are phonologically bound to the verb. This suggests that Kisar may be developing new bound prefixes from the short pronouns.

While phonological attrition and subsequent disambiguation of homophonous forms is a highly likely explanation for the change from ambiguous to syntactic agreement marker, it cannot be the only one. There are languages which display a good deal of homophony in their person affixes but which do not require that they be accompanied by a corresponding independent form. For instance, as illustrated in chapter three (see example (2)), in the Surmic language Chai there is homophony between the first- and second-person singular and also between the third-person singular and plural. Yet Last and Lucassen (1998:396) state that independent person forms are used only for emphasis. Conversely, there are languages in which the affixal person paradigms exhibit no syncretic forms but which require or strongly favour the use of independent person markers together with the affixal forms. This is the case in Au and Fehan, for example.[7]

What then are the other reasons for the development of syntactic agreement? One diachronic scenario that comes to mind in the context of Western European languages is syntactic, namely the emergence of a verb-second constraint. This is seen to be the source of grammatical agreement in Old High German, medieval French and some of the Romansch dialects. The claim is that independent person markers came to be used obligatorily to avoid declarative clauses with initial verbs. Subsequently, the use of independent person forms spread from initial position to other positions, resulting in grammatical as opposed to ambiguous agreement. Support for the rise of grammatical agreement as a response to a V2 constraint comes from the fact that, in medieval French and Old High German, whenever

---

[7] Particularly interesting in regard to the ambiguous vs syntactic agreement distinction are Standard German and Bavarian. Gilligan (1987:170) points out that while they have the same agreement paradigms, in the former the agreement is syntactic, in the latter ambiguous. Unfortunately, I have not been able to verify this in relation to Bavarian.

the V2 constraint was satisfied by another sentential constituent, that is by a topic in TVX declaratives or was inoperative, as in interrogatives, the independent subject person forms were generally omitted. The use of dummy subjects such as the English *there*, German *es* and French *il* in impersonal clauses, though not synchronically associated with the V2 constraint, is also seen as a reflection of its diachronic relevance. Another possible source of grammatical agreement is diffusion. Independent person forms may begin to occur in non-focal contexts under the influence of language contact and the agreement affixes may over time simply fall into disuse.

The rarity of syntactic person agreement is rather surprising. Given the ubiquity of person agreement in the world's languages, one would expect there to be more languages exhibiting person markers at a late stage of grammaticalization. The fact that there are not suggests that languages tend to develop new person agreement markers once the old ones lose or start losing their referential potential. This can be currently observed in Colloquial French and some of the Rhaeto-Romance dialects, both of which have developed subject clitics, despite the presence of vestiges of person marking on the verb. The frequent presence of independent person markers in the Papuan language Kobon accompanying the person marking (fused with tense) on the verb may be another manifestation of this phenomenon. The independent person markers may occur even in the presence of an NP, as in (45b) where they redundantly mark the NP as definite.

(45)   Kobon (Davies 1981:152, 151)
 a.   Hane ihariŋ ñiŋ-ag-mɨd-un.   hane lau ñiŋ-mɨd-un.
      We just eat-NEG-HAB-1PL:PAST we eat-HAB-1PL:PAST
      'We do not eat it raw, we eat it cooked.'

 b.   Ales nipe Abonain ar-öp
      Ales he Abonain go-3SG:PERF
      'Ales has gone to Abonain.'

7.3 Language externally driven changes in person marking

The changes in person markers resulting from the influence of other languages vary greatly from the borrowing of an individual person form or even just a semantic distinction such as gender or inclusivity to the total overhaul of the person system. The type of sociolinguistic situations which may lead to sporadic instances of borrowing are too numerous to contemplate. The more extensive type of changes tend to occur in prolonged situations of intense language contact (i.e. in bi- or multilingual societies) or in language obsolescence. Prolonged language contact may underlie both the acquisition and loss of person markers. Language obsolescence, on the other hand, tends to involve only loss or simplification of person paradigms, in the latter case typically in the direction of the dominant language of the area.

It is not always easy to determine whether a particular change in person marking is due to the influence of another language or to language-internal factors. This is especially so in cases of reduction or loss, which may be the result of ongoing processes of grammaticalization. Consequently, some of the instances of change attributed to language contact to be discussed below are necessarily of a speculative nature.

7.3.1 Borrowing of person markers

The borrowing of person markers is in itself a contentious issue. Some linguists are of the opinion that person markers are almost never borrowed (e.g. Nichols & Peterson 1996). Others, such as Campbell (1997) maintain that this is not so. The issue is of special relevance to genetic linguistics as it bears on the diagnostic value of person markers in the establishing of the genetic relatedness between languages. If person markers are not resistant to borrowing, considerably less store can be put on the existence of similarities in the person systems of two candidates for genetic relatedness than if person forms are highly unlikely to be borrowed. My investigations reveal quite a few instances of the borrowing of person markers. However, I am not in a position to judge whether these instances of borrowing qualify as common or as incidental relative to the borrowing of other grammatical categories.

Most examples of the borrowing of specific person forms come from closely genetically related languages. Thus Old English substituted the old *hie*, *hiera* and *him* by *they*, *their*, *them* borrowed from Scandinavian. The Central Dravidian language Kolami borrowed the second-person singular independent marker *niv* from Old Telugu and most probably also the second-person plural marker *ir*, which then by analogy with the second-person singular form became *nir*. The independent forms subsequently gave rise to the second-person singular suffix *-iv* and the second-person plural suffix *-ir*, respectively (Subrahmanyam 1971:411). The Northern Interior Salish language Lillooet seems to have borrowed from the Coast Salish languages the marking of transitive predicates by the third-person suffix *-as* (Kroeber 1999:20). Sayula Popoluca, a Mixtecan language of Mexico, borrowed from Zoquean the first-person prefix *na-* and with it the distinction between inclusive and exclusive (Wichmann 1995:91). Interestingly enough, in Sayula Popoluca, *na-* is the first-person inclusive, while the closest form currently attested in Zoquean, in Soteapan Zoque, is *an-*, which is the first-person exclusive. Campbell (1997:340) mentions that the Misumalpan language Miskito, spoken in Nicaragua, appears to have borrowed its first *yaŋ* and second-person *man* independent pronouns from other Misumalpan languages of Nicaragua and Honduras, namely Northern Sumu (*yaŋ* and *man*). Donohue and Smith (1998:72) observe that Mlap, a Nimboran language spoken in northern Irian Jaya, has borrowed from its sister language Kemtuik the non-singular number suffix *-naŋ* and used it in the creation of plural person markers. Güldermann (2001) argues that the Khoekhoe languages (!Ora, Eini, Nama) typically referred to as Central

Khoisan, have borrowed from the !Ui-Taa-family (Southern Khoisan) the first-person non-singular form *si* and in doing so innovated the inclusive/exclusive distinction.

Borrowing of person morphemes from languages belonging to quite different phyla is also attested. Some instances of such borrowing involve the colonial Standard Average European (SAE) languages. For example, Chamorro (Topping 1973:107) seems to have borrowed the first-person absolutive prefix *yo-* from Spanish. Ambonese Malay has borrowed the second-person singular form *ose* from Portuguese (Donohue & Smith 1998:82). Thai (Cooke 1968:11) has added to its list of forms for person reference the English *ʔaj'* and *juu'* and Vietnamese (Cooke 1968:114) the French *moa* (*moi*) and *toa* (*toi*). An instance of borrowing between different families of Amerindian languages is reported by Newman (1980:156), who notes that Okanagan-Colville borrowed a first-person subject pronoun from Kutenai (Kutenai *ku* → Okanagan $k^w o$ and Colville $k^w u$). Several instances of the borrowing of person morphemes have been observed between Austronesian and Papuan languages. For instance, West Makian (Voorhoeve 1982:16), a West Papuan language of the North Halmahera stock, spoken in north Moluccas, borrowed from its Austronesian neighbour East Makian the first-person exclusive form *mi* (Austronesian *kami). A quite extensive case of borrowing of person forms is found among the Omotic languages, which constitute one of the branches of Afro-Asiatic. It seems to be generally accepted (Bender 2000:163, 200) that some of the Omotic languages have borrowed person markers from the Nilotic languages. This is exemplified in (46) on the basis of the Omotic languages Ari and Hamer and two Nilotic languages Nuer and Teso. The reconstructed Proto-Omotic forms are included for comparison.

(46)   Aroid Languages (Bender 2000:163, 199)

	Ari	Nuer	Hamer	Teso	*Omotic
1SG	ʔitá	γän	inta	ɛɔŋɔ	in
2SG	aaná	jin	ya	ıjɔ	ne
3SGM	nó(o)	jɛn	kisi	ŋesi	is/is+i
3SGF	náa				
1PL	wo(o)tá	kɔɔn/kɔn	wosi	ɔnı(INCL)	nu
				ıs(y)ɔ(excl)	
2PL	yetá	yɛn	yesi	yɛsi	int
3PL	ketá	kɛn	kosi	kɛsi	ist

The borrowing is reflected in the plural forms of the markers, which manifest the typical Nilotic pattern of w/y/k first consonants. As shown in (46), the forms in Ari seem to be based on West Nilotic, exemplified by Nuer, those of Hamer more on East Nilotic, exemplified by Teso. The forms in both Ari and Hamer are obviously quite different from the reconstructed proto-Omotic forms.

Sometimes it is not the actual person forms that are borrowed but rather just a particular feature of the person system. For instance, Kakua, a Maku language spoken in Colombia near the Brazilian border, is the only language in the family to have gender distinctions in third-person independent person markers and in the subject prefixes. Martins and Martins (1999:258) suggest that this is borrowed, or acquired under the influence of East Tucano. The inclusive/exclusive distinction appears to be particularly amenable to borrowing. Jacobsen (1980) attributes the presence of this distinction among the North American languages of the Great Basin, particularly in Numic and Washo, to contact with the Penutian languages. Van der Voort (2000:158) suggests that the inclusive/exclusive distinction in Kwaza has been borrowed from the Tupi-Guarani languages. The occurrence of the inclusive/exclusive distinction in a few Indo-Aryan languages, namely Gujarati, Marathi and Sindhi is seen to be the result of contact with the Dravidian languages, in which inclusivity, in contrast to Indo-European, is widely attested. Anêm (Thurston 1994:594), a non-Austronesian language of north-west New Britain, displays the inclusive/exclusive distinction in the object suffixes, but not the subject prefixes, which are sensitive to tense and are clearly older forms. Thurston suggests that the inclusive/exclusive distinction has been borrowed from the Austronesian languages. Gimira, Amaaro and Dasenech are the only Ethiopian Omotic-Cushitic languages to have the inclusive/exclusive distinction. Breeze (1986:49) suggests that it is acquired under the influence of the Nilo-Saharan languages in the area.

A particular radical instance of borrowing is the borrowing of person agreement systems. This is alleged to have happened quite regularly among the languages of Australia. Australianists (e.g. Blake 1990) consider the clitic or affixal person agreement marking found in many languages of the continent to be of relatively recent origin and to have spread via areal diffusion. The diffusion is seen to be of the indirect type, that is involving not concrete morphemes but rather structural patterns, in this case the phenomenon of bound person marking.[8] The most widely cited instances of the diffusion of person agreement are those involving contact between the non-Pama-Nyungan languages of Arnhem land and their Pama-Nyungan neighbours. The non-Pama-Nyungan languages have an elaborate system of person clitics or affixes. The Pama-Nyungan languages vary; some do have bound person markers others do not. For example, all but two of the languages of the Yuulngu subgroup of Pama-Nyungan lack person clitics or affixes. The two languages that do have them are Ritharngu and Djinang, which are spoken on the edges of the Yuulngu area. Heath (1978:126) attributes the presence of person enclitics in Ritharngu to the influence of the non-Pama-Nyungan languages to the south, Nunggubuyu and Ngandi, both of which have person prefixes.[9] Dixon makes the same suggestion for Djinang. Another Pama-Nyungan language which is seen to have acquired its bound person markers due to contact with non-Pama-Nyungan languages, most probably Mara

---

[8] The term diffusion is used by some scholars as a synonym for borrowing. Others use it only for instances of indirect borrowing. An illuminating discussion is provided in chapter four of Heath (1978).

[9] An example of the person enclitics in Ritharngu was given in chapter 4, example (61).

and/or Garawa, is Yanyuwa (Blake 1990:447), spoken in the Northern Territory and Queensland.

Diffusion of person markers appears to have also occurred among the Pama-Nyungan languages. A particularly interesting case is that of the presence of person suffixes in Gunya but not Margany (Breen 1981), which are dialects (now extinct) of the same language, spoken in east-central Queensland. Breen (1981:324) considers the Gunya person suffixes to be in an early stage of development since they seem to be in the main derived from the free person markers by deletion of the first syllable, and a few suffixes exhibit some variation in form. Moreover, as (47) illustrates some suffixes are lacking, most notably the first-person P forms.

(47)   Gunya (Breen 1981:304)

	Indep	S/A Suffix	Indep	P Suffix
1SG	ŋaya	-ya/-iya	ŋana	
2SG	inda	-nda/-inda	inana	-nana
3SG	ṉula	-la	nuṉuṉa	-na
1DU	ŋali	-li/-iŋali	ŋaliṉa	
2DU	ibalu	-ibalu	ibaluṉa	-baluna
3DU	bula	-bula/-ibula	bulaṉa	-bulana
1PL	ŋana		ŋanaṉa	
2PL	yuṟa/yu:lu	yurana		
PL	ḍana	-idana/-dana	ḍanana	-ṉḍanana

Unfortunately, Breen does not speculate on the diffusional basis of the person suffixes.

7.3.2 Loss of person agreement

The absence of person agreement in a language may be due to loss or the fact that it never developed. The same holds for incomplete person agreement paradigms; they may be the result of reduction or conversely, they may be still under construction, so to speak, as (potentially) in the case of Gunya, illustrated above in (47). Often it is difficult to determine which of the above two possibilities holds. Typically the presence of a person agreement in closely genetically related languages is taken as indicative of loss and the nature of this agreement system as the yardstick for any assumptions pertaining to reduction or development. But if person agreement is not consistently distributed throughout a genetic grouping, absence of agreement or what appears to be a reduced form of agreement may be just as well a retention as an innovation. This problem may be illustrated by the concrete example of Yingkarta (Dench 1998), a Pama-Nyungan language spoken on the fringe of the Western Desert in Western Australia. Yingkarta, like several other languages in the region, has an incomplete set of person clitics which attach to the first constituent in the clause. These, together with the forms occurring in the closely related language Wajarri, are depicted in (48).

(48)   Yingkarta   Wajarri
                s/A forms
       1SG -rna   -rna
       1PL -rtu   -tu, tuju
       2SG -npa   -n
       3pl -ya   -ya
                P forms
       2SG -nta   -nta

Other Pama-Nyungan languages to the immediate north of Yingkarta do not have any person clitics or affixes, while languages further to the east have well-established sets. Thus Dench (1998:37) states that the person clitics in Yingkarta and also Wajarri may be an innovation relative to the languages in the north or, alternatively, they may constitute a retention and the lack of person clitics in the languages to the north may be an innovation. Moreover, both the loss or conversely potential development of the person clitics may be due to language-internal factors or to areal diffusion; in the case of loss, areal diffusion from the north, and in the case of development, areal diffusion from the east.

Given the above, clear instances of the loss of person agreement are difficult to come by. Some cases in point are: the loss of subject agreement in Swedish, the Dravidian language Malayalam and Colloquial Sinhalla; the loss of P(sp) enclitics/suffixes in the Arawakan languages Bare, Tariana, Resigaro and !Yawalapiti; and the loss of P(sp) prefixes in the Tupi-Guarani language Uruubu Kaapor. Rarer still are clear cases of loss of person agreement owing to the interference of other languages. The loss of inflection, both nominal and verbal, in Swedish is considered by some to have been exacerbated by contact with Middle Low German (Haugen 1976:314) but to the best of my knowledge none of the other just-mentioned examples of loss involve language contact.[10]

A potential instance of complete loss of person agreement due to language contact has been noted by W. Adelaar (2002) in North Chibchan. Virtually all of the North Chibchan languages, namely Ika, Kogu, Damana and Musica-Duit have person prefixes and Chimilla has person suffixes. Cuna and Tunebo, however, have neither. Adelaar suggests that these two languages have lost the person affixes under influence of Chocolan languages, which have no affixal person marking. Adelaar further mentions that Chimilla presumably was also affected by a comparable loss and only subsequently innovated the person suffixes. That the person suffixes of Chimilla are an innovation is evidenced by their phonological distinctiveness from the person affixes of the other North Chibchan languages.

---

[10] I have no information on the factors underlying the loss of the P(sp) markers in the Arawakan languages or in Uruubu Kaapor. As for Malayalam, all the Dravidian languages except for Malayalam have person agreement suffixes for the S/A, most of which have been inherited from the proto-language. According to Subrahmanyam (1971:403–5), loss of these person suffixes in Malayalam is a recent innovation. Clear evidence of their former existence in the language can be found in the literary records. There is even a fourteenth-century grammar of Malayalam which quotes verbs with personal endings. And even today some person suffixes are still in use in Aminidiv Malayalam, a dialect spoken by the Moplahs of the Aminidiv and Lakkadiv islands.

This can be appreciated on the basis of the person markers of the P in Ika, Damana and Chimilla depicted in (49).

(49)   Northern Chibchan P affixes
              Ika   Damana   Chimilla
          1SG   nʌ-   nï-   -nu
          2SG   mi-   nai-   -d^{z}u/ču-
          3SG   Ø   ma-   -wi
          1PL   niwi-   mai-   -nu-ra
          2PL   miwi-   Ø-/a-   -d^{z}u-ra
          3PL   winʌ-   ihkï-   -(n)ne

Another case of loss of person agreement marking as a result of language contact can be observed among the North Halmahera languages, which are West Papuan languages, but are spoken in an Austronesian area, that is in North Moluccas, Indonesia. Under the influence of Malay and Indonesian the person agreement system in these languages is eroding, but at a different rate in different languages. Voorhoeve (1994) divides the North Halmahera languages into two families: the North Halmahera family consisting of Sahu, Ternate-Tidore, which are classified as borderline dialects of one language but could equally well be considered as borderline languages, and North-east Halmahera (a dialect chain comprised of six dialects) and West Makian, which is a family-level isolate. This genetic composition of the North Halmahera languages is depicted in (50).

(50)   The North Halmahera languages
          North Halmahera   West Makian
          Sahu Ternate-Tidore   North-east Halmahera
                                              Pagu, Tobelo, Galela,
                                              Loloda, Modole, Tabaru

The person agreement system in the North-east Halmaheran dialects seems to be relatively intact. They exhibit person agreement with the S, A and P by means of verbal prefixes. In transitive clauses this is manifested by only partially segmentable combinations of the A and P. In Galela, for instance, there are forty-two such prefix combinations. In comparison to North Halmaheran, Sahu exhibits some decay of the person agreement system. Instead of the forty-two combinations of the A and P there are only thirty. Moreover Visser and Voorhoeve (1987:30) note that younger speakers tend to simply leave the prefixes out and use just the independent person forms. This is particularly common with respect to the P prefixes but can even be observed with third-person S markers. In Ternate and Tidore as well as West Makian there are no P prefixes. Ternate and Tidore clearly once did have P prefixes as they are attested in some older texts. Whether this also holds for West Makian is not clear. Voorhoeve (1994:659) states that since the only West Papuan languages which have P affixes on the verb are Northeast Halmaheran, it is possible that West Makian did not lose its P prefixes like

Ternate and Tidore but simply never had them. In Tidore the decay of person agreement has progressed even further in that, as shown in (51), the S/A prefixes are no longer obligatory.

(51)   Tidore (Van Staden 2000:81)
    a.   Ngofa ngge peka tora
        child there fall go downwards
        'The child fell down.'

    b.   Ngofa ngge yo-peka tora
        child there 3SG-fall go downwards
        'The child fell down.'

According to Van Staden (2000:71, 89), there are no clear pragmatic or semantic factors which underlie the use of S/A prefixes in current Tidore. Nor are prefixes more characteristic of higher registers. What is significant, though, is that there are dialects (in the vicinity of Rum) in which the person prefixes are virtually absent. Thus in these dialects the loss of person prefixes is nearly complete.

It is possible that the just-discussed reduction and near loss of person markers may be due not only to language contact, but also, at least in part, to language atrophy. Unfortunately, language atrophy or obsolescence has been a regular consequence of language contact, particularly with SAE in Africa, the Americas, Australia and Austronesia. In cases of language atrophy, person markers appear to be one of the most easily effected grammatical markers. In the words of Mühlhäusler (1996:296):

> Because pronoun systems are typically dependent on an existing social order and cultural beliefs, cultural changes can have dramatic consequences in this area of grammar. These consequences include
> 1. formal simplification
> 2. large-scale loss of pronouns indexing culturally rather than situationally relevant information
> 3. the addition of new pronouns signalling the social asymmetries between coloniser and colonised
> 4. typological convergence with SAE six pronoun systems
> 5. inconsistent usage.

A language, which according to Bavin (1992:267) is not yet a dying language, but which has nonetheless undergone significant changes and simplifications in its person agreement systems under the influence of Australian English, is Walpiri. Walpiri is currently still spoken by a relatively large community numbering around 3,000 persons. The most significant changes in the person system that have been observed are in the speech of children. Like many Australian languages, Walpiri has both independent person markers and clitic ones, the latter attached to an auxiliary base. In the traditional system there are twenty-one clitic forms for the S/A and for the P, some of which in transitive clauses are fused. Both in the independent forms and the clitics a distinction is made between singular, dual and plural in the first and second persons and in the first person there is an inclusive/exclusive opposition in the dual and plural.

Bavin reports on the results of a survey on person usage conducted among 166 Walpiri speakers. The survey revealed that all the speakers over the age of thirty-seven (around 40 persons), still utilize the full set of first-person independent and clitic forms, i.e. altogether fifteen forms, but no person under the age of seventeen does so. One of the reductions that has taken place in the person system of the younger speakers is loss of the inclusive/exclusive distinction. For example, of the 37 children between the ages of nine and sixteen, the use of the exclusive for the inclusive in the dual of independent forms occurred in 52.3 per cent of the speakers, in the plural of independent forms in 59.1 per cent of the speakers and in the dual of S/A clitics in 45.5 per cent of the speakers. The uses of the inclusive forms for exclusive were particularly notable in the P clitics; 52.3 per cent of the relevant speakers used inclusive forms for exclusive ones in the plural, and 29.5 per cent in the dual. Another change that has occurred is the substitution of the non-singular second-person forms by more morphologically transparent forms; instead of the traditional *nyumpala* and *nyurrula* the forms *nyuntu-jarra* and *nyuntu-rra* respectively are used, where *nyuntu* is the second-person singular form and *-jarra* and *-rra* the dual and plural markers used elsewhere in the grammar. A third notable difference that the survey revealed is the levelling of allomorphy of the second-person S/A clitic; 50 per cent of the younger speakers used the *-npa* allomorph in contexts where older speakers used the *-n* allomorph.

Reductions in person inventories including of person agreement systems may also be observed in pidgins and creoles relative to their lexifier languages. Several cases in point are discussed in Mühlhäusler and Harré (1990:ch. 10) and Aikhenvald (2000:398–9). For instance, whereas Standard Fijian has over 130 person forms, Plantation pidgin Fijian employs only 6. And while Kikongo displays person and gender/class agreement both with verbs and nouns, the creole based on it, Kituba, has no agreement.

The partial or complete loss of person paradigms (including of person agreement markers) or of semantic oppositions within paradigms is not an issue which has as yet been systematically explored. The assumption seems to be that the process of loss is not the mirror-image of developmental scenarios, since the factors underlying loss are essentially of an external, political/social nature rather than language internal. This may well be so. Nonetheless, the external nature of the factors underlying loss does not preclude there being any patterns in which forms or distinctions are lost. Whether there are indeed any remains for future research to reveal.

Appendix 1 List of languages in the sample by macro-area

Eurasia 55

Abkhaz, Ainu, Akkadian, Albanian, Armenian (Eastern), Basque, Brahui, Burushaski, Chepang, Chinese (Mandarin), Chukchi, Crimean Tatar, Dagur, Dong, Dutch, English, Evenki, Finnish, French, Garo, Georgian, German, Greek (Modern), Hindi, Hittite, Hungarian, Hunzib, Ingush, Irish, Italian, Japanese, Ju-chen, Kannada, Kashmiri, Ket, Khalkha, Korean, Kurdish (Central), Lak, Latvian, Lezgian, Mundari, Nenets, Nivkh, Ossetic, Persian, Polish, Remo, Russian, Spanish, Sumerian, Turkish, Udihe, Welsh, Yukaghir (Kolyma)

Africa 81

Amharic, Ani, Arabic (Egyptian), Babungo, Bagirmi, Bambara, Bari, Beja, Berta, Bilin, Bimoba, Boni(Jara), Burunge, Coptic, Dagaare, Diola-Fogny, Dizi, Dogon, Dongolese Nubian, Doyayo, Ewe, Fula, Fur, Geez, Grebo, Gude, Hamar, Hausa, Hebrew, Igbo, Iraqw, Kana, Kanuri, Katla, Kera, Kisi, Koh (Lakka), Kolokuma (Ijo), Koma, Kongo, Koromfe, Koyra Chiini, Kreol (Mauritian), Krongo, Kuku, Kunama, Lango, Lele, Luvale, Maale, Maba, Mbay, Mende, Mesalit, Mumuye, Mupun, Murle, Nama, Nandi, Ndonga, Ngiti, Nkore Kiga, Noon, Nupe, Oromo (Harar), Pari, Sandawe, Sango, So, Songhay (Koyraboro), Supyire, Swahili, Tamazight (Ayt Ndhir), Turkana, Wolaytta, !Xu, Yaoure, Yoruba, Zande, Zulu

South-East Asia and Oceania 62

Acehnese, Adzera, Anejom, Atayal, Bawm, Burmese, Byansi, Chamorro, Chrau, Dehu, Fijian, Hmong Njua, Indonesian, Kaliai Kove, Kapampangan, Karo Batak, Kayah Li, Khasi, Khmer, Khmu, Kilivila, Kiribatese, Konjo, Kusaiean, Ladakhi, Lahu, Larike, Lepcha, Limbu, Lolo (Nesu), Lushai, Malagasy, Maori, Meithei, Mlabri (Minor), Mono Alu, Muna, Nakanai, Paamese, Paiwan, Palauan, Rapanui, Rawang, Samoan, Savu, Sema, Semelai, Sundanese, Taba, Tagalog, Temiar, Thai, Tidore, Tinrin, Tolai, Tsou, Tukang-Besi, Uma, Ura, Vietnamese, Woleaian, Yapese

List of languages in the sample by macro-area   283

Australia and New Guinea   76

Abun, Alamblak, Amele, Anem, Arabana, Asmat, Au, Awtuw, Bandjalang, Barai, Broken, Bukiyip, Cape York Creole, Daga, Dani (Lower Grand Valley), Ekari, Gapun, Gooniyandi, Gumawana, Guugu Yimidhirr, Hatam, Hua, Imonda, Kalkatungu, Kapau, Kayardild, Kewa, Kobon, Koiali (Mountain), Koiari, Labu, Lavukaleve, Maisin, Makian (West), Malak Malak, Mangarayi, Maranungku, Marind, Martuthunira, Maung, Maybrat, Nasioi, Ngalakan, Ngankikurungkurr, Ngiyambaa, Nunggubuyu, Nyulnyul, Panyjima, Pitjantjatjara, Sahu, Salt (Yui), Selepet, Sentani, Suena, Tauya, Tawala, Tehit, Tigak, Tiwi, Una, Ungarinjin, Uradhi, Vanimo, Wambaya, Wambon, Wanuma, Wardaman, Waskia, Yava, Yeletnye, Yessan-Mayo, Yidin, Yimas, Yukulta, Yulparija, Yuwaalaraay

North America   68

Achumawi, Acoma, Atakapa, Cahuilla, Chalcatongo Mixtec, Chinantec Lealao, Chocho, Chumash Barbareño, Comanche, Comox, Copala-Trique, Cora, Cree (Plains), Greenlandic (West), Haida, Halkomelem, Hanis Coos, Jacaltec, Jamul Tiipay, Jicaque, Karok, Kiowa, Koasati, Kutenai, Lakota, Makah, Maricopa, Mohawk, Mountain Maidu, Navajo, Nez Perce, Nootka, Oneida, Otomi (Mezquital), Passamaquoddy, Pipil, Quileute, Salinan, Seri, Sierra Popoloca, Slave, South-eastern Pomo, Squamish, SS Miwok, Takelma, Tarascan, Tepehuan (Northern), Tetelcingo Nahuatl, Tlingit, Tonkawa, Totonac (Misantla), Tsimshian (Coast), Tunica, Tzutujil, Umpqua (Lower), Wappo, Wasco-Wishram, Washo, Wichita, Wikchamni, Wintun, Yaqui, Yuchi, Yupik, Yurok, Zapotec San Lucas, Zoque (Copainala), Zuni

South America   60

Abipon, Amuesha, Apurina, Araona, Arawak (Lokono Dian), Awa Pit, Aymara, Barasano, Bororo, Bribri, Campa (Axininca), Candoshi, Canela Kraho, Capanahua, Carib, Cavineña, Cayuvava, Chacobo, Cubeo, Epena Pedee, Guarani, Guaymi, Hixkaryana, Ika, Iquito, Jaqaru, Karitiana, Kawesqar, Kwaza, Macushi, Mapuche, Marubo, Mataco, Miskito, Mura Pirahã, Nadeb, Nambikuara, Ndyuka, Palikur, Paumari, Pech, Quechua Imbabura, Rama, Retuarã, Sanuma, Saramaccan, Selknam, Shipibo Konibo, Teribe, Tiriyo, Trumai, Uruubu Kaapor, Waorani, Warao, Warekena, Wari, Waura, Witoto (Muinan), Xokleng, Yagua

Appendix 2 Genetic classification of languages cited in the text

The genetic classification below is based on Ruhlen (1987) with modifications introduced by various scholars over the past two decades. The classification is somewhat simplified with various sub-branches removed. Some of the groupings in the classification are quite controversial. These are in italics. The actual languages cited are in bold.

KHOISAN
  Sandawe
  !UiTaa: Taa: **!Xu**
  Khoe:
    Kalahari: **Ani**
    Khoekhoe: **Eini, Nama, !Ora**

NIGER-KORDOFANIAN
  Kordofanian: **Katla, Krongo**
  Niger-Congo:
    Mande:
      Northern-Western: **Bambara, Kono, Kpelle**
      Southern-Eastern: **Boko, Bokobaru, Busa, Yaoure,**
    Niger-Congo Proper:
      West Atlantic:
        Northern: **Diola-Fogny, Fula, Wolof, Noon**
      Central Niger Congo:
        North Central Niger Congo:
          Kru: **Godie, Grebo**
          Dogon: **Dogon**
        Gur: **Dagbani, Supyire, Koromfe, Bimoba, Dagaare, Koma**
        Adamawa-Ubangian:
          Adamawa: **Doyayo, Koh Lakka, Mumuye, Yaga Dii**
          Ubangian: **Gbaya, Ngbaka, Sango, Zande**
      South Central Niger-Congo:
        Ijo-Defaka: **Kolokuma**
        Kwa (Western): **Ewe**

Eastern:
  Nupoid: **Nupe**
  Defoid: **Yoruba**
  Igboid: **Igbo**
  Cross: **Kana**
  Benue-Zambesi:
    Nyima: Plateau: **Fyem**
    Wel: Bantoid:
      Broad Bantu: Grassfields: **Babungo, Mundani**
      Narrow Bantu:
        Northwest Bantu: **Akɔɔse**
        Central Bantu: **Nyamwezi, Shambala, Swahili, Chi-Mwi:ni Kongo, Haya, Kinyarwanda, Luvale, Nkore Kiga, Bemba, Chichewa, Ndonga, Shona, Sotho, Zulu, Nkore Kiga**

NILO-SAHARAN
Songhai: **Koyra Chiini, Songhay (Koyraboro)**
Saharan: **Kanuri, Tuburi**
Maban: **Mesalit**
Fur: **Fur**
East Sudanic:
  Eastern:
    Nubian: **Dongolese Nubian**
    Surma: **Baale, Murle, Chai**
  Nilotic:
    Western: **Dho-Luo, Lango, Pari, Nuer**
    Eastern: **Bari, Kuku, Teso, Turkana**
    Southern: **Nandi**
Kuliak: **So**
Central Sudanic:
  West Central: Sara-Bagirmi: **Bagirmi, Mbay**
  East Central:
    Moru-Madi: **Moru, Avukaya, Keliko, Logo, Lugbara**
    Mangbetu-Efe: **Ngiti**
Berta: **Berta**
Kunama: **Kunama**

AFRO-ASIATIC
Ancient Egyptian: **Old Egyptian, Coptic**
Berber: Berber Proper:
  Tuareg: **Tăhăggart Berber, Tamachek Berber**
  Northern: **Kabyle, Ntifa, Shilha, Tamazight (Ayt Ndhir), Tarifit**

Chadic:
  East: **Kera, Lele**
  Biu-Mandara: Group A: **Margi, Mandara, Podoko, Daba, Gude**
  West: Group A: **Hausa, Angas, Kofyar, Mupun, Pero**
Omotic:
  South: **Ari, Galila, Dime, Hamar**
  North:
    Dizoid: **Dizi**
    Mao: **Hozo, Sezo**
    Gonga-Gimojan:
      Ometo-Gimira: **Gimira, Basketo, Maale, Wolaytta, Welamo, Amaaro, Koré, Zaysé**
Cushitic:
  Beja: **Beja**
  Cushitic Proper:
    Central: **Awngi, Bilin, Kemat**
    Eastern: **Burji, Boni (Jara), Dasenech, Oromo**
    Southern: **Burunge, Iraqw**
Semitic: West:
  Central:
    Aramaic: **Biblical Aramaic**
    Arabo-Canaanite: **Hebrew, Classical Arabic, Arabic (Egyptian, Gulf, Syrian)**
  South: Ethiopic: **Geez Amharic, Harari**

NAKH-DAGHESTANIAN
  Nakh: **Batsbi**
    Chechen-Ingush: **Ingush**
  Daghestanian
    Avro-Andi-Dido: **Avar, Zakatal', Akhvakh, Megreb, Hunzib, Tsez**
    Lak-Dargwa: **Lak, Dargwa**
    Lezgian: **Lezgian, Tsakhur**

NORTHWEST CAUCASIAN
  Abkhaz-Abaza: **Abaza, Abkhaz**

KARTVELIAN
  South: **Georgian**
  Zan: **Laz**

INDO-HITTITE
  Anatolian: **Hittite**
  Indo-European
    Armenian: **Modern Easter Armenian**

Indo-Iranian
  Indic
    Sinhalese-Maldiviab: **Colloquial Sinhalese, Literary Sinhalese**
    Northern India: **Kashmiri, Poguli, Marathi, Sindhi, Bangala,**
      Gujarati, Hindi, Punjabi, Nepali, Maithili, Oriya, Bengali
  Iranian: **Ossetic, Roshani, Kurdish, Persian**
Albanian: **Albanian**
Greek: **Ancient Greek, Modern Greek**
Italic:
  Latino-Faliscan: **Latin**
  Romance: **Sardinian, Rumanian, Italian, Romansch, French,**
    Portuguese, Brazilian Portuguese, Spanish
Celtic: Insular: **Breton, Irish, Welsh**
Germanic: **Gothic, Danish, Faroese, Icelandic, Norwegian,**
  Swedish, Afrikaans, Dutch, English, German (Standard, Bavarian),
  Swiss German
Balto-Slavic:
  Baltic: **Latvian, Lithuanian**
  Slavic: **Russian, Czech, Polish, Slovak, Upper Sorbian, Bulgarian,**
    Serbo-Croatian, Slovene

URALIC-YUKAGHIR
  Yukaghir: **Kolyma Yukaghir**
  Uralic:
    Samoyed: **Nenets**
    Finno-Ugric:
      Ugric: **Hungarian, Ostyak**
      Finnic:
        Permic: **Komi, Udmurt**
        Volgaic: **Erzya Mordvin, Mari**
        North Finnic: **Finnish, Estonian**

ALTAIC
  Turkic: **Turkish, Crimean Tatar**
  Mongolian-Tungus
  Mongolian: **Buryat, Daur, Khalka Mongolian**
  Tungus: **Evenki, Ju-Chen, Udihe**
  Korean-Japanese-Ainu
    Korean, Ainu
  Japanese-Ryukyuan: **Japanese**

CHUKCHI-KAMCHATKAN
  Chukchee

ESKIMO-ALEUT
  Aleut: **Aleut**
  Eskimo:
    Inuit: **West Greenlandic**
    Yupik: **Central Yupik**

ELAMO-DRAVIDIAN
  Dravidian Proper
    Central: **Kolami, Telugu**
    South Tamil-Kannada: **Kannada, Tamil, Malayalam**

SINO-TIBETAN
  Sinitic Chinese: **Mandarin**
  Tibeto-Karen
    Karen: Sgaw-Bwe: **Sgaw Karen, Kayah Li**
    Tibeto-Burman
      Qiangic: **Tangut**
  Bodic
    Digaro-Midu: Idu-Digaru: **Idu**
    Dhimal-KhamToto: **Dhimal**
    Adi-Nishi: **Lepcha**
    Bodish: **Jiarong, Classical Tibetan, Lhasa Tibetan**
    Central Himalayan: **Chepang, Kham (Gamale, Takale)**
    West Himalayan: **Kinnauri, Byangsi, Darmiya, Gahri, PaTani, Rangpa, Tinani**
    East Himalayan: **Hayu, Yamphu, Athpare, Belhare, Chamling, Limbu**
  Baric
    Bodo-Garo: **Garo, Kokborok**
    Chang-Tangsa: **Nocte**
  Burmic
    Kuki-Naga: **Bawm Meithei, Mikir**
      Naga: **Chang, Khiamnungan, Konyak, Sema**
      Kuki-Chin: **Mizo, Tiddim**
    Kachin-Luic: **Rawang**
    Burmese-Moso: Burmese-Lolo
      Burmic: **Atsi, Burmese, Maru, Pola**
      Lolo: **Nosu, Sani, Jinuo, Lahu, Akha**

AUSTRIC
  Austroasiatic:
    Munda: **Mundari, Santali**

Genetic classification of languages cited in the text

Mon-Khmer:
  North: **Khasi, Khmu, Vietnamese**
  East: **Katu, Chrau, Sedang, Khmer**
  South: Aslian: Semang-Senoic: **Semelai**

Austro-Thai:
  Daic: Li-Kam-Tai: Be-Kam-Tai: **Thai**
  Austronesian:
    Tsouic: **Tsou**
    Paiwanic: **Paiwan**
    Malayo-Polynesian:
      Western Malayo-Polynesian: **Chamorro, Palauan, Yapese**
        Northern Philippines: **Illocano, Pangasinan, Kapampangan**
        Meso-Philippine: Central Philippine: **Tagalog**
        Celebes: **Uma, Padoe, Konjo, Muna, Tukang Besi, Malagasy**
        Sundic: **Javanese, Karo Batak, Toba Batak, Madurese, Minangkabau, Indonesian, Acehnese**
      Central-Eastern Malayo-Polynesian:
      Central Malayo-Polynesian:
      Central Maluku: East: Seram: **Nuaulu, Larike**
      Southeast-Maluku: **Kei**
      Timor-Flores: **Maumere, Fehan, Kisar**
      Bima-Sumba: **Kamberra**
    Eastern Malayo-Polynesian:
      South Halmahera-Northwest New Guinea: South Halmahera-Geelvink Bay:
      South Halmahera: **East Makian**
      Geelvink Bay: **Biak, Wandamen**
      Oceanic: **Maisin**
        Siassi:
          Sepik-Madang: Sepik: Eastern: **Kariru, Manam**
          Rai Coast-Northwest New Britain:
            Bariai-Ngero: **Kabana, Kove, Lusi**
            Huon Gulf: **Jabem, Labu**
        Milne Bay – Central Province: Milne Bay: Western: **Gapapaiwa, Gumawana, Tawala, Kilivila**
        Kimbe: **Nakanai**
        New Britain: **Bali Vitu**
        New Ireland: **Lihir, Sursurunga, Tolai, Tigak, Mussau**
        Admirality Islands: Eastern: **Manus: Loniu**
        Bougainville: East: **Mono Alu**
        New Georgia: **Roviana**
        Santa Isabel: **Kokota**
        Santa Cruz: **Asumboa, Buma, Tanimbili**

Southern New Hebrides: **Anejom, Sye (Erromangan), Ura, Southwest Tanna**
New Caledonia: Southern: South: **Tinrin**
Loyalty Islands: **Iai, Dehu, Nengone**
Remote Oceanic:
    Micronesian: **Gilbertese, Kiribatese, Kusaiean, Ponapean, Pulo Annian, Puluwat, Trukese**
    Southeastern Solomons: **Gela, Kwaio**
    Central and Northeastern New Hebrides: **Big Nambas, Vinmavis, Mota, Raga, Paamese**
    Central Pacific:
        Rotuman-Fijian: **Fijian**
        Polynesian: **Samoan, Tikopia, Tuvaluan, Rapanui, Maori**

INDO-PACIFIC
Trans-New Guinea:
Main Section:
    Central and Western New Guinea:
        Finisterre-Huon: Huon: **Kâte, Ono, Selepet**
        East New Guinea Highlands: **Kobon, Gadsup, Tairora, Bena Bena, Fore, Kamanugu, Kuman, Salt Yui, Enga, Kewa**
        Central and South New Guinea: **Asmat, Kombai, Wambon**
        Angan: **Kapau, Menya**
        Marind: **Marind**
        Sentani: **Sentani**
        Dani-Kwebra: **Grand Valley Dani**
        Wissel Lakes-Kemandoga: Ekagi-Wodani-Moni: **Ekari**
    Eastern:
        Binanderean: **Suena**
        Koiarian: **Koiari, Mountain Koiali, Barai**
        Dagan: **Daga**
    Madang-Adelbert Range:
        Madang: Mabuso: Gum: **Amele**
        Adelbert Range: **Mauwake, Wanuma, Waskia, Tauya**
    Eleman: **Tate**
        Mek: **Una**
        Northern: **Imonda, Berik**
        Nimboran: **Mlap, Kemtuik**
        Timor-Alor-Pantar: **Kolana**
    West Papuan: **Maybrat**
        Bird's Head: West: **Tehit**
        Borai-Hatam: **Hatam**

Northern Halmahera: **West Makian**
  North: **Sahu, Ternate, Tidore**
  Northeast: **Pagu, Tobelo, Galele, Loloda, Modole, Tabaru**
Geelvink Bay: **Yava**
Sko: Vanimo: **Vanimo**
Torricelli: **Au, Bukuyip**
Sepik-Ramu: **Gapun**
  Sepik: **Awtuw, Yessan Mayo, Alamblak**, Ndu: **Abelam, Boikim, Iatmul, Manambu, Ngala, Yelogu**
  Nor-Pondo: Pondo: **Yimas**
East Papuan:
  Yele-Solomons–New Britain:
    Yele-Solomons: **Yele, Baniata, Lavukaleve, Anêm**
    Bougainville: East: **Nasioi**
    Reef Islands–Santa Cruz: **Reefs, Nanggu**

AUSTRALIAN
  Anindilyakwa, Mangarayi, Murinypatya, Ndjébbana, Nunggubuyu, Tiwi, Yanyuwa
  Yiwaidjan: **Ilgar, Maung**
  Gunwinyguan: **Jawony, Rembarnga, Ngalakan, Ngandi**
    Gunwinygic: **Gunwinggu, Bininj Gun-wok**
    Yangmanic: **Wardaman**
  Burarran: **Burarra**
  Maran: **Alawa, Mara**
  West Barkly: Wambayan: **Wambaya**
  Garawan: **Garawa**
  Daly: **Ngankikurrungkur, Maranungku, Malak Malak**
  Bunaban: **Bunuba, Gooniyandi**
  Nyulnyulan: **Nyulnyul, Warra**
  Wororan: **Ungarinjin, Worora**
  Pama-Nyungan: **Kalaw Kawaw Ya, Bandjalang, Wangaybuwan**
    Yuulngu: **Djinang, Dhuwal, Djambarrpuyngu, Ritharngu**
    Tangic: **Kayardild, Lardil, Yukulta**
    Paman: **Uradhi, Nganhcara, Wik Munkan**
    Yalanjic: **Guugu Yimidhirr, Gugu Yalanji**
    Yidinyic: **Djabugay, Yidin**
    Maric: Mari: **Biri, Gunya, Margany**
    Gumbaynggiric: **Gumbaynggir**
    Wiradhuric: **Ngiyambaa**
    Ngarinyeric-Yithayityhic: **Narinjari**
    Karnic: **Arabana, Wangkangurru, Badjiri, Wangkumara**

Wagaya-Warluwaric: Wagaya: **Wagaya**
Kalkatungic: **Kalkatungu**
South-West: **Djaru, Gurindji, Walmatharri, Nyangumarta
Ngarluma, Panyjima, Yingkarta, Wajarri, Pitjantjatjara, Pintupi,
Yulparija, Walpiri, Adynyamathanha, Kuyani**

NA-DENE
  Haida
  Continental Na-Dene:
    Tlingit
    Athabaskan-Eyak: Athabaskan: **Lower Umpqua, Slave, Navajo**

AMERIND
  North Amerind:
    Almosan-Keresiouan:
      Almosan: **Kutenai**
        Algic:
          Algonquian: Algonquian Proper: **Cree, Passamaquoddy**
        Mosan:
          Chimakuan: **Quileute**
          Wakashan: **Makah, Nootka**
          Salish: Salish Proper:
            Coast: **Comox, Squamish, Halkomelem, North Straits**
            Interior: **Lillooet, Colville, Okanagan, Kalispel**
      Keresiouan:
        Keresan: **Acoma**
        Siouan-Yuchi: **Yuchi, Assiniboine, Biloxi, Lakhota**
        Caddoan: **Caddo, Wichita**
        Iroquoian: Northern: **Mohawk, Oneida, Tuscarora**
    Penutian:
      Coast Penutian: **Coast Tsimshian**
        Chinookan: **Upper Chinook, Wasco-Wishram**
        Oregon: **Takelma, Hanis Coos**
        Plateau: Sahaptin – Nez Perce: **Sahaptin, Nez Perce**
        California:
          Wintun: **Wintun**
          Maiduan: **Mountian Maidu**
          Miwok: **Southern Sierra Miwok**
        New Mexico: **Zuni**
        Gulf:
          Tunica-Chitimacha: **Chitimacha, Tunica, Atakapa**
          Yuki-Wappo: **Wappo**
          Natchez-Muskogean: Muskogean: **Choctaw, Creek, Alabama,
            Koasati, Hitchiti**

Mexican:
   Totonacan: **Misantla Totonac**
   Mixe-Zoque: **Sayula Popoluca, Sierra Popoluca, Copainala Zoque**
   Mayan:
     Huastecan: **Huastec**
     Yucatecan: **Itza Mayan**
     Greater Tzeltalan: Cholan: **Chorti**
     Greater Kanjobalan: Kanjobalan: **Acatec, Jacaltec**
     Eastern: **Mam: Sacapultec, Tzutujil**

Hokan
  Northern: **Achumawi, Eastern Pomo, Southeastern Pomo, Central Pomo, Washo**
  Salinan-Chumash: **Salinan, Chumash**
  Seri-Yuman, **Seri, Maricopa, Jamul Tiipay, Walapai**
  Coahuiltecan: **Tonkawa**
  Southern: **Jicaque, Tlappanec**

Central Amerind:
  Tanoan: Kiowa-Towa: **Kiowa**
  Uto-Aztecan:
    Numic: **Comanche, Kawaiisu**
    Takic: Cupan: **Cahuilla**
    Pimic: **Papago, Northern Tepehuan, Southeastern Tepehuan**
    Taracahitic: **Yaqui**
    Corachol: **Cora**
    Aztecan: **Pipil, Nahuatl, Tetelcingo Nahuatl**
  Oto-Manguean:
    Otomian: **Pame**
    Mixtecan: **Copola Trique, Chalcatongo Mixtec, Ocotepec Mixtec, Silacayoapan Mixtec**
    Popolocan: **Mazatec, Chocho**
    Chinantecan: **Lealao Chinantec**
    Zapotecan: **San Lucas Zapotecan**

Chibchan-Paezan:
  Chibchan: **Tarascan, Pech**
  Yanoman: **Yanomani, Sanuma**
Nuclear Chibchan:
  Misumalpan: **Miskito, Northern Sumu**
  Talamanca: **Teribe**
  Rama: **Rama**
  Aruak: **Chimilla, Ika, Kogu, Damana**
  Cuna: **Cuna**
  Chibchan Proper: **Musica-Duit, Tunebo**

Pazean: **Warao, Itonama**
Mura: **Mura Pirahã**
Nuclear Pazean: Barbacoan: **Awa Pitt**
Andean:
  Urarina-Waorani: **Waorani**
  Cahuapanan-Zaparoan: Zaparoan: **Iquito**
  Quechuan: **Imbabura Quechua, Cuzco, Inga**
  Aymaran: **Aymara, Jaqaru**
  Southern: **Mapuche, Kawesquar, Selknam**

Equatorial-Tucanoan:
  Macro-Tucanoan: **Kwaza**
    Nambiquaran: **Nambiquara**
    Puinave-Maku: Maku: **Kakua**
    Tucanoan: **East Tucano, Tuyuca, Southern Barasano, Cubeo, Retuarã**
  Equatorial: **Trumai**
    Jivoran: **Achuar, Candoshi**
    Kariri-Tupi: Tupi:
      Arikem: **Karitiana**
      Tupi-Guarani: **Wayampi, Kamaiura, Guajajara, Guarani, Munduruku**
    Macro-Arawakan: Arawakan:
      Arawan: **Arawa, Paumari, Sorowaha**
      Chapacuran: **Wari, Uruubu Kaapor**
      Maipuran:
        Parecis-Sereveca: **Parecis**
        Pre-Andine: **Amuesha, Apurina, Asheninca, Campa**
        Eastern: **Palikur, Waura, !Yawalapiti**
        Northern: **Carib, Resigaro, Warekena, Bare, Arawak (Lokonong Djang), Tariana**

Ge-Pano-Carib:
  Macro-Carib:
    Peba-Yaguan: **Yagua**
    Bora-Witotan: **Bora, Ocaina, Muinan Witoto, Murui Witoto**
    Carib:
      Northern: **Galibi, Garifuna, Apalai, Tiriyo, Waiwai, Macushi**
      Southern: **Hishkaryana**
  Ge-Pano:
    Macro-Panoan:
      Mataco-Guaicuru: **Mataco**
      Pano-Tacana: Panoan: **Chacobo: Capanahua, Marubo**
    Macro-Ge: **Rikbaktsa, Guato, Karaja, Kipea, Yate**
    Bororo: **Bororo**

Ge-Kaingang:
    Kaingang: **Kaingang, Xokleng**
    Ge: **Canela Kraho, Timbíra, Xerente**

ISOLATES
Basque, Burushaski, Ket, Nivikh, Sumerian

CREOLES
    Kituba (Kikongo based, Africa), **Mauritian Kreol, Ndyuka**

References

For a more complete bibliography see:
http://www.ling.lancs.ac.uk/staff/anna/anna.htm

Abbott, Miriam. 1991. Macushi. In: Desmond Derbyshire and Geoffrey Pullum (eds.), vol. III, 23–160.
Acharya, Jayaraj. 1991. *A Descriptive Grammar of Nepali and an Analyzed Corpus.* Washington DC: Georgetown University Press.
Adelaar, Willem F. H. 2002. Solving the South American puzzle: a reappraisal of basic lexicon comparison in genealogical linguistics. Paper presented at The Language Blueprint Workshop, Nias, Wassennar, 11–13 January 2002.
Agee, Daniel and Marlett, Stephen. 1987. Indirect objects and incorporation in Mazatec. *Working Papers of the Summer Institute of Linguistics. University of North Dakota*, 59–76.
Aikhenvald, Alexandra Y. 1995. *Bare*. Munich: Lincom Europa.
   1998. Warekena. In: Desmond C. Derbyshire and Geoffrey K. Pullum (eds.), *Handbook of Amazonian Languages*, vol. IV. Berlin: Mouton de Gruyter, 225–439.
   2000. *Classifiers*. (Oxford Studies in Typology and Linguistic Theory) Oxford: Oxford University Press.
Aikhenvald, Alexandra Y. and Dixon, R. M. W. 1999. Other small families and isolates. In: R. M. W. Dixon and Alexandra Y. Aikhenvald (eds.), 341–84.
Alexander, Ruth Mary. 1988. A syntactic sketch of Ocotepec Mixtec. In: C. Henry Bradley and Barbara E. Holenbach (eds.), *Studies in the Mixtecan Languages*. Dallas: Summer Institute of Linguistics and University of Texas at Arlington, 151–304.
Allan, Keith. 2001. *Natural Language Semantics*. Oxford: Blackwell.
Allan, Robin., Holmes, Philip and Lundskær-Nielsen, Tom. 1995. *Danish: A Comprehensive Grammar*. London and New York: Routledge.
Ambrazas, Vytautas (ed.). 1997. *Lithuanian Grammar*. Vilnius: Baltos Lankos.
Ameka, Felix. 1996. Body parts in Ewe grammar. In: Hilary Chappell and William McGregor (eds.), 783–840.
Amha, Azeb. 2001. *The Maale Language*. Leiden: CNWS Publications.
Amritavalli, R. 2000. Lexical anaphors and pronouns in Kannada. In: Barbara C. Lust et al. (eds.), 49–112.
Anagnostopoulou, Elena. 1999. Conditions on clitic doubling in Greek. In: Henk van Riemsdijk (ed.), 762–98.
Andersen, Torben. 1988. Ergativity in Pari, a Nilotic OVS language. *Lingua* 75:289–324.
Anderson, Stephen R. 1993. Wackernagel's revenge: clitics, morphology, and the syntax of second position. *Language* 69:68–98.
Ariel, Mira. 1990. *Accessing Noun Phrase Antecedents*. London: Croom Helm.
   2000. The development of person agreement markers: from pronouns to higher accessibility markers. In: M. Barlow and S. Kemmer (eds.), *Usage-Based Models of Language*. Stanford: CSIL Publications, 197–260.

Asher, R. E. 1982. *Tamil* (Descriptive Grammars Series). London: Croom Helm.
Asher, R. E. and Kumari, T. C. 1997. *Malayalam* (Descriptive Grammars Series). London: Routledge.
Ashton, E. O. 1944. *Swahili Grammar.* Second Edition. London: Longmans, Green Camp Co.
Austin, Peter and Bresnan, Joan. 1996. Nonconfigurationality in Australian Aboriginal languages. *Natural Language and Linguistic Theory* 14:215–68.
Baker, Mark. 1996. *The Polysynthesis Parameter.* Oxford: Oxford University Press.
Banfield, Ann. 1982. *Unspeakable Sentences. Narration and Representation in the Language of Fiction.* Boston: Routledge and Keagan Paul.
Bavin, Edith. 1992. Some lexical and morphological changes in Walpiri. In: Nancy. C. Dorian (ed.), *Investigating Obsolescence. Studies in Language Contraction and Death.* Cambridge: Cambridge University Press, 267–86.
Beaumont, Clive H. 1979. *The Tigak Language of New Ireland* (Pacific Linguistics, B-58). Canberra: ANU.
Bender, Lionel M. 1996. *Kunama.* Munich: Lincom Europa.
  2000. *Comparative Morphology of the Omotic Languages.* Munich: Lincom Europa.
Benveniste, Emile. 1971. *Problems in General Linguistics.* Translated by Mary Elizabeth Meek. Cora Gables, FA: University of Miami Papers.
Besnier, Niko. 2000. *Tuvaluan* (Descriptive Grammars Series). London: Routledge.
Beyer, Stephan 1992. *The Classical Tibetan Language.* Albany, NY: State University of New York Press.
Bhatt, D. N. S. Forthcoming. *Pronouns.* Oxford: Oxford University Press.
Bhatia, Tej K. 2000. Lexical anaphors and pronouns in Punjabi. In: Barabara C. Lust et al. (eds.), 637–714.
Biber, Douglas, Johansson, Stig, Leech, Geoffery, Conrad, Susan and Finegan, Edward. 1999. *Longman Grammar of Spoken and Written English.* London: Longman.
Bickel, Balthasar. 2001. Introduction: Person and evidence in Himalayan languages. *Linguistics of the Tibeto-Burman Area* 23.2:1–11.
Bickel, Balthasar, Bisang, Walter and Yadava, Yongreda, P. 1999. Face vs empathy: the social foundation of Maithili verb agreement. *Linguistics* 37:481–518.
Bitner, Maria and Hale, Ken. 1996. Ergativity: toward a theory of heterogeneous class. *Linguistic Inquiry* 27.4:531–604.
Blackwell, Sarah, E. 2000. Anaphora interpretations in Spanish utterances and the neo-Gricean pragmatic theory. *Journal of Pragmatics* 32:389–424.
Blake, Frank R. 1934. The origins of pronouns of the first and second person. *American Journal of Philology* 55:244–8.
Blake, Barry J. 1977. *Case Marking in Australian Languages.* Canberra: ANU.
  1990. The significance of pronouns in the history of Australian languages. In: Philip Baldi (ed.), *Linguistic Change and Reconstruction Methodology.* Berlin: Mouton de Gruyter, 435–50.
Blansitt, Edward L. 1988. Datives and allatives. In: Michael Hammond, Edith A. Morarcsik and Jossica R. Worth (eds.) *Studies in Syntactic Typology.* Amsterdam: John Benjamins, 175–91.
Blood, Cindy. 1992. Subject-verb agreement in Kisar. *NUSA, Linguistic Studies of Indonesia and Other Languages in Indonesia* vol. 34, Jakarta: Badan Penyelenggara NUSA, 1–21.
Blondeau, Hélène. 2001. Real-time changes in the paradigm of personal pronouns in Montreal French. *Journal of Sociolinguistics* 5/4:453–74.
Bodomo, Adams. 1997. *The Structure of Dagaare.* Stanford: CSLI Publications.
Borgman, Donald M. 1990. Sanuma. In: Desmond C. Derbyshire and Geoffrey K. Pullum (eds.), vol. II, 15–248.
Bradley, David. 1993. Pronouns in Burmese-Lolo. *Linguistics in the Tibeto-Burman Area* 16.1:157–215.

Braun, Friederike. 1988. *Terms of Address: Problems of Patterns and Usage in Various Languages and Cultures*. Berlin and New York: Mouton de Gruyter.
Breen, Gavin. 1976. Wagaya. In: R. M. W. Dixon (ed.), 590–4.
  1981. Margany and Gunya. In: R. M. W. Dixon and Barry J. Blake (eds.), *Handbook of Australian Aboriginal Languages*, vol. II. Canberra: ANU, 275–351.
Breeze, Mary J. 1986. Personal pronouns in Gimira. In: Ursula Wiesemann (ed.), 47–70.
Bresnan, Joan. 1987. LSA Summer Institute classes lectures. Stanford University.
  2001a. *Lexical Functional Grammar*. Malden, MA and Oxford: Basil Blackwell.
  2001b. The emergence of the unmarked pronoun. In: Geraldine Legendre, Jane Grimsha and Stig Vikner (eds.), *Optimality-Theoretic Syntax*. Cambridge, MA: MIT Press, 113–42.
Bresnan, Joan and Mchombo, Sam A. 1987. Topic, pronoun and agreement in Chichewa. *Language* 63:741–82.
Brown, Cheryl. 1983. Topic continuity in written English. In: T. Givón (ed.), 313–63.
Brown, Penelope and Levinson, Stephen. 1987. *Politeness: Some Universals in Language Usage*. Cambridge: Cambridge University Press.
Brown, Roger. 1965. *Social Psychology*. New York: The Free Press.
Brown, Roger and Gilman, Albert. 1960. The pronouns of power and solidarity. In: Thomas Sebeok (ed.), *Style in Language*. London: Wiley and Sons, 253–76.
Burquest, Donald A. 1986. The pronoun system of Chadic languages. In: Ursula Wiesemann (ed.), 70–102.
Burridge, Kate. 1996. Yulparija sketch grammar. In: W. McGregor (ed.), 15–69.
Burzio, Luigi. 1998. Anaphora and soft constraints. In: Pilar Barbarosa, Danny Fox, Paul Hagstrom et al. (eds.) *Is the Best Good Enough? Optimality and Competition in Syntax*. Cambridge, MA: MIT Press, 93–113.
Bybee, Joan. L. 1985. *Morphology*. Amsterdam: John Benjamins.
Bybee, Joan L. and Hopper, Paul (eds.). 2001. *Frequency and the Emergence of Linguistic Structure*. Amsterdam: John Benjamins.
Bybee, Joan L., Pagliuca, William and Perkins, Revere. 1990. On the asymmetries in the affixation of grammatical material. In: W. Croft, K. Denning and S. Kemmer (eds.), *Studies in Typology and Diachrony*. Amsterdam: John Benjamins, 1–42.
  1991. Back to the future. In: Elizabeth Closs Traugott and Bernd Heine (eds.), 17–58.
Camp, Elizabeth and Liccardi, Millicent. 1967. Itonama. In: Esther Matteson (ed.), *Bolivian Indian Grammars*, vol. II. Norman: Summer Institute of Linguistics and the University of Oklahoma, 257–351.
Campbell, Lyle. 1985. *The Pipil Language of El Salvador*. New York: Mouton.
  1997. Amerind personal pronouns: a second opinion. *Language* 73.2:339–51.
Capell, A. 1969a. *A Survey of New Guinea Languages*. Sydney: Sydney University Press.
  1969b. The structure of the Binandere verb. *Papers in New Guinea Linguistics* 9:1–32 (Pacific Linguistics, C-38). Canberra: ANU.
Cardinaletti, Anna and Starke, Michael. 1999. The typology of structural deficiency. In: Henk van Riemsdijk (ed.), 145–233.
Carlin, Eithne. 1993. *The So Language*. Cologne: Institute of African Studies, University of Cologne.
Casad, E. H. 1984. Cora. In: Ronald W. Langacker (ed.), *Studies in Uto-Aztecan Grammar*, vol. IV. Dallas: Summer Institute of Linguistics and University of Texas at Arlington, 151–459.
Caughley, Ross. C. 1982. *The Syntax and Morphology of the Verb in Chepang* (Pacific Linguistics, B-84). Canberra: ANU.
Chafe, Wallace L. 1976. *The Caddoan, Iroquoian and Siouan Languages*. The Hague: Mouton.
  1977. The evolution of third person verb agreement in the Iroquoian languages. In: Charles N. Li (ed.), 493–524.

1990. Use of defocusing prefixes in Caddo. *Anthropological Linguistics* 32:57–68.
Chaker, Salem. 1983. *Un Parler Berbere D'Algerie* (Kabylie). Aix en Provence: Publications Université de Provence.
Chapman, Shirley and Derbyshire, Desmond C. 1991. Paumari. In: Desmond C. Derbyshire and Geoffrey K. Pullum (eds.), vol III, 161–351.
Chappell, Hilary and McGregor, William (eds.). 1996a. *The Grammar of Inalienability*. Berlin: Mouton de Gruyter.
   1996b. Introduction. In: Hilary Chappell and William McGregor (eds.), 3–30.
Chomsky, Noam. 1981. *Lectures on Government and Binding*. Dordrecht: Foris.
Chung, Sandra. 1984. Identifiability and null objects in Chamorro. *Proceedings of the Annual Meeting of the Berkeley Linguistic Society* 10:116–30.
Cinque, Guglielmo. 1999. *Adverbs and Functional Heads: A Cross-Linguistic Perspective*. New York: Oxford University Press.
Clements, George N. 1975. The logophoric pronoun in Ewe: its role in discourse. *Journal of West African Linguistics* 10.2:141–77.
Comrie, Bernard. 1981. *Language Universals and Linguistic Typology*. Chicago: University of Chicago Press.
   2001. Recipient person suppletion in the verb "give". Paper given at the 4th International Meeting of the Association of Linguistic Typology, Santa Barbara, 19–23 July 2001.
Cook, Walter A. 1965. A descriptive grammar of Mundari. PhD dissertation, Georgetown University.
Cooke, Joseph R. 1968. *Pronominal Reference in Thai, Burmese, and Vietnamese*. (University of California Publications in Linguistics, 52). Berkeley: University of California Press.
Cooreman, Anne. 1988. The antipassive in Chamorro: variations on the theme of transitivity. In: Masayoshi Shibatani (ed.), *Passive and Voice*. Amsterdam: John Benjamins, 561–94.
Corbett, Greville. 1991. *Gender*. Cambridge: Cambridge University Press.
   2000. *Number*. Cambridge: Cambridge University Press.
Cornish, Francis. 1999. *Anaphora, Discourse and Understanding*. Oxford: Oxford University Press.
Corston, S. H. 1998. *Ergativity in Roviana, Solomon Islands* (Pacific Linguistics, B-113). Canberra: ANU.
Cowan, H. K. J. 1965. *Grammar of the Sentani Language*. The Hague: Martinus Nijhoff.
Craig, Collette C. 1977. *The Structure of Jacaltec*. Austin: University of Texas Press.
Croft, William. 1990. *Typology and Universals*. Cambridge: Cambridge University Press.
   2000. *Explaining Language Change*. London: Longman.
Crowley, Terry. 1983. Uradhi. In: R. M. W. Dixon and Barry J. Blake, (eds.), *Handbook of Australian Languages*, vol. III. Amsterdam: John Benjamins,
   1996. Inalienable possession in Paamese grammar. In: Hillary Chappell and William McGregor (eds.), 383–464.
   1998. *An Erromangan (Sye) Grammar*. Honolulu: University of Hawaii Press.
   2002a. *Serial Verbs in Oceanic. A Descriptive Typology*. Oxford: Oxford University Press.
   2002b. Vinmavis. In: John Lynch, Malcolm Ross and Terry Crowley (eds.), *The Oceanic Languages*. Richmond: Curzon, 638–49.
Culy, Christopher. 1997. Logophoric pronouns and point of view. *Linguistics* 35:845–59.
Curnow, Timothy J. 1997. A grammar of Awa Pit (Cuaiquer): an indigenous language of south-western Colombia. University Ph.D. dissertation, Australian National University.
Cysouw, Michael. 2000. The paradigmatic structure of person marking. PhD dissertation, Catholic University of Nijmegen.
Das Gupta, K. 1971. *An Introduction to the Nocte Language*. Shillong: North-East Frontier Agency.
Davies, John. 1981. *Kobon* (Descriptive Grammar Series). Amsterdam: North Holland.

Dench, Alan. 1998. *Yingkarta*. Munich: Lincom Europa.
Derbyshire Desmond C. and Pullum, Geoffrey K. (eds.). 1986. *Handbook of Amazonian Languages*, vol. I Berlin: Mouton de Gruyter.
(eds.). 1990. *Handbook of Amazonian Languages*, vol. II Berlin: Mouton de Gruyter.
(eds.). 1991. *Handbook of Amazonian Languages*, vol. III Berlin: Mouton de Gruyter.
Dik, S. C. 1989. *The Theory of Functional Grammar. Part 1. The Clause*. Dordrecht: Foris.
Dimitrova-Vulchanova, Mila and Hellan, Lars. 1999. Clitics and Bulgarian clause structure. In: Henk van Riemsdijk (ed.), 469–514.
Dimmendaal, Gerrit J. and Last, Marco (eds.). 1998. *Surmic Languages and Cultures*. Cologne Rüdiger Köppe Verlag.
Dixon, R. M. W. (ed.). 1976. *Grammatical Categories in Australian Languages*. Canberra: Australian Institute of Aboriginal Studies.
1988. *A Grammar of Boumaa Fijian*. Chicago: University of Chicago Press.
1999. Arawá. In: R. M. W. Dixon and Alexandra. Y. Aikhenvald (eds.), 293–306.
Dixon, R. M. W and Aikhenvald, Alexandra Y. (eds.). 1999. *The Amazonian Languages*. Cambridge: Cambridge University Press.
(eds.) 2002. *Word. A Cross-Linguistic Typology*. Cambridge: Cambridge University Press.
Długosz-Kurczabowa, Krystyna and Dubisz, Stanislaw. 1999. *Grammatyka Historyczna Jçzyka Polskiego*. Warsaw: Warsaw University Press.
Doble, Marion. 1987. A description of some features of Ekari language structure. *Oceanic Linguistics* 26:55–113.
Dol, Philomena. 1999. A grammar of Maybrat: a language of the Bird's Head, Irian Jaya, Indonesia. PhD dissertation, University of Leiden.
Donaldson, Bruce C. 1993. *A Grammar of Afrikaans*. Berlin: Mouton de Gruyter.
Donohue, Mark. 1999. *A Grammar of Tukang Besi*. Berlin: Mouton de Gruyter.
Donohue, Mark and Smith, John Charles. 1998. What's happened to us? Some developments in the Malay pronoun system. *Oceanic Linguistics* 37:65–84.
Dressler, Wolfgang U. and Barbaresi, Lavina Merlini. 1994. *Morphopragmatics. Diminutives and Intensifiers in Italian, German, and Other Languages*. Berlin: Mouton de Gruyter.
Dryer, Matthew S. 1986. Primary objects, secondary objects, and the antidative. *Language* 62:808–45.
Du Bois, John W. 1987. The discourse basis of ergativity. *Language* 63.4:805–55.
Du Feu, Veronica. 1996. *Rapanui* (Descriptive Grammars Series). London: Routledge.
Duranti, Alessandro. 1979. Object clitic pronouns in Bantu and the topicality hierarchy. *Studies in African Linguistics* 10:31–45.
1984. The social meaning of subject pronouns in Italian conversation. *Text* 4.4:277–311.
Durie, Mark. 1985. *A Grammar of Acehnese*. Cinnaminson: Foris.
Dutton, Tom E. 1996. *Koiari*. Munich: Lincom Europa.
Dutton, Tom E. and Tryon, Darrell T. (eds.). 1994. *Language Contact and Change in the Austronesian World*. Berlin: Mouton de Gruyter.
Eades, D. 1979. Gumbaynggir. In: R. M. W. Dixon and Barry J. Blake (eds.), *Handbook of Australian Languages*, vol. II. Canberra: ANU, 244–361.
Ebert, Karen H. 1990. On evidence for the relationship Kiranti-Rung. *Linguistics of the Tibeto-Burman Area* 13.1:57–78.
Eckert, Paul, and Hudson, Joyce. 1988. *Wangka Wiru: A Handbook for the Pitjantjatjara Language Learner*. Underdale, Australia: Aboriginal Studies and Teacher Education Centre.
England, Nora. 1983. *A Grammar of Mam, a Mayan Language*. Austin: University of Texas Press.
Erguvanli-Taylan, Eser. 1986. Pronominal versus zero representation of anaphora in Turkish. In: Dan Isaac Slobin and Karl Zimmer (eds.), *Studies in Turkish Linguistics*. Amsterdam: John Benjamins, 209–31.
Evans, Nicholas D. 1995. *A Grammar of Kayardild*. Berlin: Mouton de Gruyter.

2000. Iwaidjan, a very un-Australian language family. *Linguistic Typology* 4.1:91–142.
2002. The true status of grammatical object affixes: evidence from Bininj Gun-wok. In Nicholas Evans and Hans-Jürgen Sasse (eds.), *Problems of Polysynthesis*. Berlin: Akademie Verlag, 15–50.
Everett, Daniel L. 1986. Piraha. In: Desmond C. Derbyshire and Geoffrey K. Pullum (eds.), vol. I, 200–325.
Everett, Daniel L. and Kern, Barbara. 1997. *Wari* (Descriptive Grammars Series). London: Routledge.
Everaert, Martin. 2000. Types of anaphoric expressions: reflexives and reciprocals. In: Z. Frajzyngier (ed.), *Reciprocals. Forms and Functions*. Amsterdam: John Benjamins, 63–83.
Ezard, Bryan. 1997. *A Grammar of Tawala* (Pacific Linguistics, C-137). Canberra: ANU.
Facundes, Sidney. 2000. The language of the Apurina people of Brazil. PhD dissertation, State University of New York, Buffalo.
Fattah, Muhammad Maruf. 1997. A generative grammar of Kurdish. PhD dissertation, University of Amsterdam.
Feldman, Harry. 1986. *A Grammar of Awtuw* (Pacific Linguistics, B-94). Canberra: ANU.
Foley, William A. 1986. *The Papuan Languages of New Guinea*. Cambridge: Cambridge University Press.
   1991. *The Yimas Language of New Guinea*. Stanford: Stanford University Press.
   1997. *Anthropological Linguistics*. Oxford: Blackwell.
Foley, William and van Valin, Robert D. 1984. *Functional Syntax and Universal Grammar*. Cambridge: Cambridge University Press.
Forchheimer, P. 1953. *The Category of Person*. Berlin: Walter de Gruyter.
Foreman, Velma. 1974. *Grammar of Yessan Mayo*. Santa Anna (California): Summer Institute of Linguistics.
Foris, David Paul. 2000. *A Grammar of Sochiapan Chinantec*. Dallas: Summer Institute of Linguistics and University of Texas at Arlington.
Fox, Barbara. 1995. The category "S" in English conversation. In: Werner Abraham, Talmy Givón and Sandra A. Thompson (eds.), *Discourse Grammar and Typology. Papers in Honor of John W.M. Verhaar*. Amsterdam: John Benjamins, 153–78.
Frachtenberg, Leo J. 1922a. Coos. In: Franz Boas (ed.), *Handbook of American Indian Languages, Part II*, Smithsonian Institution Bureau of American Ethnology Bulletin 40. Washington: Government Printing Office, 297–429.
   1922b. Siuslawan (Lower Umpqa). In: Frans Boas (ed.), *Handbook of American Indian Languages. Part II*. Smithsonian Institution Bureau of American Ethnology Bulletin 40. Washington: Government Printing Office, 431–629.
Frajzyngier, Zygmunt. 1993. *A Grammar of Mupun*. Berlin: Dietrich Reimer Verlag.
   2001. *A Grammar of Lele*. Stanford: Stanford Monographs in African Languages.
Frajzyngier, Zygmunt and Curl, Traci S. (eds.). 1999. *Reflexives. Forms and Functions*. Amsterdam: John Benjamins.
Frank, Paul. 1990. *Ika Syntax* (Studies in the Language of Colombia 1). Dallas: Summer Institute of Linguistics and University of Texas at Arlington.
Friberg, Barbara. 1996. Konjo's peripatetic person markers. *Papers in Austronesian Linguistics* 3:137–71.
Gary, Judith and Keenan, Edward. 1977. 'On collapsing grammatical relations in universal grammar'. In: P. Cole and J. Sadock (eds.), *Syntax and Semantics 8. Grammatical Relations*, New York: Academic Press, 83–120.
Gasser, Michael. 1983. Topic continuity in written Amharic narrative. In: Talmy Givón (ed.), 95–139.
Georgopoulos, Carol. 1991. *Syntactic Variables. Resumptive Pronouns and A' Binding in Palauan*. Dordrecht: Kluwer Academic Press.

Gildea, Spike. 1994. Semantic and pragmatic inverse: inverse alignment and inverse voice in Carib of Surinam. In: Talmy Givón, (ed.), *Voice and Inversion*. Amsterdam: John Benjamins, 187–230.
  1998. *On Reconstructing Grammar: Comparative Cariban Morpho-Syntax*. New York: Oxford University Press.
Gilligan, Gary M. 1987. A cross-linguistic approach to the pro-drop parameter. PhD dissertation, University of Southern California.
Givón, Talmy. 1976. Topic, pronoun and grammatical agreement. In: Charles N. Li (ed.), *Subject and Topic*. New York: Academic Press, 151–88.
  (ed.). 1983. *Topic Continuity in Discourse*. Amsterdam: John Benjamins.
  1984. Direct object and dative shifting: Semantic and pragmatic case. In: Frans Plank (ed.), *Objects*. London: Academic Press, 151–82.
  1990. Syntax. *A Functional Typological Introduction*, vol. II Amsterdam: John Benjamins.
Glidden, Suellyn H. 1985. The Koh verbal system. *Working Papers of the Summer Institute of Linguistics, University of North Dakota* Session 29:223–82.
Gordon, Lynn. 1987. *Maricopa Morphology and Syntax* (University of California Publications in Linguistics 108). Berkeley: University of California Press.
Greenberg, Joseph H. 1963. Some universals of grammar with particular reference to the order of meaningful elements. In: Joseph H. Greenberg (ed.), *Universals of Human Language*. Cambridge: MIT Press, 73–113.
  1978. How does a language acquire gender markers? In: Joseph H. Greenberg, Charles A. Fergusson and Edith Moravcsik (eds.), vol. III, 47–82.
  1988. The first person dual as an ambiguous category. *Studies in Language* 12:1–18.
  1993. The second person is right so called. In: Mushira Eid and Gregory Iverson (eds.), *Principles and Prediction: The Analysis of Natural Language. Papers in Honor of Gerald Sanders*. Amsterdam: John Benjamins, 9–24.
Greenberg, Joseph H., Fergusson, Charles A. and Moravcsik, Edith (eds.) 1978. *Universals of Human Language*, vols. I–IV. Stanford: Stanford University Press.
Gregores, Emma and Suarez, Jorge A. 1967. *A Description of Colloquial Guarani*. The Hague: Mouton.
Grice, H. P. 1975. Logic and conversation. In: P. Cole and J. Morgan (eds.), *Syntax and Semantics 3: Speech Acts*. London: Academic Press, 41–58.
Grosz, B. J., Weinstein, S. and Joshi, A. K. 1995. Centering: a framework for modeling the global coherence of discourse. *Computational Linguistics* 21.2:203–25.
Groves, Terab'ata R., Groves, Gordon W. and Jacobs, Roderick. 1985. *Kiribatese: An Outline Description* (Pacific Linguistics, D-64). Canberra: ANU.
Gruzdeva, Ekaterina. 1998. *Nivkh*. Munich: Lincom Europa.
Guirardello, Raquel. 1999. A reference grammar of Trumai. PhD thesis, Rice University, Texas.
Güldemann, Tom. 2001. Die Entlehnung pronominaler Elemente des Khoekhoe aus dem! Ui-Taa. MS., University of Leipzig.
Gundel, J. K., Hedberg, N. and Zacharski, R. 1993. Cognitive status and the form of referring expressions in discourse. *Language* 69.2:274–307.
  2000. Cognitive status and definite descriptions in English: why accommodation is unnecessary. MS., University of Minnesota, Simon Fraser University and NTNU, Trondheim, New Mexico State University.
Haas, Mary. R. 1977. From auxiliary verb phrase to inflectional suffix. In: Charles N. Li (ed.), 525–37.
Hagège, Claude. 1974. Les pronoms logophoriques. *Bulletin de la Société de Linguistique de Paris* 69:287–310.
Haiman, John. 1980. *Hua: a Papuan Language of the Eastern Highlands of New Guinea*. Amsterdam: John Benjamins.
  1985. *Natural Syntax*. Cambridge: Cambridge University Press.

Hale, Ken. 1966. Kinship reflections in syntax. *Word* 22:318–24.
Hall, C. J. 1988. Integrating diachronic and processing principles in explaining the suffixing preference. In: John A. Hawkins (ed.), *Explaining Language Universals*. Oxford: Basil Blackwell, 321–49.
Hamel, Patricia J. 1994. *A Grammar and Lexicon of Loniu, Papua New Guinea* (Pacific Linguistics, C-N103). Canberra: ANU.
Hardman, M. J. 2000. *Jaqaru*. Munich: Lincom Europa.
Haspelmath, Martin. 2001. Ditransitive alignment. Paper presented at the 4th International Meeting of the Association of Linguistic Typology, Santa Barbara, 19–23 July 2001.
Haugen, Einar. 1976. *The Scandinavian Languages*. London: Faber and Faber.
Hawkins, John A. and Gilligan, G. 1988. Prefixing and suffixing universals in relation to basic word order. *Lingua* 74:219–59.
Head, Brian F. 1976. Social factors in the use of pronouns for the addressee in Brazilian Portuguese. In: J. Schmidt-Radefeldt (ed.), *Readings in Portuguese Linguistics*. Amsterdam: North Holland, 289–347.
  1978. Respect degrees in pronominal reference. In: Joseph H. Greenberg et al. (eds.) vol. III, 151–211.
Heath, Jeffrey. 1978. *Linguistic Diffusion in Arnhem Land*. Canberra: Australian Institute of Aboriginal Studies.
  1991. Pragmatic disguise in pronominal affix paradigms. In: Frans Plank (ed.), *Paradigms. The Economy of Inflection*. Berlin: Mouton de Gruyter, 75–90.
  1996. Pragmatic skewing in 1<–>2 pronominal combinations in native American languages. *International Journal of American Linguistics* 64.2:83–104.
Heine, Bernd. 1999. *The Ani: Grammatical Notes and Texts*. Cologne: Institute of African Studies, University of Cologne.
Heine, Bernd, Claudi, Ulrika and Hunnemeyer, Frederike. 1991. From cognition to grammar-evidence from African languages. In: Elizabeth Closs Traugott and Bernd Heine (eds.), 149–87.
Heine, Bernd and Reh, Mechthild. 1984. *Grammaticalization and Reanalysis in African Languages*. Hamburg: Helmut Buske Verlag.
Helmbrecht, Johannes. 1996a. On the grammaticalization of 1st and 2nd person pronominal affixes in North American Indian languages. *Proceedings of the Berkeley Linguistic Society* 22:69–77.
  1996b. The syntax of personal agreement in East Caucasian languages. *Sprachtypologie und Universalienforschung (STUFF)* 2:127–48.
  2001. Grammar and function of we. Ms., University of Erfurt.
Hercus, Luise. 1994. *A Grammar of the Arabana-Wangkangurru Language Lake Eyre Basin, South Australia* (Pacific Linguistics, C-128). Canberra: ANU.
Hetzron, Robert. 1976. The Agaw Languages. *Afroasiatic Linguistics* 3.3:1–45.
Hewitt, B. G. 1979. *Abkhaz* (Descriptive Grammars Series). Amsterdam: North Holland.
Hock, Hans Henrich. 1986. *Principles of Historical Linguistics*. Berlin: Mouton de Gruyter.
Hofling, Charles Andrew. 2000. *Itzaj Maya Grammar*. Salt Lake City: University of Utah Press.
Holmes, Philip and Hinchliffe, Ian. 1993. *Swedish: A Comprehensive Grammar*. London and New York: Routledge.
Hopkins, Elizabeth B. 1986. Pronouns and pronoun fusion in Yaouré. In Ursula Wiesemann (ed.), 191–203
Hopper, Paul and Traugott. Elizabeth Closs. 1993. *Grammaticalization*. Cambridge: Cambridge University Press.
Hoskinson, James T. 1983. *A Grammar and Dictionary of the Gude Language*. Ann Arbor: University Microfilms.
Huang, Yan. 2000. *Anaphora: A Cross-Linguistic Study*. Oxford: Oxford University Press.

Hutchisson, Don. 1986. Sursurunga pronouns and the special use of quadrual number. In: Ursula Wiesemann (ed.), 1–20.
Hyman, Larry and Duranti, Alessandro. 1982. On the object relation in Bantu. In: Paul J. Hopper and Sandra A. Thompson (eds.), *Syntax and Semantics 15: Studies in Transitivity*. New York: Academic Press, 217–39.
Ingram, David. 1978. Typology and universals of personal pronouns. In: Joseph, H. Greenberg et al. (eds.), vol III, 213–47.
Irwin, Barry. 1974. *Salt-Yui Grammar* (Pacific Linguistics, B-35). Canberra: ANU.
Jacobsen Jr, William H. 1979a. Why does Washo lack a passive? In: Frans Plank (ed.), *Ergativity*. New York: Academic Press, 145–60.
  1979b. Noun and verb in Nootkan. In: Barbara S. Efrat (ed.), *The Victorian Conference on Northwestern Languages* (British Columbia Provincial Museum Heritage Record No. 4). Victoria BC: British Columbia Provincial Museum, 83–155.
  1980. Inclusive/exclusive: a diffused pronominal category in native western North America. In: J. Kreiman and A. E. Ojeda (eds.), *Papers from the Parassession on Pronouns and Anaphora*. Chicago Linguistic Society, Chicago: University of Chicago, 204–27.
Jacquesson, François. 2001. Person-marking in TB languages of North-East India. *Linguistics of the Tibeto-Burman Area* 24.1:113–44.
Jakobi, Angelika. 1990. *A Fur Grammar: Phonology, Morphophonology, and Morphology*. Hamburg: Helmut Buske.
Jakobson, Roman. 1971. Shifters, verbal categories, and the Russian verb. In: Roman Jakobson (ed.), *Selected Writings*, vol. II. Den Haag: Mouton, 130–47.
Järvinen, Liisa. 1991. The pronoun system of Mauwake. In: Tom Dutton (ed.), *Papers in Papuan Linguistics* no.1 (Pacific Linguistics, A-73). Canberra: ANU, 57–95.
Jayaseelan, K. A. 2000. Lexical anaphors and pronouns in Malayalam. In: Barbara C. Lust et al. (eds.), 113–68.
Jelinek, Eloise. 1998. Prepositions in North Straits Salish and the noun/verb question. In: Ewa Czaykowska-Higgins and M. Dale Kinkade (eds.), *Salish Languages and Linguistics*. Berlin: Mouton de Gruyter, 325–46.
Jelinek, Eliose and Demers, Richard A. 1983. The agent hierarchy and voice in some coast Salish languages. *International Journal of American Linguistics* 49.2:167–85.
Jensen, John Thayer. 1977. *Yapese Reference Grammar*. Honolulu: University of Hawaii Press.
Jhaa, Subhadra. 1958. *The Formation of the Maithilii Language*. London: Luzac and Company.
Jones, Linda K. 1986. The question of ergativity in Yawa, a Papuan language. *Australian Journal of Linguistics* 6:37–56.
Jones, Michael A. 1993. *Sardinian Syntax* (Descriptive Grammars Series). London: Routledge.
Jones, Ross, McCallum. 1998. *The Boko/Busa Language Cluster*. Munich: Lincom Europa.
Jones, Wendell and Jones, Paula. 1991. *Barasano Syntax*. Dallas: Summer Institute of Linguistics and University of Texas at Arlington.
Judge, Anne and Healey, Frank George. 1985. *A Reference Grammar of Modern French*. London: Edward Arnold.
Kaiser, Elsi. 2000. Pronouns and demonstratives in Finnish: indicators of referent salience. In: Paul Baker, Andrew Hardie, Tony McEnry and Anna Siewierska (eds.), *Proceedings of the Discourse Anaphora and Reference Resolution Conference* (DAARC 2000), Lancaster: UCRAL, 20–28.
Kalstrom Dolson, Marjorie, Austin Krumholz, Ewan, Austin Krumholz, Jeanne, Bartholomew, Doris. 1995. *Gramatica del Popoloca se San Juan Atzingo*. Tucson: Summer Institute of Linguistics.
Kamp, H. and Reyle, U. 1993. *From Discourse to Logic*, parts 1 and 2. Dordrecht: Kluwer Academic.

Kärkkäinen, Elise. 1996. Preferred argument structure and subject role in American English conversational discourse. *Journal of Pragmatics* 25:675–701.
Keegan, John M. 1997. *Mbay*. Munich: Lincom Europa.
Keesing, Roger M. 1985. *Kwaio Grammar* (Pacific Linguistics, B-88) Canberra: ANU.
Kenesei, Istvan, Vago, Robert M. and Fenyvesi, Anna. 1998. *Hungarian* (Descriptive Grammars Series). London: Routledge.
Kibrik, Andrej A. 1991. Maintenance of reference in sentence and discourse. In: Winfred P. Lehmann and Helen-Jo Jakusz Hewitt (eds.), *Language Typology 1988*. Amsterdam: John Benjamins, 57–84.
Kimball, Geoffrey. 1991. *Koasati Grammar*. Lincoln, NA: University of Nebraska Press.
King, John T. 2001. The affinal kin register in Dhimal. *Linguistics of the Tibeto-Burman Area* 24.1:163–83.
König, Ekkehard and Peter Siemund. 1999. Intensifiers and reflexives: a typological perspective. In: Zygmunt Frajzyngier and Traci S. Curl (eds.), 41–74.
Kornfilt, Jaklin. 1997. *Turkish* (Descriptive Grammars Series). London: Routledge.
Kozintseva, Natalia. 1995. *Modern Eastern Armenian*. Munich: Lincom Europa.
Kroeber, Paul D. 1999. *The Salish Language Family*. Lincoln and London: University of Nebraska Press.
Kuno, Susumu. 1972. Pronominalization, reflexivization, and direct discourse. *Linguistic Inquiry* 3:161–95.
1987. *Functional Syntax. Anaphora, Discourse and Empathy*. Chicago and London: University of Chicago Press.
Kutsch, Lojenga Constance. 1994. *Ngiti: A Central-Sudanic Language of Zaire*. Cologne: Rüdiger Koppe Verlag.
Laidig, Wyn D. 1993. Insights from Larike possessive constructions. *Oceanic Linguistics* 32:312–51.
Lakoff, George. 1987. *Women, Fire and Dangerous Things: What Categories Reveal About the Mind*. Chicago: University of Chicago Press.
Lambertii, Marcello and Sottile, Roberto. 1997. *The Wolaytta Language*. Cologne: Rüdiger Köppe Verlag.
Langacker, Ronald W. 1977. *Studies in Uto-Aztecan Grammar*, vol. I. Dallas: Summer Institute of Linguistics and University of Texas at Arlington.
LaPolla, Randy J. 1992. Anti-ergative marking in Tibeto-Burman. *Linguistics of the Tibeto-Burman Area* 15.1:1–9.
1994. Parallel grammaticalizations in Tibeto-Burman languages: evidence of Sapir's drift. *Linguistics of the Tibeto-Burman Area* 17.1:61–79.
Last, Marco and Lucassen, Deborah. 1998. A grammatical sketch of Chai, a Southeastern Surmic language. In: Gerrit Dimmendaal and Marco Last (eds.), 375–436.
Laycock, D. C. 1965. *The Ndu Language Family* (Linguistic Circle of Canberra Publications). Canberra: ANU.
Lee, Cher Leng. 1999. The implications of mismatched personal pronouns in Chinese. *Text* 19.3:345–70.
Lee, Kee-Dong. 1975. *Kusaiean Reference Grammar*. Honolulu: University of Hawaii Press.
Lehmann, Christian. 1982. Universal and typological aspects of agreement. In: Hans-Jakob Seiler and J. Stachowiak (eds.) *Apprehension. Das sprachliche Erfassen von Gegenständen*, vol. II. Tübingen: Gunter Narr, 201–67.
1995. *Thoughts on Grammaticalization: A Programmatic Sketch*. Munich: Lincom Europa.
Li, Charles N. (ed.). 1977. *Mechanisms of Syntactic Change*. Austin: University of Texas Press.
Lichtenberk, Frantisek. 1983. *A Grammar of Manam*. Honolulu: University of Hawaii Press.
Love, J. R. B. 2000. *The Grammatical Structure of the Worora Language of North-Western Australia*. Munich: Lincom Europa.

Lust, Barbara C., Wali, Kashi, Gair, James W. and Subbarao K. V. (eds.). 2000. *Lexical Anaphors and Pronouns in Selected South Asian Languages*. Berlin: Mouton de Gruyter.
Lynch, John. 1982. Anejom grammar sketch. *Papers in Linguistics in Melanesia* 4:93–154.
Lyons, John. 1977. *Semantics* (vols. I and II) Cambridge: Cambridge University Press.
Macaulay, Monica. 1996. *A Grammar of Chalcatongo Mixtec* (University of California Publications in Linguistics 127). Berkeley: University of California Press.
MacDonald, Lorna. 1990. *A Grammar of Tauya*. Berlin: Mouton de Gruyter.
MacKay, Carolyn Joyce. 1991. A grammar of Misantla Totanac. PhD dissertation, University of Texas at Austin.
MacPhail, R. M. 1983 [1953]. *Introduction to Santali*. Calcutta: Firma KLM Private Ltd.
Mahootian, Shahrzad. 1997. *Persian* (Descriptive Grammars Series). London: Routledge.
Marchese, Lynell. 1986. The pronominal system of Godie. In: Ursula Wiesemann (ed.), 217–55.
Marlett, Stephen A. 1990. Person and number inflection in Seri. *International Journal of American Linguistics* 56:503–41.
Martins, Silvana and Martins, Valteir. 1999. Makú. In: R. M. W. Dixon and Alexandra Y. Aikhenvald (eds.), 251–67.
Maslova, Elena. 1999. A grammar of Kolyma Yukaghir. Habilitation thesis, University of Bielefeld. To appear in the Mouton Grammar Library.
McClelland, Clive W. 2000. *The Interrelations of Syntax, Narrative Structure, and Prosody in a Berber Language*. Lewiston: Edwin Mellen Press.
McGregor, William. 1994. *Warrwa*. Munich: Lincom Europa.
1996a. *Nyulnyul*. Munich: Lincom Europa.
(ed.). 1996b. *Studies in Kimberley Languages in Honour of Howard Coate*. Munich: Lincom Europa.
McKay, Graham R. 1979. Pronominal person and number categories in Rembarrnga and Djeebana. *Oceanic Linguistics* 17:27–37.
1996. Body parts, possession marking and nominal classes in Ndjebbana. In: Hilary Chappell and William McGregor (eds.), 293–326.
Meira, Sergio, S.C.O. 1999. A grammar of Tiriyo. PhD dissertation, Rice University, Texas.
Michailovsky, Boyd. 1988. Hayu typology and verb morphology. *Linguistics of the Tibeto-Burman Area* 1.1:1–26.
Miller, Amy. 2001. *A Grammar of Jamul Tiipay*. Berlin: Mouton de Gruyter.
Miller, Wick R. 1965. *Acoma Grammar and Texts*. Berkeley: University of California Press.
Mistry, P. J. 2000. Lexical anaphors and pronouns in Gujarati. In: Barbara C. Lust et al. (eds.), 333–96.
Mithun, Marianne. 1991. Active/agentive case marking and its motivations. *Language* 67: 510–46.
1993. Switch-reference clause combining in central Pomo. *International Journal of American Linguistics* 59:119–36.
1994. The implications of ergativity for a Philippine voice system. In Barbara Fox and Paul J. Hopper (eds.), *Voice, Form and Function*. Amsterdam: John Benjamins, 247–77.
1996. Multiple reflections of inalienability in Mohawk. In: Hilary Chappell and William McGregor (eds.), 633–50.
1999. *The North-American Indian Languages*. Cambridge: Cambridge University Press.
2003. Pronouns and agreement: the information status of pronominal affixes. *Transactions of the Philological Society* 101.2: 235–78.
Moravcsik, Edith A. 1978. Agreement. In: Joseph H. Greenberg et al. (eds.), vol. IV, 331–74.
Mühlhäusler, Peter. 1996. *Linguistic Ecology. Language Change and Linguistic Imperialism in the Pacific Region*. London and New York: Routledge.
Mühlhäusler, Peter and Harré, Rom. 1990. *Pronouns and People: The Linguistic Construction of Social and Personal Identity*. Oxford: Basil Blackwell.

Mulder, Jean Gail. 1994. *Ergativity in Coast Tsimshian (Sm'algyax)* Berkeley: University of California Press.
Munro, Pamela and Lopez Felipe H. 1999. *San Lucas Quiavini Zapotec Dictionary.* Los Angeles: Chicano Studies Research Centre.
Murthy, B. Lalitha and Subbarao, K. V. 2000. Lexical anaphors and pronouns in Mizo. In: Barbara C. Lust et al. (eds.), 776–835.
Muysken, Peter. 1994. Inflection and agreement properties of quantifiers in Quechua. In: Peter Cole, Gabriella Hermon and Mario Daniel Martin (eds.), *Language in the Andes.* Newark: University of Delaware, 180–204.
Newman, Paul. 2000. *The Hausa Language.* New Haven: Yale University Press.
Newman, Stanley. 1980. Functional changes in the Salish pronominal system. *International Journal of American Linguistics* 46.3:155–67.
Nichols, Johanna. 1985. The grammatical marking of theme in literary Russian. In: R. D. Brecht and M. S. Flier (eds.), *Issues in Russian Morphosyntax.* Columbus: Slavica, 170–86.
    1988. On alienable and inalienable possession. In: W. Shipley (ed.), *In Honor of Mary Haas: From the Haas Festival Conference on Native American Linguistics.* Berlin: Mouton de Gruyter, 557–609.
    1992. *Linguistic Diversity in Space and Time.* Chicago and London: University of Chicago Press.
Nichols, Johanna and Peterson, David A. 1996. The Amerindian personal pronouns. *Language* 72.2:336–71.
Nikolaeva, Irina. 1999. Object agreement, grammatical relations and information structure. *Studies in Language* 23.2:331–76.
Nikolaeva, Irina and Tolskaya, Maria. 2001. *A Grammar of Udihe.* Berlin. Mouton de Gruyter.
Noguchi, Tohru. 1997. Two types of pronouns and variable binding. *Language* 73:770–97.
Nordbustad, Froydis. 1988. *Iraqw Grammar: An Analytical Study of the Iraqw Language.* Berlin: Dietrich Reimer Verlag.
Nordlinger, Rachel. 1998. *A Grammar of Wambaya, Northern Territory (Australia).* (Pacific Linguistics, C-140). Canberra: ANU.
Oates, William and Oates, Lynnete. 1968. *Kapau Pedagogical Grammar* (Pacific Linguistics, C-10). Canberra: ANU.
Olawsky, Knut J. 1999. *Aspects of Dagbani Grammar.* Munich: Lincom Europa.
Olson, Cliff. 1992. Gumawana (Amphlett Islands, Papua New Guinea): grammar sketch and texts. *Papers in Austronesian Linguistics* 2:251–430.
Olson, M. 1975. Barai grammar: highlights. In: Tim E. Dutton (ed.), *Studies in Languages of Central and South-East Papua* (Pacific Linguistics, C-29). Canberra: ANU, 471–512.
Omondi, Lucia Ndong'a. 1982. *The Major Syntactic Structures of Dholuo.* Berlin: Dietrich Reimer Verlag.
Osborne, C. R. 1974. *The Tiwi Language.* Canberra: Australian Institute of Aboriginal Studies.
Osumi, Midori. 1995. *Tinrin Grammar.* Honolulu: University of Hawaii Press.
Pandharipande, Rajeshwari V. 1997. *Marathi.* London: Routledge.
Parker, Elizabeth. 1986. Mundani pronouns. In: Ursula Wiesemann (ed.), 131–65.
Payne, Doris L. 1990. *The Pragmatics of Word Order: Typological Dimensions of Verb-Initial Languages.* Berlin: Mouton de Gruyter.
Payne, Doris L. 1992. Nonidentifiable information and pragmatic order rules in O'odham. In: Doris. L. Payne (ed.), *Pragmatics of Word Order Flexibility.* Amsterdam: John Benjamins, 137–66.
Peeke, Catherine. 1994. Waorani. In: Peter Kahrel and René van den Berg (eds.), *Typological Studies in Negation.* Amsterdam: John Benjamins. 267–90.
Penalosa, Fernando. 1987. Major syntactic structures of Acatec. *International Journal of American Linguistics* 53:281–310.

Plank, Frans. 1989. On Humboldt on the dual. In: Roberta Corrigan, Fred Eckmann and Michael Noonan (eds.), *Linguistic Categorization*. Amsterdam: John Benjamins, 293–333.
Plank, Frans and Schellinger, Wolfgang. 1997. The uneven distribution of genders over numbers: Greenberg Nos. 37 and 45. *Linguistic Typology* 1.1:53–101.
Polinsky, Maria. 1996. The double object construction in Spoken Eastern Armenian. In: Howard Aronson (ed.), *NSL. 8. Linguistic Studies in the Non-Slavic Languages of the Commonwealth of Independent States and the Baltic Republics*. Chicago: University of Chicago Press, 307–35.
Quesada, J. Diego. 2000. *A Grammar of Teribe*. Munich: Lincom Europa.
Quizar, Robin. 1994. Split ergativity and word order in Chorti. *International Journal of American Linguistics* 60:120–38.
Radin, Paul. 1935. Notes on the Tlappanecan language of Guerrero. *International Journal of American Linguistics* 8:44–72.
Redden, James E. 1966. Walapai II: morphology. *International Journal of American Linguistics* 23:141–63.
Reed, Judy and Payne, David L. 1986. Asheninca (Campa) pronominals. In: Ursula Wiesemann (ed.), 323–31.
Reesink, Ger. R. 1999. *A Grammar of Hatam* (Pacific Linguistics, C-146). Canberra: ANU.
Rehg, Kenneth. 1981. *Ponapean Reference Grammar*. Honolulu: University of Hawaii Press.
Reichle, Verena. 1981. *Bawm Language and Lore Tibeto-Burman Area*. Bern\Frankfurt am Main\Las Vegas: Peter Lang.
Reinhart, Tanya and Reuland, Eric. 1993. Reflexivity. *Linguistic Inquiry* 24:657–720.
Rijkhoff, Jan and Bakker, Dik. 1998. Language sampling. *Linguistic Typology* 2:263–314.
Roberts, John R. 1987. *Amele* (Descriptive Grammars Series). London: Croom Helm.
Roberts, Ian. 1999. Agreement marking in Welsh and Romance. In: Henk van Riemsdijk (ed.), 621–38.
Robertson, John S. 1993. The origin and development of the Huastec pronouns. *International Journal of American Linguistics* 59:294–314.
Robins, R. H. 1967. *A Short History of Linguistics*. London: Longman.
Romankevicius Costa, Raquel Guimaraes. 1998. Aspects of ergativity in Marubo (Panoan). *Journal of Amazonian Linguistics* 1:50–103.
Roncador, Manfred von. 1992. Types of logophoric marking in African languages. *Journal of African Languages and Linguistics* 13:163–82.
Rosen, Joan M. 1986. Phonemes, verb classes and personal endings in Maumere. *NUSA Linguistic Studies in Indonesia and Languages in Indonesia* vol. 25. Jakarta: Badan Penyelenggara NUSA, 39–69.
Ross, Malcolm. 1980. Some elements of Vanimo, a New Guinea Tone language. *Papers in New Guinea Linguistics* 20:77–109.
Ross, Malcolm and Natu Paol, John. 1978. *A Waskia Grammar Sketch and Vocabulary* (Pacific Linguistics, B-56). Canberra: ANU.
Rude, Noel. 1993. Dative shifting in Sahaptin. *International Journal of American Linguistics* 59:316–21.
Rupp, James E. 1989. *Lealao Chinantec Syntax*. (Studies in Chinantec Languages 2) Dallas: Summer Institute of Linguistics and University of Texas at Arlington.
Saltarelli, Mario. 1988. *Basque* (Descriptive Grammars Series). London: Croom Helm.
Schaub, Willi. 1985. *Babungo* (Descriptive Grammars Series). Dover, NH: Croom Helm.
Schebeck, Bernhard. 1973. The Adnjamathanha personal pronoun and the Wailpi kinship system. *Papers in Australian Linguistics*. no. 6 (Pacific Linguistics, A-36), 1–45.
Schuster-Šewc, H. 1996. *Grammar of the Upper Sorbian Language* (translated by Garry H. Toops). Munich: Lincom Europa.

Schwartz, Linda J. 1986. The function of free pronouns. In: Ursula Wiesemann (ed.), 405–36.
Scorza, David. 1985. A sketch of Au morphology and syntax. *Papers in New Guinea Linguistics* 22:215–73.
Seiler, Hansjakob. 1983. *Possession as an Operational Dimension of Language*. Tübingen: Gunter Narr.
Shibatani, Masayoshi. 1985. Passive and related constructions. *Language* 61:821–48.
Siegel, Jeff. 1984. Introduction to the Labu Language. *Papers in New Guinea Linguistics* 23:83–157.
Siewierska, Anna. 1988. *Word Order Rules*. London: Routledge.
  1998. Nominal and verbal person marking. *Linguistic Typology* 2:1–53.
  1999. From anaphoric pronoun to grammatical agreement marker: why objects don't make it. *Folia Linguistica* 33.2:225–51.
  2000. On the origin of the order of agreement and tense markers. In: J. C. Smith and Delia Bentley (eds.), *Historical Linguistics 1995*, vol. I *General issues and non-Germanic Languages*. Amsterdam: John Benjamins, 377–92.
  2003. Person agreement and the determination of alignment. *Transactions of the Philological Society* 101 2:339–70.
Siewierska, Anna and Bakker, Dik. Forthcoming. Inclusive/exclusive in free and bound person forms. In: E. Filiminova (ed.), *Inclusivity*. Amsterdam: John Benjamins.
Silverstein, Michael. 1976. Hierarchy of features and ergativity. In: R. M. W. Dixon (ed.), 112–71.
  1978. Deixis and deducibility in a Wasco Wishram passive of evidence. Proceedings of the Berkeley Linguistic Society 4:238–53.
Smith, Ian and Johnson, Steve. 1985. The syntax of clitic cross-referencing pronouns in Kugu Nganhcara. *Anthropological Linguistics* 27:102–11.
Sohn, Ho-Min. 1975. *Woleaian Reference Grammar*. Honolulu: University of Hawaii Press.
  1994. *Korean* (Descriptive Grammars Series). London: Routledge.
Solnit, David B. 1997. *Eastern Kayah Li: Grammar, Texts, Glossary*. Honolulu: University of Hawaii Press.
Sridhar, S. N. 1990. *Kannada* (Descriptive Grammars Series). London: Routledge.
Stassen, Leon. 1997. *Intransitive Predication*. Oxford: Oxford University Press.
Steele, Susan. 1978. Word order variation: a typological survey. In: Joseph H. Greenberg et al. (eds.), vol. IV, 585–623.
Stephens, Janig. 1993. Breton. In: Martin J. Ball (ed.), *The Celtic Languages*. London: Routledge, 349–409.
Stirling, Leslie. 1993. *Switch-Reference and Discourse Representation*. Cambridge: Cambridge University Press.
Storto, R. Luciana. 1999. Aspects of Karitiana grammar. PhD dissertation, MIT.
Strom, Clay. 1992. *Retuarã Syntax* (Studies in the Languages of Colombia 3). Dallas: Summer Institute of Linguistics and University of Texas at Arlington.
Subbarao, K. V. and Murthy, B. Lalitha. 2000. Lexical anaphors and pronouns in Telugu. In: Barbara C. Lust et al. (eds.), 217–73.
Subrahmanyam, P. S. 1971. *Dravidian Verb Morphology*. Tamilnadu, India: Annamalai University Annamalainagar.
Sugamoto, Nobuko. 1989. Pronominality: a noun-pronoun continuum. In: Roberta Corrigan, Fred Eckman and Michael Noonan (eds.), *Linguistic Categorization*. Amsterdam: John Benjamins, 267–91.
Swanton, John R. 1929. A sketch of the Atakapa language. *International Journal of American Linguistics* 5.2–4:121–49.
Taylor, C. 1985. *Nkore-Kiga* (Descriptive Grammars Series). London: Croom Helm.
Taylor, John R. 1996. *Possessives in English*. Oxford: Clarendon Press.

Terrill, Angela. 1998. *Biri*. Munich: Lincom Europa.
  2000. A grammar of Lavukaleve: A Papuan language of the Solomon Islands. PhD dissertation, Australian National University.
Thomas, David. 1955. Three analyses of the Ilocano pronoun system. *Word* 11:204–8.
Thomsen, Marie-Louise. 1984. *The Sumerian Language*. Copenhagen: Akademisk Forlag.
Thráinsson, Höskuldur. 1991. Long-distance reflexives and the typology of NPs. In: Jan Koster and Eric Reulan (eds.), *Long-Distance Anaphora*. Cambridge: Cambridge University Press, 49–75.
Thurston, William R. 1994. Renovation and innovation in the languages of north-western New Britain. In: Tom Dutton and Darrell T. Tyron (eds.), 573–609.
Tiffou, Etienne and Pesot, Jurgen. 1989. *Contes du Yassin: Introduction au bourouchaski du Yasin avec grammaire analytique*. Paris: Peeters and Société d'Etudes Linguistiques et Antropologiques de France.
Topping, Donald M. 1973. Chamorro Reference Grammar. Honolulu: University of Hawaii Press.
Traugott, Elizabeth Closs and Heine, Bernd (eds.). 1991. *Approaches to Grammaticalization* vols. I and II. Amsterdam: John Benjamins.
Tryon, Darrell T. 1967. *Nengone Grammar* (Pacific Linguistics, B-6). Canberra: ANU.
  1968. *Iai Grammar* (Pacific Linguistics, B-8). Canberra: ANU.
  1994. Language contact and contact-induced language change in Eastern Outer Islands, Solomon Islands. In: Tom Dutton and Darrell T. Tryon (eds.), 611–47.
Tsunoda, Tasaku. 1981. *The Djaru Language of Kimberley*. (Pacific Linguistics, B-78). Canberra: ANU.
Tuggy, David H. 1979. Tetelcingo Nahuatl. In: Ronald W. Langacker (ed.), *Studies in Uto-Aztecan Grammar*, vol. II. University of Texas at Arlington: Summer Institute of Linguistics, 1–140.
Uhlenbeck, E. M. 1978. *Studies in Javanese Morphology*. The Hague: Martinus Nijhoff.
Van Riemsdijk, Henk (ed.). 1999. *Clitics in the Languages of Europe*. Berlin: Mouton de Gruyter.
Van der Voort, Hein. 2000. A grammar of Kwaza. PhD dissertation, University of Amsterdam.
Van Driem, George. 1987. *A Grammar of Limbu*. Berlin: Mouton de Gruyter.
Van Staden, Miriam. 2000. Tidore. A linguistic description of a language of the North Moluccas. PhD dissertation, University of Leiden.
Visser, L. E. and Voorhoeve, C. L. 1987. *Sahu-Indonesian–English Dictionary and Sahu Grammar Sketch*. Dordrecht: Foris.
Vogt, H. 1940. *The Kalispel Language*. Oslo: Norske Videnskaps-Akademi.
Voorhoeve, C. L. 1982. The West Makian language, North Moluccas, Indonesia: a field report. In: C. L. Voorhoeve (ed.), *The Makian Languages and Their Neighbours* (Pacific Linguistics, D-46). Canberra: ANU, 1–74.
  1994. Contact-induced change in the non-Austronesian languages in the North Moluccas, Indonesia. In: Tom Dutton and Darrell T. Tryon (eds.), 649–74.
Vuorinen, Paula. 1995. Person marking in Padoe. *NUSA Linguistic Studies in Indonesia and Languages in Indonesia* vol. 33. Jakarta: Badan Penyelenggara NUSA, 97–121.
Wales, Katie. 1996. *Personal Pronouns in Present-Day English*. Cambridge: Cambridge University Press.
Wali, Kashi. 2000. Lexical anaphors and pronouns in Marathi. In: Barabara C. Lust et al. (eds.), 513–74.
Wali, Kashi and Koul, Omkar N. 1997. *Kashmiri: A Cognitive-Descriptive Grammar* (Descriptive Grammars Series). London: Routledge.
Wali, Kashi, Koul, Omkar N., Hook P. E. and Koul, A. K. 2000. Lexical anaphors and pronouns in Kashmiri. In: Barbara C. Lust et al. (eds.), 471–512.

Wash, Suzanne. 2001. Adverbial clauses in Barbareno Chumash narrative discourse. PhD dissertation, University of California at Santa Barbara.
Watters, David E. 1993. Agreement systems and syntactic organization in the Kham verb (Nepal). *Linguistics of the Tibeto-Burman Area* 16.2:89–112.
  2002. *A Grammar of Kham.* Cambridge: Cambridge University Press.
Wichmann, Søren. 1995. *The Relationship Among the Mixe-Zoquean Languages of Mexico.* Salt Lake City: University of Utah Press.
Wiesemann, Ursula (ed.). 1986a. *Pronominal Systems.* Tübingen: Gunter Narr.
  1986b. The pronoun system of some Jê and Macro-Jê languages. In: Ursula Wiesemann (ed.), 437–64.
  1986c. Grammatical coreference. In: Ursula Wiesemann (ed.), 359–80.
Williams, Edwin. 1981. Argument structure and morphology. *The Linguistic Review* 1:81–114.
Wiltschko, Martina. 2002. The syntax of pronouns: evidence from Halkomelem Salish. *Natural Language and Linguistic Theory* 20:157–95.
Wise, Mary Ruth. 1986. Grammatical categories of Preandine Arawakan languages of Peru. In: Desmond C. Derbyshire and Geoffrey K. Pullum (eds.), vol. I, 567–642.
Wolfart, H. C. and Caroll, J. F. 1981. *Meet Cree: A Guide to the Cree Language* (2nd edition). Lincoln, NA: University of Nebraska Press.
Wu, Chaolu. 1996. *Daur.* Munich: Lincom Europa.
Xiong, Xueliang. 1998. First person anaphor as a cognitive unit in Chinese. *Word* 49.3:383–401.
Yamamoto, Mutsumi. 1999. *Animacy and Reference.* Amsterdam: John Benjamins.
Yigezu, Moges and Dimmendaal, Gerrit J. 1998. Notes on Baale. In: Gerrit Dimmendaal and Marco Last (eds.), 273–318.
Zigmond, Maurice L., Booth, Curtis G. and Munro, Pamela. 1990. *Kawaiisu.* Berkeley: University of California Press.
Zribi-Hertz, Anne. 1989. A-type binding and narrative point of view. *Language* 65:695–727.
Zwicky, Arnold M. 1985. Clitics and particles. *Language* 61:283–305.
Zwicky, Arnold M. and Pullum, Geoffrey K. 1983. Cliticization vs. inflection: English n't. *Language* 59:502–13.

Author index

Abbott, 123
Acharya, 229
Adelaar, 278
Agee, 25
Aikhenvald, 17, 19, 106, 107, 134, 139, 161, 248, 281
Alexander, 219, 248
Allan, K., 10
Allan, R., 218, 222
Ambrazas, 109
Ameka, 144
Amha, 70, 73
Amritavalli, 196
Anagnostopoulou, 158
Andersen, 252
Anderson, 29
Ariel, 46, 173, 174, 175, 176, 177, 262, 264, 265, 266, 267
Asher, 216, 218
Ashton, 104, 167
Austin, 124, 125

Baker, M., 124, 164, 167
Bakker, 15, 86
Banfield, 205
Barbaresi, 93, 94
Bavin, 280
Beaumont, 254
Bender, 88, 96, 252, 256, 257, 275
Benveniste, 4, 8
Besnier, 211, 213, 220
Beyer, 231
Bhatt, 249, 250
Bhatia, 203, 225, 227
Biber, 267
Bickel, 64, 241, 242–244
Bisang, 241
Bitner, 167, 168
Blackwell, 194
Blake, F. R., 249
Blake, B. J., 55, 276, 277
Blansitt, 61
Blondeau, 212
Blood, 271, 272

Bodomo, 109
Booth, 249
Borgman, 35, 36
Bradley, 6
Braun, 214
Breen, 277
Breeze, 182, 276
Bresnan, 8, 9, 19, 37, 122, 124, 125, 126, 193
Brown, Ch., 265
Brown, P., 214, 217, 237
Brown R., 214, 217
Burquest, 260
Burridge, 169
Burzio, 195
Bybee, 164, 166, 268

Camp, 111
Campbell, 81, 274
Capell, 95, 100, 259, 260
Cardinaletti, 8, 19, 37, 38
Carlin, 83
Carroll, 150
Casad, 31, 32, 62
Castren, 132
Caughley, 24, 112
Chafe, 236, 239, 260
Chaker, 109
Chapman, 142
Chappell, 143, 144, 145
Chomsky, 8, 122, 173, 185, 186, 190, 197, 198
Chung, 45
Cinque, 172
Clements, 204
Comrie, 44, 56, 63, 137
Cook, 46, 254
Cooke, 13, 228, 229, 235, 275
Cooreman, 134
Corbett, 75, 81, 90, 91, 92, 93, 95, 103, 120, 147, 148, 219, 220, 221
Cornish, 173, 174
Corston, 41
Cowan, 93, 113, 166
Craig, 249

Croft, 57, 142, 246, 266
Crowley, 5, 84, 139, 140, 146
Culy, 204, 205, 206
Curnow, 47, 48, 261
Cysouw, 75, 82, 85, 86, 87, 93, 95, 97–103, 110, 112

Das Gupta, 55
Davies, 99, 221, 273
Demers, 239
Dench, 277, 278
Derbyshire, 142
Dik, 160
Dimitrova-Vulchanova, 4, 157
Dimmendaal, 24
Dixon, 17, 25, 91, 134, 276
Dlugosz-Kurczabowa, 258
Doble, 78, 135
Dol, 73
Donaldson, 244
Donohue, 219, 274, 275
Dressler, 93, 94
Dryer, 57
Dubisz, 258
Du Bois, 40, 41
Du Feu, 95
Duranti, 170, 171, 208, 209
Durie, 130, 222, 244, 247
Dutton, 77, 269

Eades, 188
Ebert, 241
Eckert, 27
England, 62
Erguvanli-Taylan, 198, 199, 200
Evans, 66, 124, 125, 159, 184
Everett, 40, 79
Everaert, 190, 191
Ezard, 141, 147

Facundes, 78, 161
Fattah, 30, 163
Feldman, 69
Foley, 66, 91, 92, 169, 175, 215, 230
Forchheimer, 75, 93, 96
Foreman, 62
Foris, 144, 234
Fox, 41
Frachtenberg, 55, 130
Frajzyngier, 202, 203
Friberg, 31, 160

Gary, 52
Gasser, 179
Georgopoulos, 154
Gildea, 128, 151, 153

Gilligan, 127, 164, 165, 272
Gilman, 214
Givón, 46, 137, 166, 173, 262, 264, 265
Glidden, 49
Gordon, 139, 140, 270, 271
Greenberg, 75, 79, 82, 88, 106, 107
Gregores, 119, 130
Grice, 177
Grosz, 173
Groves, R., 41, 42
Groves, W., 41
Gruzdeva, 117
Guirardello, 29, 45
Güldemann, 111, 274
Gundel, 173, 175, 176, 177, 183, 185, 192

Haas, 258–259
Hagège, 201
Haiman, 142, 143, 155, 266
Hale, 3, 167, 168
Hall, 164
Hamel, 91
Hardman, 238
Harré, 214, 281
Haspelmath, 57
Haugen, 278
Hawkins, 164, 165
Head, 209, 214, 215, 219, 224
Healey, 222, 237
Heath, J., 154, 237, 239, 240, 276
Hedberg, 173
Heine, 44, 61, 246, 248
Hellan, 4, 157
Helmbrecht, 93, 149, 237, 240, 249
Hercus, 3
Hetzron, 257
Hewitt, 145, 168
Hinchliffe, 222, 236
Hock, 217
Hofling, 260
Holmes, 218, 222, 236
Hopkins, 69, 83
Hopper, 246, 268
Hoskinson, 44
Huang, 173, 188, 189, 190, 191, 195, 196, 200, 204
Hudson, 27
Hutchisson, 91

Ingram, 75, 96, 97
Irwin, 6

Jacobs, 41
Jacobsen Jr, 7, 79, 147, 276
Jacquesson, 4, 65
Jakobi, 4

Järvinen, 212
Jayaseelan, 190, 195, 197, 218, 225
Jelinek, 8, 20–21, 239
Jensen, 118
Jhaa, 225
Johnson, 27
Jones, L., 89
Jones, M., 30
Jones, P., 114
Jones, R. M., 38, 39, 204, 255, 256
Jones, W., 114
Joshi, 173
Judge, 222, 237

Kaiser, 180
Kamp, 173
Kärkkäinen, 41
Karjalainen, 212
Keegan, 20, 202, 203
Keenan, 52
Keesing, 90
Kenesei, 226
Kern, 40
Kibrik, 180
Kimball, 72, 140
King, 3
König, 69, 73
Kornfilt, 70, 192, 226
Koul, 68, 225
Kozintseva, 94
Kroeber, 274
Krumholz, 219
Kumari, 218
Kuno, 206, 207, 208, 242
Kutsch Lojenga, 71, 189

Ladig, C. J., 90, 113
Lakoff, 217
Lambertii, 58
Langacker, 146, 147
LaPolla, 61, 252
Last, 76, 272
Laycock, 106
Lee, Ch. L., 219, 221
Lee, K.-D., 155
Lehmann, 120, 122, 246
Levinson, 214, 217, 237
Liccardi, 111
Lichtenberk, 148
Lopez, 234
Love, 90, 108
Lucassen, 76, 272
Lundskær-Nielsen, 218
Lynch, 269
Lyons, 5, 10

Macaulay, 28, 80, 86, 87, 161
MacDonald, 53, 68, 70, 138
MacKay, 25
MacPhail, 221
Mahootian, 156
Marchese, 26, 104
Marlett, 24, 25, 175
Martins, S., 276
Martins, V., 276
Maslova, 184
McClelland, 116
McGregor, 101, 143, 144, 145
Mchombo, 8, 122, 126
McKay, 142
Meira, 92, 117
Michailovsky, 64
Miller, A., 60, 115, 141
Miller, W. R., 40
Mistry, 188
Mithun, 54, 57, 140, 156, 159, 211
Moravcsik, 82, 120
Mühlhäusler, 214, 280, 281
Mulder, 50
Munro, 234, 249
Murthy, 68, 80, 180, 181, 192, 193, 194, 196, 205, 218
Muysken, 147, 148

Natu, 44, 129
Newman, P., 105, 189
Newman, S., 275
Nichols, 56, 75, 128, 143, 210, 274
Nikolaeva, 7, 138, 152, 179
Noguchi, 9, 10, 11, 12
Nordbustad, 52, 106
Nordlinger, 6, 252

Oates, L., 114
Oates, W., 114
Olawsky, 104
Olson, C., 23, 120, 122
Olson, M., 78
Omondi, 153
Osborne, 117
Osumi, 157, 220

Pandharipande, 225
Parker, 74
Payne, David L., 250
Payne, Doris L., 41, 90, 161
Peeke, 50
Penalosa, 145
Pesot, 145
Peterson, 274
Plank, 95, 96, 108, 109, 115

Polinsky, 58
Pullum, 26

Quesada, 48, 134
Quizar, 41

Radin, 95
Redden, 90
Reed, 250
Reesink, 83
Reh, 246, 248
Rehg, 89
Reichle, 28, 158
Reinhart, 190, 191, 197, 201
Reuland, 190, 191, 197, 201
Reyle, 173
Rijkhoff, 15
Roberts, J. R., 76, 136, 144, 172, 211, 244
Roberts, I., 152
Robertson, 260, 274
Robins, 164
Romankievicius Costa, 28, 135
Roncador, 201
Rosen, 33
Ross, 44, 129, 269, 270
Rude, 60
Rupp, 71

Saltarelli, 253
Schaub, 183
Schebeck, 3
Schellinger, 96, 108, 109, 115
Schuster-Šewc, 223
Schwartz, 69
Scorza, 25, 108
Seiler, 142, 143
Shibatani, 227
Siegel, 270
Siemund, 69, 73
Siewierska, 61, 86, 136, 143, 164, 171
Silverstein, 63, 137, 168, 172
Smith, I., 27
Smith, J. C., 274, 275
Sohn, H., 34, 35, 163
Sohn, H-M., 210, 231-233, 244
Solnit, 248
Sottile, 58
Sridhar, 178, 225, 244
Starke, 8, 19, 37, 38, 39
Stassen, 129, 131, 132, 144
Steele, 120
Stephens, 94
Stirling, 202, 203, 205
Storto, 133, 134
Strom, 166

Suarez, 119, 130
Subbarao, 68, 80, 180, 181, 193, 194, 196, 205, 218
Subrahmanyam, 274, 278
Sugamoto, 9, 12
Sulkala, 212
Swanton, 77

Taylor, C., 209
Taylor, J. R., 265
Terrill, 107, 171, 181
Thomas, 84
Thomsen, 54
Thráinsson, 207
Thurston, 255, 276
Tiffou, 145
Tolskaya, 7, 138, 179
Topping, 275
Traugott, 246
Tryon, 39, 89, 233, 253
Tsunoda, 34, 155
Tuggy, 226, 227

Uhlenbeck, 230, 231

Van Driem, 81, 240, 241
Van Staden, 235, 248, 280
Van Valin, 175
Visser, 279
Voorhoeve, 275, 279
Vogt, 131
Vuorinen, 73

Wales, 208, 210, 217, 218, 222, 236
Wali, 68, 193, 225, 228
Wash, 118
Watters, 6, 96
Weinstein, 173
Wichmann, 260, 274
Wiesemann, 106, 202, 203
Williams, 164
Wiltschko, 8, 21, 167
Wise, 171
Wolfart, 150
Wu, 94

Xiong, 235

Yadava, 241
Yamamoto, 22, 178, 208, 210, 235
Yigezu, 24

Zacharski, 173
Zigmond, 249
Zribi-Hertz, 71, 207
Zwicky, 17, 26

Language index

Abaza, 105
Abelam, 105
Abkhaz, 63, 105, 137, 145, 167, 168, 212
Acatec, 145, 147
Acehnese, 42, 49, 50, 55, 62, 63, 130, 132, 137, 155, 222, 244, 247, 248
Achuar, 250
Achumawi, 113, 119
Acoma, 40, 41, 42, 55
Adnyamathanha, 3
Afrikaans, 244
Ainu, 93, 168, 223, 257
Akha, 88
Akhvakh, 77
Akɔɔse, 203
Alabama, 258
Alamblak, 257
Alawa, 239
Albanian, 114, 157
Aleut, 88, 96
Algonkian, 7
Altaic, 255
Amaaro, 276
Amele, 76, 136, 144, 168, 172, 211, 244
Amharic, 103, 168, 179, 217, 223
Amuesha, 42
Anejom, 42, 92, 117, 119, 134, 135, 137, 151, 163, 253, 268, 269, 270
Anêm, 30, 137
Angas, 105, 106, 260
Ani, 43, 44, 105, 108, 116
Anindilyakwa, 239
Apalai, 56, 127–128
Apurina, 55, 62, 63, 78, 93, 137, 161
Arabana, 3, 65, 92
Arabic, 105
Arabic, Classical, 96, 136
Arabic, Gulf, 212
Arabic, Syrian, 212
Aramaic, Biblical, 109
Arawa, 248
Ari, 256, 275
Armenian, 162

Armenian, Modern Eastern, 94, 217
Armenian, Spoken Eastern, 57, 58
Asheninca, 250
Assiniboine, 88
Asumboa, 252
Atakapa, 77
Athpare, 208, 211
Atsi, 88
Au, 24, 25, 42, 76, 108, 268, 272
Avar, 133, 149
Avukaya, 248
Austronesian, 276
Awa Pit, 47–48, 261
Awngi, 257
Awtuw, 69
Aymara, 87
Ayt Ndhir, 108 (*see also* Tamazight)

Baale, 24
Babungo, 183, 211
Badjiri, 54
Bagirmi, 137
Bali-Vitu, 118
Bandjalang, 65
Bangala, 61, 73, 189
Baniata, 110
Bantu, 156, 171
Barai, 43, 44, 77, 78
Barasano, 76, 114
Bare, 135, 161–162, 254, 278
Bari, 43, 128, 135
Basketo, 257
Basque, 5, 63, 74, 167, 235, 249, 253
Batsbi, 54
Bavarian, 272
Bawm, 28, 29, 157, 158, 163
Beja, 105, 163
Belhare, 64, 211
Bemba, 223
Bena Bena, 77
Bengali, 217
Berber, 115
Berik, 92
Berta, 134, 163
Biak, 96, 109, 110

316

Language index

Big Nambas, 93
Bilin, 162, 257
Biloxi, 238
Bimoba, 43, 134, 163
Binandere, 100
Bininj Gun-wok, 125, 159
Biri, 89, 95, 168, 171
Boikin, 105
Boko, 38, 39, 203, 204, 256
Boko-Busa, 135
Bokobaru, 255–256
Boni, 78, 119, 163
Bora, 107
Bororo, 137
Breton, 94
Bulgarian, 4, 62, 137, 149–151, 157, 168
Bukiyip, 55
Buma, 102
Bunuba, 88
Burarra, 89
Burji, 48
Burmese, 8, 61, 128, 247
Burunge, 46, 76, 105, 106
Burushaski, 145–146, 162
Buryat, 94
Busa, 38
Byansi, 53, 118

Caddo, 211, 236, 238
Cahuilla, 63, 137, 168
Campa, 87, 171
Candoshi, 30, 163
Canela Kraho, 42, 87, 133, 211
Capanahua, 50, 76, 115
Carib, 139, 255
Carib of Surinam, 151
Catalan, 209
Central Pomo, 54
Chacobo, 77, 128, 150, 163, 168
Chai, 76, 272
Chalcatongo Mixtec, 28, 29, 80, 86–87, 92, 161
Chamling, 95, 241
Chamorro, 42, 45, 134, 275
Chang, 65
Chepang, 24, 61, 112, 113
Chermis (*see* Mari)
Chibchan, 278
Chichewa, 151, 156
Chimilla, 278–279
Chi-Mwi:ni, 156
Chinookan, 66, 88, 136, 137, 167, 172, 238
Chitimacha, 77
Chocolan, 278
Choctaw, 137, 258
Chorti, 41

Chrau, 87
Chukchee, 77
Chumash, 30, 42, 63, 118, 119, 137
Coast Tsimshian, 49, 50, 62, 63
Colville, 275
Comanche, 5, 134, 249
Comox, 61, 66
Coos, 89, 119, 130, 132, 238
Copainala Zoque, 53 (*see also* Zoquean)
Copa Moca, 61
Copola Trique, 53, 150, 235
Coptic, 163
Cora, 31–32, 49, 62, 67, 137
Cree, 115, 150–151
Creek, 258, 259
Cubeo, 105, 106
Cuna, 278
Cushitic, 257
Czech, 180, 209, 217

Daba, 135
Daga, 137, 168
Dagaare, 109
Dagbani, 30, 103, 104, 134
Damana, 278, 279
Dani, Grand Valley, 42, 259
Danish, 217, 218, 222, 223
Dargwa, 93
Darmiya, 76, 77, 150
Dasenech, 276
Daur, 94, 114
Dehu, 38, 92, 114, 150, 233
Dhimal, 3
Dho-Luo, 153
Dhuwal, 96
Dime, 77, 92
Diola Fogny, 30, 136
Dizi, 83, 88, 96, 143
Djabugay, 65
Djambarrpuyngu, 220
Djapu (*see* Dhuwal)
Djaru, 34, 53, 155, 217
Djinang, 276
Dongolese Nubian, 143
Doyayo, 135, 136, 168
Dravidian, 276
Dutch, 49, 67, 73, 76, 114, 180, 208, 223, 224, 248, 268, 269

East Makian, 275
East Tucano, 276
Eastern Pomo, 54, 217, 223
Egyptian, Old, 134
Eini, 274
Ekari, 62, 77, 78, 118, 119, 135, 168, 268, 269
Enga, 137

English, 1–2, 3, 4, 5, 7, 9–12, 13, 16–19, 22, 23, 26, 41, 49, 61, 69, 70, 71, 73, 76, 77, 79, 82, 86, 93, 100, 103, 105, 114, 115, 121, 122, 123–126, 129, 147, 150, 159–160, 177, 181–182, 185–188, 189, 192–195, 201, 207, 208, 210, 212, 216–217, 218, 222, 227, 236, 251, 263, 265, 267, 268, 269, 273, 275, 280
English, Old, 274
Erromangan, 146–147 (see also Sye)
Erzya Mordvin, 211
Estonian, 212
Evenki, 42
Ewe, 144, 203, 204–205

Faroese, 268
Fehan, 223, 268, 272
Fijian, 2, 90, 91, 217, 223, 281
Finnish, 44, 180, 208, 212, 217
Fino-Ugric, 213
Fore, 77
French, 7, 37–38, 209, 210, 211, 212, 216, 217, 218, 220, 222, 223, 236–237, 268, 269, 272, 273, 275
Frisian, 79, 268
Fula, 88
Fur, 4, 109, 128
Fyem, 135

Gadsup, 77
Gahri, 235
Galela, 279
Galila, 256
Galibi, 56
Gamale, 6 (see also Kham)
Gapapaiwa, 155
Gapun, 42, 77
Garawa, 277
Garifuna, 103
Gbaya, 217
Geez, 42, 163
Gela, 157, 158
Germanic, 78, 210, 211, 212
German, Middle Low, 278
German, Old High, 272
German, Standard, 73, 114, 223, 236, 268, 272, 273
German, Swiss, 268
Gilbertese, 135
Gimira, 182–183, 276
Godie, 26, 103, 104, 211, 212
Gooniyandi, 88, 168
Gothic, 212
Greek, Modern, 119, 157, 162, 188, 211, 213, 217
Greek, Ancient, 96
Greek, New Testament, 209
Guajajara, 56

Guarani, 62, 63, 119, 130, 132, 137, 163
Guato, 93
Gude, 44, 87, 137
Gugu-Yalanji, 89
Gujarati, 73, 188, 189, 276
Gumawana, 23, 24, 30, 120, 122, 123–126
Gumbaynggir, 188
Gunwinggu, 169, 239
Gunya, 277
Gurindji, 223
Guugu Yimidirr, 87

Haida, 55, 143
Halkomelem, 8, 21, 46, 66, 167
Hamer, 76, 275
Harari, 217
Hatam, 83, 87
Hausa, 105, 189, 210, 219
Haya, 136, 170–171
Hayu, 64
Hebrew, Modern, 105, 212
Hindi, 61, 73, 212
Hishkaryana, 42, 211
Hitchiti, 258, 259
Hittite, 54
Hozo, 256
Hua, 53, 77, 137, 154, 155
Huastec, 260
Hungarian, 62, 211, 212, 226
Hunzib, 50, 76

Iai, 38, 39
Iatmul, 105
Icelandic, 77, 191, 195, 207, 268
Idu, 77
Ika, 50, 55, 63, 77, 137, 278, 279
Ilgar, 66
Illocano, 84
Imbabura Quechua, 5, 44, 150, 226, 235
Imonda, 55, 87
Indonesian, 115, 134, 217, 244, 279
Inga, 69
Ingush, 53
Iraqw, 50, 52, 78, 105, 106
Italian, 49, 67, 68, 208–209, 213, 223
Itonama, 102, 105, 110, 111, 116
Itzaj Maya, 260

Jabêm, 113
Jacaltec, 62, 63, 167, 249, 254
Jamul Tiipay, 60, 115, 141, 150, 250
Japanese, 8, 9, 12–13, 22–23, 73, 178, 206, 209, 210, 232, 235
Jaqaru, 87, 238, 250
Javanese, 215, 230–231
Jawony, 239

Jiarong, 89
Jicaque, 163
Jinuo, 89
Ju-chen, 114

Kabana, 102, 255
Kabylie or Berber, 108, 109
Kaingan, 211
Kairiru, 155
Kakua, 275
Kalaw Kawaw Ya, 106, 110
Kalispel, 131, 132, 239–240
Kalkatungu, 77
Kamaiura, 56
Kamanugu, 92, 100
Kambera, 136, 157
Kannada, 68, 178, 196, 224, 225, 244
Kanuri, 168
Kapampangan, 50, 87, 156, 157, 167, 217
Kapau, 77, 107, 114
Karaja, 105, 106, 116, 150
Karitiana, 43, 63, 133–134
Karo Batak, 43, 223, 235
Kashmiri, 48, 68, 73, 168, 192, 211, 212, 223, 225, 250
Kâte, 95, 259–260
Katu, 109
Kawaiisu, 87, 249
Kawesquar, 88
Kayah Li, 128, 150, 248
Kayardild, 184
Kei, 102
Keliko, 248
Kemat, 257
Kemtuik, 274
Kera, 30, 110, 134, 135, 163
Ket, 119, 132
Kewa, 44, 55, 63, 77, 137
Kham, 6, 61, 63, 96
Khasi, 217, 235, 251
Khiamnungan, 65
Khmer, 247
Khmu, 105
Kikongo, 281
Kilivila, 134, 151, 162, 211
Kinnauri, 89, 114
Kinyarwanda, 52, 136, 151
Kiowa, 88, 113, 119
Kipea, 150
Kiranti, 173–211
Kiribatese, 41–42, 45, 109, 113, 119, 134, 151, 163
Kisar, 271–272
Kituba, 281
Koasati, 42, 55, 63, 65, 72–73, 74, 140, 168, 254, 258, 259

Kobon, 49, 74, 77, 99, 113, 114, 162, 221, 273
Kofyar, 106
Kogu, 278
Koh Lakka, 49, 87, 128
Koiari, 77, 78, 87, 114, 268, 269
Kolana, 133
Kokota, 118
Kokborok, 61, 128
Kolami, 274
Kombai, 259
Kombon, 211
Komi, 211, 212
Konjo, 31, 50, 63, 157, 160–161, 163, 235
Kono, 38
Konyak, 65
Koré, 252, 257
Korean, 73, 189, 207, 210, 231–233, 244
Koromfe, 136, 211, 212, 217
Kove, 255
Koyfar, 105
Koyra Chin, 49, 212
Kpelle, 38
Kuman, 77, 92–100
Kunama, 88, 92
Kurdish, 30, 163, 211, 212
Kusaiean, 45, 48, 114, 135, 146, 154, 155, 233
Kutenai, 46, 115, 275
Kuyani, 3
Kwaio, 90
Kwaza, 63, 87, 276

Labu, 50, 92, 102, 117, 268, 270
Lahu, 89
Lak, 5, 63, 133, 149
Lakhota, 55, 63, 65, 87, 114
Lango, 42, 63
Lardil, 3
Larike, 55, 63, 90, 92, 108, 113, 260
Latin, 162, 209
Latvian, 114, 217
Lavukaleve, 6, 88–92, 107, 114, 119, 137, 181, 249
Laz, 54
Lele, 87, 105, 163, 203, 210
Lealao Chinantec, 70
Lepcha, 44, 137
Lihir, 91
Lillooet, 274
Limbu, 63, 80–81, 95, 115, 173–211, 240
Lithuanian, 108, 109, 116
Logo, 248
Loloda, 279
Loniu, 90, 91
Lower Umpqua, 46, 50, 55, 88

Lugbara, 248
Lummi, see North Straits Salish
Lusi, 255

Maale, 70, 73, 114, 134, 257
Macushi, 63, 122, 123–126, 211, 212
Madurese, 2
Maisin, 50
Maithili, 225, 241–244
Maká, 106, 107
Makah, 147
Malak Malak, 42, 53, 87
Malay, 100, 223, 247–248, 275, 279
Malayalam, 73, 137, 189–190, 195, 197, 217, 218, 225, 250, 278
Mam, 62
Manam, 136, 148
Manambu, 105, 116
Mandak, 61
Mandara, 38, 135
Mandarin, 73, 190, 196, 200, 207, 212, 219–220, 221, 235
Mande, 38, 217
Mangarayi, 92, 119, 137
Mao, 256
Mao Naga, 252
Maori, 88
Mapuche, 119, 150
Mara, 277
Maranungku, 42, 87, 118, 119
Marathi, 207, 212, 225, 227–228, 276
Margany, 277
Margi, 38, 135
Mari, 211
Maricopa, 6, 88, 139, 140, 270–271
Marind, 114, 168
Maru, 89
Marubo, 28–29, 48, 135
Mataco, 115
Maumere, 32–33
Maung, 143
Mauritian Kreol, 48
Mauwake, 48, 154, 155, 212, 250
Mayan, 248
Maybrat, 73, 212
Mazatec, 25, 33
Mbay, 20, 119, 134, 151, 163, 202, 203
Megreb, 77
Meithei, 128
Menya, 77
Mesalit, 48, 168
Mikir, 252
Minangkabau, 105, 106
Miskito, 274
Mizo, 68, 80, 137, 192–194
Mlap, 274

Modole, 279
Mohawk, 88, 119, 140, 142
Mono Alu, 63
Moru, 203
Mota, 220
Mountain Koiali, 134
Mountain Maidu, 87, 118
Mumuye, 143
Muna, 135, 162
Mundani, 74, 211, 212
Mundari, 46, 88, 114, 155, 254
Munduruku, 54
Mupun, 62, 201, 202, 203, 252
Mura Pirahã, 79, 86
Murinypatya, 53
Murle, 113, 119, 168
Musica Duit, 278
Muskogean, 258, 259
Mussau, 157, 158

Nakanai, 88
Nama, 105, 108, 110, 111, 114, 116, 254, 274
Nambiquara, 83, 96, 113, 114
Nandi, 137
Nanggu, 150
Narinjari, 54
Nasioi, 55, 63, 114, 119
Navajo, 118, 168, 217
Nauhatl, 136
Ndjébbana, 110, 142
Ndonga, 168
Ndyuka, 74, 217
Nenets, 211
Nengone, 38, 233
Nepali, 217, 229–230
Nez Perce, 65, 115
Ngala, 105, 106
Ngalakan, 53
Ngandi, 53, 238, 276
Nganhcara, 27, 29
Ngankikurungkurr, 89
Ngarluma, 217
Ngbaka, 203
Ngiti, 71, 87, 137, 189, 249
Ngiyambaa, 64, 88, 137, 168, 217
Nilo-Saharan, 276
Nilotic, 275
Nivkh, 43, 87, 117
Nkore Kiga, 136, 209, 211, 212
Nocte, 55–56, 150, 151
Noon, 43, 136, 155, 163
North Straits Salish, 8, 20–21, 239
Northern Sumu, 274
Northern Tepehuan, 67
Norwegian, 223
Nosu, 6, 89

Ntifa, 108
Nuaulu, 113
Nuer, 275
Numic, 276
Nunggubuyu, 110, 239, 276
Nyamwezi, 219
Nyangumarta, 88
Nyulnyul, 63, 114, 119, 144

Ocaina, 107
Ocotepec Mixtec, 219, 248
Okanagan, 275
Ometo, 256
Omotic, 275
Oneida, 55, 63, 88, 113, 119
Ono, 259
!Ora, 105, 110, 111, 116, 274
Oriya, 73
Oromo, 78
Ostyak, 152

Paamese, 62, 90, 92, 119, 137, 139, 140, 146, 163, 220, 253
Padoe, 73
Pagu, 279
Paiwan, 128
Palauan, 44, 63, 109, 153, 157, 253
Palikur, 42, 43, 62, 133, 137, 163
Pame, 76
Pangasinian, 217
Panyjima, 43, 88, 150
Papago, 41
Parecis, 150
Pari, 163, 252
Passamaquoddy, 119
PaTani, 114, 235
Paumari, 119, 142, 143
Pech, 87, 118, 137
Pero, 250
Persian, 156–157, 211, 217
Pintupi, 53
Pipil, 42, 81, 168
Pitjantjatjara, 27, 29, 34, 150
Podoko, 38, 135
Poguli, 105
Pola, 89
Polish, 9, 11–12, 32, 33–34, 49, 59, 60, 67, 68, 73, 94, 114, 124, 125, 137, 162, 184, 192–195, 198–199, 209, 212, 224, 245, 251, 257–258
Ponapean, 46, 89, 135, 253
Popoloca, 240
Portuguese, 209, 248, 275
Portuguese, Brazilian, 224
Pulo Annian, 135
Puluwat, 135
Punjabi, 203, 225, 227

Quileute, 119, 168
Quechua (Cuzco), 147

Raga, 113
Rama, 49, 134, 163
Rangpa, 92
Rapanui, 88, 95
Rawang, 89, 118
Reefs (Ayiwo), 253
Rembarnga, 53
Resigaro, 107, 278
Retuarã, 30, 42, 119, 134, 150, 163, 166, 168
Rhaeto-Romance, 268, 273
Rikbaktsa, 105, 116
Ritharngu, 154, 276
Romance, 30, 209, 210, 211, 212
Romansch, 268, 272
Roshani, 48
Roviana, 41
Rumanian, 61, 155, 157, 158, 213, 217
Russian, 73, 180, 208, 209, 217, 219, 245, 268

Sacapultec Mayan, 41
Sahaptin, 54, 59, 60
Sahu, 279
Salinam, 42
Salish, Coast, 274
Salishan, 64, 147
Salt Yui, 6, 88, 92
Samoan, 88
Sango, 4
Sani, 89
Santa Cruz, 150
Santali, 221
Sanuma, 35–36, 37, 102
Sardinian, 30, 61, 213
Sayula Popoluca, 274
Sedang, 89, 96
Selepet, 168
Selknam, 87
Sema, 43, 163, 250
Semelai, 55, 135
Sentani, 77, 93, 113, 162, 166, 168, 254
Seri, 24, 171
Sezo, 256
Sgaw Karen, 252
Shambala, 136, 170
Shilha, 108
Shona, 156, 217
Sierra Popoloca, 63, 219
Silacayoapan Mixtec, 217
Sindhi, 276
Sinhalla, Colloquial, 278
Slave, 136, 250
Slavonic, Slavic, 211, 213
Slovak, 67, 179, 180

Slovene, 221
So, 83, 150, 252
Sochiapan Chinantec, 144, 234
Somali, 210
Sorowahá, 25
Sotho, 223
South Eastern Pomo, 128
Southern Sierra Miwok, 61, 250
Southwest Tanna, 253
Southeastern Tepehuan, 46
Spanish, 59, 60, 61, 68, 77, 108, 146, 156, 157, 162, 194, 209, 213, 224, 248, 275
Spanish, Latin American, 213
Spanish, Porteno, 157, 158
Suena, 50
Sumerian, 42, 54
Supyire, 74
Sursurunga, 91, 150, 220
Swahili, 104, 167, 168
Swedish, 217, 222, 223, 236, 237, 278
Sye, 113

Taba, 135, 163
Tabaru, 279
Tagalog, 87, 223
Tăhăggart Berber, 108, 109
Tairora, 93
Takale, 6 (*see also* Kham)
Tamachek Berber, 105
Tamazight, 105 (*see also* Ayt Ndhir)
Tamil, 73, 189, 211, 216, 218
Tangut, 252
Tanimbili, 89, 117, 119, 253
Tarascan, 87, 114, 168
Tariana, 108, 135, 278
Tarifit Berber, 105, 107, 116, 213
Tate, 116
Tauya, 53, 68, 70, 76, 113, 119, 137, 138, 143, 208
Tawala, 141, 147, 211
Tehit, 88, 117
Telugu (also Old), 180–181, 196, 205, 207, 217, 218, 274
Teribe, 48, 49, 134, 163
Ternate, 279–280
Teso, 275
Tetelcingo Nahuatl, 226–227
Thai, 8, 9, 13, 189, 228–229, 231, 236, 247, 275
Tibetan, Classical, 231
Tibetan, Lhasa, 55
Tibeto-Burman, 61
Tiddim, 4
Tidore, 235, 248, 279–280
Tigak, 38, 46, 63, 92, 135, 254
Tikopia, 220
Timbira, 150
Tinani, 96

Tinrin, 157, 210, 220
Tiriyo, 92, 117, 137, 153, 249
Tiwi, 87, 117, 119, 168
Tlappanecan, 95
Tlingit, 55, 163
Toba Batak, 223
Tobelo, 279
Tolai, 92
Tonkawa, 42, 63, 119
Totonac, Misantla, 25, 33
Trukese, 135
Trumai, 29, 45, 63, 88, 114, 133, 150
Tsakhur, 77, 150
Tsez, 137
Tsou, 34, 55, 135
Tuburi, 202, 203, 204
Tukang Besi, 211, 217, 219
Tunebo, 278
Tunica, 63, 105
Tupi-Guarani, 276
Turkana, 63, 114
Turkish, 70, 74, 192, 198, 199–200, 211, 212, 226, 250
Tuscarora, 240
Tuvaluan, 212, 220, 223
Tuyuca, 261
Tzutujil, 137, 167

Udihe, 7, 73, 138–139, 179, 250
Udmurt, 210, 211
!Ui-Taa, 275
Uma, 42, 63, 87
Una, 53
Ungarinjin, 90, 92, 117
Upper Sorbian, 217, 223
Uradhi, 84, 85, 87
Uruubu Kaapor, 278
Uto-Aztecan, 139, 147, 255

Vanimo, 88, 92, 105, 110, 114, 268, 269
Vietnamese, 8, 189, 247, 275
Vinmavis, 5, 77

Wagaya, 65
Waiwai, 56
Wajarri, 277
Wakashan, 147
Walapai, 90
Walmathari, 53
Walpiri, 53, 280–281
Wambaya, 6, 66, 88, 252
Wambon, 77, 162
Wandamen, 109
Wangaybuwan, 54
Wangkangurru, 3
Wangkumara, 55

Language index 323

Wanuma, 156, 162
Waorani, 50, 254
Wappo, 48, 143
Warao, 250
Wardaman, 53, 87
Warekena, 19, 55, 63, 103, 137, 254
Wari, 40, 41, 68
Warrwa, 100, 101
Wasco-Wishram, *see* Chinookan
Washo, 42, 64, 79, 88, 115, 143, 167, 276
Waskia, 44, 88, 118, 129, 137
Waura, 150, 163
Wayampi, 56
Welamo, 217
Welsh, 49, 152–153
West Greenlandic, 63, 162, 167
West Makian, 136, 279–280
Wichita, 55, 65, 87, 163, 257
Wik Munkan, 89
Wintun, 115, 150
Witoto, 114
Witoto, Muinan, 107
Witoto, Murui, 107, 108
Woleaian, 34–35, 36, 37, 46, 135, 163
Wolof, 136
Wolaytta, 58
Worora, 3, 90, 92, 107, 108, 143

Xerente, 92
Xokleng, 93
!Xu, 110

Yaga Dii, 203
Yagua, 41, 55, 89, 90, 161
Yamphu, 64, 208
Yanomani, 134
Yanyuwa, 277
Yaoure, 69, 83, 84, 87, 88
Yapese, 46, 62, 88, 118, 119, 135, 253
Yaqui, 146
Yate, 105
Yava, 55, 63, 89
!Yawalapiti, 278
Yelogu, 105
Yessan Mayo, 62, 128
Yidin, 88
Yimas, 66, 90, 91, 118, 169
Yingkarta, 277–278
Yoruba, 49, 217
Yuchi, 55, 63, 143
Yukaghir, Kolyma, 44, 137, 150, 184
Yukulta, 65, 119, 169
Yulparija, 53, 88, 113, 169
Yuman, 139
Yuwaalaraay, 64
Yupik, 62, 63

Zakatal', 77
Zande, 49, 219, 248, 249
Zapotec, San Lucas, 234
Zapotecan, 150
Zaysé, 252
Zoquean, 274

Subject index

accessibility, 46–47, 62, 67, 68, 173–185, 191–197, 207
  and encoding, 46, 57, 173–185, 207, 265
  and grammaticalization, 262, 264–266, 267
  hierarchies, 46–47, 175, 178, 191, 198, 199
  marking scale, 175–176, 191, 197, 207
affix, 4, 24, 26, 80, 127, 135, 251, 262, 265, 266
  (*see also* bound forms)
  circumfix, 24
  infix, 25
  order, 137 (*see also* alignment)
  prefix, 24
  suffix, 24
  tonal, 25
agreement, 8, 21, 103
agreement, conditions on (*see* controllers, targets of)
agreement, controllers of, 120, 121, 148
  objects, 150, 151, 263, 265
  possessors, 150, 264, 265
  subjects, 120, 121, 151, 152, 263, 264, 265, 267, 271–272
agreement, markers of, 120, 162
  location of, 136, 139–140, 162, 163, 166
  formal affinities between, 143, 146–147
  (*see also* phonological identity of)
  number of, 133
  omission of, 129, 242
  order of, 136–137, 166–172
  phonological identity of, 136–137, 140–141, 168
agreement, obligatoriness of, 121, 124, 153, 162
agreement, and order, 153, 161
agreement, targets of, 120, 121, 127–148
  adpositions, 127–128, 137, 145, 151
  other, 145, 147–148
  predicates, 127–137
  possessed nouns, 127–128, 138–145, 146, 147, 151
agreement, types of
  ambiguous, 126, 151, 156, 157, 162, 262, 268, 269, 272

anaphoric, 122, 123, 126–128, 134, 138, 263, 264–268
  grammatical, 122, 123, 126, 127–128, 158, 263, 264, 265, 266, 272
  pronominal, 126, 151, 156, 157, 162, 262
  local vs non-local, 120–122
  syntactic, 126–127, 151, 162, 262, 268, 272
Agreement universal, 131
alignment, 50
  of agreement markers (*see* of dependent person markers)
  of dependent person markers, 19–21
    ditransitive, 135–137, 169–171
    (*see also* indirective and secundative)
  of independent person forms
    monotransitive, 51–57, 133–135
alignment, and affix order, 52, 136
alignment, splits in, 51, 53, 63–66, 151
alignment, types of, 133
  active, 51, 53, 54, 56, 57, 59, 61, 63, 65, 135, 154
  accusative, 51, 52–54, 56, 63–66, 133–135, 154, 167–168
  ergative, 51, 53–54, 56, 59, 63–66, 133–135, 167–168
  hierarchical, 51, 53, 55, 56, 60, 150–151, 239
  indirective, 61–63, 66, 135, 168
  neutral, 21, 51–52, 56, 61, 63, 65, 136
  and person, 63–66
  secundative, 59, 61–63, 66, 135–137, 154, 168
  tripartite, 51, 53, 55, 56, 59, 61, 65–66
anaphor (*see* binding conditions)
anaphora, 7, 174
anaphoric expression, 7
anaphoric pronoun, 120
  vs agreement marker, 121–127, 137, 156, 159
animacy, 60, 61–62, 90, 103–104, 108, 137, 138, 156, 179, 250
animacy hierarchy, 149, 154–156, 168
argument prominence, 42–47
  hierarchy of, 43–46
aspect, 1–2, 38–39, 54, 147, 162
augmented inclusive, 85, 88, 101, 102, 103, 117
Avoid Pronoun Principle, 198

Subject index

binding conditions, 8, 173, 185, 186, 193, 198
  and referent accessibility, 191–197
  reinterpretation of, 190–191
bound forms, 22–26, 43–47, 51, 57, 67
bound pronouns, 8, 67, 156 (*see also* affix, bound forms, dependent forms)

case, 3
case marking, 6, 46–47 (*see also* independent forms, syntactic functions)
  analytic, 47
  suppletive, 47, 48–49 (*see also* stem change)
  suprasegmental, 47
  synthetic, 47
clause linkage, 175, 191
clitic, 4, 22, 24, 26–34, 43–47, 51, 67, 127, 251, 257–258, 262, 265, 266, 273, 277
  as agreement markers, 158, 162
  vs. bound forms, 26, 27, 31–34, 150
  typology of, 29–31
  vs. weak forms, 37–38
competition between referents, 179–182, 183
contrast, 67, 68, 69, 159, 183, 200
coordination, 18, 19, 22–58, 199
coreference, 185, 187–188, 189, 192–197, 198, 202–207
cross-referencing, 126, 127 (*see also* agreement)

definiteness, 3, 10, 124, 156, 163, 174, 196
deixis, 3, 7, 174
deicitc expression, 7, 201
demonstratives, 5, 7, 180, 208, 247, 249–251
dependent person markers, 16, 21–40, 42–47, 60, 61–63, 112, 123
diachronic syntax hypothesis, 164–166
discourse function, 67 (*see* focus hierarchy)
dual, 83, 84–85, 87, 88–92, 95–96, 102, 107, 110, 113, 118, 220–221, 269

eight-person paradigm, 85–88, 97
ellipsis, 18, 22, 37 (*see also* zero forms)
emphasis, 67–74, 200, 272
  degrees of, 74
emphatic person forms, 20, 67–74, 227, 254, 255–256
emphatic reflexives, 67, 69, 71, 72, 189, 207, 226
empathy, 174, 197, 200–201, 207–210, 224, 241, 244
explicitness hierarchy, 99, 101, 102
evidentiality, 205, 207, 260–261

face, 237, 241, 244
first person complex, 83–88
focus, 67, 163, 166, 183, 243
focus hierarchy, 137, 159–161
fourth person, 7

free form (*see* independent form)
frequency driven morphologization, 262, 266–268
function-argument biuniqueness, 124

gender, 3, 7, 103, 113, 114, 115–116, 119, 214, 250, 276
  and inclusive/exclusive, 110–112
  and number, 107–110, 115–116
  and person, 104–107, 115–116
  sex based vs non-sex based, 103–104, 107–108, 109–110, 113
  universal, 106
generic use, 2, 11, 124, 163, 210, 236
  pronominal root, 19–20, 254
givenness hierarchy, 176–177
grammaticalization, 40, 162, 166, 185, 192, 246, 247, 251, 261–273, 274

head-marking, 126
head ordering principle, 164–166
homophony, 30, 70, 75–79, 92, 97–103, 268, 269–272 (*see also* syncretism)
  horizontal, 97, 100, 102
  horizontal homophony hierarchy, 102
  in singular, 97, 102
  vertical, 97, 102 (*see also* explicitness hierarchy)
honorification, 215, 224, 228–235 (*see also* social deixis)
  and agent defocusing, 227–228
  levels of, 222–223, 225, 228, 229, 231–233, 241
humanness, 37, 40, 60, 61–62, 103–104, 108, 113, 137, 138–145, 154, 170, 196, 198, 205, 206, 208, 250 (*see also* animacy)

iconicity, 142
impersonal use, 2, 174, 210–213, 217, 235, 236–237
  of first person, 175
  of second person, 211–212
  of third person, 211, 212–213
inalienability hierarchy, 143, 144
inclusive/exclusive, 79, 83, 85, 87, 89, 91, 92, 100, 102, 112, 113, 114, 116–117, 119, 214, 274, 275, 276 (*see also* minimal augmented)
independent forms, 4, 16–21, 34, 40–42, 87, 112, 123, 152, 251, 268
  case marking of, 47, 49–50, 56, 61–63
  lack of, 19–21, 42 (*see also* pronoun, universality of)
indexation, 126, 127
information status, 159
intensifiers, 67, 68, 69–73, 226, 227

326 Subject index

inter-clausal semantic relation hierarchy, 175
inverse marker, 55, 151

kinship, 235, 244–245, 247
kin terms, 13

logocentric verb hierarchy, 202, 203
logophoricity, 67, 197–200, 201, 202, 203, 204, 205 (*see also* long-distance reflexives)

markedness, 19
maxim of quantity, 177, 183, 192
minimal augmented, 85, 87, 100, 101, 116
minimal inclusive, 85, 87, 99, 101, 102, 103, 117
mood, 1–2, 147, 162
 imperative, 22
 irrealis, 73
 realis, 134
morpho-phonological form, 4, 16, 162–163 (*see also* syntactic function)
negation (*see* polarity)

nominal hierarchy, 149, 151–154
NP-detachment analysis, 262, 263–264, 266, 267
null subject, 23 (*see also* pro-drop)
number, 214
 hierarchy, 170
 interpretation of, 82, 92, 93, 117
 lack of, 79–81, 114–115
 and person hierarchy, 7, 92–96, 101
 universals of, 107, 108

object, 40, 43, 203
 oblique, 40, 43
only inclusive, 86, 87, 92, 117
overt pronoun constraint, 11

paradigm, 4
 structure of, 5, 75, 214
parallel paths hypothesis, 246
patient, 43
paucal, 90, 102, 118, 220
person agreement, *see* agreement
person, differentiation of (*see* homophony)
person hierarchy, 55, 60, 149–151, 154, 168, 169–171
person indexation, 149–151
person markers (*see also* independent forms, dependent forms)
 acquisition of, 273
 borrowing of, 273, 274, 276
 changes in, 278
 loss of, 263, 268, 272, 273, 274, 277–281
 diffusion of, 273, 276–277, 278

omission of, 235–245
order of, 6
phonological form of, 6
sources of, 247–261
substitution of, 215
universality of (*see* pronoun)
perspective (*see* point of view)
plural, 84
 of majesty, 218–219
 of modesty, 218–219
point of view, 197, 200–207 (*see also* logophoricity)
polarity, 1–2
politeness, 247, 248 (*see also* social status)
possessed noun hierarchy, 138, 143
possession, 138–145, 152, 154
 alienable vs inalienable, 138, 143
possessive forms, 30
possessor, 203
predicates, types of, 129
predicate hierarchy, 127, 128
processing ease, 164
pro-drop, 126, 213
pronoun, personal
 as bound variables, 11
 lack of, 8
 modification of, 10, 12, 13, 18, 37
 referential status of (*see* reference)
 universality of, 8
 vs. lexical NP, 8–13 (*see also* pronominality scale)
pronominal (*see* binding conditions)
pronominal argument analysis, 41, 123–124, 125
pronominality scale, 9–13
pronominalized nouns, 223–224

quadral, 91

recipient, 43, 44 (*see also* indirective and secundative alignment)
reflexives, 70, 186–187, 188, 189, 191, 192–197, 224–228, 265 (*see also* emphatic reflexives)
 long-distance, 188, 195, 201, 205, 207 (*see also* logophoric)
reference, 10, 137, 174, 215
 of agreement markers, 124–125
 arbitrary (*see* generic)
 and encoding, 174
 of pronouns, 9, 10–11
referential conflict (*see* competition between referents)
referential hierarchy, 149, 156–159
r-expression (*see* binding conditions)
relevance, principle, 166, 171

saliency, 174–175, 178–183, 191, 197
semantic predicate hierarchy, 132
serial verbs, 146
shifters, 7
six person paradigm, 97, 103
social deixis, 11, 214
   address, 216, 218, 219–223
   self-reference, 216, 218, 236, 237, 240
   third parties, 216, 218
   via variation in number, 215–221, 238
   via variation in person, 222–224
social status (*see* social deixis)
style, 4, 12
stem change, 10, 24, 25, 33, 44, 94, 269
subject, 40, 43, 198, 203, 205
suffixing preference, 164–166
suppletion, 80, 137, 237
switch-reference, 179
syntactic functions, 40–66, 118, 202, 267
   (*see also* argument prominence)
   morpho-phonological form of, 40–47
   (*see also* alignment)

tense, 38–39, 54, 64, 135, 147, 162, 269, 270, 276
theta-criterion, 124
titles, 224, 235, 244–245, 247
topicality, 67, 143, 159
   topic, 178, 198, 200
   topic shift, 179, 183, 263, 264
trial, 87, 90, 96, 102, 107, 110, 118, 269

unity, 174, 175, 178, 183–185, 191, 197

verbal inflection, 178, 179, 181, 198, 199, 212
verb-second constraint, 272–273

Wackernagel's Law, 166
weak form, 22, 34–38, 43–47, 51, 67, 127, 135, 162
word status, 16–19

zero form, 4, 22–24, 43–47, 58, 178, 184, 198, 200, 212, 235, 239, 265